P9-CAB-471

We Are Not Such Things

We Are Not Such Things

*The Murder of a Young American, a South
African Township, and the Search for
Truth and Reconciliation*

Justine van der Leun

SPIEGEL & GRAU

NEW YORK

Published in the United States by Spiegel & Grau, an imprint of Random House, a division of Penguin Random House LLC, New York.

SPIEGEL & GRAU and Design is a registered trademark of Penguin Random House LLC.

Grateful acknowledgment is made to the following for permission to reprint previously published material:

Darhansoff & Verrill Literary Agents: "No foreign sky . . ." from "Requiem 1935–1940" from *Poems of Akhmatova* by Anna Akhmatova, selected, translated, and introduced by Stanley Kunitz with Max Hayward (Mariner Books, an imprint of Houghton Mifflin Harcourt, 1997), copyright © 1967, 1968, 1972, 1973 by Stanley Kunitz and Max Hayward. All rights reserved. Reprinted by permission of Darhansoff & Verrill Literary Agents.

Harper's Magazine: Excerpt from "To Those Who Follow in Our Wake" by Bertolt Brecht, translated by Scott Horton, copyright © 2008 by Harper's Magazine. All rights reserved. Reprinted from the January 2008 issue by special permission of *Harper's Magazine.*

HarperCollins Publishers: Excerpt from "Long You Must Suffer" from *The Essential Rilke,* selected and translated by Galway Kinnell and Hannah Liebmann, translation copyright © 1999 by Galway Kinnell and Hannah Liebmann. Reprinted by permission of HarperCollins Publishers.

LIBRARY OF CONGRESS CATALOGING-IN-PUBLICATION DATA
Names: Van der Leun, Justine, author.
Title: We are not such things: the murder of a young American, a South African township, and the search for truth and reconciliation / by Justine van der Leun.
Description: First edition. | New York: Spiegel & Grau, 2016.
Identifiers: LCCN 2015045138| ISBN 9780812994506 |
ISBN 9780812994513 (ebook)
Subjects: LCSH: Biehl, Amy—Death and burial. | South Africa. Truth and Reconciliation Commis-
sion. | Murder—Political aspects—South Africa—Cape Town. | Anti-apartheid activists—Crimes
against—South Africa. | Fulbright scholars—Crimes against—South Africa. | South Africa—Race
relations—Political aspects—History—20th century. |
Gugulethu (Cape Town, South Africa)—Social conditions—History.
Classification: LCC DT1974.2 .V35 2016 | DDC 305.8009687355—dc23 LC
record available at http://lccn.loc.gov/2015045138

Printed in the United States of America on acid-free paper

spiegelandgrau.com

2 4 6 8 9 7 5 3 1

First Edition

Book design by Caroline Cunningham

Map by Jeffrey L. Ward

Frontispiece photo: Nofemela family archives

For Samuel David Choritz

STATE LAWYER: You see what I am going to suggest
to you, Mr. Nofemela, is that the attack and brutal
murder of Amy Biehl could not have been done with
a political objective. It was wanton brutality, like a
pack of sharks smelling blood. Isn't that the truth?

EASY NOFEMELA: No, that's not true, that's not true.
We are not such things.

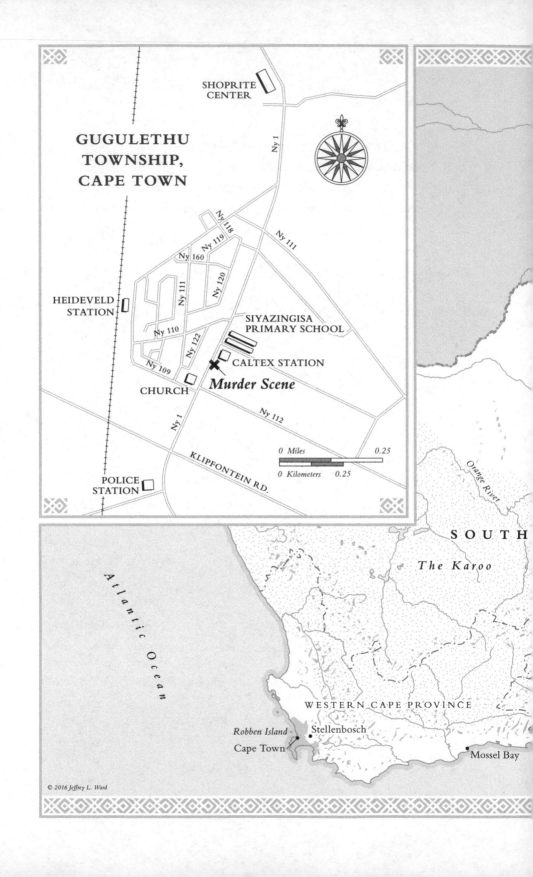

GUGULETHU
TOWNSHIP,
CAPE TOWN

SHOPRITE
CENTER

Ny 1

Ny 118
Ny 119
Ny 160
Ny 111
Ny 120
Ny 111

HEIDEVELD
STATION

Ny 110
Ny 122
Ny 109

SIYAZINGISA
PRIMARY SCHOOL

CALTEX STATION

Murder Scene

CHURCH

Ny 1

Ny 112

KLIPFONTEIN R.D.

0 Miles 0.25
0 Kilometers 0.25

POLICE
STATION

© 2016 Jeffrey L. Ward

Atlantic Ocean

SOUTH

The Karoo

Orange River

WESTERN CAPE PROVINCE

Robben Island
Cape Town

Stellenbosch

Mossel Bay

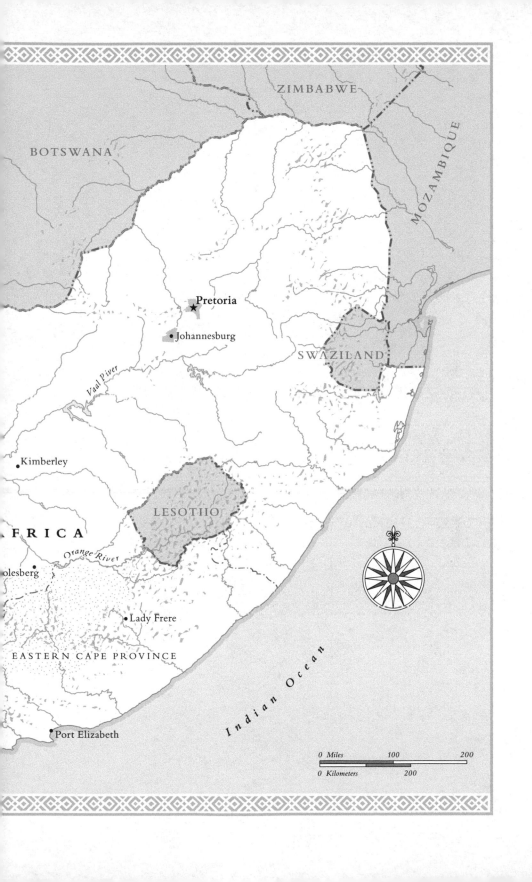

ZIMBABWE

BOTSWANA

MOZAMBIQUE

★ **Pretoria**

• Johannesburg

SWAZILAND

Vaal River

• Kimberley

LESOTHO

FRICA

Orange River

olesberg

• Lady Frere

EASTERN CAPE PROVINCE

Indian Ocean

• Port Elizabeth

0 Miles   100   200

0 Kilometers   200

1.

Some stories are true that never happened.

—Elie Wiesel

The journalists and documentarians and small-time film producers filed out of the van and toward St. Columba Anglican Church, a gray-brick building on the corner of NY1 and NY109 in Gugulethu, a township eleven miles outside Cape Town city center. Easy and I stayed behind, he in the driver's seat and me on the passenger's side. Easy was a short, compact man with butterscotch skin and a large, round, clean-shaven head. At forty-two, he had this weird ability to shape-shift. Did he look like a hardened old gangster? Yes, some days. Did he look like an adorable, harmless child? Yes, some days. In one of the photos I've snapped of him over the years, he is menacing, crouching on the ground with a cigarette between his thumb and forefinger, his band of brothers behind him, one of them holding up a disembodied sheep's head. But in the next, he's curled on a small stool, cradling his infant son and smiling as his ten-year-old daughter drapes herself over his shoulder.

Easy laughed generously, from the belly, and moved in quick spurts. His features were framed by a constellation of small dark scars: from a knife fight, a stick fight, an adolescent bout with acne, that time he crashed a van into a horse in the middle of the night and then fled, that time the taxi he was riding in collided with a hatchback, and a recent incident involving a scorned ex-girlfriend with long nails and a vendetta. His arms were dotted with fading ballpoint-pen tattoos—one pledging devotion to a long-defunct street gang, one to a prominent prison gang, and one to an old flame named Pinky. The first one had become infected immediately, when he was fifteen, and his mom had spent months tending to it. After that, for a few years at least, Easy felt like it made him look particularly tough.

I liked Easy very much. I won't pretend otherwise. But then again: precisely twenty years before our meeting in the van, on August 25, 1993, and approximately fifteen yards away, Easy had been part of a mob that had hunted down a young white American woman. If you plucked her out of that moment in history and slotted me in, my fate would have likely been the same. Easy chased her through the streets, chanting the slogan "One settler, one bullet," and hurled jagged bricks at her. He stabbed at her as she begged for her life. She died, bleeding from her head and her chest, on the pavement just across the road.

At least this is the crime Easy repeatedly claimed to have committed. He was convicted of her murder, and sentenced to eighteen years in jail. He'd done it, he publicly stated, because "during that time my spirit just says I must kill the white." The dead woman was named Amy Biehl, and she was twenty-six years old.

Once we finished our conversation, Easy and I hopped out of the van. He locked the door and patted the hood. The vehicle was a shiny silver donation from a local auto dealership that said across the side in bold letters: THE AMY BIEHL FOUNDATION.

We walked toward the church together, but as I stepped toward the door, Easy lingered in the winter sunshine. "I'm coming now," he said. This was South Africanese for "I'll be right back."

I went on without him. A sorry-eyed man in an ill-fitting suit motioned me into a pew. I slid in and scanned the room, its high ceilings, its tall burning votives. On a portrait nailed high above on the wall, a white Jesus, as lithe and glossy as a Hollywood star, reclined among a small herd of angelic lambs. Behind the pulpit hung an enormous cross.

I could see Amy Biehl's mother, Linda, sitting several rows ahead, her sharp platinum bob distinct in a dark sea of cornrows, weaves, wraps, curls, and towering church hats. Linda was the sort of woman who swept into town, and then swept into rooms, and then swept around rooms, her lipstick and eyeliner painted in broad, unbroken lines. She was nearly seventy. She liked to tell stories to rapt audiences. She always set her jaw and held her head high, and when I had first met her, just over a year earlier, I had found her to be impossibly composed. But with time, I came to notice that her body betrayed her attempts at imperturbable dignity: her shoulders slumped forward and she seemed, often, to be fighting against a great weight that threatened to drag her down.

Her friends, a pair of white American filmmakers, flanked her in the pew. She held in her arms a three-year-old black girl, hair cropped close to the head, dressed all in purple. The father of the girl was a man named Ntobeko Peni. According to all available reports, court records, and his own voluntary confession, Ntobeko had joined Easy and two other men in the attack on Amy. Back then, Ntobeko was a teenager and Easy and the other men were in their early twenties.

South Africa was in the final, fiery days of apartheid, when the entire country seemed poised for civil war. The young men, in the stories they would later repeat to various officials and commissions and journalists, had just left a political rally for a fringe militant party called the Pan Africanist Congress of Azania, or the PAC. Ntobeko and Easy were among around one hundred young people marching down NY1, the street where the church still sits. After forty-five years of state-sanctioned racial segregation, which saw black South Africans stripped of basic human rights and contained in slums, Nelson Mandela was poised to be the first black president of the country. Apartheid was on its way to being dismantled.

Amy, a Fulbright scholar at a Cape Town university, had spent nearly a year researching the rights and roles of disadvantaged women and children of color in this transitioning new democracy. That day, she had agreed to give two black students a lift home to the townships. As she drove by, the marchers spotted her, her long dirty-blond hair a bull's-eye. The crowd, knowing nothing about her, decided she looked very much like the oppressor. Her death, they claimed to believe, would further their cause to bring African land back to indigenous Africans: *One settler, one bullet.* Or maybe they were just looking for revenge on a pretty afternoon. They pulled Amy from her car, chased her down the road, and stoned and stabbed her to death on a little patch of grass in front of a gas station.

Four men—Easy and Ntobeko among them—were tried and convicted of Amy's murder and were sentenced to eighteen years in prison. But in 1997, they applied for amnesty at the Truth and Reconciliation Commission, South Africa's experiment in restorative justice. Chaired by Archbishop Desmond Tutu, the commission offered release and a clean slate to those who, upon taking responsibility, fully and honestly, for their apartheid-era crimes, could prove that their misdeeds were politically motivated.

In 1993, Linda, a stay-at-home mom turned clothing saleswoman, and her husband, Peter, a businessman, lived in a wealthy California coastal suburb. They had never before set foot on the African continent, but soon after Amy's death they flew to Cape Town. They immersed themselves in the rapidly changing country. They educated themselves on its complex political situation. They threw themselves into social welfare programs and spent time with the political elite of the African National Congress, Nelson Mandela's party and the party Amy had admired.

"We want to carry on where our daughter left off," Peter told a TV reporter. "We want to assist at the grassroots level anyone who's working for human rights and women's rights in particular. We want to be just as active as she was."

The ANC, for its part, took the Biehls into their fold. Amy had been a "comrade," the ANC announced. Moreover, she had been a martyr for their cause: liberty for all, racial harmony, and equality. Also, it looked good to have these two appealing, well-off Americans stand up for the ANC. Eventually Linda and Peter became friendly with a bunch of the liberation-era luminaries: Mandela himself; Archbishop Tutu; deputy president and soon-to-be-president Thabo

Mbeki; and Ahmed Kathrada, who had been sentenced to life imprisonment with Mandela in 1964.

In 1997, when the men convicted of killing Amy sat before the Truth and Reconciliation Commission, the Biehls, too, attended. They decided that Amy, who often wrote of the importance of reconciliation and moving forward in post-apartheid South Africa, would have wanted them to respect the processes of this new democracy. And so, unlike many families of victims, the Biehls did not oppose amnesty for Amy's killers, and the men were released from prison in 1998, after serving between three and five years.

A University of California at Berkeley anthropologist named Nancy Scheper-Hughes—who now sat near Linda in a pew in St. Columba Church—had been working in South Africa in 1993. She had written about the crime and the trial in several academic papers. In the ensuing years, when Nancy was not tracking an international ring of organ traffickers or looking into infant mortality rates in the Brazilian favelas, she was investigating violence in post-apartheid South Africa. She had grown especially intrigued by Easy and Ntobeko, and in August 1999 she hired a guide to take her to Gugulethu, where the men were staying after their release from prison. Nancy interviewed them, and they expressed to her an admiration for Peter Biehl and the desire to meet him in person, and to apologize face-to-face.

"I thought that there was one thing that could possibly make me better," Ntobeko confessed to Nancy. "I wanted to tell Mr. Biehl that I did not take the death of his daughter lightly. That this thing has weighed heavily on me. And I wanted him to know that he is a hero father to me. If I could just get Peter Biehl to listen to me and to forgive me to my face—why that would be as good as bread."

Nancy called Peter, who was staying at a Cape Town hotel at the time, and arranged for such a meeting.

"He probably thought I was a real buttinski," she recalled.

Peter, Nancy, and Nancy's guide proceeded to drive to Gugulethu for what began, Nancy told me, as a "tense meeting, on a miserable, rainy day." She stood to the side, taking copious notes and snapping photos, as a sullen, skinny Ntobeko and a sullen, skinny Easy patted down a grave Peter Biehl, checking him for a gun in case he took this meeting as an opportunity for a couple of revenge killings. Then the men ushered Peter into a shack they had claimed as their "club-house," a drafty hovel with a couple of small chairs and a love seat. The three spoke to each other, gruffly at first, but soon they soft-ened. Easy served Peter tea. Easy and Ntobeko explained to Peter that they were starting a youth group; the bunch had already climbed Table Mountain together and they'd designed T-shirts. They nick-named Nancy "the bridge" for her role in connecting the two worlds. They asked to meet Linda, who was in America, where her youngest daughter, Molly, had just given birth to a baby boy. Soon thereafter, Linda arrived in Cape Town and accompanied Peter to Gugulethu. Ntobeko and Easy were waiting for her. Easy showed her a photograph of his six brothers. Linda in turn showed him a photograph of her new grandson.

"Makhulu," Easy said.

"What does that mean?"

"Grandmother."

From then on, Easy and Ntobeko addressed Linda and Peter as Makhulu and Tatomkhulu, respectively: Grandmother and Grandfa-ther in the Xhosa language, honorifics used to express reverence. Linda and Peter spent a lazy Sunday evening as guests of honor at the official launch of Easy and Ntobeko's youth club; mostly it in-volved sitting outside and watching kids dance and give speeches. Next, the Biehls invited the men to dinner.

"Easy's mother said we would be given such things," Ntobeko whispered when a waiter presented them menus a few days later. Until then, the young men's dining out experience had been limited to a few trips to a takeaway joint.

Easy shoveled in steak and a milkshake, leaving his vegetables pushed to the side of his plate, while Ntobeko, who had a more adventurous culinary spirit, picked at a towering pile of nachos and then watched in wonder as the remainder was gathered into a package called a "doggie bag." The four ambled over the wide, sanded docks by the ocean and into the mall. During apartheid, the men had had limited access to white-designated areas, the sorts of places that boasted ritzy shops and restaurants. When apartheid fell, they were in prison. Since they'd left prison, they hadn't had a penny to their names. The Biehls bought four tickets to an IMAX film about water, and then the group wandered around the adjacent BMW dealership, admiring the shiny cars until showtime. After that, the Biehls bought four tickets to *Austin Powers: The Spy Who Shagged Me*. Linda fell asleep during the movie. It was too late for the men to catch a taxi, so the Biehls drove into the township at night and deposited the men at their homes.

The next morning, Easy called Linda at her hotel to inform her that, in a rare turn of events, a small tornado had swept through the township in the early morning hours, flattening shacks. He was checking to see that the Biehls had gotten back safely. He also wished to tell the Biehls that his family was furious at him, since Ntobeko had returned home with leftover nachos to share, while Easy had returned empty-handed. The legend of the doggie bag had then been disseminated through the families and has endured. Years later, while dining with Easy and Ntobeko and their relatives, Linda once excused herself to go to the restroom; when she returned, her meal, which she had not finished, was boxed up and sitting in front of one of the guests.

The Biehls developed a warm relationship with Easy and Ntobeko, which they maintained felt entirely natural. They took them to dozens of restaurants, taught them how to tip, introduced them to wine. Soon, they employed the two men to work at the foundation they had established in Amy's name.

The Amy Biehl Foundation, initially funded largely by the American government, was supposed to work to prevent violence, create jobs, develop the area, provide food, and offer recreation opportunities within Cape Town's townships. But these days, the foundation focused on after-school classes for local kids. The staff taught dance and reading and music, and handed out jam sandwiches.

Over time, Ntobeko rose in the ranks at the foundation. Without a high school degree, he began as a security guard on a bakery truck, but by 2013, Ntobeko was an office manager who lorded over the employees (most of them black), despairing at their lack of ambition, reading *The Seven Habits of Highly Effective People,* and idolizing Henry Ford. His old socialist days were long gone, and he was a capitalist now. He even had a couple of sidelines: school transport, wholesale chicken distribution, soft-serve ice cream, and a little wash-and-fold laundromat run from his garage. Easy, meanwhile, had risen from security guard to sports coordinator, and then had been dubbed unreliable and demoted to driver, a position he had accepted with resignation and relief.

The two men had grown up together. Ntobeko was a friend of Easy's younger brother and had spent many nights at the Nofemela house. They had grown closer in prison and, bonded by the experience, spent a great deal of time together upon their release. But these days, with Ntobeko acting as Easy's boss, the two only saw each other at work.

"We're just colleagues, not friends," Easy said. "If a person choose his own direction, I don't blame him."

The men visited the Biehls in America, and were invited to speak at conferences across the country. They were disappointed that they did not meet many of "the Black Americans," whom Easy expected—as per a lifetime of watching TV shows and movies, particularly *Big Momma's House,* starring the "great actor and great guy" Martin Lawrence—to say things like, "Yeah, mah maaannn, wussup, mah maaannn!" and "Mudder*fucker*!" Easy and Ntobeko preferred the New Jersey suburbs to the towering New York buildings, and once looked upon a swath of untamed Massachusetts land and noted that they could build an African village there. They were pleased to stay near a Manhattan police station, which they referred to as "NYPD Blue" and had their snapshots taken with mustachioed cops. Easy discovered that his favorite cuisine was the American buffet, which allowed a person to eat as much meat as desired for no additional fee. The men were impressed by hotels, and in particular, hotel bathrooms, which were the polar opposite of Gugulethu outhouses. During one trip, they took a series of photographs of each other dressed in color-coordinated b-boy outfits, lounging on the marble sink and striking a pose by the glass-encased shower. Easy kept these pictures, along with several stand-alone portraits of toilets and bathtubs, in a photo album.

After Peter died of aggressive colon cancer at age fifty-nine in 2002, Ntobeko and Easy helped arrange a Gugulethu memorial service in his honor. The two marched Linda around the township, one man on each arm, trailed by a crowd of mourners. As they had done before Peter's death, the men continued to accompany Linda to paid engagements in Europe and the United States, where their relationship was held up as an example of the power of forgiveness, reconciliation, and redemption.

At least—with the exception of some blogs run by disapproving white-power enthusiasts who, upon relating Amy's story, gleefully claimed, "liberalism can get you killed!"—that was how the story had always gone, repeated ad infinitum in over a thousand national and international newspaper and magazine articles, in award-winning documentaries, on talk shows, on radio shows, on TV shows. And why wouldn't it? Its stars played their parts, and confirmed the arc and breadth of the distinct narrative: black South Africans, loving by nature but distorted into rampage by apartheid, who had been reformed and redeemed through the grace of an inspirational if puzzling pair of good-looking white Americans.

Now it was the twentieth anniversary of Amy's death. Press interest had waned years ago. Before, the top journalists at major international papers had covered the ongoing story, but now the only foreign press was a reporter from Linda's hometown paper, *The Orange County Register*, jotting down notes. During this trip, Linda had one radio interview, which was in turn picked up by a single website. The press had largely forgotten about Amy and the Truth and Reconciliation Commission, and were busy looking into the more immediate potty protests, during which angry township residents who wanted to relieve themselves in flush toilets instead of the communal sludge buckets they currently employed, had taken to throwing human feces at the mayor's vehicle and dumping the contents of their latrines near Parliament. CAPE TOWN POO WARS, the BBC headline shouted.

Regardless, the people in St. Columba's church that day were focusing on Amy's too-brief life. The foundation loyalists, women who had known and worked for Linda for fifteen years, snuck into the church late, one with her hair tied into knots so tight that her scalp was pulled and red, one intently applying lip gloss with a wand. Ntobeko's wife, wearing a pale gray skirt and top with her hair in ringlets, and their two older daughters in freshly pressed dresses, sat to the back. Ntobeko himself was not there. A haze of incense settled near the ceiling; I could feel the perfume spreading through my lungs.

"Jesus was a teacher, Jesus was a rector, Jesus was everything!" a lady preacher in colorful patterned Xhosa garb began.

"Yes!" said the congregants. They were mostly women, ranging in age from thirty to ninety, in African-print dresses, cardigans, shawls, blazers. A minority of men and children were scattered few and far between.

"Whom do I trust?" the preacher asked rhetorically. "Jesus!"

"Mmmm hmmm," the ladies said.

The preacher launched into Xhosa, then reverted to English. She introduced Linda as "Amy Biehl's mother."

"Hiiii," the ladies said in unison. In these parts, for the older generation, the name Amy Biehl required no explanation.

The preacher said she'd organized a speaker on the occasion of American guests but the speaker had disappointed her by bailing, so she herself would be speaking today. Don't we all know about disappointment? Everyone nodded vigorously.

"Amy was a hero," the preacher said uncertainly. She was winging it. "That was the plan of God. That she must die the way she did." The preacher turned to Linda. "Thank you for having heart to show peace and love."

"Amen," the ladies said solemnly. Linda bowed her head slightly.

A male preacher, dressed in a heavy robe, took over.

"You are here for a reason, Amy was here for a reason," he said to Linda. "We wish you a good day and we will always remember you in our prayers."

"Amen," said the ladies.

I looked around for Easy, then recalled that he was allergic to churches, and so probably would not make an appearance after all. Then again, he sometimes, without great enthusiasm, talked about how Jesus died for his sins, which usually signaled that his evangelical uncle had succeeded in dragging him to a service. So perhaps Easy was, more accurately, allergic not to churches but to the annual memorials to Amy that were held in churches. A year earlier, to the day, at a Catholic church nearby, I had also looked up from the service to find Easy missing. I'd slipped out of the pew and found him pacing nervously on the lawn. He took me into a back room and showed me a bare wall, where local kids used to watch projector movies; he was a sentimentalist, and he remembered, with characteristic nostalgia, not having the five-cent admission fee and sneaking in through a bathroom window.

Now, as the women sang hymns, I went outside to look for Easy, but he was gone, and he had taken the van. I stood in the sunlight, trying to get warm. August is chilly in Cape Town, winter in the Southern Hemisphere. A gray-haired white lady was cutting hearts out of fabric on a bench nearby, assisted by a pretty black teenage girl who called her Grandma. They offered me a heart and a safety pin decorated with colorful beads.

"They symbolize love over violence," the girl explained as I stuck the pin to my sweater.

Some months earlier, the country had been in an uproar about

Anene Booysen, a plain-looking brown-skinned seventeen-year-old
from a poor Western Cape town who was gang-raped and disem-
boweled on an abandoned construction site. An even more newsworthy victim, and one who would captivate the nation's attention
for years to come, was Reeva Steenkamp, the radiant blond thirty-
year-old model and reality TV star shot to death through a bathroom door by her boyfriend, the Olympian and double-amputee
Oscar Pistorius. These fabric hearts, the lady said, honored Anene
and Reeva and Amy, too, and all the thousands of women injured,
murdered, and violated by men each year.

I wandered down NY1 to Amy's memorial statue, by the Caltex
gas station and garage where she was killed. From across the street, I
could see the dry grass, the old cars piled up for repair, the low stone
wall that had long ago replaced the white fence that Amy had leaned
on during the attack. The memorial statue was a slick gray marble
cross erected in 2010 by the Fulbright Foundation, unveiled to
vague fanfare by the U.S. ambassador at the time. On the base of the
memorial, carved into stone in elegant capitals, were the words:

AMY BIEHL

26 APRIL 1967 - 25 AUGUST 1993

KILLED IN AN ACT OF POLITICAL VIOLENCE.

AMY WAS A FULBRIGHT SCHOLAR AND TIRELESS

HUMAN RIGHTS ACTIVIST.

A disheveled old man usually spent his days leaning against the
cross, sleeping rough with his three dogs, but the man had been
temporarily relocated to a nearby field. I spotted Ntobeko standing
on the pavement above, by the gas pumps. His childhood nickname
was Blacks, for he was so dark-skinned that from afar his features
were hard to make out. Up close, he was a rotund, somber-looking
man in his late thirties, with a narrow face and a weak chin. His head
was shaved and rubbed with lotion. His small, glistening eyes were
intelligent and suspicious, his nose long and Roman. He was neither

tall nor short, and he wore his black Amy Biehl Foundation logo polo shirt stretched tight over his expansive belly.

Ntobeko used to be the scrawniest kid, a pencil neck sticking out of an oversized T-shirt, often borrowed. Now he owned a home, the chicken wholesale business, and two minivans that he used to transport upwardly mobile township children to schools in the city or the suburbs. He was married to his childhood sweetheart and had three daughters. He was a manager, which in Gugulethu held a grand allure—no longer was he merely bossed around, no, finally he got to do the bossing. Ntobeko ate meat nearly every day. His old friends to whom he no longer spoke remembered that he had been a naughty kid who ran around the streets and lived in a tiny house full of extended family. He would miss his household curfew and supper, and find himself locked out for the night. "He was a wild boy who slept in the trees," one such friend once told me. Ntobeko saw me from across the road and, as always, averted his gaze.

Ntobeko was helping two other foundation staffers arrange a group of children before two marimbas. Marimbas are wooden xylophone-like instruments that originated in Africa and were introduced by sixteenth-century slaves to Latin America, where they were redesigned and spread around the world. A few kids were expertly hitting the bars with mallets, the chimes whipped up into the wind. A chorus swayed behind them, biding their time, singing half-heartedly. I turned back and went to wait outside the church.

Soon, the doors opened and Linda followed the stream of church-goers. She wore a black pleated skirt, just above the knee, a black top, black pumps, a coral blazer, and a silk coral scarf. Her hair was, as always, perfect: short, angular, gleaming white-blond, and stick-straight.

A ragtag group of people gathered around her, comprised of a couple of academics Amy had known when she studied in Cape Town; the ambulance driver who had tried unsuccessfully to treat Amy as she died; the fabric-heart-making lady and girl; the reporter for Linda's hometown paper and the photographer who accompa-

nied her; some Los Angeles–based college graduates making a short
film starring black South Africans whose hope against all odds would
stun and inspire any audience; several people involved in some form
of media; and Nancy Scheper-Hughes, the anthropologist who had
introduced Easy and Ntobeko to the Biehls.

Nancy was an elfin sixty-something woman with a pert nose and
short gray hair; she radiated a nervous intellectual energy. She was a
woman molded by the 1960s free love movement, who tended
toward all views radically left-wing and, "being an old Wobbly socialist," actually celebrated Labor Day. Nancy had been working at
the University of Cape Town when Amy was killed, though she'd
left the country soon after. Back then, Nancy had joined a band of
furious women of all different races and marched the streets of Gugulethu in protest, waving placards demanding that the brutality
cease. Now Nancy and her husband had flown out from California,
carrying the old cardboard signs from that 1993 peace march, which
Nancy had saved for all these years and handed out to anyone who
wanted one. Nancy was the director of the Program of Medical An-
thropology at UC Berkeley, and had published three books significant in her field, but she appeared not to mind bad spelling: a couple
of the handwritten signs read STOP THE SENCELESS VIOLENCE and AMY
BIEHL, OUR COMERADE.

The small group walked down the street toward the marimba
music. Linda wore her sunglasses; she would have made a great first
lady, at once regal and Midwestern, warm but removed, with the
looks of an aging, corn-fed beauty queen. Everyone followed. Locals, sitting on low walls and smoking on milk crates, watched with
little interest. A young man in long shorts stood outside the TyreMan
Tyre Shop and clapped without knowing why.

Ntobeko, who saw the group coming, walked slowly away, expertly disappearing into the township. His daughter, the little girl in
purple, grabbed Linda's hand tightly. She wasn't even in kindergarten, but she knew the drill. The full-color image promptly appeared

in *The Orange County Register*, accompanying a story on love and reconciliation in South Africa:

Linda Biehl, front left, walks with Avile Peni, 3, the daughter of one of the four men convicted and imprisoned for her daughter Amy Biehl's death on August 25, 1993.

The group arrived at the marble cross, the kids stopped playing, and everyone briefly grappled with what to do next. Somebody had placed upon the memorial a blown-up old photo of the late Peter Biehl, a smiling, white-haired man with the chunked-out build of a retired college football player, flanked by a young Easy flashing a peace sign and a young Ntobeko grinning broadly; it had been taken during their first meeting and was weighed down with a cracked brick, of the sort that had been used to bludgeon Amy. Amy's old Cape Town university colleagues had offered to arrange a memorial day a while back but hadn't done anything, so this whole makeshift show had been put together on the fly in the days since Linda had landed a week earlier.

"Who wants to give a speech?" Linda asked. A curly-haired former colleague of Amy's stood up, said a few words about her departed friend, let out a sob, and threw herself into Linda's arms. Linda patted her while maintaining a close-mouthed smile; the photographer snapped away. Some others filed before the small crowd and spoke about the loveliness of Amy, the strength of Linda, and the importance of grace and transformation. Nancy, holding her STOP THE SENCELESS VIOLENCE sign, took the stage for twenty minutes, during which her husband shot her a stream of "cut-it-short" glares, which she ignored.

"Amy was a beautiful soul!" Nancy said. She wore wire-rim glasses and long colorful earrings.

I stood away from the group and leaned against a white sedan. Mzi Noji, a middle-aged, unemployed ex-militant, ex-con, and army veteran, arrived on foot, wearing his green cap, embroidered with the phrase UNIVERSAL MESSAGE over a Rastafarian flag. Mzi was a lifelong social activist, raised during the height of the anti-apartheid struggle. Even today, when he claimed that he wanted to get on with his life, he continually found himself embroiled in protests, marches, negotiations, meetings, neighborhood committees, and organizations.

I'd met Mzi by chance a year earlier, and he had become an unexpected kindred spirit, as well as my guide, my translator, my friend. He accompanied me on my expeditions and investigations into the Amy Biehl story, often driving my car and dredging up forgotten people from within the depths of the townships. Mzi was also to be my key to unraveling the truth, or as much truth as possible, of what really happened on that fateful day twenty years before.

Until I met Mzi at a burger shop downtown, I had been tracking the same story that every journalist before me had written, except that my aim had been to tell for the first time the full tale as it stretched over two decades. But Mzi informed me that he believed that this long-accepted story of the circumstances of Amy's death was not exactly accurate. His revelation had led me, in a series of nearly unbelievable coincidences, to a meeting I had had the day before. After months of frenzied searching, I had finally found an old and ruined man who had also been in Gugulethu on August 25, 1993, though few remembered him. Nobody had ever told his account of that day, nor made the chilling links between what had happened to him and what had happened to Amy Biehl five hours later and a quarter mile away. The old man knew something about brutal mobs and racial violence, and he was the final piece in the jigsaw I had been painstakingly piecing together for two years.

Mzi sidled up next to me, his cap pulled low over his deep-set eyes. He was tall and strong, with a little paunch he was self-conscious about, so he was always abstaining from chocolate milkshakes even though he loved them. We each crossed our arms on the roof of the sedan and rested our chins on our forearms. By then, Easy had reappeared and parked the van to the side of the memorial, and was hiding behind us, hoping he would not be called on to talk. He was mumbling: Man, he hoped Makhulu did not make him stand up before the group.

"Amy was an accidental hero," Nancy said.

Mzi's hands were shaking. He looked down at them, and so did I.

"Her death was a Shakespearean tragedy!" Nancy said.

The old lady and the girl had hit up everyone, I noticed. Every lapel boasted a beaded pin and a cutout heart.

"Linda is strong, charismatic, beautiful," Nancy said.

I looked around. I felt a surge of fury, inexplicable in its intensity. I moved closer to Mzi. In a few days, his great-aunt's house would burn down, with his great-aunt inside. Just like his own mother's house back in the old days of politics and firestorms, when the ANC kids in the neighborhood shot it full of lead and set it alight with petrol bombs. Now there was no liberation movement to blame, no just cause or grand scheme, no enemies intent on your demise. Just faulty wiring and cheap petroleum heaters. Mzi was listening intently to Nancy, his face set in that practiced flat expression of his, composed specifically to shroud the fact that he was almost always overwhelmed by various emotions.

Nancy praised Easy and Ntobeko. This was a story of "gentle forgiveness," she said. "Of lived apology!"

When she finished her speech, the crowd applauded.

Linda stood before her guests. She looked for Easy and Ntobeko. Ntobeko was long gone, so she called for Easy. A sharp intake of breath, back straightened, and then he emerged from behind us and went to her. Easy hooked his arm in Linda's and stood with her as a local reporter scribbled, a pair of student videographers filmed, the hometown newspaper photographer snapped away. Linda began to say her part. Easy and I looked at each other for the briefest of moments, eye-to-eye above the small crowd, and then he turned back to smile for the cameras.

2.

They tell me: eat and drink. Be glad to be
   among the haves!
But how can I eat and drink
When I take what I eat from the starving
And those who thirst do not have my
   glass of water?
And yet I eat and drink.

—BERTOLT BRECHT, "To Those Who
   Follow in Our Wake"

When I went to live in South Africa in November 2011, I didn't know what to expect, and I didn't reflect on it. My husband, Sam, then my fiancé, wanted to return on sabbatical to the country he had left at age eighteen, so I followed. Career-wise, I was untethered. Years earlier, I had published a light travel memoir to nobody's notice, and since then I had no real writing prospects as far as I could tell. Every single article I pitched to magazines was rejected. I kept submitting short stories set in Montana to literary journal contests, in the hopes of winning $500, but I only came in as runner-up twice, so I actually lost money, since it usually cost $20 to enter. To make ends meet, I had taken to editing a celebrity doctor's website, despite having no medical knowledge. If Sam wanted to move across the world, I had no argument against it.

Soon after Sam took off to find us a place in Cape Town, I sold the old SUV I'd had for years, moved my boxes to a storage locker in New Jersey, packed an oversized duffel bag full of clothes, forced my flailing dog into a travel-safe crate at the JFK cargo terminal, and hurtled fourteen hours across the ocean to Johannesburg. Sam met me at Arrivals. We planned to drive the nine hundred miles to Cape Town rather than put the dog on another connecting flight, so we rented a car and cut through the Karoo desert.

Karoo, which means "land of thirst" in the indigenous Khoikhoi language, is a vast, bleak scrubland that stretches through the country, searingly hot in the afternoon and cold as steel at night. Sheep roam across its inhospitable terrain, dotted with rugged little shepherds' dwellings where young boys with hard feet spend months alone. I sat in the passenger seat and gazed out the window at the monotonous landscape. It looked like a place picked over, as if anything of value, anything lush or desirable or even a little bit sweet or pretty, had been collected by a determined band of looters sweeping across the plain, leaving behind only dry bush and dust. The N1 highway slices through that rugged expanse, wide and smooth and lonely.

Only a few hours from Johannesburg, we came upon a gruesome car accident. The remains of a car sat diagonally across two lanes, its mangled hood smashed into its windshield, its roof sliced clean off. The pavement was strewn with glass, sparkling like crystals in the high spring sun, and a couple of truckers had pulled to the side to call for help and to snap cellphone photos. Some merciful soul had rolled a heavy woolen blanket across the top of the car to try to conceal three bodies sitting upright.

The image lingers bright and precise in my mind: two men flank a woman in the back of the ruined car, which was slammed—by what? a tractor trailer?—with such force that the passengers must have died on impact but were not ejected from their seats, perhaps because they were packed so tight in there. All three are slender with dark brown skin, and young, judging by their builds. The woman wears a pink T-shirt. Her hair is jet black and plaited into stiff shoulder-length braids that stick out in all different directions—like Pippi Longstocking, I remember thinking.

From then on, we drove slowly and anxiously to the guesthouse where we planned to stay the night. It was situated in the stark Northern Cape desert town of Colesburg, the halfway point between Johannesburg and Cape Town, where it seemed every other home offered a bed for weary travelers. The owner, an elderly man of British ancestry, led us to our room, a white square filled with pink floral pillows, a pink comforter marred by a tiny blood spot, and a knitted woolen throw so rough that the dog used it to scratch her back. The decoration was minimal: a single straw hat, pinned with a fake rose, nailed to the wall.

That night, we drove through the town, which gave the impression of overwhelming flatness—flat roads, flat land, flat houses—and ate tasteless, mushy vegetables at a pub patronized only by white people. After, we stopped for snacks at a local twenty-four-hour shop. As I stood in line to pay for chips and a drink, a tired-looking light-brown-skinned woman at the register spoke to me in a heavy Germanic-sounding language I couldn't understand. She was, Sam explained, a colored woman, a term that sounds offensively retrograde to Americans but is in fact the designation for the population of mixed-race South Africans. The language she had directed at me was Afrikaans, a derivation of Old Dutch spoken mainly by South Africa's colored people and white Afrikaners, the descendants of early European settlers.

The next day, as we were leaving, we chatted with our host, a former school principal who said he had taken a buyout package for state employees when the black majority came to power in 1994. He had retired early to run this unique interpretation of an inn.

"So, what's the population of Colesburg?" Sam asked.

"Two thousand whites, five thousand coloreds, and fifteen thousand blacks," the man answered. That was how he automatically understood his hometown—as a collection of people broken into racial categories. We herded the dog into the car and headed toward our final destination: Cape Town.

The Western Cape contains the southernmost tip of the African continent. European explorers and kings and queens had long agreed that if they could only round the Cape, they would be able to sail northeast to India and open a sea route to Asia, with its silks and spices and gemstones and teas. Such a route would prove lucrative to European powers, which had so far only managed to arrange an arduous and dangerous trade trek through the Middle East, which was teeming with bandits and costly middlemen. The only problem, as the Europeans saw it, was the Cape's habit of swallowing ships.

On February 3, 1488, the square-jawed Portuguese voyager Bartolomeu Dias and his crew anchored near a freshwater spring in a fishing village known today as Mossel Bay. Dias had departed Lisbon seven months earlier in an attempt to chart a new southern route to Asia, and he and his haggard crew had just survived a harrowing storm. Above, watching from a bluff, stood a group of Khoikhoi tribesmen, indigenous cattle farmers with yellow-brown skin, standing around five feet tall.

The Khoikhoi, grazing their animals by the sea on that day in the fifteenth century, watched as a vessel full of ashen humans docked in their watering hole and started taking water. The Khoikhoi were not a particularly warmongering group, but, angry and frightened, they pelted the explorers with rocks. The whites responded with gunshots, killing a Khoikhoi before sailing away.

Though Dias wished to continue charting the eastbound journey, his bedraggled crew threatened mutiny, and so the ship stopped at what is now known as Bushman's River, where Dias planted a Portuguese flag and then turned homeward. One cold comfort for Dias was that he had at least laid eyes on the meridional tip of Africa, a rocky point of land where waves crashed relentlessly against the shore and heavy winds blew through tough grasses and low, hardy scrubs. The balmy currents of the Indian Ocean here meet the arctic currents of the Atlantic. From a height, one can see the two bodies of water tangle together in a shaky line of wild white foam that stretches past the horizon.

These waters had pushed Dias blindly out to sea, and Dias, returning home after seventeen months with his men, named the area Cabo das Tormentas, or Cape of Storms. King John II of Portugal, who saw the Cape as a stop on the profitable opening to the East, rebranded it Cabo da Boa Esperança, or Cape of Good Hope. But Dias had been prescient: twelve years later, on another journey, he and his crew were swallowed whole by the Cabo das Tormentas, their sunken ship never found.

Dias's bearded compatriot Vasco da Gama was more successful. In 1497, he was the first to navigate an all-water eastern passage. Da Gama rode the winds down the African coast, then arced into the Atlantic and swept back toward land, docking for supplies and water in an inlet on the Western Cape today known as St. Helena Bay. There, the threatened Khoikhoi again attacked, spearing da Gama in the thigh. Undeterred, da Gama and his crew continued down the coast and rounded its tip. Again, they came upon a tribe of Khoi-khoi, but this time they enjoyed better relations, offering gifts. Da Gama even danced with some locals.

The good vibes were short lived. As was the Portuguese habit, da Gama took water supplies without asking the chief for permission. The Khoikhoi, aghast at da Gama's slight, readied themselves to at-tack, and da Gama quickly sailed off to the western coast of India, which he would reach in 1498 with the help of an Arab navigator he picked up in East Africa. In 1510, the Khoikhoi slaughtered sixty-five Europeans, including a Portuguese viceroy heading home after his term in the East—a massacre that resulted in a century during which ships gave the Cape a wide berth.

This was the inauspicious beginning of the relationship between blacks and whites in South Africa, a relationship that began with whites taking natural resources that both groups assumed were rightfully theirs. In a foretelling of events to be replayed in centuries to come, the blacks threw stones, and the whites responded with bullets.

A year before landing in Cape Town, I'd been to South Africa on holiday. Those days in the Karoo had offered me a hint that living in the country would be nothing like that three-week vacation, when we took a safari just outside of Kruger Park and saw a pride of lions, dozens of elephants, the far-off silhouette of a leopard, and a pack of endangered spotted African wild dogs chilling out in the bush, licking their balls and nuzzling each other like regular pets, except that they could run at forty miles an hour to gut and devour a gazelle. In Cape Town, we lay about on palm-tree-lined beaches, which were too sunny for my New England tastes. The white people on the beaches—and there were mostly white people on the wealthy stretch of beachside suburbs known as the Atlantic Seaboard—looked like descendants of Russian oligarchs, *Baywatch* actors, and/or the cast of your average reality television program: lots of enhanced breasts and chiseled six-packs, displayed with unabashed vanity.

But when I settled in Cape Town for two years, I found the city disconcerting. I landed in a white enclave by the seaside, where my husband's Jewish family and their insular, tight-knit community lived in the houses typical of well-off South Africans: pale-colored cement rectangles surrounded by high walls lined with barbed coils, electric shock wire, or shards of broken glass.

The white Capetonians I met at first had been raised in a country steeped in racist policy and educated according to a racist curriculum. History books reinvented colonial commandos who slaughtered indigenous people as heroes. During apartheid most whites had never seen the living conditions of blacks. Opposition groups were banned, their leaders in exile or prison. The media was heavily censored. In 1977, for example, 1,246 publications, 41 periodicals, and 41 films were banned in South Africa—most of them putting forth an anti-apartheid view. The government also controlled TV, radio, and, to some extent, newspapers. After apartheid, most whites still turned away from the reality of daily life for their black compatriots, never visiting townships, denying or justifying the continued inequities between the races. Therefore, most white South Africans of a certain age, and accordingly their children, had become—

through grand design, through osmosis, and through their own choice to accept the status quo—entrenched in racism.

A friend of mine once suggested that an anthropologist would do well to study the ways of the white tribes of South Africa. The white Capetonians I met liked working out, getting their hair done, shopping, displaying large diamonds, driving flashy cars, eating sushi, and cooing at their dogs, both pedigreed and rescued. They referred to things that tickled their fancies as "stunning," "spectacular," "unreal," and "*out* of this world." They dished local gossip and talked about money and business. They discussed families who had been lucky enough to emigrate to the major white South African resettlement destinations: the States, the U.K., Israel, Australia, Canada. No matter how many assets a person possessed in South Africa, he was guaranteed to moan about the country going to pot, and how a trailer in Sydney was better than a mansion in the most beautiful city of the most advanced country on this doomed continent.

They peppered mundane conversation topics with casual mentions of the black majority, most of whom they feared and few of whom they knew on a personal level. South Africa has no ingrained culture of "political correctness," and so, on the subject of race, many people are generally far more forthright, nonchalant, and openly offensive than Americans. The white South Africans I met casually attributed to black people a number of negative characteristics: laziness, dishonesty, savagery, stupidity, ungratefulness, ugliness. They were puzzled by my sputtering protests, and regarded me as a naive foreigner (which I was, but for other reasons). They blamed all the problems in modern-day South Africa not on an intricate and complex set of political and socioeconomic issues running back centuries, but rather on the intrinsically hideous qualities of blacks. If the country was going to pot, this was because black people were fundamentally incapable of leadership. Presenting them with an endless list of horrible white leaders throughout history did nothing to change their minds.

"Blacks are lazy, and you'd know that if you worked at a corporate. I'm not being racist, I'm just stating the facts."

"Sponsor a black child to go to school? Oh, right, because they end up being such *model citizens.*"

"I sure as hell *am* racist. The difference for you liberal Americans is your population is fifteen percent of them, but ours is nearly ninety percent."

"It's about the trees. They came down from the damn trees."

"It's not racist to be scared of black people. It's realistic."

The people who said such things were not dropouts from the boonies. Rather, they were well educated and widely traveled: a lawyer, a businessman, a designer, a farmer, a small business owner. And they were decent people, too. The racists of South Africa are a kindly lot, who are helpful and resourceful, community-minded and polite. They're a good laugh, fine company, and fantastic to have by your side if you're in a pickle. These very bigots, many of whom I hardly knew, have driven me across the country, saved my dog's life, provided me top-notch medical care, given me free room and board when I needed it most, generously hosted me in their homes, and cooked me meals. And they don't just help other white people. I have seen them feed the poor colored beggars, even as they roll their eyes; offer free and compassionate legal advice to the very black people for whom they have previously expressed disdain; put their gardener's children through school; and buy beautiful houses for their maids, complete with furniture.

Usually, when the racists know black people personally, they are capable of seeing them as individuals. But on a larger level, to them black South Africans seem to meld together with their inept, corrupt black leaders, into an indiscernible mass, a majority that is steering the country toward mayhem: economic free fall, widespread violent crime, a crumbling public healthcare system, a broken government peopled with cronies. It is this mass—not specific members of it—that is the enemy. Before the mass existed (or more accurately, when it was disempowered and hidden), white South Africans lived in a kind of utopia: agreeable dirt-cheap labor, all the fruits of a gifted land, beauty everywhere for the taking, lovely neighborhoods with open doors, and all the suffering contained behind borders at a good distance.

Once I asked Easy about a friend of his whose actions were inconsistent. What he said makes as much sense as anything: "He's a human being. Sometimes he's good, sometimes he's evil. Sometimes he is *comme ci*. Sometimes he is *comme ça*."

I met plenty of exceptional white South Africans, of course. I came to know a yoga teacher whose many boyfriends spanned the racial spectrum, and a corporate mom born into a conservative Afrikaner family who married a Congolese basketball player. I spent time with some of the old white freedom fighters, who remained as committed to racial equality and justice as ever. I hung around a bunch of my husband's high school friends, well-off thirty-something men who were focused on their various apolitical endeavors, like creating a Burning Man–type festival in Africa or bringing Cape Town its first New York–style Jewish deli or attending ayahuasca ceremonies for spiritual healing. And I knew plenty of young white activists who worked with the country's most disadvantaged, including a man fluent in the Zimbabwean tongue of Shona who had devoted his life to helping African refugees gain footing in a new land.

However, according to the wealthy white citizens I met at first, townships—the impoverished zones created by the apartheid government to segregate black South Africans—were the epicenters of the crime epidemic sweeping the country, the places out of which black badness oozed. During apartheid, people of color had little access to white areas, generally allowed in during the day to work but banned after close of business. Once the laws that controlled people's movement had been dismantled, that violence spilled out, affecting whites as well as everyone else (though whites complained most vigorously, crime actually affected them far less than it did their dark-skinned compatriots). South Africa, with its soaring crime rate, was now among the world's most violent countries, with a murder rate five times that of the global average. Every day across the country there were 502 assaults, 475 robberies, 172 sexual offenses, 47 murders, and 31 carjackings. Every day, 714 houses were burgled, 202 businesses were robbed, and 349 cars were broken into.

Instead of seeing these daily terrors as the result of tyranny, many South African whites came to associate them with the enduring *swaart gevaar*, or black danger. The threat of the *swaart gevaar*—the concept of an overwhelming and inherently bloodthirsty black majority that needed to be contained lest it consume everything in its path—had been used to persuade a white electorate to vote into power in 1948 the National Party, whose platform came to be known as apartheid.

I could see these townships, Gugulethu in particular, from the highway leading away from the airport: a glimmering sea of corrugated tin shacks separated from the road by only a strip of grass, upon which I once saw a man squatting for a shit while casually flipping through a magazine. This accounted for the faint fecal stink that wafted out from the slums, especially on hot days. I was eager to see inside, but I was informed, repeatedly, of the dangers of those ghettos, which teemed with ruthless gangs high on a type of rough local crystal meth called *tik*.

In an old *Lonely Planet* guidebook I found, nestled between reviews for the extravagant high tea at the pink Mount Nelson Hotel and a most pleasant ride up the aerial cableway to Table Mountain, I read a quick note on the townships, which were situated in the Cape Flats, a depressed belt of sand and bedrock southeast of the city known as "apartheid's dumping ground":

> For the majority of Cape Town's inhabitants, home is one of the grim townships of the Cape Flats: Gugulethu, Nyanga, Philippi, Mitchell's Plain, Crossroads, or Khayelitsha. Visiting without a companion who has local knowledge would be foolish. If a black friend is happy to escort you, you should have no problems.

Lacking an amenable black escort at the time, I waited until one day, less than a month into my stay, an opportunity to pass over those allegedly dangerous borders presented itself. Sam was setting up a project aimed at improving the delivery of basic social services for the poor, and he had been invited by an NGO to see the conditions in Khayelitsha, a sprawling township of nearly 400,000 people just north of Gugulethu. He asked me if I'd like to come along.

On that hot day in November, we met two women at the organization's headquarters off a main road, a chilly refurbished municipal building surrounded by barbed wire and guarded by a groundskeeper and his two sooty dogs. The lead guide was a fat and pretty black lady, with a flawless complexion and a short ponytail. Her assistant, also black, was a grave, slender woman with cropped hair and glasses; the left side of her body, running from her chin to her hand, had been consumed by fire long ago, and the skin was knotted with scar tissue.

Townships are divided, roughly, into formal and informal areas. The formal areas are generally those built up with simple cement houses along paved streets. Most were constructed years ago by the apartheid government, and have been, over time, expanded by their inhabitants, repainted various colors, remodeled and tricked out or neglected and allowed to fester. Some were constructed more recently by the new black-led government under the Reconstruction and Development Programme, which aimed to help close the massive gap between the rich and poor, and white and brown. These are known as "RDP houses," and tend to be small, relatively new, identical matchbox homes clustered together. The key to such a house is obtained by languishing on a waiting list. Woven between, behind, and among the legal homes is a web of backyard shacks, built by homeowners and rented out in an underground township economy.

The formal areas also contain hostels taken over by squatters. During apartheid, companies housed black migrant laborers in single-sex dormitory-like structures, carting them to and from manual jobs each day and allowing them one month a year to visit their families in the rural areas designated for most blacks. In the late 1980s and early 1990s, as apartheid edged toward its demise and the townships became increasingly ungovernable, the companies abandoned these buildings and the workers and their families took over. Twenty years later, they still live in cramped, deteriorating quarters under faded signs bearing the names of the original owners: WJM CONSTRUCTION CORP, UME STEEL LTD, DAIRY-BELLE PTY. Pigeons roost in the broken shower stalls. Once in a while, a police tow truck pulls out from a hostel's courtyard, dragging a stolen car behind it.

Informal settlements are plots of previously barren urban land upon which people squat, usually in haphazard tin shacks. They are meant to be temporary, but often become permanent as their inhabitants, mired in poverty, fail to either score an RDP house or rent a better spot. The settlements rise up on township borders and on undesirable land within. They contain a mixture of city-born locals, migrants from the underdeveloped South African countryside, and refugees, asylum seekers, and undocumented aliens from repressive Zimbabwe, impoverished Ethiopia, war-torn Somalia, war-torn Democratic Republic of the Congo, and war-torn Burundi. Since the settlements are not government-approved, they receive little in terms of services and once in a while are unceremoniously torn down.

Our guides lived in one such settlement, a maze of makeshift matchbox houses set on gray sand. The plumper woman lived in a tidy single room with her husband, a few children, and the inevitable rat or two. She called her young son, a shirtless ten-year-old with a mischievous smile, and instructed him to watch our car, which we parked in a dirt yard. We would conduct the tour on foot, since the pathways far into the shantytowns—tiny, potholed roads that passed through insecure territories—weren't built for vehicles. We were deep inside Khayelitsha now, invisible to the outside world.

"See how we are living," a woman called from behind a low wire fence as we trudged through the sand. In her shack, a flat-screen TV played a daytime soap, and a bunch of people sat on stools, drinking brandy, waving at us. "Come in, come see how we live."

Trash piled up in a stagnant, water-filled ditch beside the houses. Children with crusty faces played by a pile of refuse, where a herd of goats feasted. The garbage was laced with rat poison. During the rainy season, when water seeped into the shacks and sewage spilled into the streets, kids came down with diarrhea. A pack of dogs slunk by, all grown in the township canine mold: of medium size, sporting short pale-brown fur, with pointy ears pressed low against the head. A few weeks earlier, a different rogue pack of mutts had broken into a shack and mauled a child to death, so the people were in the mood to stone them. A barefoot white man with dreadlocks and a long beard lay in the lap of a black woman, her hair tied back with a violet scarf. They wore stained pajamas and faced the sun.

We passed a low swampland on the border of the highway, shacks built among the reeds; in the rain, pungent murky water rose up through the floors of each house, whose lightbulbs were powered by a spaghetti of ragged lines jury-rigged from the power poles. The shack dwellers were unmoved by posters urging South Africans to KEEP OUR COUNTRY POWER-FUL, part of a nationwide campaign to curb electricity theft.

Toilets were often buckets or the fetid fields by the highway, where people squatted in the open as cars whizzed by, the worlds so separate that neither the drivers nor the defecators seemed concerned by each other's humanity. Some portable toilets had been provided by companies that had won city contracts, but they were rarely cleaned or emptied, and the resulting indignities had led, in part, to the Poo Wars. Worse, such toilets could easily be toppled, as the installers sometimes skimped on cash by failing to secure them to the ground. Local criminals pushed the unstable toilets over while people were inside, reached in, grabbed cellphones or cash, and left their victims scrambling amid a soup of age-old human waste and neon-blue chemical sludge. Kids on their way to pee in the pitch-black night were hit by cars or snatched off a path and molested. Adults who needed to expel before a morning shift at work were mugged for their cellphones as they hiked in the dim predawn light.

The whole area shared a dozen or so communal taps. I tried to figure out how a person could bathe, the dwellings pressed so close
together.

"What about privacy?" I asked the assistant.

"Privacy?" She let out a bitter laugh. "There is no privacy."

The women led us past a row of yellow three-room houses built
by an Irish charity. I admired the houses, popping out cheerfully
from the mass of gray corrugated tin and old timber, the address
numbers painted in pastels by the front doors, accented by a little
cartoon flower. The assistant pointed to a ramshackle two-story gray
manor at the path's corner, its roof supported by uneven columns. At
the base of the manor was an austere grocery shop manned by an
aging grocer in a white hat.

"He was the chairman in charge of these charity houses," she said,
grabbing my arm. "He takes the money and eats it. Look at his
house. He takes the cement from the other houses, so now they
begin to fall apart." I scanned the yellow houses; their year-old ex-
teriors were indeed already beginning to chip at the edges. I imagined the butcher scooping up a portion of each material allotment
and patching it together, bit by bit, until his own home took shape,
towering above the rest.

We walked on. Teenage boys laughed and shared cigarettes by a
little spaza shop, a bodega that sells soda, candy, chips, phone cards. A
man shaved his friend's head on a stoop, dipping his razor and soap
in and out of a bucket. Children brightened as we passed, reached
for our hands. Finally, we came upon the tour's ultimate destination:
a square of sand, smoke rising from its edges. People were bringing
buckets of water and pieces of wood and iron back and forth.

"It burned last night," the guide explained, ushering us into the
smoldering lot. Of the three shacks that previously stood here, only
outlines on the ground remained, debris all around. Nobody knew
how the fire had started—a cigarette in bed? An electrical outage? A
gas stove? Or maybe somebody had a grudge; it was not unheard of
to lock an enemy in his shack and set it alight, leaving him to pound

at the door as he burned. Once a spark caught, all nearby shacks could be consumed by flames; in these tight quarters, built of thin flammable materials, fire spread fast, and sometimes it took out hundreds of shacks before a fire truck could arrive and control the blaze. Whole neighborhoods were flattened and rebuilt on the regular. Our guide had twice lost her home to fire and once lost her shack when the city council resettled her whole block to make room for a new power plant. She had come home to find a slash of red spray paint across her door, marking her place as one to be removed.

"They just painted my door," she said, shaking her head. I imagined the municipal worker, living in some nicer part of town, brandishing his red can of paint as he strode down these sandy paths, past shelter after shelter patched together, he assumed, with garbage. What's the difference if you slash a red mark across a mound of trash?

At the empty lot, a group of women stood at an incline. One was tall and busty, in her fifties, wearing a long skirt and a T-shirt that displayed her pendulous breasts. Her arm was wrapped around a smaller, darker woman with thin shoulders and short hair. The guide explained to us: it was this smaller woman whose house had burned and whose father had died in the smoke and fire. She was silent, standing among the remains of her home, staring at us with red-rimmed eyes.

We had been joined on the tour by a gangly ginger-haired American research fellow who, within three minutes of meeting a person, compulsively conveyed that his wife was a black South African.

"Can I give money?" he asked awkwardly, his face reddening. The guide grew equally uncomfortable and shrugged.

We passed the assistant's shack on the way out. She called her six-year-old daughter to come meet us. The girl had a heart-shaped face, a missing front tooth, and short hair in little twists.

"Hello," I said. "What is your name?"

"Yes, teacher, thank you, teacher," she said, batting her eyelashes.

Later, as Sam and I drove away, the streets grew wide and smooth as the township receded. Heavy-bottomed palm trees lined the road. The people were soon lighter and taller, as if to match the ivory buildings that rose along the crashing sea. The restaurants were full of diners ordering calamari and chicken caesar salads. In the distance, along the promenade, the iconic red-and-white-striped Mouille Point lighthouse sparkled, and silky dogs ran after tennis balls in its shadow.

At the time, we were living in a dull, cold rental apartment, which was angled so that not even the smallest beam of sun could enter, ever. On one side, shaded windows overlooked a golf course, and on the other side, small, high windows overlooked an open hallway that circled an interior courtyard. These windows above the courtyard presented an acoustic nightmare that sent the din of a radio in another apartment or the low pitch of a conversation in the common area directly into our living room at top volume. I hated the place, with its walls coated in mold in the winter and its unflattering fluorescent lights. In the basement, the storage areas used by residents had once been rooms where black and colored maids would sleep. A few communal bathrooms, which included toilets and showers, had been built in the hallways during apartheid so that the help did not use their boss's private facilities.

But on that day, the flat took on new characteristics. It was luxury, pure and simple, with its sturdy walls, its two secure locks, windows to protect against the elements, plentiful electricity, and a bathroom and toilet of its own. I stood in a scalding hot shower and felt filthy rich. I never wanted to go back to the townships and I wanted to go back immediately.

But you couldn't just wander aimlessly around there. It was too far from town for a pop-in, and there weren't, for example, coffee shops with Wi-Fi where a person could hang out. So I started to research various NGOs that did work there. I asked around, again surveying the people I knew, but I was only met with gestures of concern. It seemed that I was a not uncommon species of foreigner who thinks a bleeding heart or a hankering for a taste of "real Africa" will keep her safe as she wanders, smiling dimly and handing out lollipops, through destitute black areas. So in my search for volunteer work, I was met, several times, with the same question, uttered with a mixture of irritation and concern:

"Haven't you heard of Amy Biehl?" people said. "Better not come down with Amy Biehl Syndrome."

I was twelve when Amy Biehl was killed, and not up on international news, so I had never heard of her. Now, with no friends in South Africa and only a bit of freelance work trickling in, I had plenty of time to burrow into that Internet rabbit hole. I began to look into the story of the young white scholar attacked by the black mob. The tale had been covered at length, with over 100,000 search results on Google. For days, I read articles and studied images. The murder had been so odd, the fury so misplaced, and the choice of victim so ironic. The story, as it rolled out before me in backlit print, conveniently followed along the country's timeline for the past nearly two decades: oppression, inequality, activism, protest, race-based violence, imprisonment, freedom, amnesty, reconciliation. Over the years, the headlines themselves traced the arc of recent history:

A BRUTALIZED GENERATION TURNS
ITS RAGE ON WHITES
(*The New York Times,* 1993)

THREE BLACKS FOUND GUILTY OF "RACIST" KILLING
(*The Herald,* Glasgow, 1994)

SOUTH AFRICANS APOLOGIZE TO FAMILY OF
AMERICAN VICTIM
(*The New York Times,* 1997)

4 SOUTH AFRICAN KILLERS OF U.S. STUDENT
GET AMNESTY
(*Chicago Tribune,* 1998)

BIEHL PARENT, APARTHEID FIGHTER BRIDGE GAP
(*The Santa Fe New Mexican,* 2004)

IN SOUTH AFRICA, AN IMPROBABLE TALE
OF FORGIVENESS
(*Los Angeles Times,* 2008)

This was a microcosm of South Africa for twenty years, and it was the hopeful story people liked to tell and be told. The oppressed, once driven to wanton disorder, now displayed an unreal spirit of forgiveness. They were led by Mandela himself, who, after twenty-seven years in prison, forgave his oppressors. At his inauguration, his jailer was given VIP seating. The end result was white people and black people who had endured a terrible time locked in an embrace. As far as stories go, Amy Biehl's was pretty perfect in terms of PR for South Africa, the rainbow nation. And America, with its generous ambassadors in the form of Linda and Peter and martyred activist Amy, didn't come out too badly either. The whole thing was so peculiar that I couldn't stop reading about it.

Over dinner, I reported my findings to Sam, who had been fourteen at the time of Amy's death and eighteen during the Truth and Reconciliation Commission hearings, and so remembered her name and the basics of the story, but not much more. I went over the murder, the particularly undeserving victim, the famed amnesty, the remarkable show of mercy, the close relationship between the mother and the men, who even called Linda Biehl "Grandmother" in Xhosa.

I mentioned it to my conservative in-laws, who didn't understand why anyone would ever reward their daughter's killers with a job. Their dinner guests were equally unimpressed by the tale—the general story they knew by heart but the details they only vaguely remembered. One posited that such a gesture might encourage other black folks to kill white girls in order to score jobs, and she could not be dissuaded by the fact that over the course of nearly twenty years, nobody had ever done such a thing. Later that week, as Sam and I sat in the park by the sea, I expounded upon the story again.

"You sound pretty interested in this," he finally said. "Why don't you write about it?"

In the following days, I tried to locate a book on the subject, convinced that surely somebody had already covered this singular story at length. Indeed, many journalists had filed reports in all forms of media. There had been documentaries and talk shows. A South African playwright, inspired by Linda Biehl's act of compassion, had even written a fictionalized account, *Mother to Mother*, which she then adapted into a one-woman play that toured every few years. But nobody had ever written a book.

So I drafted a letter to Linda, and sent it to an email address at her Cape Town–based foundation. I explained myself: *I would like to examine the story of Amy's life, her death, and what happened after—including your and Mr. Biehl's forgiveness of and relationship with Easy Nofemela and Ntobeko Peni, and the continued work of the foundation—and to write about it, possibly something book-length. I'd like to explore who Amy was and how she got here, as well as what her life and legacy means for South Africa today, nearly twenty years after her death and the end of apartheid.*

Thirteen hours passed and then a little red circle appeared on my mail app: *I would be happy to chat . . . almost 20 years has passed since the event occurred and the story like South Africa is very complicated. You are welcome to call.*

3.

Show me a hero and I will write you a tragedy.

—F. Scott Fitzgerald

I called Linda Biehl in January 2012, a day after receiving her email. After her husband's sudden death from colon cancer ten years earlier, Linda had sold her Newport Beach house and had thus far not settled down elsewhere. She kept no permanent residence, and instead hopped around the States, flashing her Delta gold card, crashing with her three surviving children in Florida, Pennsylvania, and California, and helping out with the grandkids—and there were six, divided among the households. Once or twice a year, she bought a ticket to South Africa and went to check up on her foundation. Universities and private organizations sometimes hired her to give a speech on reconciliation. Journalists writing about South Africa or forgiveness or an activist's murder called her once in a while for a quote.

I'd expected a reticent woman, soft-spoken and probably super-Christian. How else, I wondered, but for a serious devotion to biblical standards with which I was admittedly unfamiliar, could a person so intensely forgive and love those who had so powerfully sinned against her?

"No, I find Christianity to be as hypocritical as anything in the world can be," Linda said during our first conversation. I hadn't asked her a thing about religion; Linda had just offered it up.

Linda was an engaging storyteller whose tales were dotted with full names of individuals both grand and obscure. She repeated her favorite stories at length, their details precise and unwavering, before she veered off, and I was left with notebooks full of loops, question marks, and arrows. And though she rarely paused long enough for anyone to interrupt her, I soon found that she would eventually, unaided, answer any question I might have, and more. Simply put, she spoke so much and had presumably been asked the same predictable questions so many times that she ended up covering nearly every relevant topic without being asked.

"Religion has nothing to do with it," she said during the first conversation.

I wanted to ask: So what *does* have to do with it? But she was already talking about her fascination with traditional Xhosa beliefs, and about how she once got sick swilling home brew in an unsealed clay mug in the township. She talked about how the white dinner party circuit bored and upset her; she recalled how a wealthy Cape Town hostess had once asked her to lie silently on a reclining chair in the parlor of a mansion and listen to classical music before eating delivery pizza—a misguided attempt at highbrow entertaining.

"I blame sanctions!" she said. Apartheid-era sanctions were imposed on the country by an international community that had, by the 1980s, become increasingly disapproving of the country's race-based legislation. Sanctions deprived South Africans of Western popular culture, prevented their beloved Springbok rugby and cricket teams from competing internationally, stymied the economy, and forced the elite to make up their own weird interpretations of European-style sophistication. White people tended to be obsessed with Europe and America, and they craved the fancy mores practiced in those far-off lands. But they were separated from them, and could only turn to each other. The result, which endured, seemed to be that a group of people, using rumors passed down from those who had visited abroad, had more or less imagined a collection of styles and manners. The older set still adored frilly and opulent furniture set up in odd configurations and stared down upon by a collection of stern, literal oil paintings.

Linda talked about her love of jazz and art history and about her grandkids. One was an actress. Two were star athletes. One played the drums. Her youngest granddaughter, then five years old, reminded everyone of a little Amy: spirited, energetic, sweet. Sometimes the little girl, absorbed in play, would look up and say, "I'm with Aunt Amy now."

In 2012, Linda was trying to pull out of the foundation and devote herself entirely to her family in America, but she seemed incapable of truly making the move, tethered to the country that took her daughter from her. She talked affectionately about Easy and Ntobeko, whom she seemed to care for as if they were her own occasionally wayward and disobedient middle-aged man-children. Ntobeko was her favored son; his many accomplishments, large and small, filled her with pride. She talked about how these new relationships had cost her friends from the old days, people who had known her before she became, suddenly, a part of South African history and a paragon of reconciliation.

"I myself am a figure of curiosity and controversy," she said, sighing. "Sometimes I wonder how and why did I ever do this?"

For the next four months, in an attempt to acquire a satisfactory answer to the question Linda had posed, I interviewed her over the phone. I visited a professor at the University of Cape Town and convinced him to sign off on a guest researcher pass. I spent weeks in the airy college library, combing through files, books, old clippings, and reports. I relentlessly chased after Easy and Ntobeko, with varying degrees of success, as they both tried politely to avoid me.

After a few months of research, I was convinced that I'd stumbled upon a story that needed telling—or, perhaps more honestly, that I desperately needed to tell. Amy was my entrée into this strange world. She had come here with purpose, just twenty-five years old when she left home, and she had tried her best to understand a pulsing South Africa in the midst of revolution. She had died in her quest. I had come here without any such noble purpose, thirty years old, and now I, too, wanted to understand a new South Africa.

The men I would be writing about were the ultimate "other": poor, black, South African men, convicted murderers, reformed rad-

icals living in a sort of modern wasteland, at once nursing the
wounds of apartheid and—if you believed the "Africa Rising" magazine covers that hit the stands annually, emblazoned with the acacia
tree set against an incandescent setting sun—heading toward a
brighter future. The men had grown up with little education in an
urban tribal culture that placed abiding value on ancient Xhosa traditions. And they now lived in this new rainbow nation, that enduring nickname given to post-apartheid South Africa by Archbishop
Desmond Tutu, who was trying to celebrate the country's racial and
cultural mishmash. I hoped that in understanding these men, I could
understand how a country broken apart by a system of colonization,
segregation, and dehumanization could heal, reconcile, and move
forward. This small, fierce story would tell the larger story of the
New South Africa, and of the redemptive power of forgiveness in
the face of tragedy.

But you won't read about that here. That old narrative, the one I
was following as I began my research, fell ill early on and perished
about a year in. In its stead, a different story emerged.

When I started my work, I didn't understand the complexities of
the Truth and Reconciliation Commission, or of South Africa, or, I
suppose, of true-life stories in general. I assumed there were clear-
cut narratives in the country, with good and bad protagonists and
antagonists, and that I would simply tell one of them. But as the
Johannesburg-born journalist Rian Malan wrote, "In South Africa,
it's like a law of nature: there's no such thing as a true story here. The
facts might be correct, but the truth they embody is always a lie to
someone else. . . . Atop of all this, we live in a country where mutu-
ally annihilating truths coexist amicably. We are a light unto nations.
We are an abject failure. We are progressing every day as we hurtle
backward."

Early on, I became convinced, naively, that with enough frenzied
effort, I could find the Big Truth about the Amy Biehl story. I was
after the objective truth: that elusive creature, a forensic reality that
conformed to proven or provable facts, something mathematical and

scientific and doubtless. But Easy, the man who over the years brought me closest to this truth and led me farthest from it, broke it down for me.

We were sitting across from each other at a linoleum table at the Hungry Lion fast food establishment in downtown Cape Town. Easy was wearing his buttercup-yellow Paul Smith polo, which he bought from a Nigerian who dealt in cut-rate fine garments, which were either stolen or counterfeit, it was hard to tell. He was drinking a ginger soda and I was spitting questions at him.

Months earlier, Easy had christened me Nomzamo, a Xhosa name. All Xhosa names have literal meanings that are reflections of a person's character or the hopes of the parent for the child. Nomzamo comes from the Xhosa word *zama*, "to try." It can be interpreted as "she who strives and perseveres" or, probably, in my case, "pain in the ass." Easy had explained it as: "You always try, try, try. It's a good name."

"What do you really want to know?" he finally asked, looking at me with a mixture of compassion and bewilderment. He was wiping the grease from his fingers onto a paper napkin.

"I want to know the truth!" I exclaimed.

Easy studied me for a moment and then broke into guttural laughter.

"Nomzamo, Nomzamo, Nomzamo," he said. "The truth is not anymore existing for years and years."

4.

He who fights with monsters should
be careful lest he thereby become a
monster.

—Friedrich Nietzsche

In 1652, the Dutch, in their colonial trading heyday, established an outpost of the Dutch East India Company on the Cape, the purpose of which was to replenish passing ships with vegetables, meat, and water. To get the enterprise started, three boats of Dutch men (and a smattering of women) were sent to Africa. Several months after embarking, the crew docked in a natural bay that sat below an enormous mountain, dotted with knotty bushes and flowers. The broad black mountain was unique: it seemed as though it had been sliced in half with an enormous knife, and instead of a peak, it sported a long, flat top. The Dutch called it Tafelberg, or Table Mountain. They named the chilly water beneath it Tafelbaai, or Table Bay. Today the dense clouds that spread across are called "the tablecloth."

The group, having heard rumors of aggressive locals, arrived armed and determined. They immediately fashioned a large fort of mud, clay, and timber just inland, and dubbed it Fort de Goede Hoop, or Fort of Good Hope. They began to farm the surrounding area, and in their spare time they dressed in pinafores and suits and performed swooping Dutch folk dances on the African vista.

They swiftly took over increasing swaths of land. Threatened Khoikhoi mounted various small wars over the next decades, but they were almost always defeated by modern weapons. Resistant Khoikhoi were branded with irons, assaulted, and imprisoned— some on Robben Island, just off the coast, where, around three hundred years later, Nelson Mandela would toil as a political prisoner. Bit by bit, day by day, the Khoikhoi lost the land they had once used to graze their cattle. The cattle were then sold to or stolen by Europeans until the tribespeople were shattered. Lacking their traditional means of survival, many Khoikhoi took to working in poor conditions on Dutch farms.

But there were not enough Khoikhoi to work the land; their numbers were small anyway, and in 1713 they would be nearly wiped out by a wave of imported smallpox. While the initial goal of the Dutch East India Company had been only to act as a rest stop for sailors, the European newcomers now decided to construct the basic infrastructure of a colony, growing fruit and grain and raising livestock. The powerful trading company set up its own governmental structure: it made laws, appointed governors, and granted land, with no regard for the indigenous people except as they related to the use or nuisance of the colonists.

Europeans, mostly from the lower rungs of Dutch society, drizzled in, including a small group of persecuted French Huguenots and a smattering of German, Swedish, and British scientists, naturalists, and missionaries. Schools were not a priority, and generations lacked much more than basic elementary educations. As the white population grew, the colonists decided they needed more free labor to build up their fledgling community, and sent word back home. In 1658, the first batch of slaves was led ashore, followed by a flood of ships filled with captives from Mozambique, Madagascar, Indonesia, India, and Sri Lanka.

Slaves labored as artisans and fishermen and gardeners. They served in homes as maids and nannies. They constructed roads, hospitals, and bridges, tilled fields, and picked produce. By the 1770s, white Cape Town residents were referred to widely as "baas," from the Dutch word for boss.

The relationship between slave and owner, especially in a contained area with a small population, was not clear-cut. Depending on their masters and positions, the slaves were treated alternately as lowly but beloved members of a family or as animals that deserved to be whipped into submission. Masters took to baptizing their slaves, but those who committed crimes were executed with deliberate brutality in the center of town: one slave who killed his owner was tied to a cross, his skin burned with smoldering metal, his limbs broken, and his head cut off and fastened to a pole. Some escaped, but those who were caught were punished. The members of one captured group, who sought to found a "free village," had their Achilles tendons sliced or their feet broken; their leader, sentenced to "death by impalement," committed suicide. Here was the early relationship between master and servant, white and brown, set between the mountain and the sea: one of use and abuse, where violence or its threat was the universal mode of communication.

As time progressed, the relationships blurred further. White farmers took female slaves as their mistresses. The male settlers, who greatly outnumbered female settlers, also had sex—both forced and voluntary—with local Khoikhoi women who worked their farms, and several settlers married freed female slaves. Many female slaves were forced into prostitution, the market for which was robust, as sailors docked in the Cape for replenishments. Some escaped slaves formed their own communities, while others ran north and were integrated into indigenous tribes—which also, evidence suggests, accepted white members, often criminals who had absconded from the colony to escape punishment.

The outcome of all such interbreeding, intermingling, and time away from Europe was a growing population and a new language. The children of slaves and slave owners, of prostitutes and sailors, of illicit interracial love affairs, were a population of people who were neither white nor black. The language that emerged from all this mixing was the forefather of today's Afrikaans: a gruff version of Dutch that evolved as the early settlers simplified their mother tongue to communicate with Khoikhoi employees and foreign slaves. Khoi, Xhosa, Zulu, and Indonesian words made their way into the language.

Meanwhile, settlers began encroaching on new tracts of land. A hardy offshoot of pioneers dubbed themselves trekboers ("semi-nomadic pastoral farmers") and headed north and east in ox wagons, searching to claim better land, cutting through the Karoo, camping and setting up bare-bones dwellings described by one visitor as "tumble-down barns." The nights were bitterly cold and arid, and the days were so hot that dogs had to be transported in wagons, for their paws would burn if they touched the ground. The dusty nomads burrowed into the interior of the country, alternately employing, warring against, and trading with those whose paths they crossed. They sold butter, sheep, cattle, elephant ivory, and animal hides. They bought tobacco, coffee, and sugar.

Their most valued possessions were their guns and packets of gunpowder. Remote groups of indigenous people still lived within the Karoo, usually near water holes, and so to gain access to that water, trekboers often killed adult members of the Khoikhoi and San (a tribe of bushmen scattered throughout Southern Africa). They spared their children, whom they sold, traded, or raised as slaves. The trekboers also interacted with the Xhosa people who lived in the eastern Cape: tight-knit clans of farmers who kept livestock, tilled subsistence crops, and organized themselves loosely around local chiefs.

The Xhosa people, as the first settlers noted, were a healthy, friendly group. They were not averse to fighting to defend what was theirs, but they weren't warriors. They preferred to farm their fields of tobacco, grain, and produce, and to graze their livestock. They slaughtered animals for frequent ceremonies, drank rich homemade beer, and smoked pipes and cigarettes. Above all, the Xhosa people nurtured their families. An early Dutch explorer noted, in 1689, the strength of the Xhosa bonds: "It would be impossible to buy slaves there, for they would not part with their children, or any of their connections for anything in the world, loving one another with a most remarkable strength of affection."

In the 1790s, as Europe was plunged into crisis by the French Revolution, the British temporarily turned the nearly bankrupt Dutch trading outpost into a naval base. The British hoped to protect the Cape colony, their valuable midway point on the Europe-

Asia trade route, from being overtaken by the French. While the Cape held no grand financial promise in and of itself (it exported a little wool, some animal hides, and elephant tusks), the British soon found another use for the growing outpost: as a source of job creation for Brits struggling in the wake of the Napoleonic Wars. British citizens, mostly those of the desperate lower classes, could be resettled on Xhosa farmland, thereby quelling potential social unrest in England.

The British knew that for the Xhosa, cattle had been, from time immemorial, the main marker of wealth. According to a Dutch colonial employee, cattle were, to the Xhosa patriarch, "practically the only subject of his care and occupation, in the possession of which he finds complete happiness."

British Parliament therefore sent over orders for their people to execute homicidal commando raids of "kaffir" villages ("kaffir" was initially used to refer to non-Christians, but eventually became a derogatory term for a black person), during which women and children were slaughtered and cattle stolen. Desperate Xhosa guerrillas nearly won a battle to reclaim land, but were ultimately dispossessed of even more territory and lost 23,000 cattle. After leading conquests in 1811 and 1812, the Cape's governor, Sir John Cradock, cheerily reported back to London on the success of these attacks: "I am happy to add that in the course of this service, there has not been shed more Kaffir blood than would seem necessary to impress on the minds of these savages a proper degree of terror and respect."

In 1820, four thousand British citizens—poor artisans, mostly, unaware of the battles being fought in South Africa and hoping for their own property allotment—were shipped over and handed one hundred acres each of the rough and wild eastern Cape. These inexperienced farmers found themselves out of luck: they were stranded in the middle of a simmering series of frontier wars, about which they had not been informed when they applied to go to Africa. To add insult to injury, the grasslands were difficult to cultivate without the generational wisdom the Xhosas possessed. Within a few years, many of the sour-grass plots were abandoned as the British took refuge in the settlements of Grahamstown, Port Elizabeth, and East London.

For their part, the Xhosas were fractured, grief-stricken, plunged into poverty: over the years, they had lost their land, many of their animals, and their communities to settlers. Unable to come to terms with their sudden reversal of fortune, they became convinced that this onslaught of misery had been brought on by furious ancestors. A young female prophet reported that if the tribe slaughtered their remaining livestock and stopped planting crops, they would be forgiven and rise again, and so the desperate people abided by her word. By 1857, the population was starving. The Xhosa people would mount various offenses to secure the return of their land, but ultimately the majority of them realized that their only survival option was to work at a pittance for the white farmers who now tilled their former land.

Amy Elizabeth Biehl came into the world 315 years after the Dutch landed on the Cape and 110 years after the Xhosa people faced what then seemed to be their darkest hour. She was born on April 26, 1967, in Chicago, Illinois, to loving, upper-middle-class parents. It was a cool and hazy spring Wednesday, and a light rain drizzled down on the lakeside city. She died on August 25, 1993, in Gugulethu, Cape Town, at the hands of a violent mob of students, gangsters, and unemployed young people. It was a clear winter Wednesday, 78 degrees and unseasonably sunny.

Journalists often misidentified Amy as a "volunteer," an "aid worker," or an "exchange student." Some referred to her as an "angel" or a "golden girl." When she died, the headlines were melodramatic and simplistic:

A WOMAN WHO GAVE HER LIFE TO AFRICA

PRAISES SUNG BY ALL

DEATH OF AN IDEALIST

POOR AMY

In fact, Amy was a serious academic and an activist, but she didn't present as the widely held caricature of the intellectual, at least not in photos. Amy was female, first of all, and she was conventionally pretty. She had long dirty-blond hair, straight teeth, and a spray of freckles across her delicate nose. She had fashionable clothes bought by her father and a sense of style inherited from her mother, who in her later years became a couture saleswoman at Neiman Marcus in well-heeled Newport Beach. She was slender from years of competitive sports. She was confident in her opinions but modest and allergic to causing offense. She had good posture and a decent handshake. She was not above telling a bad joke.

Amy had not wandered blindly into Gugulethu that August day, some ignorant missionary who thought her smile could cut through the fury of a disenchanted and dispossessed generation of blacks. She knew there was a storm brewing in South Africa. She'd majored in African Studies at Stanford, and at graduation she had plastered the words FREE MANDELA in masking tape across her cap, which her grandmother, a Midwestern Republican, kept trying to pick off. After Stanford, as an employee of the nonprofit National Democratic Institute, Amy had traveled to South Africa, Zambia, the Ivory Coast, Ethiopia, Burundi, and what is today the Democratic Republic of the Congo. In 1989, she spent time in Namibia, which was holding free elections as it transitioned to independence from South African rule. She traveled there again in 1991 to study the early workings of a new parliamentary democracy. She even went on a jog through Lusaka, Zambia's capital, with Jimmy Carter.

By the time Amy landed in South Africa in September 1992, she was well versed in the long-standing issues of liberty, race, and rights that had shaped postcolonial African discourse. She was especially interested in the country as apartheid began to crumble and Nelson Mandela's rise to the presidency became increasingly inevitable. She wanted to be in the middle of the action. So when Amy landed her Fulbright, she packed her bags and Linda drove her to Los Angeles International. In the waiting area, Amy fell into an engrossing conversation with another passenger, who was also up-to-date on South African politics. Distracted, she hugged Linda goodbye. Though they spoke on the phone during Amy's ten months in South Africa, the last words Amy delivered to Linda in person were a parting command as she boarded the plane: "Don't cry, Mom."

In Cape Town, Amy immersed herself in her research topic: the rights and roles of women, primarily black and colored women, in an emerging democracy. She traveled into the depths of the townships and witnessed firsthand the squalor in which black people were forced to live under apartheid law. Diplomatically inclined and tactful, Amy rarely expressed, verbally, the effect this inequality and racism had on her. Perhaps she knew it was not her place to complain, that the emotions of a white American on the subject of state-sanctioned racism were hardly relevant. But sometimes she let it rip. Once Amy and her boyfriend, Scott Meinert, who was visiting from the States for a couple of weeks, wandered into an all-white bar wearing T-shirts emblazoned with Mandela's face. The patrons unhappily received two white kids with a black opposition leader plastered across their chests, and some spit a few under-the-breath comments at the pair: "Like the darkies, do you?" Amy ignored them, drank her beer, and strode back to the parking lot, where she got in her car and started hitting the dashboard with all her might and letting fly a stream of profanities. She was furious at herself for taking the high road.

While in Namibia, Amy met some rising ANC dignitaries, including Brigitte Mabandla, who would become minister of justice and constitutional development in post-apartheid South Africa. The late 1980s and 1990s were prime periods in the history of what is referred to as the Struggle, or the long fight for freedom. Back then, high-ranking ANC members were often also professors, and Mabandla headed up the Community Law Center at the University of the Western Cape. Inspired, Amy chose to conduct her South African Fulbright-funded research at the University of the Western Cape instead of the more prestigious and whiter University of Cape Town. At UWC, a university historically designated for students of color, she drafted memos for Dullah Omar, Mandela's lawyer who would become the president's minister of justice, and for Rhoda Kadalie, an intellectual and activist who would become Mandela's commissioner of human rights. Rhoda was then a single mother in her late thirties, and she and Amy grew especially close over the months, discussing politics, feminism, policy—and boyfriends, sex, and gossip. On the day of her death, Amy was clearing out her workspace at UWC, organizing her papers, and packing up any spare notes as she prepared to head back to America. She used a university phone to call Rhoda, who was working from home that day, and they spoke for nearly two hours.

"Rhoda, I'm so sentimental for this place," Amy said as their conversation finally neared an end. She had filled her suitcases with patterned cloths for friends at home and CDs of local musicians. She had sold her car, which she planned to deliver to the buyer the next day. Rhoda and Amy agreed to meet up for lunch one last time before Amy flew out. As they hung up, Rhoda told Amy to stay away from the townships. The radio was abuzz with news of protests, rallies, and stonings. Marching kids were smashing up government property and attacking government-employed health workers. Amy knew all this. She was lucky, she remarked, that she'd made it all this time without anything ever happening to her.

"There's a lot of unrest," Rhoda ordered in her clipped voice. "You will not go in today. Do you understand?"

Amy said she understood. She was well aware of the thousands of lives lost, most of them black, in the fireballing political strife of the last several years—the early 1990s, after Mandela was released from prison and negotiations for the first inclusive democratic elections began, saw the country on the brink of a civil war. Anyway, she didn't have time to go to the townships. She had been renting a room from a friend and colleague named Melanie Jacobs, and lived with Melanie and Melanie's teenage daughter in a small flat in the relatively diverse suburb of Mowbray, about eight miles from the townships. Amy needed to go back to Mowbray to see her friends; she had less than forty-eight hours before she hurtled toward California, where she planned to go with her family to consume margaritas at her favorite Mexican restaurant, Mi Casa. You can't get a proper margarita in South Africa.

Amy didn't know that Scott planned to propose to her when she arrived. On the evening of August 25, on the west coast of America, Scott had a dinner date planned with Peter Biehl, to ask for his blessing. Amy was a liberal feminist, but Scott suspected she wanted a traditional engagement: Dad's permission, one knee, Champagne. If life had taken a different turn, would Amy have said yes?

"We don't know that," Linda told me.

"Oh yeah," her college friend Miruni Soosaipillai countered. "I have a memory of her saying that she felt like she was ready. They had been together for something like six or seven years."

But no matter what, Amy would only be home for a few days, just enough time to see some friends, her mom and dad and sisters and brother, and pack her bags again. She was heading for Rutgers University in New Jersey. She had recently been awarded a fellowship to pursue a PhD in international women's studies. After that, she would become an academic—or perhaps a policy adviser in government. In her dreams, she would launch her own NGO, a serious, research-based organization that would help protect the rights of women and children in African countries that were transitioning from colonial oppression to free democracy.

A half mile from Amy's office, two UWC students, Sindiswa Bevu and Maletsatsi Maceba, stood on the main road, trying to hitch a ride. A friend had promised to drive them home, but had forgotten about them, and now they were a pair of young black women, arms out, looking to be dropped near an area deemed unsafe by most locals. For the past week, the radio had been reporting that the townships were burning and high school kids were trying to kill cops and overturn government vehicles.

There was also the quotidian township violence, stoked by the political situation. The day before Amy's death, somebody was stoned and two people were attacked in Gugulethu. Two hours before Amy entered the township, a homeless man was robbed by an unknown assailant. A half hour before Amy drove in, several more people were stoned. At various points throughout the day, three men were separately attacked. That afternoon, two residents were robbed, two homes were burglarized, and somebody was arrested for "possession of ammunition." There were two separate reports of "public violence" and one report of "grievous bodily harm." Of all the other crimes that were committed in Gugulethu on August 25, only one man was arrested: according to police records, a "non-white" squatter camp resident had stabbed another "non-white" squatter camp resident to death, for which he was sentenced to just five years in prison.

For the most part, the victims and perpetrators were black and colored residents of various townships and their misfortunes warranted minimal attention. One exception to the rule occurred at around eleven that morning, five hours before Amy was attacked. A white man employed by the city had been helping to fix a buzzing light out by Heideveld train station. Heideveld station straddles the colored area of Heideveld and Gugulethu, the tracks connected by an overhead footbridge. The white man, working on the Gugulethu side, was pulled from his truck by a mob of young black locals, stomped, stabbed, and left for dead. Despite the race of the victim, that crime, too, escaped the attention of law enforcement or media. There was neither an investigation nor a single arrest. Later, I was to find out a heretofore unreported and improbable link between that obscure, forgotten crime, with its two decades of pain and suffering that followed, and what happened to Amy that day.

Sindiswa and Maletsatsi waited forty-five minutes, but nobody would pick them up, so the women trudged back to campus. There they found Amy clearing out her office. They asked her for a lift. Despite her promise to Rhoda to stay away from the townships, Amy agreed to drive Sindiswa and Maletsatsi home.

"I always say she went because she forgot she was white," Rhoda told me. As a white person who has spent years doing research and interviews in Gugulethu, I find this alleged slip of memory to be nearly impossible. I am never quite so searingly aware of the color of my skin as when I am in the township.

In the parking lot, Amy passed by Evaron Orange, a nineteen-year-old cousin of Amy's roommate, Melanie. He was a baby-faced colored kid with a caterpillar mustache and oiled black hair. He also needed a lift, and so Amy agreed to take Evaron to Athlone, the nearby colored neighborhood where he lived.

The four loaded into Amy's dinged-up beige Mazda. Evaron sat in the passenger seat and the two women slipped into the back. The Mazda was all muddy tones: tan fabric seats, dull brown carpeting, a dark brown dashboard. Its only pop of color was a bright yellow Cape Town license plate, its only adornment a squat rectangular sticker plastered on the back right bumper, just below the taillight, printed with unadorned black capital letters: OUR LAND NEEDS PEACE.

Amy drove her friends southwest on Modderdam Road, passing the bleak industrial yards of Parow and the Bishop Lavis ganglands. She drove by the flat, crumbling pastel houses that lined the broad thoroughfare, and at the four-way intersection that separates the black townships of Gugulethu, KTC, and Crossroads from the colored townships of Bonteheuwel and Valhalla Park, she turned left onto NY1. NY stands for Native Yard, the lingering apartheid designation for streets in black townships, all of which were simply initialed and numbered: Native Yard 32, Native Yard 58, Native Yard 79, Native Yard 111.

Amy had been to the townships dozens of times, to drink and dance at the clubs and shebeens, the taverns that provided relief from the daily grind of apartheid and poverty, and to visit friends and conduct research. Driving along NY1, she passed the brown-brick Shoprite Center. She continued over a small overpass that stretches above the N2 highway and connects the northern corners of Gugulethu to the rest of the world. On that day, as rush hour neared, traffic was congested on NY1, which offers only a single slender northbound lane and a single slender southbound lane, hemmed in between sidewalks. After the turnoff, Amy followed a small truck down NY1.

She drove past the shoulder-high grass on the outskirts of Gugulethu. She slowed down as she went by the police barracks contained behind razor wire, past the long municipal buildings that comprised the elementary school. Now there was traffic. She edged nearer to the Caltex service station laid out on the corner of NY1 and NY123. The station was positioned just off the road, its six pumps sheltered by a red cement overhang and set next to a low gray-brick building where the cashiers worked behind bulletproof glass.

A quarter mile past the Caltex sat the Gugulethu police station. Amy planned to drop the women near the police station, where she could safely turn around and go off to Athlone with Evaron. But just before Amy reached the Caltex, the truck in front of her stopped short. She pressed the brake.

"Ride, ride," Evaron said.

"I can't." Amy gestured before her at the truck, which was shaking. In South Africa, as in the U.K., people drive on the left, so to

Amy's left was a sidewalk, and to her right was a line of bumper-to-bumper cars traveling in the opposite direction. Ahead, they could make out a group of young people, some of whom seemed to be pressing against the truck.

A man from that group turned and zeroed in on Amy, her pale face shining. The man yelled out and the other young men swiveled around. There is a word in Xhosa, *iqungu*. It's similar to the English term bloodlust. It means "the joy in killing."

The men and boys were speaking Xhosa, yelling to each other. Amy and her friends sat, paralyzed and uncomprehending. One man held in his hand a cracked brick, tan in color, plucked from construction refuse on the side of the road. No, many of them had bricks, almost all of them had bricks or stones clutched in their hands. Now Amy and her friends could see that up the road, ahead of the truck, the crowd was moving, chanting. That first man raised his brick and hurled it toward Amy, fast and straight. The force shattered the windshield, which exploded with a loud cartoon pop. Droplets of glass flew across the car's interior, coating the seats, the floor, wedging in the clutch, getting stuck in clothes and hair and shoes. Later that night, when Evaron took a bath, he found shards of glass nestled in the seams of his underwear.

Unthinking, disoriented, Amy drove onward. Another brick came, this one on a perfect trajectory, with no windshield to break its flight. It connected with Amy's face, hitting her square above her right eyebrow. Her head snapped back and then forward. The brick cracked her skull easily, like an eggshell. It left a three-centimeter-long piece of bone, shaped like an arrowhead, hanging loose. The arrowhead bone briefly pressed against her soft pink brain, now exposed.

Blood poured from Amy's forehead, drenching her hair. She drove a few more yards down NY1, her right arm dangling from the window, before she stopped. A skinny young boy popped up near her. He looked at the four of them sitting there, slipped the watch off Amy's limp wrist, and melted back into the crowd.

From inside the car, it seemed that the sun had disappeared and the sky had gone black. The stones hailed down. In the backseat, Sindiswa and Maletsatsi began to scream. Evaron pulled Amy onto his lap.

"Oh dear Lord, help me," he whispered.

There were people all around, shouting. Now you could make out the words, if you listened.

"One settler, one bullet," the people chanted.

"Africa for Africans."

"Kill the farmer, kill the boer."

"Boer" is the Dutch word for farmer. In South Africa, farmers, primarily Afrikaners, grabbed swaths of land that previously belonged to indigenous people and then employed blacks as sharecroppers or low-paid laborers and kept the profits.

A woman stood on the sidewalk across the way. She yelled at Amy and her friends over the slogans.

"Get out!" she implored. "Run, run, run!"

"Run," urged other disembodied voices, locals standing at a distance who had seen this grisly show before, though never starring a white woman. If a mob surrounds you, you only have one sorry choice: Run, run, *run*.

More young people were pouring in from NY109, where a path from the train station met NY1. Others were already ahead, blocking traffic. There seemed to be more than a hundred of them, or perhaps it was just eighty. They were engaged in a *toyi-toyi*, a beautiful, terrifying march-dance originally from Zimbabwe, in which a coordinated group of people lift their knees up high and wave their arms above their heads as they chant and move in protest. As Amy lay on Evaron's lap, the chants grew louder and clearer and some kids began to lift the car up, hoping to roll it.

"One settler, one bullet."

Amy, bewildered, her blood-soaked shirt sequined with glass shards, opened the car door and stepped out onto the street.

"Settler, settler!" the mob erupted.

Evaron, Maletsatsi, and Sindiswa toppled out of the car now, too, yelling frantically. The two women appealed to the crowd in Xhosa, insisting that Amy was a student, a comrade, a member of their ANC-aligned National Women's Coalition. They were waving around their membership cards like tiny laminated shields. A handsome, broad-faced man tried to grab Maletsatsi's purse, but she shoved him away. A few days later, her back sore, she went for an X-ray and found that her rib had been fractured.

Like most colored South Africans, Evaron spoke English and Afrikaans but did not understand Xhosa. He had never even been to Gugulethu before; he didn't know these streets. He turned to a man standing nearby.

"What do I do?" he pleaded.

"They just want the settler," the man explained. Not Evaron, a colored boy—only that fleeing white woman. It didn't matter that Amy wasn't a settler, wasn't even South African.

Evaron was too scared to go to Amy, surrounded as she was by the mob. It would have been futile, and he would likely have been attacked, and so he stood back, edging toward the Caltex as Amy began to run. First she ran west, away from the gas station and across the dotted line separating the lanes in the road. She pressed her hand above her eye, felt the warm blood, the way her skull gave way, and she let out a scream.

Above NY1 at the Caltex is a barren field, strewn with trash and dotted with tufts of dry grass. A team of twelve-year-old boys had been practicing soccer there when they heard a commotion. They sprinted over to the Caltex and stood by the gas tanks, some on their tiptoes, craning their necks. They had grown up in a world steeped in violence, perpetrated by the white government, their black relatives, their black neighbors, the colored gangsters across the way, their parents' white employers, white strangers, the white and black and colored and Indian cops, white soldiers, bands of black vigilantes, and political leaders of all colors. This pale, wounded lady was certainly a curious display, worth witnessing, but she was not the first person these kids had seen attacked, perhaps not even that day, and she would not be the last. The fact that she was white, however, made the scene particularly memorable; nobody could name the last time a white person had been taken down like this. Not here, in the middle of Gugulethu.

"There was blood, people throwing stones," remembered one of the soccer-playing boys, now a grown man. "I can't say I was happy. I can't say I was angry."

Over at the elementary school, children had just been released from the nursery, and their parents and guardians had arrived to pick them up. Now they stood on the corner, holding babies and toddlers in their arms or by the hands, and they, too, stopped to watch.

One man, a three-year-old child propped on his hip, briefly surveyed the scene, in which two black women pleaded with a crowd as a mob attacked a young white woman. The crowd was shouting, "Down with white sympathizers!" He watched as if in a dream, until the child cried, pulling him back to reality. He turned and hurried away with the child in his arms. He didn't feel too cut up about the whole thing.

"Black people were being murdered by white people, so we weren't sorry," he told me years later. He wondered about Amy's friends, though: "Why would these black people bring a white person here? They knew what was happening in our location."

As the mob surrounded Amy, an old man stormed out of his house, shouting at the attackers, demanding that they leave her be. The mob pushed him away, and he stumbled to the sidewalk. A grandmother ordered her children inside and locked the door. Her grandson, then seven, pressed his hands and nose to the plate glass window.

"She wasn't really running fast, she was confused," the grandson remembered twenty years later, sitting in that same living room. "Her hair was not tied. It was loose."

Evaron and the two women started to pound on the doors of the Caltex, where the station employees had barricaded themselves. The

employees shook their heads. Eventually, with no place to run, Evaron, Sindiswa, and Maletsatsi returned to the gas pumps, where they
stood next to the soccer team and watched as their friend was
hunted.

At first, Amy was heading toward the mob, as though they might
save her. Then, perhaps realizing her error, she swerved away. The
mob broke into spontaneous groups. Some were upon her abandoned car, trying to pour out the petrol and burn the thing. A young
boy yanked open the door and grabbed some of Amy's books, Evaron's backpack and sweater, Amy's bag, and a camera. He took off in
a sprint for his mom's house on NY111. Others stopped and held
their stones limply as the scene unfolded, having lost their taste for
murder. The majority of young people stood back on the sidewalk
by the houses, spectators now, chanting still: "One settler, one bullet."

A group of men and boys—some say it was eight, some say
fifteen—pursued Amy. Residents of NY1, lured by the noise, walked
out of their houses and stood now by their gates. Mostly, they were
older women, and in the background, blaring from their TVs but
muted by the frenzy on the street, was a dialogue of romance and
scandal from the afternoon soap operas. The women were joined by
people returning from the center of town, who had walked among
the mob and had then stopped as an unexpected scene unfolded
before them. With the exception of the old man, only one onlooker
tried to save Amy.

Pamela was a pretty, curvy twenty-year-old with straight black
hair in a short ponytail. She had been hanging out in her backyard,
off the main street, when the mob marched by, full of boys and girls
she recognized from the neighborhood. When Pamela heard music,
something boiled inside her and she had to move, so she joined in
the singing and toyi-toyi-ing. Sometimes a protest was just an excuse to do something, to escape the boredom and grind of township
life. But when they hit NY1, Pamela realized that this was no normal, peaceful march; to the contrary, this group was in an electric,

destructive mood. From a distance, she saw a white person driving toward them.

Pamela watched as the mob began throwing stones. She watched as Amy, bleeding, fell from her car, as the men chased her. Pamela had never before seen Amy, but as Amy ran, Pamela stepped out of the crowd and began, too, to run. Pamela still doesn't know why she did it. When the cops came to her door days later, she denied all knowledge of the event, and even seasoned officers couldn't break her resolve.

She ran toward Amy, reaching out her arms. Now Amy and Pamela were running to each other. Pamela touched Amy, she grabbed at her, their hands met, their eyes met, too. Pamela was holding Amy, feeling the blood on Amy's hands. She and Amy were about the same size—small and athletic—but for a moment Pamela shielded Amy with her body.

But then the men and the boys were there, chanting and yelling and whooping, and bearing down on both of them, waving stones and knives. Pamela knew these boys, but they pushed her aside. Amy pulled away, and Pamela's hand slipped from hers. Pamela stood on the gravel now, alone, as Amy and the boys ran on.

"It was a very cruel scene to watch," she told me in 2013.

Amy crossed back over the street at a diagonal to avoid those behind her. She headed in the direction of the gas station. Now she was slower, less steady. The mob was trying to throw stones at her as they ran, and the combination of two efforts—running and pitching—made them less effective at both. She reached a patch of grass just before the white fence and turned around, her hands extended, as if to appeal to her attackers, to offer peace or surrender. Then the handsome, broad-faced man who had tried to steal Maletsatsi's bag put his foot out to trip her.

Amy pitched backward, but a childhood of gymnastics classes ten thousand miles away had burned balance into her muscle memory, and she fell to the ground in a sitting position, her arms out. She looked up at the mob, her back pressed against the fence, and pushed her hair away from her eyes. The curtains parted; the men looked down at Amy's face. Her blue eyes stared into theirs. For a moment, impossible to measure, the mob stepped away in one coordinated wave, their expressions registering something like fear.

"Why? I don't know," Easy later told me. "I try my entire life to understand why they are scared."

Then they set upon her. Sindiswa, her cheeks slick with tears, broke away from the gas pumps and pushed up against the men, protesting, until one turned to her and sliced her hand with a knife, and she retreated again. Another boy, unable to muscle into the mob, turned to find Evaron quivering on the asphalt. He was colored, which meant he was enough of a target in a pinch. The boy ran at Evaron, stabbing in his direction. Evaron was neither a fighter nor an athlete, but he moved calmly away from each swoosh, some unknown instinct or force guiding him.

"When you see death in front of your face, you don't care if you believe in God or not: you pray," Evaron told me. "I prayed, and I think my prayers were answered."

After a few seconds, the eyes of Evaron's assailant widened with shock and he ran away without explanation. Evaron turned again toward Amy. "She was being butchered to death."

A scrawny slip of a teenager with dark skin had grabbed a bunch of Amy's hair to steady her, and, balancing himself upon her legs, rained down on her head with a brick, slamming it into her skull once, twice, three times. He stood up and kicked her with all the strength he could muster, landing a blow to her torso, and then bent down again with his brick.

"Like wild animals," Amy's friend Maletsatsi told an American news team several years later.

Others muscled in, some short, light-skinned boys with bricks. They wanted a part of the action. Then the handsome man who had tripped Amy pushed his way into the center of the mob and he, too, brought down a large stone upon her head. He turned to a friend on the outskirts of the group.

"Give me your knife," he demanded in Xhosa. His friend handed over a six-inch switchblade. The others stepped away to give the man space. He knelt down on Amy's thighs.

"What did I do?" Amy asked. "I'm sorry."

He plunged the knife, all the way to its hilt, into Amy's body, just beneath her left breast, puncturing the soft blue-white skin, inserting the blade straight into her heart.

The Gugulethu police station on NY1 is about a quarter mile from the Caltex. At around 4:40 P.M. that winter Wednesday, a rangy young cop named Leon Rhodes was sitting in a police truck. Back in the 1990s, the South African Police often drove small yellow pickups with narrow cages built into the back flatbeds, where criminals were placed for transport. They still have similar trucks, and I once saw one at that very Caltex, where a cop was filling its tires with air. A shirtless handcuffed man, missing a couple of teeth, sat in the back, wailing loudly. I peered in, before the cop waved me away.

"Will they take the handcuffs off soon?" I asked Easy, who was with me at the time.

"No, they gonna punish him, throw tear gas in, leave him until someone feel for him and unlock him," Easy said, with some exaggeration. "Now he's facing layers and layers and layers of pain."

Rhodes was one of the only white police officers in Gugulethu, twenty-nine years old and a ten-year veteran. He'd been working in Gugulethu for most of his career. He had just returned to the station from following up on a radio call that reported a truck being stoned in a far corner of the township. Rhodes sat in his vehicle in the driveway, filling out paperwork. Suddenly, a harried man rushed through the open metal gates and rapped on the driver's side window. Rhodes looked up.

"You must seriously and urgently go down the road," the man
said in Afrikaans, a language black people were required to learn at
school. "They're stoning a vehicle with a white lady by the Caltex."

Rhodes revved the car and took a sharp turn out of the station,
immediately crossed the light at Lansdowne Road, and sped north
toward the garage. He could see stones and glass glinting on the road
in the distance. A crowd of people was gathered around the gas station, spanning up and down the street. On the residential side, to
Rhodes's left, young people were chanting and toyi-toyi-ing. The
people in the street made way, and Rhodes drove through.

As the yellow police vehicle approached, the mob by the station
broke up, its members disappearing into the slim side streets, over
back fences, over walls, through alleys, into settlements, into houses.
The toyi-toyi of some spectators grew less enthusiastic and the
chants diminished. Rhodes could see a white woman now, standing,
supported by two black women and a colored man. Her small chest
rose and fell. She let out no words, only sobs.

A battered car lay on its side, pitted by stones, splattered with petrol. Rhodes parked near the exit where Amy stood.

After nearly a decade in Gugulethu—and one of the deadliest in
South African history, at that—Rhodes was used to death and mayhem. He knew his colleagues of all colors smacked around suspects,
and he knew vigilante cops did whatever they wished to township
residents. He had clocked dozens of hours sitting at the edges of
settlements, watching people kill each other for a variety of reasons:
girls, domestic issues, family feuds, vigilante justice, turf battles, political dustups, drunkenness, unbridled and unspecified pain and
fury, ennui. He couldn't drive back into those ganglands, since the
sandy pathways didn't allow for cars, and he was just a single cop on
the beat, a man with no interest in walking alone into a war.

So he had grown accustomed to simply watching small massacres
from the sidelines, in the vague hope that his presence might deter
some residents from killing other residents. On more occasions than
he could count, he'd rolled into work in the dawn hours to find a

body or two, revealed by the morning light, strewn across the streets. He'd seen death and ferocity up close nearly every week. All that was remarkable about this particular case was the color of the victim's skin. He had never seen a white person beaten in Gugulethu. Sure, some delivery drivers had been struck by pebbles and scratched up, maybe their vehicles damaged by bricks, but they usually sped off.

Rhodes pulled up to Amy and asked if she was okay. She let out a low moan. Her hair was so thick, Rhodes thought, and so matted with blood—was it blond or brown? Her eyes, open but blank, rolled back into her head, yet she remained standing. After such a blunt force injury, "your brain just basically dies and deteriorates," Rhodes told me, after I'd tracked him down to his modest single-level home in a small working-class neighborhood. He was a slender, clean-shaven man with a neat haircut and strong forearms. In his blue jeans, work boots, and checked shirt, he looked like he could just as well be baling hay in Kansas.

He'd stayed with the police force after the transition to a democratic South Africa, but had grown convinced that he could never rise in the ranks, and after twenty-six years serving the citizens of Cape Town he had retired early, at the lowly rank of warrant officer. Before 1994, Rhodes theorized, he worked too closely with black colleagues for the National Party to trust him; after 1994, he was too white for the ANC to promote him.

Rhodes had been working on his anger management issues since his retirement, so he quickly subverted this bitterness, composed himself, and shared with me a newspaper clipping from November 1993, headlined AMY BIEHL'S FINAL MOMENTS. His mother, bursting with pride that her son had been quoted testifying in the criminal trial on the front page of the *Cape Argus*, had kept it in a plastic folder for eighteen years. Next to the cover story was a column detailing President Bill Clinton's praise for Linda and Peter Biehl, dotted with head shots of the couple.

Rhodes sat before me on a pink velour love seat, a doily behind his head. Nearby, a rosy-cheeked ceramic maiden peeked out from between two thriving golden pothos plants in copper pots. His wife, absent that day, had arranged amber bottles along a shelf, hung a framed oil painting of a generic alpine scene above the fireplace, and dotted the room with sculptures of roosters. Two small, silken dogs whined to protest their temporary confinement in the garage.

"Looking at her, she was already a goner," Rhodes said of Amy.

His first instinct was to remove Amy from the scene, and he needed to extricate himself, too. A cop of any color could be a prime target in this sort of situation. The people were still chanting, though with waning verve, "One settler, one bullet."

Rhodes opened the back of the van and, together with Evaron, loaded Amy onto the cold metal floor. Sindiswa and Maletsatsi followed, letting out escalating howls. Rhodes's instinct was to ferry Amy to certain safety, so instead of driving to the nearby hospital, he called an ambulance to meet him at the police station down the road.

Back at the station, he parked near the rear, close to the strip of holding cells. He opened the back of the truck. There Amy lay, her eyes closed and her breathing shallow. Rhodes touched her face; she didn't respond. Evaron picked her up, a limp 117 pounds, deadweight, and set her on the asphalt beneath a low tap. Rhodes went to fetch a sparse first-aid kit from the office.

As Evaron, Sindiswa, and Maletsatsi clasped each other, Rhodes washed Amy's face, hoping to see the damage beneath the blood. He cradled her head and pushed her tangled hair away—so long, he kept thinking. He wrapped some gauze around the wound above her brow. He took a scratchy, gray government-issue blanket from a nearby holding cell and stretched it across her body. Maletsatsi, Sindiswa, and Evaron hovered nearby. How would they tell Amy's mother and father about this terrible beating? Surely Amy would be hospitalized for a week or two, considering the severity of her injuries. Would her parents have to fly across the ocean? And what about Amy's valuables—the backpack, the old Mazda itself? And where were the doctors? And why was she still lying on the pavement and not on her way to the hospital?

Victor West, a young paramedic, had been sitting in his ambulance a few miles away, chatting with his partner, when the radio cackled.

"Make your way to an urgent assault case, NY1 at the Caltex garage," came the warbled voice.

Urgent assaults were the name of the game in the Cape Flats townships where West had operated for years. To dull himself after picking up dead or nearly dead bodies from shootings and knife fights and domestic brawls, West was drinking two shots of brandy every morning before his shift and four shots after his shift. Every day, he was called to at least ten assault cases, usually including one stabbing: young people were the perpetrators and the victims. West switched on his lights and siren and headed toward Gugulethu.

"Patient is now at the Gugulethu police station," the dispatcher updated him.

Traffic was heavy, as residents of the townships headed home in dilapidated minivan taxis, in the back of pickups, in private cars. The men wore the blue jumpsuits of manual laborers—literal blue-collar workers—and the women wore their maid costumes—typically a button-down knee-length cotton dress with a small apron and a matching head scarf. They piled into and out of buses and vans. The ambulance hooted and swerved, making its way past the cars slowly. The streets were littered with the detritus of protests and rallies, bits of burned tire and rubbish.

It had been thirty minutes since the radio first cackled when West finally reached the police station. He and his partner navigated through a throbbing crowd that had gathered by the gates. The paramedics pulled up to the interior courtyard. Police were milling around, and three agitated young people stood over a form covered in a gray blanket, lying on the cement near a corner of jail cells. West hopped out of the ambulance and rushed over.

"We lifted the blanket and we were shocked to see a white person," West recalled when I met him at a mall restaurant in the upscale suburb of Claremont in 2012. Amy had been, he would later say, "the cherry on top" of the general trauma of his work; a few years later, he was hospitalized for post-traumatic stress disorder and alcohol addiction. He was long sober now, a round-faced man with jet-black curls, pale café-au-lait skin, and a toothpaste-commercial smile, who, with his wife, ran seminars for at-risk kids in the down-on-its-luck colored neighborhood in which they lived. How strange, he thought on that August 1993 day, how really unusual to see all that wet blond hair in tangles. West bent down and pressed his hand to Amy's wrist and then her neck, searching for a pulse. Nothing.

He examined her bloodied body and found what Rhodes had not: in addition to the crack above her brow, she had suffered two large fractures on the back of her head and a deep stab wound in her chest.

"What struck me most is that she had long boots on," West recalled nineteen years later. But his memory, which seemed to him so sharp and true, was flawed. In fact, the medical examiner's photographs show that Amy was wearing black lace-up oxfords with a 1990s-style square toe and square heel.

"Is she okay?" Evaron asked. Maletsatsi and Sindiswa stood behind him. Shouldn't she be taken immediately to the hospital? And then shouldn't someone call her parents? What about her car? The women were becoming increasingly hysterical, and had begun to shout questions. The paramedics didn't answer. They pulled the blanket over Amy's damp, unmoving face.

That evening, after Amy's friends had gone home, a contingent of gruff police officers swept into the small station, questioning everyone, the cops even, taking over rooms and telephones. These men, with their jowls and barrel chests and packs of quickly disappearing cigarettes and bottomless cups of black coffee, were the Riot and Violent Crimes Investigation Unit, and they would begin the inquiry into Amy's murder.

The big bosses were not thrilled about this particular crime; the entire nation was already experiencing an extended anxiety attack over the threat of mass race-based violence, and now this? The top brass was prepping for a major governmental transition, and everyone was hoping to avoid bloodshed. Nelson Mandela and other political prisoners had been freed in 1990, after twenty-seven years. Soon thereafter, he and his comrades conducted protracted negotiations with the apartheid leadership, with the end goal of free, democratic elections in which people over eighteen of all races could vote. Everyone recognized that in a country with, roughly, a 10 percent white population and a 90 percent nonwhite population, free elections would mean the end of minority rule. The country remained in flux.

Foreign governments disapproved of apartheid and so South Africa had been subject to trade and arms embargoes. The country's leadership and its white citizens had become global pariahs. Apartheid had become the *cause du jour* among American and European pop stars and actors. Mandela was an international hero and, despite laws and legal titles, his influence extended to most black South Africans, as well as a growing number of white, colored, and Indian South Africans. Anti-apartheid political violence was spiraling. Protests, strikes, and rallies were being held almost daily. President F. W. de Klerk of the National Party could see the writing on the wall. The regime, which had recognized that Mandela was their best shot at a bloodless power handover, was negotiating with their former enemies. The ranks of the ANC were growing. In a March 1992 referendum, nearly 70 percent of the all-white electorate had voted

"Yes" to allow a process that would ease negotiations toward the dismantling of apartheid.

The election, which Mandela's African National Congress would handily win, was to be held in April 1994, in eight months' time. But in late 1993, that seemed unimaginably far away. The country balanced on a precipice; the smallest tilt and it risked collapsing into all-out civil war. Far-right white-power groups were preparing for Armageddon, and more moderate whites were panicking about how they would survive black leadership; many whites were nervous that payback was coming, and that all semblance of order would break down when that payback arrived. And while it is clear, in hindsight, that democracy was on its way, the black population was deeply distrustful of the status quo power structure and often suspected the media of spreading propaganda, as it had done for decades. They were nervous that they would be hoodwinked and would never truly see freedom, and so they continued mounting protests and rallies. For years, the apartheid government had fomented violence in black areas; the government had surreptitiously provided assistance to certain black political groups and vigilante mobs that warred against each other. Now the government had a situation—in part of their making, if indirectly—that needed to be contained, and quick. A dead white girl was bad. A dead white girl killed by a black mob was very bad. A dead pro-ANC white girl killed by a black mob was very, very bad. The absolute worst, however, was this: a dead white girl with ANC sympathies killed by a black mob, and the girl was, of all things, American. South Africa was hoping to reinvent itself in the national and international media, and this did not augur well. Within two days of Amy's death, a gunman attacked a bus running from Cape Town to Pretoria, and the *Cape Times* headline read SA WORLD'S MOST VIOLENT COUNTRY. The pressure was on.

As the sky grew dark, the detectives set up their satellite offices and barked to each other. Ilmar Pikker, a hulking chain-smoker with a curly red beard, headed up the investigation. He was a workaholic with a taste for meat, fried food, and Camel cigarettes. He loved the force more than life itself, every night rounding up punks, kicking in rickety doors, staking out terrorist meet-ups. Back then, he didn't have a complicated relationship with his job.

Journalists began to slink around outside the station, alerted to a possible cover story by the staticky noise on the police radios. In Gugulethu, the news passed from neighbor to neighbor. Those boys, they killed a white lady, they ran her down, they beat her to death by the gas station, they stabbed her. She was walking around, one witness recalled, "like a Barbie covered in ketchup."

Some township residents were buoyant, some blasé. Some were watching the news on TV with great interest. A few were busy pawning Amy's watch and books. Some took off for their auntie's place one township over because you knew the cops would come making trouble any minute now, so let them pick up some other kid. Since Amy had spent time socializing and working in Gugulethu, some residents remembered seeing her smiling face; she looked like a nice person, and it was a shame that they had killed her like that.

Some couldn't sleep that night, thinking of that innocent girl, thinking of her parents way off in America, how they must be feeling now, her mother especially. Some were ashamed of their own people, those good-for-nothing hooligans. Some were giving each other high fives; how many of us die, how many of our children are murdered, and who sings their songs? Why should we be the only ones to lose babies? Why not them, too? Some were proud. Some were heartsick. Some planned a protest march; they wanted this scourge to stop, and for people of all colors to be spared. They started painting signs demanding "Peace Now."

One slender young woman with a sleek, inky pixie cut walked down NY1. She was twenty-six at the time, like Amy. She read biographies and appreciated high fashion. She believed in black magic and women's rights. She was a serious person, rarely laughed or smiled. After the attack, she had called a cop friend and asked what had happened to the girl she saw being beaten by the Caltex, and the cop friend had told her that the girl had died.

She crossed Lansdowne Road and pushed through the crowd at the police station gate. She asked the uniformed officer for Rhodes, whom she knew. Rhodes came out of the station, looking even paler than usual, since the Riot and Violent Crimes Investigation Unit had been questioning him like he was some sort of suspect, and plus, figures of authority made him fidgety. He motioned the woman into the compound, and they stood to the side, near an anemic tree.

"I can tell you who killed the white lady," she said. "You cannot tell anyone who I am. Do you promise?"

"I promise," Rhodes said, scribbling down names on his notepad. "Thank you."

She nodded and walked straight home. She wouldn't eat for a day or so; she wouldn't sleep that night, thinking of what they did. She sat up in the dark. She could see Amy running from the men, all down that street, a fox running from a pack of dogs, then torn to shreds. For what? Not for liberation. Not for a free South Africa. Not for land or dogma. For nothing.

It was twilight at the station. Rhodes looked down at the notebook, at the sheet of paper he would soon hand over to Pikker, who would again aggressively question him, this time for the witness's name. Rhodes would always insist that he hadn't recognized her, that she'd just been an anonymous face in the crowd. Pikker would find her anyway, many months later. On the paper, there were three addresses in Gugulethu, all within a quarter mile of the murder site. Next to each address was a corresponding name:

Mongezi Manqina
Ntobeko Peni
Easy Nofemela

5.

_____

Having created the Frankenstein monster (and it is no less terrifying because it is largely illusory), the lyncher lives in constant fear of his own creation.

—WALTER WHITE, *Thirty Years of Lynching in the United States, 1889–1918*

We are betrayed by what is false within.

—GEORGE MEREDITH

One day in March 2012, I headed down the N2 highway toward Gugulethu, where Easy was waiting. It occurred to me that my gold Renault hatchback was not too different from the yellow-beige Mazda hatchback Amy Biehl had been driving on August 25, 1993. It occurred to me also that if I were to get whacked, there was no shortage of people who would roll their eyes.

As I drove toward Gugulethu, I tried to forget about the horror stories of the townships. How people kept telling me that I wasn't to think I was as "free as in America." Once, over sushi, a friend of a friend had told me about an acquaintance who had been carjacked, kidnapped, and dropped on a street corner in Soweto, Johannesburg's prominent township, the old stomping grounds of Mandela and his cadres.

"What then?" I asked.

"He put his head down and he got the hell out," the friend of a friend said.

"Didn't he ask for help?"

"You don't ask for help in there. You have a fifty-fifty chance anyway, if you're a man. If you're a woman, you have zero chance."

"Zero?"

"Zero."

"Even if I found another woman to help me?"

"Yes. You would be raped."

"And killed?"

"You'd be killed because the rape would never, ever stop. You would be raped to the point of death."

I didn't believe the guy at the restaurant, but at the same time even the slightest possibility of being raped to death is one of those things that's hard to dismiss. This dark communal bogeyman grew larger and more malicious every time he appeared.

Easy had asked me to pick him up in Gugulethu. I had met him briefly at the Amy Biehl Foundation office twice before, but had never been able to speak to him at length or in depth, so this would be my first proper interview and my first time alone with him. It would also be my first time driving into the townships by myself. Easy gave me specific directions: the exit, the left lane, the turn at the light, and I'd find him, standing outside the Shoprite. I jumped at the opportunity because obtaining time with the man had, until then, proved nearly impossible.

For weeks, I had been calling him. His phone was busy. His battery had died. He had no service. Bad network. No contract. Out of airtime. Can't send an SMS. The phone was stolen, broken, lost, found, dunked in water, dried out, spontaneously turned off, left at home, forgotten at the office, borrowed by his brother, hidden by his girlfriend, accidentally laundered by his mother, in the sofa cracks, at the bottom of his bag, in his cousin's backyard, in a friend's car. This was a new phone; how did it work? This was an old phone; it wasn't taking a charge.

When we did speak, roughly half of what we said got lost in translation. My American accent and his South African lilt were filtered through a sometimes patchy mobile network, his cheap, battered cellphone, and my old-model BlackBerry. We both spoke too fast. Easy's English wasn't great, and my Xhosa was nonexistent. When we hung up, I suspected neither of us had the first idea of what had just happened. Sometimes, he raised and dashed my hopes in a matter of seconds.

"I cannot meet today, but let's make a plan," he said one Friday.

"Great! What's the plan?"

"The plan is, you call me Monday. Then we see what's happening."

I tracked him doggedly, finding him a few times only by pure luck. He was at once the best-natured and most unreliable person I'd ever dealt with. We would arrange to meet at noon on any given day, and I would arrive at the spot, usually near his office in town. In the best-case scenario, Easy showed up two hours late. In the usual scenario, he did not show up at all. In the worst-case scenario, he not only did not show up, but his phone would be off for the next week. There were excuses, delivered kindly: His boss sent him to Main Street in a suburb, but this particular suburb had a "Main Street" and a "Main Street Road," and he could not figure out which was which, and for that reason, he'd been AWOL for three hours. His daughter had "fever"—later I'd find that the majority of township illnesses were referred to in English, generically, either as "fever" or "high blood"—and needed the doctor immediately. He was under stress from work. He was under stress from his family. He would be there in ten minutes. In another ten minutes. Just ten more minutes. But ten minutes never meant ten minutes. It meant, "Wait there," or "Don't be mad, buddy," or "I can't deal with you now."

Easy called this "African time." It derived from ancestral rituals, he explained, in which Africans welcomed their ancestors to traditional ceremonies. You couldn't very well rush an ancestor, he said, so you had to just wait around until the ancestor showed up. Also, consider transportation issues.

"There can be problems, there can face obstacles." Your horse could collapse, for example. And if your horse collapsed, you'd be pretty late.

"Easy, I don't see you riding around on a horse."

He tried a more timeless and convenient explanation: "African time is, you're not guilty. If we invite you at one, we can also start at two or three. When you arrive, we're not mad. You are there."

So when the opportunity to see Easy—better yet, to hold him captive in my car so he could not escape and would have to talk to me—presented itself, I did my best to push aside any nagging doubts. I drove in the shadow of Lion's Head peak, veered left to stay on the

N2, past the stinky old power plant and the trash-strewn fields, past Cape Town's first township, Langa, and the shacks on its outskirts, past the Joe Slovo Village of cement apartment blocks overlooking the highway beneath a faded billboard offering affordable housing that the advertisement promised would provide that ever-elusive "DIGNITY," past the broken-down horses grazing highway-side on the outskirts of Bonteheuwel. I turned off the N2 as directed and veered left along a barren strip of dry field. People were crossing the road at a clip, clutching each other's arms, as cars sped through. My palms were moist now, my back damp. Everything looked foreign and incomprehensible. An otherworldly junk dealer with dread-locks, blue eyes, and gigantic silver hoop earrings rode atop old bed frames and scrap metal piled high on a horse-drawn cart. A newspaper vendor at the stoplight held up the *Daily Sun,* an English-language tabloid with a multimillion-strong, almost entirely black readership. Today's headline: PROPHET BURNT TO DEATH.

An ancient man with a dent in his head limped to the car window, hands out, eyes vacant. I shook my head, as though I could do nothing for him despite my most sincere wishes to help. The light changed to green and I turned into Gugulethu. Here was the Shop-rite Center Amy had once passed. It contained a liquor store owned by Chinese immigrants, a KFC, a hardware store that advertised an array of gun safes, and a halal butchery, the slogan of which was "Where the Rainbow Nation Meat." Inside the actual Shoprite su-permarket, where guards armed with machine guns stood at the doors to stem the tide of perpetual stickups, a bulletin board was plastered with signs offering "cash in a flash :-) . . . forward ID num-ber, income, and name," as well as a "mobile fridge for hire . . . for weddings, funeral, church event and much more," and pleas for work:

My name is Thelma Ima Zimbabwe Im looking for a job any job household to look after children Im 24 years old.

My name is vuyadwethu. I'm xhosa girl. I'm 32 years old. I'm looking for kind of job like clean house or looking after children. The language I understand is English and Afrikaans. But I'm not perfect. I will be glad when you call me. I really need a job Thanks

Looking for a job trainee cook book keeper c work house maid

I knew Easy, I reminded myself. But then I started to wonder: do we *really* know anybody at all? Perhaps this was a game, and I was the all-too-willing pawn, lured straight into a bloody setup. Witnesses in Gugulethu kept their traps shut. There is very little worse than to be considered an *impimpi*, or snitch. In the old days—and still, in the far unseen reaches of the vigilante-controlled settlements where cops dare not set foot—groups would "necklace" a suspected impimpi or a thief or anyone tried and convicted in the local kangaroo courts. The grimly euphemistic necklace is, in fact, a gasoline-soaked tire that is secured around a victim's neck and set alight.

Nobody knew me in this part of the woods. I thought of all the terrible rumors I'd heard about the townships; I had dismissed them, though I also had evidently absorbed them. Wasn't this the Wild West? Was anyone safe here? And didn't Easy once get sentenced to eighteen years in prison for the stoning and stabbing death of a young white woman?

Then I saw Easy standing at the bus stop, waving at me, and I slowed. He was wearing a pressed teal and navy striped button-down shirt tucked into gray trousers. There were some folks waiting for the bus, mostly heavyset grandmas in long skirts, laden with grocery bags. There were a few kids holding hands with each other, a baby tied on his mom's back with a bath towel, a woman reading a book, some teenage boys kicking a soccer ball down the street. An elderly man in a newsboy cap was selling fruit beneath a ragged umbrella. A wave of pedestrians, some in high heels and some in slippers, passed back and forth from the Shoprite and over the bridge into Gugulethu. A few girls had clay smeared over their faces to protect their skin from the sun. Nobody noticed me, as far as I could tell.

Easy got in. He slumped in the seat and sneezed loudly. His nose was stuffy, his eyes puffy.

"I have flu," he announced, sniffling. "When you have flu, you need your mom to help, to listen your cough."

A young couple walked by, arms wrapped around each other, eating ice cream. I felt a tear of salty sweat trickle down my chest and settle in my belly button.

When I first arrived in Cape Town, I wore a sapphire-and-rose-gold engagement ring on my left ring finger, and when I passed black men on the street, I unconsciously turned the ring inward, so that the stone pointed at my palm. I tried to change the behavior, but even when I left the ring just as it was, I still felt that hot urge, as involuntary as a reflex. Soon, I took the ring off and put it in the safe in our seaside rental apartment, since almost every South African home has a safe welded into the back of a closet. But no matter. Today, I didn't need a circle of precious metal to expose me, if only to myself; the drive to Gugulethu had done the trick. I offered Easy a tissue and we turned back toward town.

That day, Easy and I sat on a café patio across from the ocean. The clientele at lunch hour was mostly rich moms in yoga pants; their husbands worked and their maids cooked and cleaned, and so between school drop-off and school pickup, they practiced Pilates, ordered salads, and had chemicals applied to their hair and faces to look more youthful. Easy ordered a vitamin-C-enriched sports drink "for hydration," and, deeming it the least complicated item on the menu, Chinese chicken. He tried to express to the teenage waitress that he wished only for the chicken element of the dish, minus vegetables or sauces, but she stared at him with wonder and he gave up. When his lunch arrived, he ate it daintily, picking out every sliver of red pepper and pineapple.

I started off with a long introduction, rambling on uncertainly until Easy looked at me, blew his nose, and said, not unkindly, "Just throw the question."

At the time of our first meeting, journalists both foreign and South African had been snapping photos and asking Easy questions about Amy Biehl for eighteen years. Since 1993, he had been locked in a strange relationship with the press. I later realized that despite being the subject of much media scrutiny, he rarely consumed any news and therefore was largely unaware of and unconcerned by the various representations of him.

He had no idea that *The New York Times* called him "a small man, a little imp of a guy ... his eyes are quick, set deep in his face, and can harden as fast as an African storm." He had not read Nancy Scheper-Hughes's article on suffering, published in a 1995 issue of the academic journal *Social Justice*, in which she detailed the scars etched on his young body, which told a "vivid story of township violence: stab wounds, brick bashings, machete chops, second-degree burns, scars from untreated infections and botched, discriminatory medical care." In 1994, when the press crowded around the courthouse during the criminal trial for Amy's murder, Easy emerged onto the steps and his face fell into a bashful smile, all the flashbulbs and attention on him. He wore a patterned wool sweater and a gold chain hung with a palm-sized medallion shaped like the African continent. He seemed to enjoy the taste of celebrity, no matter its origin, and he didn't understand how his grin might be perceived. At the very least, he didn't quite know what to do about all the flashing cameras except to say cheese.

Since then, Easy had forgotten how many people he'd spoken to. He gave them all similar quotes. He knew the drill. He was supposed to discuss issues facing the township, the power of forgiveness, his own shining rehabilitation, and the credit due his American benefactors, the Biehls. He was to juxtapose the old and the new, the radical and the reformed.

"At that time I was young and under the influence of the PAC," he told an American journalist, referring to the Pan Africanist Congress, the political party upon whose orders he claimed he acted when killing Amy. "Now it's democracy, and we understand each other. I'm happy, I'm free, I'm normal, I'm positive because of Makhulu and Tatomkhulu—they make me strong."

"Politics can cost you your life, family, and everything important to you," he explained to a reporter from New Zealand. "I decided it was time to look after myself and my family first."

"I know that previous it was apartheid, so once the foundation come to us, I think, this is my dream, to seek to work for my people," he explained, in halting English, to a grinning Katie Couric.

The Amy Biehl Foundation liked to sit visitors in a lightless back room and play an old *Dateline NBC* segment, "The Amy Biehl Story," narrated by Diane Sawyer, followed by a documentary that celebrated the Biehls' acts of forgiveness. Easy tended to duck out when the screen lit up; he could not bear to see his younger self on film. He had once asked a manager to stop playing the DVD to guests, but to no avail. Once, he'd been shocked to find a picture of his daughter in a Dutch magazine. Sure, some people came and snapped photos, but he hadn't understood they'd be published.

"Please take the picture out," he begged Linda, who informed him that she was not able to remove a print from a published magazine.

Since then, he'd only grown more accustomed and resigned to the media presence in his life. He was no longer thrilled by his little piece of fame. At this point, doing interviews was a way to please others, mostly his bosses at the foundation, who marched him out as a fundraising and public relations asset. Ntobeko had recused himself from such requests.

"I've lost my interest in journalists," Ntobeko informed me on the single occasion he had agreed to speak with me, at Linda's request. The breaking point, he said, was a 2005 article that began: *The mother of murdered US aid worker Amy Biehl attended the wedding of her daughter's killer and danced with the groom.* The article contained a quote by Ntobeko, though he swore he'd never given an interview. Ever since then, he'd decided that he despised journalists.

"I don't even read the news," he added. "Lately, I've just been reading motivational speakers."

Since Ntobeko refused to be paraded before the media, Easy was the foundation's best chance at putting a face to their unique story. Plus, Linda often urged Easy to speak to journalists, and he could not refuse her. And then there were the journalists themselves, many like me, who came from so far and seemed so desperate and were so easily placated. How could he deny me, a sorry character who had been, at that point, begging him for a meeting for nearly two months?

6.

The settler and the native are old acquaintances. In fact, the settler is right when he speaks of knowing "them" well. For it is the settler who had brought the native into existence and who perpetuates his existence. The settler owes the fact of his very existence, that is to say, his property, to the colonial system.

—Frantz Fanon, *The Wretched of the Earth*

Whatever happens, we have got
The Maxim gun, and they have not.

—Hilaire Belloc

Easy Nofemela was born on June 6, 1971, as Mzikhona Nofemela. Mzikhona's literal Xhosa meaning is: "We have a home [through him]." Easy's mother, Kiki, is from the Sotho ethnic group, and his father, Wowo, is Xhosa; the two met in Gugulethu in 1968.

"The time I see Kiki, I was only Kiki," Wowo remembered. "I was running after her and try and try and try, and it work."

Wowo was twenty-one. Kiki was thirteen. Within the year, she had given birth to their first son.

"If you can see her then, you can't see she is young, but I was nearly in jail for that," Wowo explained, forty-seven years later. "But I said to her family, 'I do everything for her.' And from that time, I not leave her."

They married in 1970. Mzikhona, their second son, took on the nickname Easy, for his easygoing temperament.

"Easy come, easy go. Easy to accept pain. Easy to release the pain," Easy once explained to me.

Only Kiki continued to call him Mzikhona, especially when she was cross. "Mmm-zee-KOH-na," she would say loudly, her face stern, and Easy would hop to: *Sorry, sorry.* Then he'd usually do the same wrong thing, whatever it was, the very next day, and on and on into his forties, which is to say he never stopped getting in trouble with his mom.

Kiki had her generous breasts sucked dry by the stream of ravenous babies; she put peanut butter on her nipples to get them to leave her alone, but they still cried for more. Kiki fell pregnant with a girl, but endured a stillbirth late in the pregnancy.

"If that girl was living, I got eight children," Wowo reflected.

In the end, she produced boy after boy, until she had borne six of them, from 1968 until 1982. She nearly died having her youngest child, to whom she gave birth alone while working as a maid; her boss returned home an hour later to find Kiki and the baby clinging to life in a pool of blood. Then there was an adopted son, the child of Wowo's sister, who was raised as one of the brood, too, bringing the grand total in the Nofemela household to seven boys.

Other young cousins came to stay for weeks or even years, sent to Gugulethu from the rural parts of the country, or from other townships. They lay their blankets on the floor and helped with the washing and ate the dinners of samp, a cornmeal mush, boiled together with sugar beans and onions; meat on a good day; potatoes on a bad day; and pap, the pale cornmeal staple cooked into a porridge, for nearly every meal. Everyone drank their tea weak, made instant coffee with lukewarm water, and took three tablespoons of sugar, at least.

The seven brothers, and eventually their children, remained the center of Kiki and Wowo's world. The main decor in the house was a framed, poster-sized collage of family photos, compiled with glue and cardboard by Wowo, a neat and precise retired gardener who also liked to sketch. In the middle, he had pasted a portrait of a young Wowo and Kiki, a sturdy and handsome pair in formal wear, staring out, unsmiling in the way of those unaccustomed to being the subject of a picture. Below, he pasted a large print of his own late parents and his wizened grandmother standing in a row on a tile floor, decades of hard labor and loss and crappy mattresses etched on their faces. Next to them, Wowo pasted a snapshot of Kiki's late mother, glowing and vigorous, smiling next to a birthday sheet cake. Wowo inserted, wherever there was space, baby pictures of various grandchildren, often propped up on couches.

Then Wowo made a border around the photos, using large, rectangular grade-school portraits of each of his sons. They wore their V-neck sweaters and finest collared shirts and posed against blue backgrounds. Xola, the adopted cousin-brother, stands out against the rest, with his broad distinctive face and upturned nose. But the other six Nofemela boys, the genetic melding of Wowo and Kiki, are indistinguishable: dainty, light-skinned faces, little noses, almond eyes, full lips. The first time I saw the collage, I studied it, trying to pick out this boy from that. It proved impossible. It didn't seem relevant to me then that I couldn't distinguish one from the next, but it would become so later on.

Today, in their thirties and forties, the brothers all look different, adulthood having stretched and molded them into unique physical specimens. Easy is the shortest and most childlike, Martin the roundest, Vusumzi, the eldest and most imposing, Misiya the tallest, Gagi the most refined. And Mongezi—Monks, for short—is the most beautiful, with a smooth movie-star face, high cheekbones, and straight white teeth, punctuated with a single gold cap on the incisor. It is hard to tell his build or his height because he was paralyzed in 2009, thrown from a minivan taxi in the early morning hours, vertebra C4 injured.

These days, Monks often reclined in a stationary Ford sedan in front of the house. He had a compulsive fear of "fever," though I later realized he was in fact terrified of contracting pneumonia, a common secondary ailment in paralyzed people, whose lungs are already compromised. He didn't know why, but he sweat constantly, and he was concerned that the combination of damp sweat and a gust of cold air could cause him illness. Everyone was convinced that Monks could outwit pneumonia by staying very hot at all times, and so the rooms in which he convalesced were outfitted with heaters, and he was constantly shuttled between a sweltering bedroom, a sweltering TV room, and a sweltering automobile, parked in the noon sun. During much of the shuttling, everyone despaired of Monks, who was always making demands and barking orders. Wowo and all the brothers pulled out their backs monthly carrying Monks from bed to couch to car. Once, Easy had said to me, unaware of the reference to the song, "He is my brother, and he is *so* heavy."

But back then, before they were marked by the ravages of time, those two Nofemela boys, Easy and Monks, looked just like each other. Months after our first conversations, for reasons I'll probably never know, Easy gave me a photograph of the two of them that eventually helped me unravel a shred of the truth about what happened on that August day in 1993, the day of Amy's death.

During Easy's childhood, there were always too many people in a small space. There were two chocolates for ten kids, one shirt mended and handed down for twelve years, shared shoes and toothbrushes. The seven brothers were almost one organism, separated only by the corporal borders of flesh and bone. They slept together on a hay-filled sack, a pleasant experience of fraternal intimacy that had one big problem, according to Easy. Time and again, an unknown miscreant was "deep, deep dreaming that he is in the toilet."

"Before we go to sleep, we talk, laughing, feeling great. But in the middle of the night, somebody is going to give you a dam of water."

"So who was the culprit?" I asked.

"We wake up and we're all suspects."

Easy was not a star student, having started school at age seven. This, he claimed, was due to an inexplicable rule that I have never found in official literature, but that has been mentioned to me several times by black men who entered the education system in the 1970s and 1980s, as well as a Nigerian friend who attended school in Nigeria during the same time: in some instances, to start attending classes, black boys had to be able to reach their right arm over their head and clutch their entire left ear, with their necks stick-straight. This, for whatever reason, meant they were ready to go to kindergarten. Easy, small of stature and short of limb, couldn't manage to grab his ear until he was nine, but, after watching kids in uniform march past his house for years, he stormed the school and announced to the principal that he wished to study.

"My only problem is my elbow," he argued, and the principal relented. Once he was there, he was taken with mathematics, physics, and geometry.

"Everything about maths is tricking people," he said.

In the mornings, Kiki made home-baked Sotho bread—sugary, dense, and steamy. The boys drank a mixture of fruit-flavored corn syrup and water, or, near the end of the month, simply water. Their favorite TV show was *Knight Rider*. Wowo coached a local soccer team, Harmony United, and taught his own kids to kick around a soccer ball as soon as they could walk. Easy played the game competitively and later somehow convinced journalists to refer to him as a "former soccer star." In reality, he wasn't half bad, but he was irritating to play with because no matter how crushing his team's defeat, if Easy had scored a single goal, he'd celebrate for hours.

"I am a hero!" he'd exclaim, running around with his arms in the air, while the others glared at him.

In the Xhosa tradition, the family elders ruled the roost, and the Nofemela household was run by Melvin Nofemela. Melvin Nofemela was Wowo's father and Easy's grandfather. He was born in 1910 in a rural Eastern Cape village and died in 1997 in Gugulethu. He navigated a lifetime marked by massive historical changes, his suffering and his struggles engineered by a succession of distant white politicians and their loyal followers, and his liberation brought about three years before his death by a party of black freedom fighters who remain in power still, their glory days marred by persistent corruption and double-dealings.

In the century before Melvin's birth, the land of his ancestors had become a battleground. Then, as in South Africa today, the fighting came down to the issue of land ownership. As white people encroached deeper into the nameless sweep of country, its borders yet drawn, wars erupted between the whites and the threatened African tribes with which they made contact. Melvin's people, the Xhosas, fought the British and colonial forces in the border wars, but by 1860, the once prosperous farmers had been shattered, concentrated in small "native" areas, and stripped of their cattle.

Meanwhile, a new wave of Dutch pioneers, infuriated by British policies in the Cape Colony, loaded their belongings into wagons and headed north, armed with rifles. They pushed the Ndebele into today's Zimbabwe. They fought the Zulus at a spot that came to be known as the Blood River, where three thousand Zulu soldiers, armed with spears, died at the hands of just over fifty pioneers, who obliterated their enemy with bullets and cannon fire. Within a generation, the Zulu kingdom, once a proud, repressive military dictatorship, had been definitively torn apart, first by civil war and next by an army of British soldiers. Meanwhile, the Sotho people, led by the famed Moshoeshoe, successfully battled Afrikaner commandos, and, years later, were allowed by the British powers to maintain a tiny mountain kingdom, an independent nation carved out of the greater South African mass and known today as Lesotho. Over time, the Pedi and the Shangaan, the Venda and the Tswana, the Tsonga and Swazi, were also dispossessed or run off their ancestral land by Dutch commandos, British army officers, or a combination of the two.

As the battles multiplied, Britain, which had once hoped only to protect a trade route, found itself pumping money into Southern Africa, trying to control numerous wars as well as a rebellious population of Dutch descendants. They had to deal with droughts and locusts and protect settler populations from angry indigenous populations. The colony had become a nuisance.

Between 1852 and 1856, Britain, in an attempt to quell restive Afrikaners, recognized two Afrikaner republics: the interior regions of the Transvaal and the Orange Free State. These land masses up to the northeast of the Cape were unenviable parcels of farmland in the middle of precisely nowhere. The Afrikaners were nonetheless pleased at this measure of autonomy, and commenced developing their republics. They were too few in number to build anything significant on their own, so Afrikaner commandos kidnapped black children. These children were often referred to as "black ivory," in reference to their value as laborers, which was soon higher than that of white ivory. It was certainly more plentiful, as the elephant population had been decimated ever since men with guns landed on the peninsula.

Then, in the year 1866, in a dusty scrubland on the outskirts of a remote agricultural village in the Orange Free State, a young boy found a shiny pebble in the dirt on his father's farm. It turned out to be a 21.25-carat diamond that was called, aptly, Eureka. Prospectors descended upon the area. In 1871, an 83.5-carat diamond was found on a hill on a property belonging to the farming De Beers family. One month later, a stampede of two thousand men had descended upon the land, and the hill was turned into an enormous depression, forty-two acres across, known as the Kimberley Mine, or, more colloquially, the Big Hole. Today, tourists gape at it.

Twenty years after the discovery of Eureka, as thousands of men marched into the Big Hole, a British carpenter wandered across a hill range in the Transvaal. He kicked a glistening stone and walked farther, scanning the land, until he happened upon a long reef of rocks, beneath which lay the biggest deposit of gold in the world. Soon, 300,000 miners would be working in this remote hinterland.

Word spread, and immigrants poured into South Africa, including thousands of persecuted Lithuanian Jews, from whom my husband is descended. European businessmen arrived with high hopes. Harbors sprang up along the coasts, as did a shipping industry. In the thirty-some years since Eureka's unearthing, workers, mostly black laborers, had laid nearly four thousand miles of railway. Johannesburg, a city built around the gold trade, exploded, and within ten years of its founding it was larger than 250-year-old Cape Town. The earth was plundered and more minerals discovered: copper, iron, and coal. By the turn of the twentieth century, South Africa was no longer a backwater colony but a place in which a white man could make a fortune.

With the discovery of gold and diamonds, Britain regretted allowing the Afrikaners to set up shop on such precious land. In 1899,
the British and the Afrikaner republics went to war. Initially shocked
and humiliated by successful Afrikaner guerrilla tactics, imperial
Britain resorted to all-out destruction: burning crops, razing home-
steads, and interning the opposition in concentration camps, where
26,000 Afrikaners died, 80 percent of them children and the rest
mostly women. In the end, the British lost 22,000 troops but prevailed.

The main result of this clash for the Afrikaners was a long-standing
hatred for the British passed down through generations, and the
birth of a particularly hard-line form of Afrikaner nationalism mixed
with Dutch Reformed Christianity. This heady mix of religion and
nationalism bloomed into a widespread belief that Afrikaners were
God's chosen people, under fire from blacks and British alike but
destined to emerge as the ruling white tribe of Africa. They sought,
then, to dominate the land in order to protect themselves and realize
a divine plan. These deep-seated beliefs would one day morph into
the formal system of governance known as apartheid.

After the Anglo-Boer War, the British and the Afrikaners negotiated a peace settlement. The British colonies merged into the Union
of South Africa, which was self-governing under the dominion of
the British government until 1961, when South Africa became a
republic. The Afrikaner general Louis Botha won the 1910 elections,
voted in almost entirely by the white British and Afrikaans minority.
Though Botha encouraged Afrikaner pride, he was pragmatic: in a
country with a black majority, the Afrikaner's best bet was to create
a white power base with his British countrymen, consolidating resources and authority in white hands.

The year of Botha's victory was the year of Melvin Nofemela's
birth, on a distant homestead on an empty bluff in the far-off village
of Lady Frere. Lady Frere was named after the wife of Britain's high
commissioner to the Cape Colony, a stately mustachioed Welshman
named Sir Henry Bartle Frere. Frere, who had previously acted as

governor of colonial Bombay, had plans to defend the Cape from a "general and simultaneous rising of Kaffirdom against white civilization," as he said, and took to crushing Xhosa rebellions and starting a bloody war with the Zulus, despite their chief's continued pleas for peace.

The exact day that Melvin came into the world was never recorded; birthdays are of little significance in old Xhosa culture. Melvin's parents were illiterate subsistence farmers who had been tending to their land for generations, worshipping their ancestors, living in huts, and visiting *sangomas,* or traditional herbal healers, when they needed healthcare. The Nofemelas had little wealth and no formal education. The only schools in rural areas were isolated missionary programs, run by evangelical European families intent on saving African souls.

Melvin's parents might have considered pursuing an education for their child, but when he was a year old, the Mines and Works Act was passed, prohibiting black South Africans from holding skilled jobs; menial labor would be their appropriate calling. By 1959, black students could only attend university with special state permission.

In that case, Melvin's family may have hoped to leave the area and purchase land elsewhere, but when he was three years old, the Natives Land Act of 1913 passed. This act barred black South Africans from buying or leasing land in white areas; instead, they were relegated to "native areas" or "reserves," undesirable and overpopulated plots. The land that blacks could legally own made up 7 percent of the total landmass of South Africa. In 1936, this was expanded to 13 percent. With the passage of the Land Act, blacks living on white-owned land were evicted. Many of them had been well-off peasant farmers, and now, if they did not make it to the reserves, they were forced to trudge from place to place, their families and downtrodden animals in tow, begging white men for a plot on which to pitch their disassembled homes in exchange for their labor.

Melvin could have headed to the cities to take a job, but by the time he was thirteen, the Native Urban Areas Act of 1923 cut short any such dreams and laid the foundations for the first townships, then called "native locations." This act defined towns and cities as the white man's turf. If blacks were ministering to white men as laborers or servants, they were permitted to live in segregated areas on the outskirts of the cities. But if a black man ceased to adequately serve the purposes and needs of whites, he could be deported back to the reserves.

Melvin, living on the bluff in Lady Frere, likely knew little of the political forces shifting his early life. But when he met and married teenage Alice, and she had their first baby in 1940 and their second in 1942, he knew he had to make money. Blacks had been surviving off the soil from time immemorial, but once their land had been reorganized and repopulated by the white government—too many people condensed on too little land, with watering holes and streams overrun—it became impossible for most residents to produce enough food on which to survive.

Melvin left his family in search of a job elsewhere, like many able-bodied black men at the time. In addition to supporting his family, he owed the government taxes, despite receiving neither rights nor representation. Along with hundreds of thousands, Melvin headed north and got a job in the expanding mines. His pay was a pittance, especially compared to a white man's doing the same work: in 1951, the white gold miner earned nearly fifteen times the wage of the black gold miner, and by 1970, white miners earned twenty-one times the wage of black miners. Because of the Mines and Works Act, Melvin could never rise above the lowest rung of the job hierarchy. He was housed in a hostel, a single-sex compound that often pressed ninety men into a single dormitory. When he left to visit his parents, Alice, and his children for three weeks a year, he was strip-searched in case he was smuggling gold.

Though the idea of unionizing was gaining traction, it was still a daunting task. In 1913 at an open-pit diamond mine in the middle of the country, a black worker offended a white foreman, who proceeded to kick him to death. When his black colleagues went on strike, white workers and cops banded together to kill eleven black miners and injure thirty-seven others. Fighting for one's rights was lethal business.

Melvin desperately missed his family, his hometown, his community. He returned annually to slowly build a small traditional house with a clay floor and straw roof. On one of his short holidays home, he took a second wife, as per Xhosa custom. His longing for his children and his hatred of the sweltering, perilous mines grew. Between 1933 and 1966, nearly twenty thousand men had died in the mines, which did not have adequate safety measures. The vast majority of victims were black. Frightened, both of death and of leaving his family destitute, Melvin searched for another job.

By that time, the Mines and Works Act had been expanded, so that white citizens would get first dibs at employment in other burgeoning industries: the railways, civil service, iron, and steel. Despite this, Melvin managed to get a job laying track for the expanding railways. First, he was based in Lady Frere, but soon the railways moved him to Cape Town. While the second wife remained in Lady Frere, Alice and the children followed, living with thousands of migrants on the outskirts of the city, pitching shacks just miles from stately white-owned 1950s-era homes with all the trappings of Western comfort and modernity. Melvin and Alice held strong against the odds. Often, defeated by distance, lacking telephones, and overwhelmed by loneliness, black men began affairs in the cities, which fractured many families and resulted in scattered children. Despite their commitment to each other, however, the Nofemelas found city living prohibitively expensive; they kept their elder children with them and sent the babies to be raised by relatives in the country.

The government, noting the unending creep of women from the reserves to the city, wished to remove "surplus females" (i.e., women who didn't serve white businesses or other white interests) and growing families from the locations. But Melvin had other plans. He was saving money with the dream of bringing all of his children back together, one by one.

Nineteen forty-eight was Melvin's thirty-eighth year. His son Wowo had just been born, and would in two years be sent to live with his uncle. Across the ocean, World War II had come to a close—of the 5,500 South Africans killed while supporting the Allies, a forgotten 25 percent were black. The world was reeling from the Holocaust, and the Nazis were on the losing side of history. But one party in South Africa was taking its inspiration from Hitler. This was the National Party, led by D. F. Malan, a Dutch Reformed cleric who campaigned on the platform of apartheid, Afrikaans for "separateness."

The central theory behind apartheid was that South Africa was not a single nation, but in fact a collection of separate nations, each populated by a certain ethnic group. Conflict in South Africa stemmed from the unreasonable attempts of these nations to meld into one, and such conflict could be eliminated if only each group existed in separate but equal spheres, free from the demands and traditions of other pesky cultures. As with all systems of segregation, however, the truth was that the founders of apartheid intended to create a society that was indeed separate, but was breathtakingly unequal. Then they could keep all the good stuff for themselves.

Malan's challenger was the incumbent Jan Smuts, a lesser racist, all things being relative. (Smuts, though opposed to giving blacks political power, helped draft the constitution of the United Nations' forerunner, the League of Nations, and met with Gandhi on the rights of Indians in South Africa.) Only coloreds in the Cape and whites could vote in the election. On May 26, 1948, Melvin watched from the sidelines as Malan took power. One of the Malan government's first orders of business was to eliminate the voting rights of coloreds.

In 1950, the National Party passed the Group Areas Act, a law that Prime Minister Malan dubbed with great reverence "the very essence of apartheid." For centuries, various colonial and white governments had been redistributing black land into white hands, so that less than 10 percent of the population owned more than 85 percent of the land. But after their victorious 1948 election, the

Afrikaner nationalists running the country started putting in place what they called *groot apartheid*, or grand apartheid.

The act aimed to forcibly separate each of the four official South African racial classifications into their own living areas. In Cape Town, whites, for the most part, inherited the beautiful city center, the leafiest suburbs, and the ocean views; Indians were bestowed with two small neighborhoods; and colored people were placed in square government matchbox houses in bleak zones that neighbored Gugulethu. Although the records are poor, some studies estimate that between 1960 and 1982, over 3.5 million South Africans were forcibly relocated, ripped from their property, and taken to townships or newly created "homelands." The apartheid dream was to eventually create a white nation free of black inhabitants.

The homelands would help realize this dream. Each homeland was intended to act as a pseudo-autonomous "nation" for a particular ethnic group, where all its members would live in peace. The homelands, which eventually numbered ten, were actually rural backwaters, where white investment was illegal. They were geographically fractured, separated by white farms, and overcrowded, set on just 13 percent of South African territory. In one central eastern homeland named QwaQwa, designated for the Sotho people, 777 people were expected to survive on the fruits of a single square mile; Easy's mother, Kiki, had been born there.

There was neither sufficient healthcare nor sanitation in the homelands, which resulted in outbreaks of cholera, tuberculosis, polio, and even the bubonic plague—in the mid- and late twentieth century. In 1974, the infant mortality rate of black children was 110 per 1,000, and the primary cause of their death was malnutrition.

"There was too much witch in the Transkei," Easy once told me, referring to the portion of today's Eastern Cape province that included his family's hometown of Lady Frere. "The women have many miscarriages."

Melvin, once a citizen of South Africa, was considered by lawmakers a member of the "Xhosa nation," and was to become a citizen of Transkei, where he was expected to settle permanently. He might work in the "European" cities or towns—and might, in the course of this work, father children in these white areas—but his family would always be temporary laborers in the greater South Africa. As the Department of Bantu Administration and Development stated in 1967: "As soon as [black workers] become, for one reason or another, no longer fit for work, or superfluous in the labour market, they are expected to return to their country of origin or the territory of the national unit where they fit ethnically if they were not born and bred in their homeland." The state, still intent on marketing the homelands as decolonized areas, installed cooperative black chiefs linked to the apartheid leadership. In 1977, Parliament granted Transkei independence. This independence was recognized by no country in the world other than South Africa.

Melvin, like many black South Africans, defied official attempts at confinement. By the late 1950s, Melvin and Alice had succeeded in bringing all of their twelve children back to Cape Town. They lived in a cramped, makeshift shack in an area called Elsie's River, on the outskirts of the city. But then, as per the Group Areas Act, Elsie's River was declared a colored area. Colored people, who had been forced from their homes—many lovely houses near the sea were handed over to whites—were relocated to crime-ridden apartment blocks or shoddy little houses on the Cape Flats. In 1960, Melvin and his family, including thirteen-year-old Wowo, were loaded onto an open truck and driven five miles south, where they were unceremoniously dumped, with their belongings, on a vast field on the border of the preexisting township of Nyanga.

For two weeks, as they built a new shack by hand, they sheltered under a table and washed and drank from a single tap installed a mile away. Nearby sat rows of houses constructed for "bachelor" men, whose purpose was to provide labor to white industry. Those dumped on the field took to calling their new neighborhood "Elsie's," since they had all been rounded up there. But soon groups of removals came from elsewhere, and the government dubbed the area Nyanga West.

In 1962, the government saw that Nyanga West was growing, teeming with new arrivals rounded up throughout Cape Town, as well as the regular migrants from the Eastern Cape. They renamed the area "Gugulethu Emergency Camp," and it would soon become the city's third official township. Gugulethu means "our pride."

"What did you do?" I once asked Wowo, as he recalled his displacement.

"You can't complain. You keep quiet."

"What did you think?"

"You can't think nothing if you want to stay alive."

The white Cape government favored coloreds, likely because Afrikaners and coloreds share a common ancestry, a language, and, often, a disdain for blacks. White people could not be expected to perform much of the menial work needed for the growing economy, and so the government's plan was to eventually expel blacks from the Western Cape and use coloreds as their cheap labor. But the endeavor proved difficult. First, the colored workforce was not big enough to meet the demand for workers; second, blacks kept illegally sneaking in across the homeland borders, squatting in the bush, and begging for work in the cities. The government soon decided it would have to build more township houses to contain such people. After eight years of squatting in the emergency camp, Melvin's name came up on the government's wait list, and the Nofemelas were allowed to rent a small house on NY6. The next year, they were shuffled to a three-bedroom house on NY41; fourteen family members took up residence in the space, sharing a lone outhouse. This overcrowding was common and enduring: in 1978, in a township bordering Gugulethu, a single bed was designated, on average, for six people.

By 1980, Wowo was thirty-three and married to twenty-five-year-old Kiki. They had five children. The house on NY41 was overflowing, and relatives had built small tin shacks in the backyard. Even if they had been financially able, they could not legally purchase property in the Western Cape, since it was not a black homeland.

Finally, Wowo was granted his own place, a two-bedroom on NY111, where he remains today; he and Kiki took one room and their sons took the other. Kiki gave birth to her youngest soon after they moved in, and Wowo's sister's boy came to live with them—eventually seven boys were sleeping together on one big straw mattress. Since obtaining the house, Wowo had slowly extended it to the furthest edges of the property line; an overhang made of uneven cement blocks abutted the edge of the sidewalk, and a series of stand-alone brick rooms pressed against the far end of the backyard.

By 2013, Melvin's grandchildren numbered fifty living souls—twenty men and thirty women, Easy among them. They were taxi drivers, clerks, housewives, hairdressers, insurance salesmen, postal workers, train conductors, cleaners, hospital workers, hotel room-service providers, supermarket checkout clerks, and employees of the South African Revenue Service. Ten were students. Five were unemployed. Nobody knew what two of them did with their days. One suffered from depression, one was disabled, and one was, according to her relatives, "a slow thinker from birth," who'd been raped and who now had to be supervised twenty-four hours a day. Some lived in the Eastern Cape province—after apartheid, the country's homelands were absorbed into the nine provinces of today—while most lived in the Western Cape, home to Gugulethu. Six had died. The number of great-grandchildren was climbing into the triple digits.

Though Melvin had no official political power, in his house, his word was law. The family considered Melvin as close to a god as they would find in this lifetime, and so as long as he was around, Wowo may have been a married father of seven, but he did not have the final say in his own household.

In the years since the first European missionary introduced Christianity to South Africa in 1737, many black preachers had taken over congregations and had created a particularly African brand of Christianity. Melvin and his wife Alice believed in Jesus Christ their Lord and Savior and in their Xhosa ancestors, who demanded animal sacrifices in return for protection. Everyone in the family followed suit, though at least one of their sons eventually disavowed traditional mores for conventional Christianity and was always grumbling about his relatives' lost souls. Easy, for one, believed halfheartedly in Jesus and wholeheartedly in the powers of his ancestors, and the meeting of the two seemed natural to him.

Melvin, "short-tempered but peaceful," according to Easy, encouraged prayer and was prone to beating disobedient kids. Alice supported this form of discipline.

"If she is angry, she get Father to beat you," Wowo recalled fondly. "She's a good wife. She like people, she like her children, but she is not funny, and if you make funny things, you make her cross."

Melvin was wise and prescient. You had best pay attention to him, because he knew what he was talking about.

"My grandfather said to one my brothers: by the end of the day if you don't want to listen you will result in prison and you will result in steal things," Easy remembered. "My brother was in and out and in and out of prison, and he get sick and pass away. My grandfather propheted that."

"Sick" in township parlance can often be a euphemism for HIV, which has a 19 percent prevalence rate among South African adults. And Easy was using the word "brother" in the black South African sense: when he said "brother" he meant "cousin." Biological brothers and sisters are not differentiated from cousins; the family structure is such that uncles and aunts have power and responsibility equal to fathers and mothers, and any local adult can discipline or direct a child—a village to raise a baby, indeed. As a Xhosa person, if your sibling dies or falls ill or simply has too much on his plate, you are expected to take in his children and raise them as your own. In this way, Wowo lived in his uncle's house from the age of three until the age of eleven, and in this way, he raised his sister's child.

Xhosa people refer to complete strangers, too, as brother or sister—*bhuti* or *sisi,* respectively. An older man is *tata;* an older woman, *mama.* Nelson Mandela, father of the nation and the world's most famous Xhosa, is referred to as Tata Mandela. Truly old men and women are addressed with great extravagance as *tatomkhulu* (grandfather, the term Easy and others used to address Peter Biehl) or *makhulu* (grandmother, the term Easy and others use to address Linda Biehl). Once, a young man addressed me as mama.

"No, call me sisi!" I said, and he looked at me blankly. I thought he was telling me that I was old, like when people stopped calling me "miss" and started calling me "ma'am." But later I learned that "mama" was simply a term of honor and respect, and the man had been trying to flatter me. To be mama is to be held in high regard, though to be bhuti or sisi isn't bad either. A Xhosa friend once explained to me that in adhering a familial term to a person, one humanizes him or her.

"Even if you don't know my name, if you call me sisi, I am *somebody.*"

By the time of his death in 1997, Melvin was a tata, or a tatomkhulu. In traditional Xhosa culture, a baby's umbilical cord and placenta are buried near their birthplace—Lady Frere, in Melvin's case. In a perfect world, a Xhosa returns to die near this very burial place, near his ancestors and relatives, on the land they all worked, completing the circle of life, from the soil and to the soil. You can live anywhere, but your home will always be where your umbilical cord rests—and in fact, when a Xhosa person recites his lineage, he usually begins by stating in Xhosa where his cord is buried.

But Melvin died and was buried in Gugulethu township; he never found the time or the money to return to his homestead and build the hut in which he wished to spend his final days. By the time Melvin died, Mandela was president and the Truth and Reconciliation Commission had commenced (in fact, Easy sat before the TRC in the year of Melvin's death). But the TRC didn't particularly register with Melvin. So much had been taken from him even before he was born; and after he was born, he was slowly stripped of most prospects he might have had. Melvin's entire life had been shaped by apartheid politics, but he remained apolitical and had not endured any terribly dramatic incident that labeled him, officially, as a victim: no police beating, no imprisonment or torture. So Melvin did not qualify as someone against whom human rights violations had been committed, and the commission was therefore irrelevant to him, and he was irrelevant to the commission.

Easy's mother, Kiki, was born Pinky Magdelene Mahula on June 6, 1955, in the tiny, depressed, overcrowded homeland of QwaQwa, that slip of earth designated for the Sotho people by the apartheid government. When Kiki was young, her family relocated to Gugulethu, where they eked out a living. Kiki left school at twelve. Her first baby, born when she was thirteen, couldn't pronounce Pinky, and called her Kiki—and the nickname stuck. By the time she was twenty, she had four kids in her care. By the time she was thirty, she had seven.

Kiki had no choice but to work, and found a job as a maid and nanny, caring for three strapping white children in a rich white suburb. Kiki's boys wished that she would wait for them with snacks and hugs when they returned home from school, like they saw TV moms doing, but she was in a Dutch-gabled home near the cricket fields, preparing sandwiches for the children of an insurance executive, and the boys had to make their own way.

The Afrikaans journalist Antjie Krog wrote of visiting an old friend who, when asked if she should provide her maid with soap or a heater during winter, claimed that maids "don't get cold like white people" and "don't like washing." When Krog asked if the maid missed her own faraway children, her friend answered, "Maids don't feel like other people about their children. They like to be rid of them." I heard similar sentiments repeated in the white community, over and over again.

These dehumanizing opinions of black people naturally boiled over into neglect and mistreatment by employers of their employees. And such mistreatment naturally caused the employees pain and humiliation, which, since they could not speak up to their employers, they often took out on their own families.

"The white person is very naughty," Easy remembered. "Our mothers are domestic workers, raising other kids. Our fathers are garden boys. When they come home, your mother push children away. Your father come home and give you harsh punishment."

Kiki was tired at the end of each long day, and she was not the hugging sort, but she still bandaged her babies' cuts, gave them baths, cooked their dinners. The elders slaughtered a goat every time a new child was born.

As they grew older, the Nofemela boys became aware of apartheid and what it meant for them. There was a shining world, they learned, outside Gugulethu, but they were not allowed there. Their parents had seen such places, but only because they worked over the city borders.

"We been blocked from town," Easy said.

In 1950, two years after the National Party took power, Parliament passed the Population Registration Act. This required all South African citizens to register as one of four racial classifications: white, Indian, colored, or black. To determine the race of ethnically ambiguous folks, the government implemented several highly scientific tests, such as the pencil test: If the pencil inserted into your hair fell out, congratulations! You're not black. Once you had been officially deemed a member of one racial classification, you would have to live, learn, love, and work among other similarly categorized people. Interracial relationships were illegal.

Perhaps more problematic, from the early 1700s until 1986, a series of laws had been passed, bit by bit, to curtail the movement of black people and maintain white control of resources and jobs. By 1956, black men and women over the age of sixteen were required to carry "reference books," or passbooks, everywhere they went. These books contained their photographs, employment records, fingerprints, ID numbers, tax details, and employment details, which had to be signed by a white employer. If a black person wished to enter a white area for any purpose other than labor, he was to request official written permission, which, if granted, would be noted in his passbook. The passbook was to be furnished to any policeman who demanded to inspect it; failure to produce the pass, or a pass that did not justify its bearer's movement, was grounds for immediate arrest. In 1975, when Easy was four years old, nearly 400,000 people were arrested for offenses related to their passes.

Taking the kids to the city was not, therefore, an easy feat. At night, from the dark townships, you could make out the sparkling city center in the distance, an unreachable world eleven miles west. When Easy did make the rare twenty-five-minute expedition to Cape Town—say, to accompany his parents to a government office or to work—he returned to Gugulethu with stories: skyscrapers, abounding electricity, seaside boardwalks, white folks in bespoke suits carrying leather briefcases, markets full of figs and peaches and whole roast chickens on the spit, rings of fried cake called doughnuts, malls displaying fashionable clothes, mansions on oak-lined streets, pruned botanical gardens full of picnickers in pretty dresses. It was the 1980s.

"You see the beautiful lights far away, you visit the city," Easy remembered. "You tell your friend, 'Yho! I was in America.'"

But once Easy had made it to this makeshift America, his experience was limited to that of an observer, alternately enraged and admiring. Easy could not step foot into the gleaming stores except to buy something and get out; so that white businesses did not lose potential customers, black people were permitted to buy food but not sit down and eat it. Easy could not walk on the same beaches as white people or sit on the same park benches or use certain toilets. Taxis, buses, trains, elevators, hotels, churches, parks, movie theaters, and restaurants were segregated. The entrances to the nice areas were marked with large signs stating a simple regulation, spelled out in Afrikaans and English, and enforced by both civilians and police, viciously if they were in the mood:

BLANKES ALLEEN

WHITES ONLY

Easy and I started to see each other more often. He allowed me to ride along with him in the cranky Amy Biehl Foundation vans. I sat to his left as he drove kids from their schools in the townships to their various lessons in the ritzier parts of town: guitar, cello, singing, ballet. The van was always full of loaves of bread, which were to be ferried from the foundation to the after-school programs. Once, we stopped at a light where an old lady stood in the rain, holding up a sign asking for help. I motioned to the pile of white bread, encased in plastic, on the floor.

"We can't give her some bread?" I asked Easy. He picked up two loaves from the floor and handed them out the window. "Is it against the rules?"

"You can see the condition," Easy said as the light turned green.

"You can break the rules." Then he thought for a moment. "In fact, is not breaking the rules. You can teach."

The foundation management, which had initially supported my research, seemed now irritated by my presence. Easy forgot a volunteer in the township one evening and was calling in sick a lot, and a couple of his bosses told me that I was a distraction. They were also warring with Linda, way across the Atlantic, over the direction of the foundation, and they seemed worried that I was a mole.

"I must ask, does Linda have any editorial power over your work?" the HR director asked me during a tense meeting. She was a broad, officious woman with a no-nonsense blond bob; she had retired from the British military and now volunteered for the foundation. The British woman additionally requested a synopsis of the book.

My concern is that Easy might not be a "true" reflection of the Foundation, the foundation's publicist wrote me in an email.

Soon enough, it became so difficult for me to access Easy via official channels that I gave up. Their attempts to block me from seeing him, however, worked in my favor. When figures of authority attempted to impose rules on Easy, he considered it "oppression" and immediately found ways to circumvent them. He believed that if he didn't use every single one of his vacation days as well as his overtime, "in a sense, is exploitation! They exploiting me!" Easy was already unhappy with the number of colored people on the management team, likening it to a "colored empire." (Other than the white managing director, Kevin Chaplin, Ntobeko, and the British woman who volunteered to work HR, the management team was colored.) Now he felt that these very people were further undermining his hard-earned freedom by trying to interface with whom he could see. He would therefore throw off the shackles and hang out with me whenever possible.

"I don't like when somebody close the door that supposed to be open," he said. "When I meet you, we became friends, we share, we continue the friendship. You ask to speak to me or Ntobeko. Nto-

beko refuse. They ask me, they say, 'Please, please, please, Easy,' crossing fingers. I said, 'Okay, I will try.' They said, 'Wow!' They were
happy. Now, end of story, they are moody. Same people who create
our friendship are same people who have problem now. I hate that."

Plus, as a man who had grown up at the height of one of the
world's greatest battles for liberation, Easy much preferred clandes-
tine meetings conducted in the spirit of rebellion to foundation-
sanctioned meetings conducted in the spirit of conformity. And so
began our lunches and day trips, many times a week, for nearly two
years.

Our regular joints included the Darling Street KFC, the Shoprite
KFC, the Sea Point KFC, or the lower level of the Hungry Lion
fried chicken establishment at the downtown Cape Town mall.
Chicken, barbecued or fried, with nary a fancy sauce, was guaranteed to please Easy. If he acquired a three-piece meal, he had a habit
of tucking one piece away to later give to his mother, to his daughter, Aphiwe, or to a friend or colleague. But twice, for his birthday,
when I presented him with what he referred to as a "birthday
chicken," an entire roasted bird, he ate it all by himself in under
thirty minutes, very neatly. Years later, I emailed him a "Happy Birthday" message, and promised to maintain our tradition when I next
came to Cape Town. *I cant wait to have my birthday chicken when you
are back in South Africa chickens are few now and thanks so much to remember my birthday chicken,* he replied.

After some time in Cape Town, I had made a smattering of friends,
a portion of them black. My black friends, for the most part, had
been born into families of modest means in the homelands. One
woman, an investment banker with an MBA, had attended school
beneath a tree. One man, a successful quantity surveyor, had believed

as a child that any newly purchased item "smelled white." Another man, an international rugby coach, had grown up without electricity. But they had been blessed with raw intelligence, luck, and determined parents who, though they may never have attended college themselves, believed in education with the extreme reverence of those for whom proper schooling had never been a given. These parents labored and pushed and persevered, with remarkable fortitude, in the single-minded determination that their children would attend university—and then, if the dream were to be expanded upon, postgraduate studies.

These friends were "black diamonds," as upwardly mobile black professionals in South Africa are called. They earned good money, invested, leased Audis, bought condos, built up designer shoe collections, and traveled to Dubai and Paris. When we socialized, I didn't notice many strange looks. The black diamonds emitted a specific, if invisible, aura of success and sophistication that allowed onlookers to comfortably, if disapprovingly, make sense of me plus them. This is a brave new world: that person sort of matches that other person.

But when I was with Easy, people stared. He was branded by the township, with scars and ballpoint pen tattoos and all of the other markings of place: a McDonald's promotional polo shirt, a heavy Xhosa accent, the barely perceptible jitters when milling around fancy stores. More than once in Easy's life, he had stood in the vicinity of a pile of newspapers on a corner, only to have an elderly white woman approach and hand him a few rand in coins. Meanwhile, I bear the markings of a comfortable white upbringing, in particular that pervasive and inbuilt sense of entitlement that radiates from the privileged. To make matters more unusual for curious onlookers, I stand five-ten and Easy stands five-five.

White people gawked; black people spoke up. At one point, near Christmas, I found myself standing in a store in Cape Town's most expensive shopping center, holding Easy's young baby, an infant so pale that he looked as if he might be mixed-race and whom Easy jokingly referred to as his "*umlungu*" baby—or white baby. The two

Xhosa saleswomen looked at me and then at Easy and then back at me, and one finally approached me to ask, "Is that your baby?"

Once, when Easy stopped to buy a peach for himself from a sidewalk vendor, an old black man admonished me. "Why you have him pick your fruit for you?" the man, sitting on a stoop, grumbled, assuming that Easy was performing some menial task for me. "Just reach in yourself!"

Easy and I spent a lot of time in Gugulethu, riding aimlessly around his area, the streets surrounding NY111. We drove past barbecue stands that specialized in sheep's head, a local delicacy, and the herbalist who could help with "weak erection, early ejaculation, court cases, lost lovers, blood pressure, ETC." We passed a man who stood on his front lawn dressed as a sensei.

"You get the energy, and that gives you the power," he orated in the direction of a dirt patch.

"He is training his students in karate," Easy told me.

"Where are they?"

"He can see them," Easy said, "but we cannot."

NY111 was our main drag. What had seemed so foreign on my first trips to the townships, I learned by heart. That slender woman, with gray hair cropped close to the scalp, who liked to dance up and down the street, was drunk first thing in the morning. Whenever she saw me, she sauntered up and asked, without any conviction, "Can you get a job for me, chummy?" She had once been the mother of six living children: five sons and one daughter. But one by one, her sons were taken down by the township: a police shooting, a shebeen shooting, HIV, a poorly treated illness of mysterious origin, and a stabbing-and-stoning incident. Only her girl remained.

"She lose her mind because she think deep thing about how other people have boys but she don't have boys now," Easy explained, and the woman didn't unnerve me anymore.

On NY111, a pile of garbage rose on a corner, a sort of open-air market for a clientele of junk dealers and junkies, who picked through it halfheartedly. Goats nibbled on diapers and moldy bread. There had been metal dumpsters here, but thieves kept carting them away in the night and selling them to scrap dealers, and so the municipality had apparently given up. Apart from the community trash heap, the street was decent enough: chipped, single-level brick-and-mortar government-issue homes running down one side of the block, a patchy field and a three-room community center on the other. Inside the community center was a bulletin board covered with photocopied pictures of African slaves taken from history books and old magazines: the severed head of a young woman, displayed on a metal platter, her eyes rolled back and her mouth hanging open; emaciated men and small boys in traditional dress chained together by their necks; a handcuffed man sitting upright inside a net, staring out; a white general commanding shirtless black men to perform push-ups; a man with a dog's muzzle tied around his mouth and a metal collar around his neck. A colorful rendering of a rosy-cheeked white Jesus with green eyes and flowing blond hair had been tacked up below the words THIS IS NOT GOD. Nearby were pasted black-and-white pictures of three African kings: King Hintsa, King Shaka Zulu, and King Sekhukhune. Scattered throughout were images of the raised, clenched fist made famous by Mandela, above the Xhosa and Zulu word for power: AMANDLA.

During these sessions, Easy talked just a little about his murder trial, and even less about his years in prison. He focused on recent times. He'd met the Biehls, gotten a job at their foundation, fallen in love with a pretty girl, had Aphiwe. Aphiwe's mom, nineteen when she gave birth, left Easy and took the baby to go live in a shack. One morning before work, Easy went to visit his daughter, whom he found alone but for an eight-year-old cousin to look after her. He bundled Aphiwe in a blanket and spirited her to his mother's house. He held her naked to his chest, "like the kangaroo."

"Is miracles, I tell you, to raise a kid," he said, shaking his head. "A small kid like this."

When Aphiwe was bored now, she sat on Easy's lap, reached down into his shirt, and twisted his nipple—a sign, he was glumly convinced, that she had not been breast-fed for long enough. Aphiwe was his universe. He would teach her to love others and to "bring a new direction. Any people must bring a new direction." In Xhosa, the name Aphiwe means "They [the family or clan] have been gifted."

But as we talked more, and delved into more difficult topics, I once wondered aloud how would he explain to Aphiwe what he had done? How could he explain to her who Linda was, and how she had come into his life? Aphiwe was growing up. One day, she'd want to know the facts.

Easy nodded. When he thought, he would become quiet, his mouth clamped shut, his eyebrows furrowed, and then he would look up, squinting, as if searching for an answer. Sometimes, upon coming to a conclusion, he'd even exclaim, *"Aha!"*

With each year, Easy said, Aphiwe grew taller and more curious. Easy knew, in some cranny of his heart, that he didn't have the wherewithal to give his child the nitty-gritty. He suspected that she would someday do her own research, since kids know how to use computers and search for information; what information, he was not entirely certain, being somewhat mystified by the Internet.

Though Easy had not read the articles that concerned him, he got the gist of what Aphiwe would come upon: a dead blond activist, an American granny-benefactor, a savage mob, Christlike love, forgiveness, redemption, and then also a bunch of hate written by white supremacists. But none of these stories captured what Easy wished to express to Aphiwe about himself, Amy, and the greater story.

For a long time, as I got to know him, Easy seemed to me forthright and open, and maybe even confessional. I attributed lapses in his stories to forgetfulness, or to language issues. I did not know that he was in fact a most secretive man. I knew that he had wooed many women and that he idolized his parents. It seemed like he knew everyone in Gugulethu; he got invited to at least one backyard party a week, attended frequent funerals, and greeted everyone he passed on the street. But later I would come to believe that Easy trusted neither his father nor his mother, neither brothers nor cousins, neither friends nor lovers. In fact, Easy trusted nobody but Aphiwe.

Aphiwe had toothpick legs and a face as precise and harmonious as a doll's. She was entirely unaware of her extreme beauty and her brown hair was in perpetual disarray. There was usually a hole in the butt of her leggings, mustard on her school shirt, a bit of wine gum stuck to her sleeve. Her temperament was perhaps her mother's, or maybe even her own, but certainly not Easy's. Where he was boisterous, outgoing, and breezy, Aphiwe was deeply, crushingly shy, and her emotional register swung from joy to misery and back, sweeping over all the in-between feelings.

Aphiwe was the great love of Easy's life, though he was useless at helping her do her hair or her homework. He wanted her to understand him fully one day. But how do you tell a story you have taught yourself to keep hidden away? Aphiwe was a good student. She had trouble speaking English, mostly because she was self-conscious, but she could read English like a pro. Easy, whose reading was labored at best, watched in wonder as she breezed through schoolbooks and volumes of fairy tales and novels. So he confessed to me a long-held and half-baked plan, which explained, a little bit, why he was talking to me so much.

"Aphiwe can read the book," he said. "Then she can understand." Which was to say: Maybe *I* would one day tell Aphiwe who her father was and what he had done. Maybe I would write it all down in this book. First, of course, I would have to figure it out.

7.

The purity of a revolution can last a fortnight.

—Jean Cocteau

Who wants to bugger up a fairy tale?

—Fergal Keane

Soon after Easy told me of his plans to communicate his history to Aphiwe using me as a proxy, I arrived on the street below the foundation offices with a bottle of peppermint cough syrup, which Easy had requested for his perpetual cough, brought on, he told me, by a week-long binge on cheap brandy and spicy meat. We drove over to Cape Town's old Company's Garden, near the foundation's office, a lush park set on the grounds cultivated by the first Dutch settlers of 1652 to provide fruit and vegetables to ships rounding the Cape and heading to Asia for the spice trade. The "Company" referred to the Dutch East India Company. Today, the garden is across the street from the courthouse where Easy was tried for murder.

We navigated our way past sprinklers, an ancient pear tree, and groups of yelping teenagers, and sat down on a bench in the gardens. Easy opened the lunch his mother had packed him, took out a chicken drumstick, ate it clean, and then winced in pain. Agony from his bleeding ulcer shot through him every once in a while, and he would grab on to some surface and bear it until it passed. I braced myself, biting my finger and watching until he turned to me and smiled brightly.

"We only have one hour," he said. He had to be back to the office soon. "So let's talk."

"Okay, Easy," I said. It was a warm day, and I had moved closer to him, out of the sun. "I want to talk about August 25, 1993. I want to talk about how, exactly, Amy died."

"Eish," he said, and mumbled something.

"Sorry?" I asked.

"I said, I love you so much right now," he said.

"Why?"

"Because finally you ask the real questions."

Easy was a member of the student wing of the Pan Africanist Congress of Azania, an offshoot of Mandela's ANC. Though they had
never garnered any significant percentage of the vote, the PAC had,
over the years, kept itself intermittently newsworthy by committing
violent acts—the most infamous targeting whites.

The ANC, founded in 1912, had steadily gathered the loyalty of
most black South Africans, a loyalty it maintains today. By the 1950s,
the formerly blacks-only party was actively reaching out to other
races. They formed an anti-apartheid coalition comprised of a range
of political groups, including Indians, black and white communists,
left-wing whites led by several famous Jews and Afrikaners, moderate coloreds, and unionists and women's rights organizations.

In 1955, the coalition, spearheaded by the ANC, adopted the
Freedom Charter, a political document upon which the current
South African constitution is broadly based. The Freedom Charter
laid out the ANC's core principles, from land reform to democratic
government to workers' rights and human rights. But the charter's
most notable commitment was to a "multiracial" South Africa. Its
now famous preamble set forth the ANC's belief that: *South Africa
belongs to all who live in it, black and white. . . . We, the people of South
Africa, black and white, together—equals, countrymen, and brothers—adopt
this Freedom Charter.*

The apartheid government immediately categorized the Freedom Charter as a dangerous communist document and tried 156
coalition members—including Mandela and many of the country's
future leaders—on charges of treason. They were ultimately found

not guilty, but would soon enough be tried for other crimes, and many would be imprisoned.

But the apartheid government was not the only group that took issue with the Freedom Charter. African nationalists within the ANC rejected the idea of multiracialism, which they felt could only result in further oppression: if you allowed nonblacks into the liberation movement, so the thinking went, they would only co-opt the Struggle for their own purposes. The PAC's founder and president was a former member of the ANC Youth League named Robert Sobukwe.

Sobukwe was an elegant, fragile-looking schoolteacher, born to poor, uneducated parents in a little Karoo desert village so dominated by Afrikaners that a local cop, defending himself in a suit that alleged he had tortured a detainee, told the judge: "I come from Graaff-Reinet, where even the dogs bark in Afrikaans." An organic intellectual, Sobukwe proved himself at the University of Fort Hare, the country's only black university and Mandela's alma mater.

When he went to college, Sobukwe was an obedient young Christian and as such he was supported in his studies by a pair of white missionaries. Having spent his youth focused only on God and grades, he had never questioned the country's race relations, and so his initial intention was to become a civil servant. To reach this goal, he majored in "Native Administration," which was the study and implementation of laws aimed at the black population. But as Sobukwe began reading, he witnessed the intricate structure of the apartheid government: its meticulously planned attempts at subjugating and ruining the black population, all in the erroneous, impossible name of "separate but equal." Up until that point, Sobukwe had lived his life within the system, but he had never peered inside the machine and seen how it had been assembled to crush the black population. He forgot about becoming a bureaucrat and slowly waded into the dangerous field of activism. He joined the ANC, but, increasingly disappointed by its open policies, eventually founded the PAC.

In his inaugural speech on April 6, 1959, in Soweto, Sobukwe argued against multiracialism before a crowd of three thousand delegates. He called it "a pandering to European bigotry and arrogance" and "a method of safeguarding white interests." Sobukwe then laid out the blueprint for his party. The political aim, he stated, was "a government of the Africans by the Africans and for the Africans."

The state newspapers, censored and often vehicles for government propaganda, immediately characterized the PAC as a "powerful splinter group" of "extremist rebels," expounding on "anti-white policy." The ANC also took a grim view of their defectors. In his memoirs, the normally even-keeled Mandela called the PAC "immature" and "naive." While the ANC and its allies initially sought to work in tandem with the PAC, the PAC seemed more interested in competing against the ANC for followers.

"Many of those who cast their lot with the PAC did so out of personal grudges or disappointments and were not thinking of the advancement of the Struggle, but of their own feelings of jealousy or revenge," wrote Mandela.

This tension came into full contrast within a year of the PAC's founding. In 1958, over 100,000 black men had been convicted and sentenced for infractions relating to passbooks, and a new law had passed, submitting black women, too, to the indignity of carrying a passbook. Since December 1959, the ANC had been meticulously planning a countrywide anti-pass campaign, during which black citizens would protest the pass laws.

The ANC's campaign was scheduled to begin on March 31 the following year, so the fledgling PAC, which refused the ANC's offer to work together, announced its own anti-pass campaign on March 21. Though protests took place across the country, the events in a township called Sharpeville put the PAC on the map and changed the course of South African history.

In Sharpeville, about fifty miles south of Johannesburg, a crowd of black civilians stood before a police station, remaining relatively peaceful and friendly, as Sobukwe had directed. But after several hours, the police arrested a demonstrator. Then the crowd, riled up, pushed against a barrier erected outside the station. Though the exact chain of events remains unclear, analysts and spectators believe that a single inexperienced policeman panicked and fired a lone shot, setting off a chain reaction of bloodshed. Most demonstrators were unarmed, but the police carried revolvers, rifles, and Sten guns, which they used to spray 705 bullets at the crowd, reloading and shooting for a full forty seconds. When the dust settled, sixty-nine black people had been killed, including forty women and eight children. Most of the dead had been shot in the back.

The images of the gruesome scene were a public relations disaster for the apartheid state. The photographs from that day are in black and white. In some, lifeless bodies of the unlucky, the slow, the first, the last, lie scattered on the same dry field or on the pebble- and bullet-strewn pavement. White policemen in pressed uniforms, guns holstered around their waists, survey the damage, leaning over to inspect victims, presumably to determine who is alive and who is dead. A woman, flanked by two friends in the uniforms of domestic workers, weeps into her hands as a barefoot boy looks on.

The United Nations Security Council recommended, for the first time, that South Africa abolish apartheid and strive for racial equality. The Johannesburg stock market plummeted and overseas investors got cold feet. Black citizens continued their protests, with the vast majority of black workers in Cape Town, Johannesburg, and Port Elizabeth staying home from work. A portion of anxious white South Africans, even those within the National Party, started to wonder about the efficacy of the approach to the "native question."

Fearing riots, Prime Minister Hendrik Verwoerd, a charming, authoritarian man with a porcine face and short white hair, declared a State of Emergency and invoked martial law. Verwoerd, who had invented the homelands, was so devoted to a separation of the races that he would have sacrificed almost anything for his project to succeed. "Rather poor and segregated than rich and integrated," he once announced.

The PAC and ANC were deemed illegal communist organizations; the punishment for membership was prison or a steep fine. Leaders were rounded up and imprisoned, starved, and humiliated. People were detained without charge. Meetings were banned, as was making anything that could be deemed a "subversive statement." Many fled into exile.

By 1963, Sobukwe was serving time on Robben Island, the two-mile-long tract of rock and sand set in Table Bay, nine miles off the Cape Town coast, where rebellious Khoikhoi had been sent three centuries earlier. Sobukwe, unlike all the other prisoners, lived in isolation. His wife and his four children were rarely able to visit. He was continually resentenced under what Parliament called "the Sobukwe Clause," which allowed them to detain a prisoner indefinitely. Upon Sobukwe's release in 1969, he was banished to house arrest in the northern mining city of Kimberley, where he died in 1978 of lung cancer. His appeals to seek treatment in the advanced hospitals of Johannesburg had been denied for too long.

Founded in 1961 in reaction to Sharpeville, Poqo (meaning "pure" in Xhosa) became the PAC's armed wing. Poqo was a disorganized assembly of militant Africanists, stoked by fury and desperation and armed with machetes and stones. In contrast to Sobukwe's peaceful ideals and intellectualism, an early Poqo pamphlet read, "The white people shall suffer, the black people will rule. Freedom comes after bloodshed."

Poqo members—and whether the group was organized enough to boast legitimate members remains debatable—took to killing black informers and policemen within the townships. In 1962, a destitute bunch of Poqo-affiliated men in the farming town of Paarl, an hour from Cape Town, attacked homes, shops, and the police station, and killed two white civilians. A few months later, members murdered two young white girls and three white adults in the Eastern Cape. In the 1960s, 101 political prisoners were executed by hanging, 100 of them black and 61 of them aligned with Poqo.

By 1967, Poqo, fractured by shoddy leadership, reinvented itself as the Azanian People's Liberation Army, or APLA. Azania, an ancient Greek term for parts of Southern Africa, had been adopted by several black nationalist groups as a noncolonial name for South Africa. Mzi, my friend, guide, and translator, who had attended the twentieth anniversary of Amy's death, was a card-carrying APLA veteran, and Easy and Ntobeko, as well as their codefendant Mongezi Manqina, claimed to have been aligned with APLA in the 1990s.

"I love you so much right now," Easy said, sitting on the bench in the Company's Garden. Then he began to recount what had happened on August 25, 1993.

He was rail-thin and round-faced, his hair trimmed into a short Afro, pimples dotting his cheeks, a caterpillar of a mustache sprouting above his lips. He had turned twenty-two a couple of months earlier but could easily have been mistaken for a fourteen-year-old. He had spent a total of eight months in Transkei homeland in APLA camps, in 1987, 1989, and 1990, training to shoot AK-47s.

"Can you take me to see the training grounds?" I asked.

"Is very risky. The PAC people who are still there might kill me."

In August 1993, Easy and PAC comrades had been moving from shack to shack, deep in the informal settlements. The cops were a constant threat to young militants, and an arrest guaranteed a beating or worse, but Easy wasn't deterred.

"Then, I never feel scared," Easy said.

"And now?"

"Now, I fear a car crash. And if I party too much, I think maybe someone will want to fight me but I can't protect myself, so I go home early. Also: tsunami."

The night before Amy was killed, Easy had only slept for a couple of hours on the dirt floor of a tin shack deep within Khayelitsha,

among seven other boys. They had wrapped themselves in heavy
coats to keep out the cold and kept on their sneakers in case they
had to run at a moment's notice. Beneath their outer layers, they
wore green T-shirts emblazoned with the PAC logo: a map of a jet-
black Africa, with a gold star on Ghana—the first African nation to
achieve independence from colonial powers in the twentieth
century—and gold lines radiating out across the continent.

Nobody in the townships had been to school in eight days, since
a teachers' strike had begun. Funding for black schools had been cut.
The regional black teachers' union wanted better pay and better
resources for their schools, and they had decided to stay home and
force the weakening white government's hand.

When Easy awoke early in the morning, a young girl was stirring
pap over a coal stove. She was a member of PAC, too, assigned to
move around the neighborhood undetected, to cook and care for
the male militants. She had already fetched a basin of water from the
tap down the road. The boys washed, ate the dry pap, rolling it with
their hands, drank tea, and shared cigarettes. Then they took off
through the depths of Khayelitsha, slinking through the thin alleys
between tin shacks.

They made their way quietly so as not to alert impimpis, informers; impimpis were everywhere, down on their luck and in need of
a few bucks from a policeman. They walked in a line out onto the
main road, where makeshift businesses had cropped up: a man
butchering a sheep, a deli with a limited inventory of cool drinks
and sweets, a line of colorfully painted barbershops, each boasting a
few plastic chairs, a tub of grease, a comb, and a pair of scissors. After
twenty minutes of hiking, the boys arrived at their destination: the
run-down train station. They boarded an old train that snaked slowly
from Khayelitsha past Gugulethu and into Langa.

Once on the train, Easy and his comrades bounced from car to
car, toyi-toyi-ing: they raised their fists in the air and sang freedom
songs. The train was full of commuters, and some of the passengers
joined the boys in song. Soon a fair-sized group had formed, and

they danced and sang around the train, picking up anyone else who might be in the mood for a protest. When the train pulled into the station, the group hopped off and headed for their assembly point at Langa Secondary School.

At around 10 A.M., Easy and his friends landed at the school, a glum brick block surrounded by rusty barbed wire. The school had been empty for the past week, but now the barren sports field was filled with people gearing up for the PAC student rally. A banner with the PAC map had been hung between two high sticks, and hundreds, maybe thousands, of people were arriving, kids from all the schools in the area. Easy waved to his friend Ntobeko, who had just been elected chairperson of the Langa Secondary School PAC student organization. At around eleven, an emcee strode out in front of the crowd, microphone in hand.

"Izwe lethu!" the emcee yelled. Our land!

"Africa!" the crowd responded.

"High discipline!" the emcee chanted.

"High morale!" the crowd replied.

Another young man took the stage. "One settler, one bullet," he hollered furiously, and the crowd erupted. In other words, the death of each white person would help them reclaim their land.

"One settler, one bullet," the crowd repeated.

"Settler! Settler! Bullet! Bullet!" the leader cried as the crowd cheered. "One settler, one bullet. One bullet, one settler!"

More youth leaders made their way into the center of the field. Before the throbbing crowd, the leaders discussed their aims to make South Africa "ungovernable." Since the success of the minority white government's policies required, in part, compliance on behalf of the subjugated majority population, that majority would refuse to comply and thereby force the government to confront a new reality. They couldn't control the people if the people refused to be controlled—or at least, it would be exceedingly difficult to do so.

"We are black tigers," the leaders said in Xhosa. The young crowd cheered. "There is no time to negotiate. Enough! Go liberate the country!"

"My spirit was brewing," Easy told me, sitting on the bench by the old pear tree. He took in a breath, and smiled at the memory. "I was feeling like, why not?"

By noon, Easy and his comrades were ready to march through the streets. They gathered together and prayed to their ancestors and to their gods to guide them, to keep them safe, and to bring them victory against their oppressors. Then they left the school yard in deliriously high spirits.

In Langa, they saw a truck driving in from the city, and pounced on it. They stopped the truck, forming a ring around it, and ordered the black driver to get out and walk away. Then they siphoned the gas out of the fuel tank and poured it around the overturned truck. The truck was carrying furniture, and they helped themselves to some chairs and sofa sets. As they were about to light a match, an armored vehicle filled with white policemen arrived, shooting, and the group split. One half took off to Langa train station and the other to Bonteheuwel. Easy and Ntobeko boarded the homebound train at Langa. Along with their friends, they began to sing again. The train cars shook. People coming back from work joined in ecstatic freedom songs.

"I was feeling like liberation is close," Easy recalled. "To bring our land back to the right owners."

Easy and Ntobeko jumped off at the Heideveld train station off NY111. From the station, Easy claimed, they hopped into the back of an old man's bakkie. They bounced down the road until they saw some kids who had taken the Bonteheuwel train dancing in the distance, swelling, a force of nature moving through the streets, unstoppable.

"Settler, settler!"

When Easy first saw Amy, she was crossing the street, a pack of people following her. She was bleeding from her face. Easy and Ntobeko hopped off the bakkie and ran into the crowd. Along with a small group that had broken away from the larger mass, they cornered Amy by the petrol station. She was trying to get away. Some asked for knives, and people gave them freely. They were standing above Amy, just inches from her. Easy kept a switchblade in his sock, so he was prepared. The men beat her, kicked her, punched her, and stabbed her. She did not die.

Amy pulled herself up again. That's when the police vehicle, driven by Officer Leon Rhodes, came flying over the sidewalk. Again, the group scattered. But Easy stayed on, pressed to the side, arms crossed, slipping into the back of the group. "I'm standing, looking, yes, feeling good," he said. "We implement one settler, one bullet."

He watched as Amy walked to the police vehicle, which would take her to the police station. "That is where she lose her life." Why, Easy had always wondered, did they ferry her to the station? Why didn't they take her to the hospital? "She could be alive, just police take time to take her to the hospital. Doctor said if they run to hospital she could be alive but they take time. She stay there and lose her life."

"Easy, did you see her face?" I asked. "When you stood above her?"

He shook his head. Her hair was so long that it covered her eyes, he said. Her arms were up as she tried to shield herself. She was blocking the blows, one by one. Easy put his hands in the air, miming her. He stopped five imaginary blows, as if in slow motion. The blows were perhaps not the only imaginary elements of this story, but I didn't know that then.

"She stabbed only one time," Easy said. He looked incredulous. He reached across the bench and touched me on the top of my left rib cage, softly. "Here."

That first time, listening to him, and for months after, I thought he meant: after such an onslaught, it was remarkable that Amy sustained only one stab wound. It did not occur to me to wonder if

Easy's story was accurate, because why would anyone admit to an act he hadn't committed—and in such detail?

It was only later that, when I started to piece together the different strands of what happened that day, I realized that I might have been wrong. When I looked through my notes, and then through old interviews and press statements dating back to the murder trial, I realized that Easy had been pointing, in his own purposely tangled way, toward a possible different "truth" about what had happened that day. He'd been doing it for twenty years, and perhaps to relieve the boredom and amuse himself, he mixed it up once in a while. But no one—not the police, not the prosecutors, not his own defense counsel, family, or friends, not the journalists—had been listening. The narrative of August 25, 1993, had quickly taken shape and was to remain stuck in the same mold for twenty years, and Easy and everyone else had gone along with it.

"Amy, she was very strong," he said, shaking his head. "Amy, she was very, very, very strong. Strong more than people think."

Rhoda Kadalie was Amy's old mentor, and the woman who had warned Amy against going into the townships. In an early issue of the Amy Biehl Foundation newsletters, Rhoda had written an essay about her love for Amy. She had at one time served on the foundation's board, and had been widely quoted in the media. She had not supported amnesty for Amy's killers, but she seemed to admire the Biehls. I assumed they were friends and I expected Rhoda to be open to an interview. Instead, I received an immediate denial: *Dear Justine, Whatever I had to say about Amy has already been captured on all kinds of media. I am estranged from this family and do not wish to be interviewed. Kind regards, Rhoda.*

I called the number on her email signature and the receptionist patched me through to Rhoda, who picked up on the first ring and listened to my rushed introduction. Then she let out a huff.

"I'm sick of it!" she exclaimed.

"Sorry?"

"I'm sick of it, I'm sick of this wretched country!" she hollered, rolling her Rs. "I'm so cynical. This wretched country!"

"Well . . . If you won't talk about Amy, would you talk to me about your cynicism?"

Rhoda let out a laugh. "I might be in an even worse place then, but okay, come next week."

Six days later, I arrived at Rhoda's office on Adderley Street, downtown's main thoroughfare, named for a British Conservative politician who in the mid-1800s had successfully staved off plans to turn the Cape into a penal colony. It was several blocks from the Amy Biehl Foundation, and the Truth and Reconciliation Commission had rented its regional headquarters here in the late 1990s. From her office overlooking the city, Rhoda ran a small NGO that provided grants to innovative social endeavors.

Rhoda greeted me from behind a desk piled with manila folders, holding her finger up in a "wait" signal as she schmoozed a donor on the phone. She was a short, sturdy woman with glossy black hair, glossy pale brown skin, glossy pink lips, and rectangular glasses. She looked a decade younger than her fifty-eight years and was wrapped in various high-quality textiles in different shades of gray. Her office was chilly and spacious, warmed by a large electric heater, decorated with heavy green drapes, and brightly lit. A photograph of Rhoda whispering into an attentive Mandela's ear was hung near a picture of her daughter at her college graduation.

"To tell you the truth, we have no money, *none*," Rhoda said over the phone. "We need your help." Hearing an affirmative answer, she smiled broadly. Soon enough, she hung up the phone, unwrapped a chicken salad sandwich, and pumped up the heater. She turned to me.

"I despair about South Africa," she said. "It will go down deep before it goes up."

Rhoda was a born contrarian, the granddaughter of the famous Malawian immigrant Clements Kadalie, a trained teacher who, after being senselessly assaulted by a policeman as he walked along a street in South Africa, became an activist and the founder of one of the country's first labor unions.

In 1993, Rhoda was a card-carrying member of the ANC. Now she was a card-carrying member of the moderate-right opposition party, the Democratic Alliance. Once Mandela's human rights commissioner, she now wrote weekly columns for the Afrikaans-language daily *Die Burger*, criticizing the ANC and bemoaning politics and society. She also spoke at various universities, where she paced back and forth in front of lecture halls, shouting, "I don't want these fuckers to govern me!"

Rhoda claimed to want to move to America and stop reading the newspapers. Her daughter and son-in-law, with Rhoda's granddaughter, had settled in California. Rhoda swore that she was ready to relocate to the Golden State any day now. There she would slip quietly into her retirement years, reading novels, playing with her curly-haired progeny, and living in a garden flat. All she had to do was sell her house, and then she'd have precisely no problem leaving, no problem whatsoever.

Only one thing: she'd only sell to the right buyer. She was certain that all the people who had made offers, and there had been many, intended to buy the gorgeous old rambling home just outside the city center to tear it down, and she would never allow that. When I saw her a year after our first meeting, she was still furiously denying potential buyers for a variety of reasons, still reading the papers, still ranting about the state of the nation, and still talking about her imminent move to America.

That first meeting occurred in August 2012, a tense time in the country. Five days earlier, a group of striking black miners had been executed by government security forces in the rural northern town of Marikana, an event that came to be known as the Marikana Massacre. The thirty-four dead miners and their seventy-eight injured colleagues were poor, uneducated men, largely hailing from the stark, underdeveloped former homelands of the Eastern Cape—including at least one miner from Melvin Nofemela's hometown of Lady Frere. They had been employed by a platinum mining conglomerate called Lonmin, headquartered in Johannesburg but listed on the London Stock Exchange. As in apartheid times, these migrants lived far from their families in grim dwellings, cooking on firewood and lighting their shacks with candles. Their murders, and their bleak living conditions, drew uncomfortable parallels between the oppressive tactics of the police under the new, black-led government and the old, white-supremacist government.

The photographs of dead black bodies, cut down in a hail of state-sanctioned bullets, reminded the country of Sharpeville and the days of strikes. Except now, instead of neatly dressed white government agents inspecting the corpses, neatly dressed black government agents inspected the corpses. In the old days, the largest and most famous strike was the 1987 National Union of Mineworkers strike, participated in by nearly a quarter million miners and led by a young firebrand lawyer named Cyril Ramaphosa, a socialist and later a favored acolyte of Mandela. By August 2012, Ramaphosa was estimated to be worth over $600 million and was a major shareholder in Lonmin (two years after I spoke to Rhoda, Ramaphosa would become deputy president of the country). The killings illuminated how, for all the promises of equality and freedom, brown-skinned laborers still marched deep into the land and drilled for the profit of a moneyed minority.

Our discussion quickly turned to the government of the day. "These people are so corrupt, they make apartheid look like a tea party," Rhoda said, shaking her head. She had suspected, when she fought to end apartheid, that the formerly oppressed would make bad democrats; it was easy for one who was so systemically victimized to feel suddenly entitled to any and all of the available perks of power. The country had no political role models, no culture of fair governance for the people. Indeed, post-Mandela, the ruling party's continuing electoral majority, despite corruption scandals that had seemingly become endemic, created an environment in which there was no accountability for corrupt wrongdoing. "What is the central theme of the ANC?" a South African friend once mused. "The central theme is: It's our turn to eat."

Mandela's successor was Thabo Mbeki, a respected, charisma-free intellectual whose reign, from 1999 to 2008, was marred by AIDS denialism. Under the influence of fringe scientists (the most prominent was from California), Mbeki insisted that AIDS was caused by an immune system collapse, not a virus, and therefore could not be treated by expensive Western drugs but would rather be treated by alleviating poverty—a stubborn assertion that one research study associated with the death of 300,000 citizens. Mbeki gave way to Jacob Zuma. Zuma is a charming Zulu populist with little education, his main credentials being a stint on Robben Island and decades in the military command of the ANC in exile thereafter. Zuma, who practices polygamy, had his own brush with AIDS denialism when he was tried for the rape of an HIV-positive woman. He claimed the sex was consensual.

"You cannot leave a woman if she is already at that stage [of sexual arousal]," he insisted at his 2006 trial.

Zuma, formerly head of the South African AIDS council, also argued against scientific evidence, noting that while he hadn't used protection, he reduced the risk of transmission by taking a shower. He was cleared of all charges and was elected president three years later.

By 2013, Zuma was in the midst of refurbishing his rural homestead, situated in the impoverished village of Nkandla in KwaZulu Natal, to the tune of about $23 million in taxpayer money (in 2016, he agreed to pay back an undetermined amount). The episode, inevitably called Nkandla-gate, had led to statements from Zuma's public works minister, who claimed that what appeared to be a new swimming pool was in fact a "fire pool," since there were no fire stations in the area, and what the press had misunderstood to be an amphitheater was simply "a structure with steps." Eventually, an in-quiry by the constitutionally mandated public protector found that public funds had been used for luxury upgrades to his personal home, and recommended that Zuma repay the government a rea-sonable portion of non-security improvements. However, the presi-dent ignored this finding. By the time this book went to print, South Africa's highest court ruled that in refusing to pay back the money, Zuma had "failed to uphold, defend and respect the Constitution as the supreme law of the land." After the ruling, Linda Biehl's friend and Mandela's confidante and fellow prisoner Ahmed Kathrada joined a growing chorus of ANC veterans calling for Zuma to step down.

In the previous decade, two consecutive police commissioners had been fired for corruption. One minister under Zuma had vis-ited a lover jailed in Switzerland under drug-related charges, spend-ing $36,000 of federal funds on the luxurious trip. And these were only some of the headline-grabbing stories to emerge.

Connections paid dividends. In Pretoria, the ANC-aligned Gupta family—owners of computer, investment, and newspaper ventures, and the employers of two of Zuma's kids—was allowed to land a chartered private plane at the capital's high-security military base, intended only for diplomats, politicians, and the armed forces. They were on their way to the lavish, multimillion-dollar, four-day family wedding of a Gupta daughter, the guest list of which included sev-eral government heavyweights. As per tradition, the resulting scandal was called Gupta-gate.

Young black millionaires and celebrities followed suit, flaunting their wealth and connections, driving Hummers and Maseratis. One tycoon, an ex-convict, had dubbed himself the "sushi king" because his favorite pastime was eating pounds of sushi off the naked bodies of models, while a self-styled black "socialite" gave an interview in which she expressed disdain for the have-nots. "If they can't put bread on their table, too bad, but I'm gonna have my croissant with my blue cheese in full public view," she announced on a talk show.

Meanwhile, in Limpopo, the country's poorest province, students went without textbooks for the 2012 school year after an intricate scandal involving crooked and incompetent officials and an unscrupulous bookmaker. And while the private medical care in South Africa remains excellent, the public system is in shambles. In a rural Eastern Cape government hospital, an otherwise healthy toddler died of pneumonia after the hospital's oxygen supply ran out. The administrator had not bothered to order more, and an ambulance from a better-stocked hospital took hours to arrive. In Free State, the provincial health minister ordered a dying woman to be booted from her ICU bed in an underserved local hospital to make way for an ANC official. In Limpopo, a housewife dislocated her ankle, was operated on in a room that had lost electricity by a government doctor who insisted that he didn't need to examine an X-ray in order to perform surgery. He botched her operation, forgot to prescribe her pain pills when he left for the weekend, and then ignored her for days as gangrene set in. Her leg was eventually amputated.

Rhoda had recently resigned from her professorship at Stellenbosch University. She claimed that she quit after an accomplished white professor lost out on the position of dean to a relatively unqualified black academic, and that the university had honored skin color and connections over capability and experience. This, Rhoda felt, was South Africa's affirmative action policy at its worst, with students the ultimate losers.

"Until I know a black person is trained, I want my gynecologist to be white and my pilot to be white!" she yelled, throwing her finger in the air.

Rhoda thought back to the days of revolution, a "tantalizing time" in South Africa, when they were fighting the good fight. Then the country was the go-to spot for activists, liberals, do-gooders, charity workers, Africanists, journalists, and anyone serious about global politics. Of course, such a fiery moment in history brought with it your regular irritating lefty activists, who parachuted into the country in their trendy blue jeans. Rhoda was unimpressed by the international students in their Mandela T-shirts, so when she first saw Amy on campus, she rolled her eyes.

"My attitude was, 'Fuck you, another American, a foreigner, just another pretty blond American.'"

But Amy tried to make a tangible contribution to the university where Rhoda served as the founder and director of the Gender Equity Unit. As one of the few students with a laptop, a rarity in 1993, Amy took notes at meetings and delved into her research on women's rights. She made friends and connections, but she also struggled. The activists she had come to work with were often too busy or distracted to provide her with any guidance. One day, she appeared at Rhoda's office door.

"I'm Amy," she said hopefully. She held a pile of papers to her chest. Rhoda just looked at her. "I'm doing research on women in South Africa and nobody can help me."

Rhoda gestured for the papers in Amy's arms, and Amy handed them over. Rhoda started paging through them, making comments, crossing sentences out, directing Amy on whom to speak with, where to find sources and subjects. Amy edged into the office, taking copious, tidy notes in her red-and-black notebook. She never interrupted Rhoda. In fact, to Rhoda's surprise, this attractive woman was the opposite of the arrogant American: rather, she was a modest intellectual, with excellent manners and a razor-sharp intellect. And Amy adored brash, outspoken Rhoda. Rhoda became Amy's mentor and friend.

"She was so sweet and generous, and a good student," Rhoda said. "She dressed well, she looked good, she was so smart. She played as hard as she worked. She partied, she did marathons, she was on the beach, she produced prolifically."

Amy's old friends remember her the same way. She worked hard at being happy, they said. She worked hard at everything. When she was sixteen, she wrote an entry in her journal, matter-of-factly outlining her goals in her tidy cursive hand. Her father read it out before the Truth and Reconciliation Commission.

I have had more homework this year than I have ever had before. In lots of ways this has helped me because I have been forced to get organized and really dig in. But I have also been forced to stay up until 11:30 or 12:00 each night, making me very cranky during the day. One thing that worries me is whether or not I will be able to keep this rigorous schedule up and still keep straight As. Every night after school, I have some activity to attend, be it diving, band, flute, or something else, and starting in November, I'll be swimming every day. I hate it when people say you should cut down your schedule, you're too busy, because I have already cut out several activities. I'm kind of addicted to exercise and get very bored if I am not constantly busy. School is very important to me but being active and well-rounded are necessary for me to be happy. I want to have a 4.0, but I also want to be an award-winning drum major, first chair flute, a State champion diver. As far as I'm concerned, why can't I? I think I will be able to make it through this year. I am a very hard worker at everything I do, and as long as I know what I want, I can get it. Besides, getting 90% on a chemistry test makes staying up all night worth it.

Amy began to walk at nine months and to read at three years, unable to bear the fact that her older sister, Kim, could do something that she could not. After entering kindergarten, she vowed that she would attend Stanford. Linda told her that if she managed that, she'd buy her a Porsche. Thirteen years later, when Amy's acceptance letter arrived, Linda bought her a chocolate bar in the shape of a sports car.

As a toddler with a bowl cut, Amy flew across the monkey bars. As a girl with her hair in tight pigtails, she competed in gymnastics tournaments, tumbling across the floor and twirling over the beam. In ninth grade at a new school, she scanned the lunchroom, her eyes homing in on a brown-haired girl.

"I met my new best friend," she told her parents. "I just haven't talked to her yet." Within weeks, she and the brown-haired girl were inseparable. A decade later, they were roommates, sending out

Christmas cards with a photo of them grinning, shoulder to shoulder, next to cartoon mistletoe.

Every day, Amy made a list of the things she wished to accomplish, and if she failed to do so, she simply switched the item to the next day's list. When she didn't understand a calculus problem, she stayed up all night, stomping around the kitchen, working the numbers in her head. Her memory was nearly photographic.

When she decided that swimming was her main passion, she ditched her other extracurriculars and trained privately with a much lauded local coach; but when she realized that an even better coach worked an hour away, she prevailed upon her mother to drive her the extra distance, and prevailed upon her less-dedicated sisters to join her.

Amy graduated to diving. She was drawn to heights, perhaps because she wanted to conquer that which daunted her. As soon as she could stand, she jumped out of her crib and broke her collarbone. Once, Linda turned away for a moment while at the playground and turned back to find eighteen-month-old Amy standing atop the highest slide, down which she had to be coaxed.

Diving is the ultimate perfectionist's sport: to master a particular dive, an athlete must repeat the same sequence hundreds of times, hurtling alone toward the water, fitting a series of specific, tightly coordinated moves into a matter of seconds. Land on it wrong and the water is as hard and unforgiving as concrete. At Stanford, Amy became captain of her diving team. She often limped away from a practice, her body blooming with purple bruises. The next day, she would return and begin again. Her prize possession was a broad gold ring set with a red garnet, a token from her victory at the 1989 Women's National Swimming Championships.

After college, lacking an Olympic-size pool, Amy stopped diving and took up running. Some days, to clear her head, she ran eighteen miles for the hell of it. In Cape Town, five months before she died, she finished the Two Oceans Ultra Marathon, a thirty-five-mile course around the peninsula, from the Indian Ocean to the Atlantic.

Amy was equally devoted to her friends, and to having fun. During her adolescence in Santa Fe, she'd become a margarita connoisseur, and for her graduation party she invited her friends to a margarita party at her house. Linda and Peter took the kids' car keys away, put out stacks of blankets, and fired up the Jacuzzi. The lime stains never came out of the wood deck.

When Amy moved to Stanford, Peter—more businessman than handyman—installed an oddly slanted margarita bar in her dorm room, topping it with a blender. Every week, she and her friends, many of them sorority sisters from Pi Beta Phi, gathered in front of the nighttime dramedy *Moonlighting,* an event they referred to as "Margaritas and Moonlighting." In D.C., she went out most nights and drank European ale and ate roasted peanuts.

In South Africa, she learned to swear in Xhosa and to drink lying down. She smoked her first joint after learning she'd been offered a four-year scholarship for a doctorate in African Studies at Rutgers University. Melanie, her roommate, took photos of her giggling all night, and Amy signed each print, "Amy's first dope experience." She also loved to go to the townships to dance and hang out.

"I remember going into Gugulethu to a shebeen on a Friday night, which is a little weird, and she was really taking me there to rattle my cage and wake me up," her boyfriend, Scott, the only American friend to visit her in South Africa, told me. "And it worked, walking into those kinds of situations with her and seeing the whole place welcome her and welcome me. She would walk into places like that and it felt very natural. Quite frankly, that's what got her killed."

Amy's ten months in South Africa were illuminating but imperfect. Amy, Rhoda recalled, was lonely. She missed Scott, and had a complicated relationship with some of her friends and colleagues, who, sensing her generosity and her privilege, tended to take advantage of her.

"Everyone is pulling at me," Amy told Linda when she called home.

Moreover, Amy had long dreamed of South Africa's righteous revolution, but upon arriving in the midst of it, she observed the contradictions of the liberation movement firsthand. The ANC, which she had long idolized, had tendencies toward sexism and misogyny, reflected today in the party's black male domination. Many of Amy's colleagues, Rhoda noted, were a "bunch of disorganized Stalinists." The scales had fallen from her eyes, but she had nowhere to turn with her observations. The opinion of a girl from California was not welcome in freedom-time activist circles.

"In the Struggle, you had to know your place," Rhoda said. "If you were a woman, even more. If you were colored, even more. If you were white, even more. If you were American, even more."

"So she knew her place?"

"She did, and she hated it."

I wondered what Amy would have thought of South Africa today, and her family's role here. But Rhoda would not speak of the Biehls on the record; according to her, their friendship had dissolved years earlier over differences of opinion. (Linda Biehl later claimed to be unaware of any conflict.) "I hate white people who bend over back-ward," she said. She was shaking her head. "Lots of things happened in the name of the Struggle. But the kids who were convicted of killing Amy were common criminals. They weren't politically moti-vated, they were bloodthirsty. A white girl was in the traffic, they took bricks, and they smashed her to a pulp."

Soon after my meeting with Rhoda, I found myself sitting on a stoop across the street from the foundation offices. I was waiting for Easy, who was nearly an hour behind schedule. Finally, he flew out the door and ran across the street, grinning.

"My friend, my friend!" he exclaimed, and hugged me with great force. He pulled away, his hands still fixed on my shoulders. I glared at him, but he was impervious to the irritation of others, which allowed him the freedom to be endlessly, gleefully unreliable.

"What is the point of your watch anyway?" I asked. For a few weeks, he had been sporting a massive, rectangular, white plastic watch that a volunteer at the foundation had brought him from the Netherlands. He was certain somebody would steal it from him in Gugulethu, so he had taken to sleeping with it on. I grabbed his wrist, hoping to make an example of this particular tardiness, when I realized that the watch could not have helped even if he had paid attention to it. It ran two hours and seventeen minutes behind, and Easy had no clue how to fix it.

"Ahhh, but soon you won't be angry," he said. He slipped off his backpack and placed it on the pavement with a flourish. Then he fished two items out of the bag. "Lucky enough," he said, extravagantly presenting me with an old photograph and a leather band.

As Easy explained, he had gone to one of the hand-hammered rooms at the back of his house, rooms filled with old dressers, odoriferous rolled carpets, and bunches of crumbling papers. The Nofemelas did not employ a filing system, and with dozens of people in and out every day, they were forever pawing through different drawers in attempts to find important papers that were always being moved, trashed, and lost. Only Wowo maintained a smidgen of organization in the form of a maroon notebook in which he diligently recorded the funeral benefits of his old colleagues from the neighborhood, all of them on the same pension fund. Funeral benefits were gold in Gugulethu, where the indignity of a pauper's ceremony was too painful to bear. The book was meticulous and never left its hallowed spot on a bookcase in the TV room, but that was pretty much the only item that didn't eventually disappear into the home's Bermuda Triangle. Despite the mess, Easy had been compelled to go rooting around, and had come up with the mementos now in my hands.

The leather band, worn and cracked, was midnight blue and

smelled as cool and fungal as a cellar. It closed with a rusted buckle. I dangled it in the air.

"It protect me from my enemy," Easy explained.

The band was the creation of a sangoma, the traditional healer of South Africa. Easy had for decades visited a sangoma he categorized as "too powerful," an obese old lady with a raging case of diabetes who lived in a dry, remote village in the Eastern Cape. There, when she was not sopping up goat stew with spongy white bread, she ministered to a clientele from across the peninsula, using herbs, powders, grasses, flowers, leaves, and potions. I later visited the sangoma with Easy. She wore a sash upon which were woven the words HERB SECRETARY and kept a room brimming with ingredients to cure ailments of the mind, body, and heart. Kiki had called several days before our arrival and explained the various family woes, and the sangoma carefully packaged up remedies, dispensed with careful directions, to be carried back to Gugulethu.

Easy tried to make the expensive, six-hour taxi journey to visit this sangoma every few years so that she could perform an elaborate cleansing ritual, purifying and fortifying him, driving away bad luck, bringing forth fortunes, and releasing sickness.

"We call it cooking you," Easy explained. "She put you in the pot and cooking you."

Decades earlier, the sangoma had inserted *muthi*—the medicine of the herbal healer—into the band I now held. The idea of the sangoma's healing muthi holds sway over a diverse collection of people: my Zimbabwean housekeeper shrieked and bolted to the other side of the room when I later held up the armband, while my Australian immigrant friend shook her head gravely and warned me to be careful. Bad muthi, they both informed me, could wreak havoc on your life.

I'd been skeptical about the powers of muthi, until one day, when Easy told me a drawn-out story about how muthi made from the powder gathered from a crushed hyena tail had the ability to render entire households unconscious for hours, during which thieves robbed them blind.

"Bullshit."

"No, my friend, is true. Check it on your computer."

I subsequently found a trove of breathless newspaper articles, in publications both respectable and less so, detailing the nationwide spate of hyena-tail robberies, conducted with the help of unethical sangomas, who were spending their days grinding the dried snout and tail of ill-fated hyenas into fine powders.

SOUTH AFRICAN HOUSE RAIDERS TURN TO WITCHCRAFT, announced the British *Telegraph*.

THIS MAN BLOWS HYENA SMOKE UNDER YOUR DOOR—THEN HE ROBS YOU! exclaimed the *Daily Sun*, which included a color photo of a disheveled man squatting by the door of a shack, exhaling through a small tube that he had wedged into a crack. Across the country, it was reported, people were wandering around their homes, minding their business, when they were knocked out cold, along with their guard dogs, only to awaken with pounding headaches to find their TVs and CD players, their couches and stoves, their shoes and de- signer jeans gone. The thieves even ate leftover food.

For his part, Easy claimed that his muthi-rich armband had shielded him during his fighting days, and it was true that he had lived through a perilous time and emerged alive.

"If it protects you, why don't you still wear it?" I asked.

"Now I'm old," he said, shrugging. "If someone really want to kill me, they can kill me." Plus, he had permanent medicine flowing in his veins, as did Aphiwe: as babies, their scalps had been lightly cut, and muthi poured in and sealed inside as the cuts healed into scars.

The other memento Easy gave me was a small photograph, yel- low from the years, water-stained, lightly spotted with mold, and torn in the right corner. I examined it. It was a photograph of three Nofemela boys perched expectantly on a parquet floor. One boy, his face partially obscured by damage to the print, wore a tiny tan suit and leather sandals. He looked about six years old. In the middle, a toddler stood atop a stool, wearing a white collared shirt and slacks. He stared out, mouth slightly open, friendly and engaged. The third boy wore an oversized beige suit and matching sneakers. He was perhaps five.

"Who am I?" Easy asked.

I pulled the photo close to my nose, squinted, and then pointed at the youngest.

"No," Easy said, delighted. "Is me here." He placed his finger on the child in the beige suit.

"So who is the one I thought was you?"

"Is Monks," he said. "My brother who is paralyze."

"But you look different now." In the photograph, the boys had carbon-copy features, identically arranged, separated only by time.

"But when we are little, like twin."

I brought the photo home and pinned it to my bulletin board. Three brothers, dressed for a formal occasion, a single snapshot. I still don't know why Easy gave me that particular photograph. Maybe it was just a coincidence or maybe there was something else guiding him, some unconscious or shrouded desire to communicate an unspoken story to me. Maybe he knew precisely what he was doing. You never could tell with that guy.

8.

If only there were evil people somewhere insidiously committing evil deeds, and it were necessary only to separate them from the rest of us and destroy them. But the line dividing good and evil cuts through the heart of every human being. And who is willing to destroy a piece of his own heart?

—Aleksandr Solzhenitsyn

Easy was only one of the many players in this long drama. He had been on one side, the militant black kid from the township accused of a heinous crime. But there was an opposing team made up of people who had put him away. The member of that team who worked the lead in the Biehl murder investigation was the hulking detective sergeant Ilmar Pikker. In a snapshot from his 1980s squad days, Pikker stands before an intricate map pinned to a board. He wears an expression of fatigue and menace, his brown eyes slightly hooded. This, combined with his mane of uncombed ginger hair sloping into a fluffy ginger beard, gives him the look of a large lounging lion. He stands with his arms outstretched, displaying an ANC flag, the symbol of the group that Pikker and his security force colleagues aimed to destroy.

Since the old days, Pikker had fallen off the grid. He was not in the phone book, and he didn't pitch up on any Google searches. As new bureaucrats of color took up state positions and old white bureaucrats took retirement, bureaucratic threads frayed. I needed to find Pikker, but months of calls, searches, and inquiries had drawn up blanks.

My only hope, then, was a sliver of civil servants I had come to regard as "the dinosaurs." These were the white government employees, most of them pushing sixty, who had stayed on through 1994, and had gone from working for a state led by the National Party to one led by the ANC. The "sunset clause," agreed upon during the 1990s negotiations, enabled white civil servants to keep their jobs for life if they so desired. Some took a buyout, but many hangers-on kept at it. I picked them out in the back rooms of prisons, working through the filing systems, or behind desks at Home Affairs. They were usually pulled into tight uniforms, name tags bearing Afrikaner monikers pinned to their chests: Botha, Coetzee, van der Merwe. With the exception of a few old-school communist sympathizers, they fell loosely into two camps: lifelong bureaucrats who couldn't bear the thought of entering the private sector or were too old or unskilled to do so, or largely apolitical worker bees who were passionate about their jobs.

One such passionate dinosaur detective led me to Pikker, finally. I had been conducting an interview with Nollie Niehaus, the prosecutor in Amy's case, who had remained a state prosecutor. When I mentioned Pikker, Niehaus racked his brain. Pikker had been making a sorry pittance his whole working life, Niehaus remembered, and as far as he knew, had left the police force at the time of Mandela's election. According to Niehaus, Pikker briefly owned a suburban "escort agency" called Partners, and, after that folded, had taken off to Dubai to pursue other sketchy endeavors.

Just then, in a lucky coincidence, a dinosaur detective passed through. He was a broad-shouldered, friendly man with a pale pitted face, large nostrils, and an aggressive military-style buzz cut. His name was Mike Barkhuizen and he had a reputation as one of the best detectives in the country. I would eventually take to meeting him for a burger once in a while. He wore three holsters on his hips: two for BlackBerrys and one for a semiautomatic pistol. Pikker and Barkhuizen had worked together in the 1980s and 1990s, Niehaus recalled. Maybe Barkhuizen could help me out?

"Ja, Pikker." Barkhuizen smiled at the memory. "Used to call me Bike Markhuizen!"

Barkhuizen remembered trolling the township streets with Pikker in the early mornings, cracking up laughing. Pikker, he said, was a real riot. As far as he knew, Pikker was indeed based in the Gulf, but he sometimes visited South Africa. He wasn't exactly dead, but he also wasn't well: last time the two had seen each other, several years earlier at a police reunion barbecue in the suburbs, Pikker had displayed a blazing scar running down his chest from open-heart surgery.

Barkhuizen had Pikker's South African number. He pulled out one of the two BlackBerrys, dialed, announced that it was "Bike Markhuizen," let out a booming guffaw, spoke animatedly in Afrikaans, and hung up.

"It's your lucky day," he said. "Pikker's on vacation now out in the suburbs and he'll talk to you." He scribbled down a number, which I dialed as soon as I left the office. Pikker agreed to meet far from town, in a fish restaurant in a big mall, and he gave me exacting directions.

I took the N1 heading toward the Northern Suburbs, a collection of largely white and colored areas stretching above and to the east of the city center. A giant bearded white man in heavy boots and long shorts plodded down the side of the highway in the boiling sun, dragging behind him a human-sized wooden cross. Nearby, a small colored boy looked longingly across the road, readying himself to jump the median and book it to the other side. Century City, a sparkling shopping development, rose up to the left, dwarfed only by the curving roller coasters of the abutting amusement park. Century City reminded me of those manufactured U.S. Sunbelt towns that crumbled when the housing bubble burst—the garish mid-priced condominiums made of plaster and designed to appeal to nouveau sensibilities, the medians lined with palm trees, the improbably circular man-made lakes. The whole development had been carved from inhospitable bush by the highway, sliced down to accommodate furniture megastores and the spiffy offices of laser-wielding cosmetic dermatologists.

I continued on toward Bellville, an Afrikaner-dominated suburb, and turned onto Willie van Schoor Avenue, named after the town's former Afrikaner nationalist mayor. Congolese and Zimbabwean immigrants and asylum seekers surrounded my car at the exit stoplight. *Hey sister, need a roll of blue garbage bags? Some cheap sunglasses? A colorful beaded rhinoceros made in China? A cellphone car charger? Sister, I'm suffering, can you please support me?*

I entered a main stretch, the commercial district of Bellville, a long strip of car dealerships, chain restaurants, and shoddily constructed apartment complexes, all built around a gray constructed lake. I parked and made my way through the mall to a sleek franchise of the fish restaurant.

At the entrance, a host approached me. "You're here to meet Mr. Pikker?" he asked. Taken aback, I nodded. "He'll be arriving shortly. Let me show you to your table."

He led me to the edge of the cavernous space, where a pair of sliding doors opened into a hermetically sealed smoking section. There, a woman in a short red bandage dress and a man in baggy jeans were sharing a plate of prawns. The host motioned to a couch, where I obediently sat.

Sitting in that hazy, fishy chamber, waiting for him to appear, I imagined Ilmar Pikker as a grand evildoer. He was remembered in the townships as part of the rough old guard, a kind of heartless white yes-man with a gun and a badge.

"Pikker, he was *rude*," Wowo once recalled.

Plus, Barkhuizen had called Pikker a jokester, after which I visualized a villain flying through the townships at night, flanked by his cruel sidekicks, laughing maniacally as he targeted various innocent black pedestrians for attack. Add to that three apparent facts: Pikker had once had an escort service with a lame name, he lived off the grid in Dubai, and he had a far enough reach to place me in the seat of his choosing in some smoky back room of a restaurant in a far-off suburb.

I was nervously sipping my rooibos tea when a clodhopper of a man ambled through the door: six feet and well over three hundred pounds, with a silver beard and a matching silver pompadour combed neatly back. He wore a tiny rectangular leather pouch strung diagonally across his body and a heavy gold chain around his neck.

"So sorry I'm late," he said gently, shaking my hand, his face rosy with exhaustion and embarrassment, his palms soft. He sat down, perching his body on the edge of a couch that suddenly looked comically small. He had a meaty, lined face and hangdog eyes, and bore a passing resemblance to a hard-living Santa Claus.

Every ex-cop and old cop I ever met in South Africa seemed to have signed a contract pledging to adhere to a common stereotype: cigarette permanently stuck in mouth, cup of coffee attached to hand. Pikker obligingly lit up and ordered a coffee with cold milk on the side.

"One of the addictions I picked up when I joined the force," he said apologetically. "I can't stop."

Pikker urged me to get anything I wanted, and then explained that the host was an old schoolmate of his son's. He had picked this place not because he wanted me alone in a sealed room, but because he knew he could smoke. And while I had half expected him to interrogate me, he instead seemed eager to reminisce and to answer any questions I had. In fact, instead of being stoic and secretive, Ilmar Pikker was extremely candid. I now think this is a quality common to people who feel they have nothing left to lose and nothing left to gain. They may as well spill the beans.

"Man, I loved being a cop," Pikker said in his soft, gravelly voice, drawing on a cigarette and thinking back to those times. "I loved it so much, it nearly destroyed everything."

Amy Biehl died when Pikker was at his peak, and his memory of the time was stitched with happy nostalgia. Back then, Pikker and his brotherhood of police officers worked most days out of what they called "the office in the bush," a makeshift clubhouse based in an old storage unit out in Bellville. The place sat among the trees, and the men barbecued and drank beers out back. They did some things Pikker wasn't proud of, and that he'd never speak of, but back then, it was all about having fun, about brotherhood and machismo and serving your country.

"You could not be weakened by emotion, and that type of indifference strengthens you, until one day, out of the blue, the dam bursts," he said.

But the dam had not yet burst in 1993, and Pikker was living the dream: hunting criminals, carrying a gun and a badge, solving cases. Pikker wasn't an Afrikaner, and so he had to exert a little extra effort to fit in. He had grown up as a first-generation South African; his father and grandparents were Estonian refugees who had fled the communist regime and had imbued in him a lifelong hatred of communism. He was raised in a modest home in the Gardens area of Cape Town, near downtown, and joined the South African Police in 1975, when he was eighteen.

Pikker had dreamed of being a cop since he was a kid, and in a sense he got to live his dream during the most exciting twenty years in South African policing history. That is, if riots, petrol bombs, and shootouts were your thing. And they were Pikker's thing. After the 1960 Sharpeville Massacre—the police killings that brought the PAC onto the world stage—the government had largely succeeded in quelling unrest by asserting its military authority, expanding apartheid policies, and banning opposition organizations. But by the time Pikker took his oath, tumult was again bubbling up.

In 1968, a twenty-two-year-old activist and medical student named Steve Biko began to espouse an ideology called Black Consciousness. Biko defined Black Consciousness as "the realization by the black man of the need to rally together with his brothers around the cause of their subjection—the blackness of their skin—and to operate as a group in order to rid themselves of the shackles that bind them to perpetual servitude."

The teachings of Black Consciousness spread across the country. On June 16, 1976, thousands of students in Soweto marched to pro-

test a new regulation that made Afrikaans language classes manda-
tory. The students, riled up but reportedly peaceful, marched,
demanding that they not be forced to learn the mother tongue of
their oppressors. Security forces ambushed them, firing tear gas. The
march erupted into a riot, which ended in a predictable haze of
police bullets. A famous black-and-white photo made the rounds in
the international media: a black man in overalls, carrying in his arms
a dying thirteen-year-old boy still dressed in his school uniform, the
boy's young sister walking next to the man, her face contorted in
grief. The world turned even more firmly against apartheid. Pikker,
only a year on the job, became more firmly committed to protecting it.

Following the uprising, seven hundred people died in political
clashes, and Biko's South African Students Organization was banned.
In 1977, thirty-year-old Biko died in police custody. Initially, the
minister of justice claimed Biko had simply died from complications
relating to a six-day hunger strike, which doctors had tried to treat.
At the subsequent inquest, security police claimed his head injuries
resulted from a "fall" against a wall during his interrogation.

Growing forms of resistance emerged in communities, schools,
and workplaces across the country. The previously fractured
brown-skinned majority—Indians, coloreds, blacks—began to
band together, often with liberal whites, to protest mistreatment
and inequality. Local anti-apartheid organizations sprang up. Protesters campaigned against social, political, and economic inequal-
ities, opposing rent increases and the imposition of "stooge"
political representatives. They mobilized communities around issues such as housing, transport, and racial segregation. There were
consumer, rent, and bus boycotts. "Collaborators" (black policemen, for example) were attacked and often killed. Local institu-
tions considered oppressive were petrol-bombed and destroyed.
Unions gathered more members willing to risk their jobs and lives
to fight for fair conditions. In 1985, more than 240,000 workers
took part in 390 strikes, and rallies and riots raged across the coun-

try; in 1987, there were 1,148 strikes. By 1986, the political situation had grown so tense that the apartheid government, which had begun to roll back some segregation laws, instituted another State of Emergency. Between five thousand and eight thousand soldiers were deployed to the townships to keep control of the roiling black population.

In 1986, during the State of Emergency, a twenty-nine-year-old Pikker was sent from the regular uniformed police to the security branch. The State of Emergency, which banned TV and radio from broadcasting rallies and protests, also allowed officers like Pikker the power to arrest, detain, and interrogate without a warrant. A study showed that 78 percent of detainees had been mentally abused, and reports of torture by security forces were widespread. Despite increasing repression through the continuing State of Emergency, the detention of thousands of activists, and the continued banning of organizations and individuals, political protests peaked in 1989 with the Defiance Campaign, during which thousands openly defied apartheid laws.

By 1990, the country was facing a stalemate. The apartheid government was unable to govern; the liberation movements were unable to seize power. President F.W. de Klerk, part of a new generation of Afrikaner, recognized the impossibility of maintaining white rule in a country with a declining white population and a rising black population—mired in a recession, hindered by sanctions and military expenditures, weighed down by a bloated bureaucracy meant to keep apartheid afloat. Mandela and the ANC recognized that they faced logistical and financial issues as the Soviet Union collapsed, denying them their main support network. Both parties would benefit from a peaceful handover of power.

So in 1990 de Klerk unbanned the ANC and PAC and released Mandela from prison. Over the following year the majority of political prisoners were released, the State of Emergency was lifted, and many apartheid laws were repealed. The ANC, in turn, suspended the armed struggle. The PAC did not. An era of political negotiations began.

Nonetheless, violence snowballed as the country navigated the rocky road from minority rule to inclusive democracy. Between 1989 and 1994, 17,426 people died in political clashes. Amy Biehl was just one of these victims, killed by a mob of young black men. The vast majority of victims, however, were black, and were killed by soldiers, police, security forces, and warring black organizations.

This was the environment in which Pikker worked, though he refused to comment on whether he tortured or killed anyone. He claimed that back when he joined the force, he was "dumb when it came to politics," but he was committed to the job. In his years on the force, Pikker had gathered information about underground groups, most specifically the ANC. He traveled hours every day to interrogate political prisoners stashed in various prisons along the peninsula. He tapped phones and gathered intelligence.

He saw burned bodies and burned children. He drove away as a grenade landed by his colleague, and turned to see a street covered in blood. One of his co-workers was attacked in Khayelitsha and dragged onto a rubbish heap, his dead body shot repeatedly. Pikker himself, after testifying against a black defendant in court, escaped being assassinated by a hit man brought in from the Eastern Cape.

"So what you do is you go buy a couple bottles of brandy, sit under the trees, and talk about it at night with other cops."

By the 1990s, Pikker was a member of the Riot and Violent Crimes Investigation Unit, working out of the "office in the bush," investigating crimes suspected to be of a political nature: murders and arsons, taxi wars, any crime that involved an Eastern Bloc weapon (the theory being that communist Russia was supplying the communist ANC opposition movement with guns).

"Whether I thought it was right or wrong is neither here or there," Pikker said softly. "They were trying to remove the government of the day with a government of their own by violent means.

This was the overthrow of the current status quo by an underground group who wanted to take over the running of the country on the communist basis." He paused and lit a cigarette. "Like the soldier, you do what you're told."

On August 25, 1993, Pikker was on standby, finishing dinner with his wife and three boys at home. His pager was on 24/7 and he was hardly ever around—sleeping off a night of boozing on Christmas morning as the boys opened their gifts; off chasing cases during a birthday party; investigating political foes during his kids' sports games. His wife picked up the slack. He balefully dubbed himself a "stay-away dad."

"I always said I had an affair with the police all my life. I couldn't wait to go back in every day. I was addicted. My wife sacrificed, and the kids sacrificed."

"Do you regret it?"

"Ja," Pikker said, nodding. "Ja."

At around 7:30 P.M., Pikker's phone rang. A white woman had been killed during a political protest in Gugulethu. The victim was American. Pikker jumped in his car and zipped over to the Gugulethu police station. He drove through the crowd outside the station gates and headed to the back, where a few of his colleagues and a bunch of local cops were milling about on the pavement. He saw Amy lying beneath a blanket. He bent down and lifted it up. She had a gash on her head, and blood on her face. Her eyes were slightly open, but she was clearly dead. Without thinking much about it, Pikker claimed his role as lead detective on the case.

"I said, 'I'll take it.' Words I'd come to regret."

After the crowds by the gate had dispersed and Pikker had adequately questioned and intimidated the edgy local cops on duty—including a humiliated Leon Rhodes, the officer who had been first to the scene, found Amy, and driven her to the police station—he drove over to the Caltex station, where the crime had occurred. The township was still and quiet, not a soul on the sidewalks. Pikker inspected the white railings smeared with blood, a lock of dark yellow hair curled on the dry grass. He walked across the way and started knocking on doors, taking statements.

As usual, few people were willing to talk, but some whispered rumors. Pikker hit up some confidential informants; he heard some accusations whispered through the grapevine. Rhodes had given Pikker the paper he'd received, with the names of the suspects scrawled on it.

"I remember Ntobeko," Pikker said. "He seemed illiterate, un-schooled. And what was his name, that guy? Easy . . . Nofemela . . . he was a local, one of the first to be identified. I know exactly what he looks like."

By dawn on August 26, less than twelve hours after Amy's death, a riot squad pulled up at Easy's house. They stormed the place and found one Mzikhona "Easy" Nofemela, age twenty-two, in his un-derwear, having been previously asleep next to his girlfriend Pinky in a back room. But you had to wonder, if Easy had spent the night before the killing hiding out in a safe house in Khayelitsha, why hadn't he returned there? Surely that would have been more practi-cal than going to his mom's place.

The cops continued to sweep the township, gathering suspects all morning and afternoon. Over the next few days, more young men were dragged in, and then let go. You could arrest whoever fit your fancy, but after forty-eight hours in holding, you were required to release a suspect if there was not enough evidence to justify his con-tinued incarceration. In fact, there was little physical evidence to back up Amy's case: no DNA and no fingerprints. People were call-ing the anonymous crime line, but township eyewitnesses, the im-pimpis, were always in short supply.

Nonetheless, Pikker and his squad had enough to keep Easy incarcerated, along with a group of seven others who had been separately rounded up. Following the crime, police had swarmed the area, plucking up at least a few suspects they could justify keeping for longer than two days, the vast majority of them from a little rectangle of streets spanning from NY1 to NY111. They hunted down Mongezi Manqina as he ran out the back of his mother's house. They snapped up Ntobeko Peni at a relative's place. Easy, Mongezi, Ntobeko: the three names on the scrap of paper that had been handed to Rhodes. In September, on a tip, cops headed to Langa and cuffed Vusumzi Ntamo in the yard of his aunt's house; he would be the fourth man convicted of Amy's murder.

Pikker's crew picked up a scrawny local teenager named Terry, who witnesses recalled had lifted items from Amy's car. They also dragged three ropy, hardened men who had gone into hiding in a southwestern coastal town called Saldanha Bay. These men were named Mena, Mankeke, and Steyn, and they were all affiliated with APLA. I'll call them the APLA trio.

On August 26 Pikker and a couple of other unwashed, bleary-eyed cops made their way west to the Salt River Mortuary, where Amy's body was held. There, a medical examiner named Gideon Jacobus Knobel performed an autopsy. Amy was placed on a metal table and cleaned off so that Knobel could properly inspect her wounds. Her hair, now wet, was tangled and slicked back from her bare, freckled face. Her eyes were closed. Her clothing, soaked with blood, had been gathered as evidence, and her body lay naked beneath a blue terry-cloth towel.

Knobel examined every inch of Amy. Her arms and legs were tanned but her torso pale white. Her height, he noted, was 1.64 meters, or just shy of five-four. Her mass, he recorded, was 53 kilograms, just under 117 pounds. He categorized her physique as "small."

"Little warrior," her boyfriend, Scott, had called her.

"Little dynamo," Peter and Linda called her.

Amy's nutrition was "good," Knobel wrote. He opened her

mouth: *Full set of teeth.* He ran his hand over her skin. *Body cool to touch. Rigor mortis fully established and posterior lividity present.*

Knobel shaved the crown of her head to examine the wounds. He peeled back the skin, opened the skull, and peered at the brain contained within. He took out a ruler and measured the stab wound to the left of her breast, the bruises on her hands and wrists, the blue blooming across her thigh. He snapped photographs of each relevant injury. He made notes on three sheets of paper that contained black-and-white sketches of the generic human body from various angles: right profile, face from the front, left profile, skull from the front, skull from above, brain, hands, palms. It was a crude map of the body, used by the examiner to keep a visual record of where each injury occurred.

Knobel marked each of Amy's wounds on the sketches. Using a pen, he marked a spot on the bridge of the nose, and wrote "old scar 0.5 cm." He marked the large, triangular wound made by a brick on her head, and drew an arrow to a more detailed rendering of the wound. He drew each cut and its corresponding measurement on the facial sketch: "0.7 cm abrasion" on her right shoulder; "3.0 cm upper edge, sharp angular edge in bone" above her right eye; "bone fragments" on the right front of the brain.

Later, Knobel sat down at his typewriter. He detailed his chief findings: the stab wound to the chest, blood that had gathered in the chest and heart, several major lacerations to the head, and two fractures of the skull. He concluded the cause of death: *Stab wound of the chest into the heart and head injuries with fractured skull and the consequences thereof.*

"She probably didn't feel much pain after the blow, even though she got out of the car and tried to speak to the mob, tried to calm them down, poor woman," Knobel later said, referring to the brick that came through her shattered windshield and hit her in the head.

Pikker recalled that Knobel had indeed blamed the initial stoning, not the stab wound, for Amy's swift and permanent demise. "He said the blow to the head could affect her gait and her speech, and it went right through the skull and damaged the brain. He was convinced that that was the cause of her death. Witnesses say she was mumbling, muttering, stumbling, reaching out in that incoherent way. Even if she had received immediate medical help for the stab wound to the chest, it wouldn't have helped for her bleeding in the brain."

Pikker left the morgue and got down to business. For the next eleven months, he worked the Amy Biehl case day and night as other files piled up on his desk, accumulating dust, and as other accused languished in jail cells. He worked twenty-hour days, transporting the remaining witnesses, making deals, seeking out evidence, searching for clues, filling out forms.

The attorney general was putting on the pressure as the story garnered attention around the world. The U.S. government was also keen on closing the case with satisfactory results. But still, testimony from township dwellers was not forthcoming. The windows of potential witnesses were broken. One witness found his dog writhing out front, its stomach split open. Soon enough, witnesses were recanting their testimony or refusing to appear in court, claiming threats and intimidation.

On October 6, 1993, seven men were indicted on charges of murder, public violence, and robbery. These included Easy, Mongezi, Vusumzi, the APLA trio, and Terry, the teenager who had nicked valuables from Amy's car. Of these seven, however, only six were in custody. Terry had been released to his mother because he was too young to be held in jail, and he had promptly skipped town.

By November 22, the APLA trio, infamous in the township for taking no prisoners, were released for lack of evidence. Witnesses refused to testify against the men, who denied any involvement in the crime. Upon hearing of their liberation, the trio ran out of the courthouse gleefully, lifted on the shoulders of their friends, saluting the PAC. Ntobeko had been hauled into the police station in late August 1993, and had stood in a lineup, but nobody could—or would—identify him, and he was let go. In old video footage, he blends into the crowd of cheering young people and helps to hoist the trio members up in the air. After a witness stepped forward, Ntobeko was rearrested, tried, and sentenced in a separate trial in 1995.

"You see, Amy thought that being in Gugulethu every day, she was well known," Pikker said. "She felt she was accepted. It often happened in the past, people who were stoned or petrol-bombed taking their domestic workers home. But Amy had this innocence. She didn't expect something like this to happen. Fortunately for the investigation, she was a prominent person. She had a political status. The kids who killed her, they thought she was just a white woman. But she worked with the ANC. If it was a normal person, the story would be out just for one day, on page five."

Every day in court, Pikker stared at the three men at the defense table: haughty Mongezi, who chewed a toothpick and wore sunglasses in court; Vusumzi, who anyone could see was struggling with intellectual disability and possibly a case of jailhouse tuberculosis; and Easy, small and uncomprehending and often racked with a cough. They kept nodding off during the proceedings, or they winked at female journalists, or they doodled on little sheets of paper.

At first, Pikker had believed they were part of a PAC-sanctioned protest, but after questioning them, he changed his mind. The accused, he decided, had simply found their way to a PAC student rally and subsequently gotten all riled up. And then they'd marched around the townships, making trouble.

The government and commercial trucks they had stopped? Sure, maybe the kids were sticking it to the white capitalists. "But also, if you stop a vehicle, you can plunder it," Pikker observed. In Langa, on their way to the scene of Amy's death in Gugulethu, many kids recalled stopping a furniture delivery truck, and those sofa sets, taken in 1993, were probably still sitting in somebody's mother's living room today. Easy had once guaranteed me as much, and we'd asked a neighbor of his to show us the items, but she scuttled away.

Amy, Pikker said, was not victimized by activists or great minds, but by a bunch of good-for-nothing low-level criminals. Once cornered in the holding cells, not one of them could articulate any ideology, as far as Pikker remembered. When he questioned them, he was surprised, and maybe even a little disappointed: it seemed that they had been far less intent on black liberation than they had been on causing chaos.

"Possibly I would have had some more respect if they had some intelligent agenda, but they weren't politicians or trained or well read," he said. "They were just bloody hooligans."

Chaos was nothing new to Pikker. Crime pulsed through the townships, where everyday life was tinged with brutality. Why? The blacks, according to Pikker, displayed a particular "savagery." He had watched people burn down an old man's house because instead of striking against the bank, the old man had continued to pay his mortgage. He had seen a father receive the news of his son's death with little surprise. Pikker rued the wretchedness of township life, but he did not connect it to his own actions. He could explain why police were reported to be laughing at dead bodies ("It's a defense mechanism, not disrespect—if you take that stuff seriously on a daily basis, you'll kill yourself") but not how a black man might remain stony-faced while a white cop delivered news of his son's death. He did not blame the violence on the apartheid government, nor did he believe that he had benefited from apartheid. To Pikker, the problems facing black South Africa were largely of their own making.

"They said we cheapened black lives, but it was a rude awakening," he mused. "Nobody cheapened black lives like they did."

Pikker also studied the Biehls from afar. He found them as alien as the black men he chased every day, perhaps more so. "The daughter's killed. Although she's basically on the other side of the fence from where I was, I felt she was following her heart and doing what she felt was right. And also in retrospect, she was doing a noble task. I put myself in the Biehls' shoes, and I thought how devastating it must have been to lose a child. I think they then wanted to believe that what they saw here in South Africa justified the actions. If it were a bunch of hooligans that took their daughter's life, it would have had less meaning. So they decided she died in political conflict, at the hands of freedom fighters. It was: 'She died for the cause.' To me, she didn't die for a cause. However you want to highlight it, and whatever foundation you want to build up around it, she died in a senseless way. There was no point in it."

Also, Pikker muttered sheepishly, the Biehls never bothered to thank him.

"You think they should have thanked you?"

"I felt it would have been in order, to appreciate my work. Although they didn't know to what extent the sacrifices I made."

"What were the sacrifices?"

"I ended up in the psychiatric ward. Twice."

In fact, the Amy Biehl case marked the beginning of a terrible time in Pikker's life. The government that employed him was crumbling, along with all the organizing principles of his life: his fraternity of cops, with a common purpose and a common enemy; a life of black-and-white and cut-and-dry. He was overworked and underpaid, transporting witnesses from the townships with no backup, walking into riots alone. Years later, he still reached for his gun if he heard a car backfire or a door slam.

Following the end of the Amy Biehl trial in October 1994, Pikker returned to his office. Mandela had been elected president six months earlier, and the government was being reshuffled. Pikker called his wife to tell her he was coming home, hung up the phone, and burst into hiccuping sobs. Two other officers eyed him uncertainly. He began to weep harder, a huge man bawling like a baby. His commander drove him home. Pikker walked into the house to find his wife watching TV.

"Help me," he said.

She took him to the police doctor, who diagnosed him as having post-traumatic stress disorder, considered an "injury on duty." He recovered at home for two weeks and then returned to the squad room—with a biweekly psychiatrist appointment as the only apparent lingering effect of his meltdown. Then, as he was wading back into work, the Amy Biehl case reemerged.

Though Easy and Linda had both claimed that Ntobeko—on the run and scared—told them that he had turned himself in, Pikker claimed that in fact one of Ntobeko's family members gave the boy up. By January 1995, Pikker was preparing for Ntobeko's trial. In the end, it was a speedy thing. A nineteen-year-old Ntobeko was tried in Afrikaans at a municipal court near Gugulethu. Chief prosecutor Nollie Niehaus sent his assistant Leon Nortier to make the case against Ntobeko, who was swiftly sentenced to eighteen years and shipped off to Pollsmoor Maximum Security Prison, a tangle of concrete buildings, guardhouses, and barbed wire set in the ritzy suburbs near the lush Tokai Forest and Constantiaberg Mountain and close to the current site of the fortresslike U.S. consulate.

Meanwhile, the police were also launching a gang investigation unit to combat the growing gang activity in the Cape Flats, and they wanted Pikker on that force. He was excellent at sitting before a judge and opposing bail, so he began to attend never-ending trials of gangsters. Case files again rose high on Pikker's desk. The sunset clause allowed for a slow but steady integration of black, colored, and Indian employees, and as new workers arrived they began to rearrange the station's layout. One day, Pikker returned from court to find that his desk had been moved into a corner. He rushed to his new space and began to search frantically for a small device his children had given him for Father's Day: a wee television with a radio function and an attached calculator. He found it atop the detritus on his desk. The radio aerial was broken.

Pikker set the splintered gadget down and walked outside to have a cigarette. "I did my part," he muttered, nonsensically. "They *promised.*"

A colleague, also having a smoke, studied him. The man had been confronting his own psychological issues, not unusual in members of the old guard. "Go phone your psychologist and make an emergency appointment," the man ordered. "Go now."

Within hours, Pikker was booked into a psychiatric institution. He'd handed over his service weapon and his vehicle. He switched off his pager for the first time in years and fell into a deep, unyielding sleep for three days. Then he cycled into a mind-numbing routine of eating, sleeping, evaluation, and medication. Initially they called his illness "burnout."

Then one day, Pikker was reading a magazine when he came upon a profile of a man that the apartheid government had designated a terrorist. Pikker remembered that the man had been categorized as "shoot to kill"—if you caught him, you were to take him out, no questions asked. Now, it seemed, this very man was a colonel in the new South African Police. Pikker tore out the picture and pinned it above his bed. When the psychologist visited him and asked about the new decor, Pikker launched into what seemed, at the time, like a reasonable rant.

"I never want to go back to the police," he said as the psychologist took notes. "That man was on the terrorist hit list. He doesn't belong. He's never made a commitment to be a policeman. Now they give him an officer's rank and he must be in charge of *me*? I'll kill him when I go back. I'll kill him."

That was when the psychologist decided Pikker was no longer fit for duty.

"They told me I can't be assimilated back into the police force and my career is finished. But I don't think I'd meant what I had said about killing the colonel. I didn't want to be finished. I had things to do, so much more to do. I was ready to normalize, study, atone for my sins."

"What sins?"

Pikker considered this. He ate a piece of shrimp and took a gulp of coffee. He didn't get into specifics on this particular subject. "You have these dreams after you leave the police. Sometimes you dream that your house is burning. That people are running around your house and you can't protect your family. You don't have the support of other police officers around you, the camaraderie and bravado, and things fall apart. After, when it's stripped away, you're raw. You get this incredible feeling of guilt, of self-loathing, that you're not worth anything and you don't deserve anything."

"Is the self-loathing related to apartheid or just police work?"

"To me it's just police work because I wasn't really a political activist."

"But who would you be sorry for, then?"

"Well, maybe I questioned a person too intensely. Maybe I could have questioned them differently." He paused. "I might be sorry for my behavior. Possibly."

"Possibly?"

"No admissions." He smiled sadly. "I miss the work, but the police made me something else. I became so indoctrinated. In base, I'm not what they made me."

"What are you?"

"What am I? A loving, good person. You know, I love music. I could play guitar and harmonica. I could maybe even have done it professionally. But straight out of school, as a student policeman, I shot my first person."

"What were you eventually diagnosed as, when you were medically boarded from the force?"

"They eventually put it down to major depression and anxiety."

"Do you think that's accurate?"

"No."

"What do you think it was?"

"I just think they broke me."

After his breakdown, Pikker cobbled together his post-transition living. He did in fact open an escort agency, Partners. He tried some gigs as a private investigator for a bit, but he could never get ahead financially. Finally, low on funds and tired of subsisting on a meager state pension, he decided to accompany his wife, a nurse, to the Middle East.

During the twentieth century, South Africa had made major medical advances, partly encouraged by the need to go it alone in a world that increasingly isolated the apartheid government. A South African doctor named Christiaan Barnard, for example, had performed the world's first successful heart transplant at Cape Town's Groote Schuur Hospital in 1967. By the mid-1990s, the country boasted a plethora of well-trained white South African medical professionals that wealthy Arab states were keen to hire for twice the price South African hospitals could pay.

So Pikker had not absconded to the Gulf, as I had imagined, and gone undercover. Rather, for the past few years, he and his wife had been living in an apartment building on an anonymous and spotless avenue in the Emirates, where Nurse Pikker went to work assisting on surgeries performed on wealthy sheikhs and ex-lieutenant Pikker sat around, missing his days on the force and the South African land: the ocean and the cool winds and the mountains and the bush.

Pikker rarely left his Abu Dhabi apartment, and the highlights of his days were the regular visits of a neighbor's cat. To avoid too much reflection, he started a correspondence course to become a hypnotherapist, but he could never find any subjects on whom to practice. He took up playing the keyboard. He got involved in untenable importing schemes—for example, he was particularly enamored of a tiny speaker, which he felt could make a splash on the electronics marketplace. He poked around on Facebook, reposting inspirational messages from pages called "Healing Hugs" and furious complaints by his white friends about the abysmal state of the new South African government. He hated rhino poachers. He loved rescue puppies. He also offered a steady stream of off-color jokes, concerning nuns having orgasms and such.

Hoping for a reason to leave the house, Pikker bought a motorcycle and imagined sailing down the wide boulevards. But the Emirati sun melted tires to the road. So he had tried to ride at night, out to the shores of the manufactured desert city, and had sometimes fished as the sun rose over the Gulf. But then the battery went flat, followed by the tires. When he fixed those, the insurance ran out. And by the time he'd renewed it, his license had expired. Finally, a year after I first met Pikker, the bike was stolen.

So much for a crime-free country! he wrote me when it happened. In any case, by 2015, Pikker was no longer fit to ride a bike—he'd been hospitalized for yet another heart attack and was wheelchairbound.

Though I offered to pick up the tab, Pikker insisted on paying. As we left, I slowed to match his pace.

"Ilmar, do you think they got the right guys, for Amy's murder?" I asked.

"No, not all of them," he said. "They said the case was a success, internationally. To me it was a fail. There was thirty people there that day, and I would have liked to see them all in prison, but we couldn't get the witnesses to talk. The four we got are just a weak consolation prize."

9.

From my weakness I drew strength that never left me.

—Jorge Luis Borges

Back in 1993, Amy's murder bloomed into an international incident, unfurling onto newspaper pages across the world. Always, they used the same shots of Amy—here with a pudgy black baby in her arms, here grinning widely, here surrounded by African women with baskets on their heads.

The trial was the first to be fast-tracked under a new act aimed at combating political violence and unrest. Other similarly political cases involving violence in the townships had been left to idle, but the local government swiftly applied the act to Amy's case. Accordingly, for the better part of the year, the accused were denied bail and the state prosecution was urged to prioritize the case.

The defendants were kept at Pollsmoor Prison, just outside Cape Town.

"The prison is beautiful outside," Easy recalled. "Nice gardens, nice flowers, very shiny. When you go inside, is cold showers, dirty beds, breakfast is porridge with one sugar, gangsters fighting and they cut your head."

When they were finally given bail of 250 rand (equivalent at the time to about $70), their families had to raise funds. Vusumzi eventually returned to prison, which transported him to the court because he couldn't afford the daily train fare to attend the trial.

The trial played against the backdrop of the Cape Town High Court, a pale gray building supported by pillars, its doors of carved, polished mahogany. The whole hullabaloo seemed a testament to colonialism. The proceedings took place in a resplendent, monochromatic room accented with wooden benches, wooden tables, and wooden paneling. The advocates wore long black robes, high white frilly collars, and powdered wigs, à la Great Britain, and everyone reverently referred to Judge Gerald Friedman as "M'Lord." Once, the local Gugulethu cop Leon Rhodes, who was accustomed to testifying in lower-level magistrates' courts, addressed Friedman as "Your Honor" instead of "M'Lord" and was roundly taken to task for disrespect as he sat there on the stand—an embarrassment he never forgot.

Set against such European-style formality, the trial became a macabre circus, especially because the PAC was experiencing trouble cobbling together a cohesive message. Some PAC leaders had sent a letter to the U.S. ambassador, expressing "regret" for Amy's murder. Meanwhile, other PAC leaders had herded some radicalized township kids into taxis and sent them to stand on the courthouse steps, kick the walls, point imaginary guns, and chant, "Settler, settler, war, war." The prosecutors snuck in and out of the back entrance to avoid them, and eventually the police erected a barbed wire barricade on the sidewalk. Pinky, Easy's girlfriend at the time, smacked a reporter with her shoe.

Ntobeko was among the crowd. Small and thin, his image was caught by the camera that time he lifted one of the men in the freed APLA trio on his shoulders. He and his other student PAC compadres from the townships stood on the steps, crowds of kids as young as ten, hamming it up for the aghast spectators, talking a good game when the microphones dangled before them, cheering each other on, repeating the PAC rhetoric—"our land," "war, war, war," "settler, settler"—and then surreptitiously eyeing the cameras to check that they were being filmed. If no one watched, they stopped dancing around, deflated, but if they had an audience, they grew ever more energetic. Invisible children, they now had the world watching them.

For a couple of days in January 1994, Linda and Amy's younger sister, Molly, pushed through the protesters as they entered the court. Peter and the other two siblings had stayed in America. The South African government had assigned the women bodyguards, a pair of poofy-haired Afrikaners whom they had nicknamed Hans and Frans. Linda, normally a zaftig woman, was thin and drawn in her various shifts, but made a point of walking with her chin angled skyward. Molly was more visibly unsettled. Hans and Frans stood guard. Later, Linda and Molly would see their bodyguards on TV, protectively flanking de Klerk, the former president who became deputy president to Mandela after the transition to democracy.

Months earlier, the PAC kids had sat in the gallery and laughed when Maletsatsi, Amy's friend who had been in the car on August 25, sat at the witness stand and spoke of Amy's last moment: how she could not speak, how she could only moan. A court clerk began to cry quietly, but the PAC kids let out whoops and giggles. Maletsatsi's friend Sindiswa, the other female passenger, broke down before her testimony.

"The witness is overcome," the judge announced, and court was adjourned.

LAUGHTER IN MURDER COURT CHILLS S AFRICA, London's *Sunday Times* announced, before bemoaning the country's "depravity": "Good was fighting evil in supreme court number one, and it looked as if this country's tide of thuggery and intimidation would triumph."

Nancy Scheper-Hughes, soon to leave South Africa for a more welcoming post in California, attended the trial in her capacity as an anthropologist. She approached the accused's attorney, Nona Goso, and asked why the spectators had laughed.

"The laughter was not acceptable to me, nor to anyone else, but it did not shock me," Goso told Nancy. "I live in a township and I know the extent to which apartheid has murdered human feelings. . . . Their own people have been killed so often that it has the effect of reducing killing to nothing."

As Linda and Molly passed the students on their way to the trial, flanked by Hans and Frans, the same students started to jeer.

"Kill Americans!" they yelled from the pavement.

"One settler, one bullet!"

Linda didn't wince, and Molly tried to follow suit.

"I've been to more intimidating Raiders football games," Linda
later told me.

Linda and Molly attended a "trial within the trial," an extensive
offshoot of the initial trial that centered on whether the defendants
had been forced to confess through intimidation and beatings. Easy's
father, Wowo, also sat in on the proceedings every day, "a small man
in a blue knit cap," as Linda remembered. "He almost looked like he
wanted to speak to me." On one of the days during which the Biehls
sat in court, the entire line of questioning concerned whether Easy
had been forced to smoke a stub of a cigarette found on the interrogation room floor.

Linda was privately anguished by this element of the trial: her
daughter had been killed, and here they were, watching people debate the provenance of a cigarette butt. Worse, Mongezi Manqina—
the handsome man accused of stabbing Amy, who chewed on a
toothpick throughout the trial—turned directly to Molly and
flashed her a broad smile.

"Was he smiling at me or laughing at me?" she wondered aloud
nervously. "I feel sorry for him."

Later, when I tracked him down, Mongezi, who still had the
toothpick in his mouth, claimed that chewing on it simply calmed
his nerves. And he had only smiled at Molly because, well, she was
Amy's spitting image; it was as if the woman he'd stabbed to death
was standing before him, a pretty walking ghost. Why that made him
grin widely, he could not explain.

After two days, the Biehls decided enough was enough, and let
the trial go on its way without them. They went to the Camps Bay
beach—the ritziest strip of sand and saltwater in Cape Town—
followed by the faithful Hans and Frans, each wearing swimming
trunks that revealed lily-white legs. They were driven out to Paarl,
the hot, rural farming and vineyard town an hour outside of Cape
Town, where the first Poqo members had marched in 1962, murdering two white citizens and wrecking property. There, the Biehls
met Mandela. Linda shook his hand; he even knew her name. Her

skirt kept blowing up in the wind and the ladies beside her kept pulling it down. Then Linda and Molly watched as Mandela commanded a throbbing, worshipful crowd at the Paarl soccer stadium, and their hair stood on end. It was history in the making. Mandela was not yet president and the country was not yet free; but he would be, and it would be, within months.

While Linda and Molly Biehl met Mandela in the Winelands, the Cape's senior prosecutor, Nollie Niehaus, was still trying to build a case, despite the fact that the senior defense attorney, the aptly named Justice Poswa, was stalling endlessly with the trial-within-a-trial tactics, spending months trying to get the defendants' confessions thrown out. More troubling was the fact that the prosecution still had very little evidence conclusively tying the accused to the murder.

Nollie Niehaus was the law to Ilmar Pikker's order and had been easy to find since he was still working for the state as a senior prosecutor. He picked up his phone on the first ring, and the next day he greeted me at the National Prosecuting Authority office downtown. Niehaus was a sprightly, salt-and-pepper-haired Afrikaner gentleman who had clearly dedicated a good portion of his life to trimming and caring for his mustache. Like most prosecutors, he was a ham and a showboater, with a healthy dose of self-confidence and a sharp mind. He was as upbeat as he was hardened; I sensed he would have no qualms about flashing you a smile before asking the judge to hang you. Through the ebb and flow of the various political tides, Niehaus had ridden the waves, putting away rapists and murderers and organized crime bosses with aplomb. He had seen a bunch of major cases in his time—including the one he'd recently wrapped up, Goldin and Bloom, about which he was eager to reminisce.

The national media was particularly enamored of certain crimes, chief among them anything that involved wealthy white people— preferably attractive and educated, and especially if the violence was senseless and arbitrary, and played into widespread fears. In the case of Goldin and Bloom, a twenty-eight-year-old comedic actor named Brett Goldin and a twenty-seven-year-old fashion designer named Richard Bloom had left a dinner party in the upscale seaside neighborhood of Camps Bay at ten one night in April 2006. I regularly strolled there after dark, and my hundred-pound mother-in-law walked her obese, docile spaniel by the sea there after dinner every evening.

But on their way to the car, Goldin and Bloom were surrounded by a group of gang-identified colored men from the Cape Flats, sleep-deprived, twitching on *tik* and loaded on liquor. Tik, or, crystal meth, makes you emaciated and wild, as evidenced by the roving bands of young addicts strutting through the townships and colored areas, followed by strung-out old addicts, limping alone down the streets. It also makes your teeth rot away.

The men had been on the lookout for a car to steal, and they had their eye on Bloom's shiny VW hatchback. In South Africa, Volkswagens are ubiquitous, and thus a draw for criminals. Many carjackers are merely working for an organized crime syndicate, which usually orders a particular make and model for a client. The carjacker targets the desired vehicle, which is immediately hustled away, its driver dead or injured or perhaps merely traumatized and standing by the side of the road. Its identifying marks are removed and it is sold to a buyer, often across the border or in a faraway city.

The men who wanted Bloom's car were too disorganized and inebriated to be working for a crime boss, but they still knew to home in on a car that might blend in undetected and appeal to a potential buyer. Why they also took Goldin and Bloom, when they could easily have simply absconded with the car, has never been fully explained. Some say it was a gang initiation, but others think it was a dumb split-second decision that snowballed into unplanned violence. Hours after the robbery and kidnapping, Goldin's and Bloom's naked bodies were found by a highway off-ramp.

Niehaus strode over to his bookshelf and rifled around, before pulling out a large photocopy of a color picture and slapping it on the desk between us: two naked young men, facedown on dry grass and pine needles, dead from a couple of shots to the head.

"It looks quite personal," I said.

"Noooo," Niehaus drawled. "They were queer though. Don't know if that had anything to do with it. Both good actors, though." Actually, only Bloom was a performer; Goldin was a fashion designer. Niehaus pointed to a close-up of a blood spatter on one man's arm. "See, that was caused by spilling from the head wound to the arm. Horrific, hey?"

He replaced the photo, sat down, and spun his chair around. Did I mind if he smoked?

I didn't mind, I said, but was that allowed?

Niehaus closed his door, cracked a window, slipped a Camel from his jacket pocket, lit it, and smiled wide. "Who guards the guardian?" he asked. Then he leaned back in his chair and focused on my questions. "Amy Biehl," he muttered.

In 1993, Niehaus's hair was chestnut brown and his neck was a little thicker, but his mustache was as full and lustrous as ever. He was working across the street in the old days. You could see his previous office from here, the building by the courthouse with the air-conditioning units on top and the red trim. Back then, Niehaus was handed the Biehl case, which would swiftly consume his life. The case was a media circus, and he was expected to do what it took to win.

He charged the suspects with murder, and asked for them to be hanged. Between 1960 and 1990 in South Africa, 2,500 men were hanged. Ninety-five percent of them were black, sentenced by white judges. As apartheid headed toward its demise, the death penalty remained on the books but was utilized less frequently, and by 1993 it was merely symbolic. Everyone knew that if the political winds continued blowing as they were, a person sentenced to death would simply rot in jail. Indeed, by 1995, a year into his presidency, Mandela abolished the death penalty completely.

Regardless, in 1993, at the beginning of the case, Mandela had still not been elected, and the courts remained a white man's domain in a white state. In South Africa, there is no jury system: a single judge hears and decides upon a case. The judge in the Amy Biehl matter was a "splendid" fellow, according to Niehaus: a distinguished white man named Gerald Friedman. These days, Friedman is a long-retired widower who lives out by the wild coastal beaches on the southern peninsula near Cape Town.

Niehaus's junior prosecutor was Leon Nortier, a socially awkward, hard-nosed young Afrikaner. After years as a prosecutor, Nortier had grown so habitually antagonistic that he had begun to cross-examine family and friends during Sunday lunch, and had subsequently moved over to a private practice. Before, he wore the shabby clothes of a lawyer on state salary, but these days he dresses as the well-paid defense attorney he is: the silky turquoise tie against the crisp white shirt, the silver watch, the shiny black shoes. He carries around an engraved silver keychain that says *I trust in your unfailing love, Psalm 13:5,* and spends much of his working day chain-smoking at his desk.

The defense attorney, Justice Poswa, was a black man whom Niehaus described as "very experienced but arrogant." Niehaus posited that the judge preferred him to Poswa because "I showed respect, I didn't make him cross." In the intervening years, Poswa had become a judge himself and then had finally retired and moved to a brick estate overlooking the red-sand beaches in Umhlanga, a vacation-slash-retirement community just outside the city of Durban adjacent to the Indian Ocean. I had visited Poswa, now in his eighties, in his silent, spit-shined home, where his diminutive wife tiptoed around, sweeping up little invisible piles of dirt. Though Poswa had told me on the phone that he had valuable information on the Amy

Biehl case, he didn't seem to remember much at all, and said sadly that his children had cleaned out his old files years earlier.

In 1993, Poswa's junior counsel was a young Xhosa woman named Nona Goso. I have never been able to find Goso, who had also represented the four men ultimately convicted of Amy's death at the Truth and Reconciliation Commission in 1997. She had allowed her bar license to lapse a few years earlier. I called an organizer of an event at which Goso had spoken in 2010, but the organizer didn't know where she'd gone. Easy told me a rumor that Goso was on the board of the regional railroad, but most of the numbers listed for the railroad were out of service. She didn't show up in any phone books and Poswa didn't know her whereabouts.

In old quotes and videos, Goso appears thoughtful and intelligent, a slender woman with close-cropped hair and a gentle manner that seemed incongruous for a litigator. She was a young black female attorney from the townships who rose up during apartheid, got herself a legal education, and made her way in a world of aggressive and immodest men of all colors who, despite their political differences and various incompetencies, believed in the common myth of their own supremacy. Whatever she had gone through, the fact remains that Nona Goso, on purpose or accidentally, had disappeared herself.

If it came down to pure legal talent, Niehaus reflected, he had been sure he could beat Poswa and Goso. But it wouldn't be so easy. After recanting early confessions, the defendants categorically denied being at the scene, and there was no evidence placing them there. Niehaus had no DNA samples, no fingerprints, and no forensic trace. One confession was thrown out, but the two remaining were weak and insubstantial. Amy's passengers weren't much help. Sindiswa had initially insisted that she'd seen Easy at the crime scene but had later testified that she was "not sure." And so far, for all the people standing on the street that day—and police claimed the number topped two hundred—no witnesses from Gugulethu had come forward to testify.

Niehaus and Pikker had tried to convince two twelve-year-old boys who had been playing soccer on the Caltex field to come forward, with little luck. At the behest of the American government, Niehaus had dispatched Pikker to offer the boys and their families a tremendous deal in return for their testimony: a new life in the United States.

"The American embassy said the government is prepared to fly this lady and her family to the States, give her a place to stay, her kid can go to school, a job, everything," Pikker told me. "Dream come true. When the court case was on they'd fly them back, put them up in a nice hotel. I said, 'Do you realize what you've been offered here? A new life, a wealthy life, a house, a brilliant education for your child.' But then they heard the dog yelping early one morning and when the mother came out, the dog's stomach had been sliced open. The dog survived, stitched up, but the woman said no. She would have had a chance to not be a menial worker."

The woman and her now grown son still remained in Gugulethu. I'd met him once to see what he remembered of Amy's murder, and he still wondered what would have happened if his mother had taken the offer. Now, in his early thirties, he had a wife and three kids whom he could barely afford to feed, and he kept getting contract jobs doing IT work that lasted only a few years. He still lived on the family lot, in an add-on to the back.

As the trial wound down, with a sure victory escaping him, Niehaus was at a loss. "The court may be on a ride to never-neverland, where it would not discover the truth, should witnesses decide what evidence to give," reported one local paper.

Niehaus turned to Pikker again. "He was at court every day, and if I needed something, I'd say, 'Go fetch!' and he would," Niehaus remembered. Now Niehaus needed Pikker to go fetch a few nice-looking, decent Gugulethu citizens who were willing to speak before a judge about what they'd seen on August 25, 1993. More important, they needed to have seen the three men sitting at the defense table in the act of killing Amy Biehl.

Pikker trolled the township and, through his network of informants, tracked down three witnesses: two sisters who had called the
tip hotline in the early days and the woman with the cropped hair
who had handed Leon Rhodes the note with the names. The women
agreed to testify behind closed doors, away from the group and visible only to the judge.

"How did you convince them to testify at all?" I asked Niehaus.

"Oh, you know, soft-soaking, telling them it was for the good of
the community."

"Did they gain anything else?"

"They get money. How much, I never know that."

Pikker estimated that witnesses in Amy's case had probably received somewhere between 10,000 and 50,000 rand each (according to the exchange rate of the day, between $3,000 and $15,000, a
massive windfall for someone living in poverty).

The woman who had handed Rhodes the note with names was
called Miss A, and she was the prosecution's most important witness.
When she testified behind closed doors in October 1994, Miss A
cinched the deal for the state. She was eloquent, she withstood cross-
examination, and she could not be intimidated by lawyers. She also
cried when she remembered Amy's murder.

"The witness is crying, shaking, when they explain story," Easy
said. "They do this on purpose. They want money."

"She was particularly good at tearing them apart," Niehaus recalled, admiringly.

She was a "poor, poor lying witness," Poswa told the papers at the
time. He insisted that Miss A was aligned with the ANC and had a
personal bone to pick with the accused, allegations Miss A contested
to the judge's stated satisfaction. Twenty years later, when I met Miss
A, I found her room peppered with ANC literature; she was a long-
time member.

Within weeks of the women's testimony, Niehaus and Poswa sub-
mitted their final arguments, and on October 24, 1994, Judge Friedman issued a 120-page verdict, condensing the nine-month trial

into a stack of typewritten words on paper. In the verdict, Friedman broke down the events of August 25, 1993, as he saw them: the mob, the beating, the injuries, the witness testimony, the defense's explanation. Throughout, he addressed all lawyers formally: Misters Niehaus, Nortier, Poswa; Ms. Goso. He addressed policemen and expert witnesses by their titles at first—Detective, Sergeant, Constable, Doctor—and then referred to them by their last names. He addressed the young black women who testified by their first names. As was standard, he referred to Mongezi Manqina as Accused 1; Easy Nofemela as Accused 2; and Vusumzi Ntamo as Accused 3. For two days, Friedman sat before the court and read aloud the logic behind his decision. At the end, he found all three men guilty of murder.

Niehaus was relieved that the long, tedious trial was over, but he felt, oddly, that he cared more about the guilty verdict than did Amy's parents. He had met them once or twice in his office, and they had seemed to him curiously disconnected from what he considered the reality of their daughter's death. He spent time with them once socially, if he remembered correctly, at a dinner at a U.S. embassy official's house in the tony suburb of Constantia, just down the road from Pollsmoor Prison, where the accused were serving time. The man, Peter Biehl, you could see he was in pain. But the woman, Linda?

Niehaus never quite understood that woman. He shook his head and furrowed his brow.

"The man was grieving, but she seemed too . . . too . . . at ease about the whole thing," he said. "They were very involved but— I couldn't understand the woman's way of reasoning, or thinking, or whatever."

"Did she seem at peace?" I asked.

"Could have been. To me, this is just strange behavior for a lady whose child got killed in such a terrible way."

Niehaus also never thought the boys would get amnesty at the Truth and Reconciliation Commission a few years later. Yes, he believed that the crime had a political element to it—the attack was unplanned, but the kids had been at an organized PAC rally before. But to Niehaus, whatever little political motivation there may have been to the commission of the crime did not make it any less gruesome or justifiable. Anyone who saw the photos could see that they'd gone after Amy Biehl with vengeance and fury.

Had the Biehls opposed amnesty at the Truth and Reconciliation Commission, Niehaus was pretty sure the men would have spent the full eighteen years behind bars, forgotten. But the Biehls sat before the country and said, "Amy would have embraced your Truth and Reconciliation process. We are present this morning to honor it and to offer our sincere friendship."

Niehaus simply couldn't wrap his mind around it.

"Unless you're such a big believer in God that you could have that much forgiveness in you . . ." He paused. "You can forgive them, but to employ them? At the Amy Biehl Foundation? Listen, I don't understand that woman's head, and I don't think anybody in their right mind that is legally orientated would ever be able to understand it."

He took a drag and blew the smoke out toward the ceiling. He would get me the file. He called his secretary and spoke briefly in Afrikaans. The file was missing, he said, hanging up. He'd give me a call when it showed up.

"This girl, she was doing what she could to uplift the blacks and she got killed." Niehaus frowned. The city unrolled behind him, sloping gently down to the shores.

10.

The weak can never forgive. Forgiveness is an attribute of the strong.

—Gandhi

Forgiveness; all that is rubbish. Oh, if only I could keep from dying.

—Leo Tolstoy, *The Kreutzer Sonata*

After six months of talking on the phone and communicating by email, I met Linda in person in July 2012. She was sitting at a hotel breakfast table in a crisp white dining room high above the swirling Atlantic, eating bran flakes and drinking black coffee. She had landed in Cape Town the evening before and was staying in a cliff-top five-star hotel in the most expensive part of town, paid for by a South African entertainment mogul friend of hers.

In that bright dining room, Linda was as distinctive and immaculate as in pictures: her crimson lipstick and platinum bob just so, a tailored silk eggplant-colored jacket, a patterned cashmere scarf of greens, oranges, reds, and purples around her neck. She wore heavy rings on her fingers, among them an oversized band punctuated with an enormous silver skull. Strung around her neck was a strand of silver that ended with a cluster of carved beads that were also, if you inspected them closely, tiny skulls. She carried a large shiny purse that, mom-style, contained various plastic Baggies full of gum, tissues, snacks, chargers, creams.

Linda had been blessed with lifelong good looks. Here was a woman who had suffered neither an awkward adolescence nor a pained old age, who had been the easy recipient of glances and compliments since childhood. Now, as she headed toward seventy, she rejected nips, tucks, paralyzing jabs, and plumping injections. She enjoyed eating, and her physique reflected this. Her face was a constellation of lines rarely witnessed on upper-middle-class American women her age. It was quite purposeful, this effect. When she was younger, Linda had seen a photograph of an aged Georgia

O'Keeffe, her tawny skin and strong features forming a landscape on her face. Linda found O'Keeffe, all wrinkles and confidence, unbearably beautiful, and had decided that she would emulate the artist as she aged.

Linda Biehl was born Linda Shewalter in Geneva, Illinois, a scenic hamlet set on the banks of the Fox River, just west of Chicago's suburbs. In Linda's childhood, and still, Geneva was the stuff of Norman Rockwell paintings: handsome shingled homes in modest colors, a red-brick courthouse, a tree-lined and spit-shined main street. The population has always been almost entirely white and financially comfortable, the school system is top-notch, there are over thirty public parks, and wildflowers bloom by the water. The town maintains a quaint little windmill, set on a square of trim, jade-green grass.

When Linda was nine years old, she met a boy named Peter Biehl at Sunday school. They went to cotillion together, she in her dress and white gloves, he in a suit with his hair slicked. In high school, Peter headed to boarding school in Connecticut, at prestigious Choate. He got in trouble for brewing liquor in the bathtub of his room, was kicked out, and transferred to another school. But every summer, Peter would return to Geneva, and he and Linda would share fries and Cokes at Rex's drive-thru.

While at college at Whittier in California, Peter performed in a production of *Bye Bye Birdie*. Linda was studying at a different college, but she traveled to see Peter onstage. At the cast party, he surprised Linda with a ring, and she accepted the proposal. They married between their junior and senior years, and Linda transferred to Whittier. They lived in an apartment near campus, where Linda was miserable and lonely, a condition made worse by the fact that their place didn't even have a telephone. In 1965, the newlyweds graduated and settled in an exquisite apartment owned by Peter's parents on Chicago's Lakeshore Drive. Peter worked first as a business consultant and later as a marketing consultant, and Linda wandered around the city's art galleries as her belly grew. Soon, she gave birth to Kim.

While Kim was still a baby, Peter was transferred to Los Angeles. Just seventeen months after Kim was born, while the young family was living in Brentwood, Amy was born. Linda took the two girls to the beach and the playground every day. By the time they had moved again, to Palo Alto, Molly had arrived on the scene: three yellow-haired girls, only a few years apart. While Peter traveled for work, Linda ran the household and, in her spare time, took ballet lessons.

Soon after they'd settled in Palo Alto, the Biehls again relocated for Peter's job, this time to the dry heat of Tucson. By the late 1970s, Zach had joined the family, the only boy, and Peter decided to leave the crush of the corporate world. The Biehls moved to Santa Fe, where they started a small Native American art gallery, situated above a bookshop on the town square. On the sidewalks below, Indians sat on colorful blankets and sold handicrafts.

By 1985, Amy was set to begin her freshman year at Stanford and Kim was already at college. Peter decided to return to consulting to help pay for his kids' higher education, and the family moved to Newport Beach, California, blocks from the Pacific. By 1993, her three girls grown and working, Linda had secured a job selling gowns to wealthy women at the local Neiman Marcus. She got herself a white Mustang convertible, and amassed an impressive designer wardrobe. She also tried to attend every single one of Zach's baseball games.

Then, one afternoon in August 1993, Linda took sixteen-year-old Zach shopping for the new school year. She rolled the top of the Mustang down and the two breezed around Newport Beach, collecting clothing and school supplies. Peter was on a business trip in Oregon, where Amy's boyfriend, Scott, was studying law. The two men arranged a dinner date, and Scott planned to ask, then, for Peter's permission to propose to Amy. Amy was due home in two days and everyone was excited for the reunion, which would take place, invariably, over tacos and margaritas at Mi Casa. The family hadn't seen Amy in ten months, though Amy and Scott had, a few months earlier, met up for a romantic week in Paris. Linda and Peter had been on holiday in Europe at the same time, and Linda had toyed with the idea of heading to France.

"I wanted to surprise her. But I didn't. Now I wish I had."

The phone was ringing as Linda and Zach walked into the house, their arms weighed down by shopping bags. Nobody had cellphones in those days. Linda answered. Kim was on the line. U.S. government representatives had tried the Biehls' home and office, but with Linda out on the town and Peter away on business, neither parent had picked up. Finally, an official reached Molly at her desk in Washington, D.C., where she worked as a congressional intern.

"Are you Amy Biehl's sister?" the official sputtered.

Molly called Kim, who lived near her parents in Newport Beach. Kim received the news and had subsequently been dialing Linda's number for nearly an hour.

"You better sit down," Kim said. "Are you sitting down?"

Linda lowered herself onto a chair.

"Amy's dead."

In contrast to the fractured PAC, the ANC boasted a smooth public relations machine that had immediately taken control of the narrative: Amy had been one of theirs, and they would simultaneously honor her and discredit the PAC. In reality, on August 25, 1993, both PAC-aligned students and ANC-aligned students had been marching down NY1. The PAC had announced that 1993 was the Year of the Great Storm around the time that the ANC announced Operation Barcelona. "Barcelona" had a circuitous meaning: it referred to the city in which the 1992 Olympics had been held, which in turn referred to the Olympic flames, which symbolized the order for ANC student members to threaten to burn government vehicles and property. Barcelona, flames, it all must burn. The march, and quite possibly the murder scene, had almost certainly included students from both political groups.

But despite an ANC element in the crowd that killed Amy, the ANC managed to quickly and successfully distance themselves from the violence and align themselves with the victim. The ANC has traditionally exercised rank-and-file rule, allowing for no dissension within the party. At a September 1993 rally in Khayelitsha, before thirty thousand supporters, Mandela himself spoke out against Amy's attackers.

"It is not military action to kill innocent civilians," Mandela said. "The people who killed Amy Biehl are no longer human beings. They are animals."

"ANC told their members to do Operation Barcelona, but when PAC youth killed Amy, the ANC went, 'Tsho tsho tsho!'" Rhoda Kadalie said, snapping three times, township style. "They said, 'Lucky they weren't us! Lucky it wasn't ours!'"

Within a day, the ANC had sent Tokyo Sexwale—then a just-released political prisoner and ANC heavyweight, now an oil-and-diamond magnate with possible presidential ambitions and a season's experience hosting the South African version of *The Apprentice*—to the Biehl household in California to express the party's sincerest condolences. Sexwale drove over from Los Angeles, where he was visiting at the time. He knocked on the door, and then sat in the living room in his tracksuit, awkwardly expressing sorrow while a flabbergasted and grief-stricken Linda offered him coffee. Many years later, Sexwale would meet with Linda again in South Africa, in more pleasant social circumstances, and she would say, "It was one of the most amazing days of my life. He told us more about world history than I could ever imagine."

To counteract the terrible international publicity South Africa had garnered from Amy's murder and to boost their reputations, the

ANC and the white mayor of Cape Town arranged for the Biehl family to visit South Africa on their dime in the fall of 1993.

The Biehls had never been to the African continent before. Amy's memorial had been held in California. On September 1, 1993, less than a week after Amy's death, Amy's roommate, Melanie, had flown to Los Angeles clutching Amy's ashes. Melanie, a poor colored single mother, and her teenage daughter stayed in an apartment donated by a friend sympathetic to the Biehls, where she ran up a $500 phone tab. Melanie was wearing a pair of expensive jeans that Linda had bought Amy; Linda suspected that Melanie had rifled through Amy's luggage, picking out a few select goodies, before the suitcases were returned to the Biehls.

"People in South Africa—and I've learned this the hard way—feel that they are entitled to things," Linda said dryly. "That money, if it's lying around, can be theirs, too." But Linda kept in touch with Melanie for years anyway.

At the memorial service, held on September 3, the Biehls walked in procession down the aisle at St. Andrew's Presbyterian Church in Newport Beach, the pews full of Amy's American friends, colleagues, teachers, family members, admirers. Linda led the procession, outfitted in a green skirt suit with a silk scarf knotted around her neck. She walked stiffly before the crowd, her face rigid, her arm hooked in the pastor's. Peter, Kim, Molly, Zach—the remaining Biehl clan—and Amy's boyfriend, Scott, followed to the somber notes of an organ.

"We are here in the memory of Amy Biehl, who was committed to carrying out these biblical instructions," the pastor said to a crowd of mourners. "Born April 26, 1967 . . ." He paused. "That's not very long ago, is it? And died August 25, 1993, in Gogo . . . gogo–ghetto township in South Africa."

"I pray for you, Amy," Melanie announced to her fellow mourners. "Please also pray for my country."

Two months later, the Biehls were headed to Gogo-ghetto town-

ship in first-class seats—courtesy of the city of Cape Town—on a
South African Airways jet. They traveled for twenty-three hours and
emerged into instant celebrity on a cold and rainy night, greeted by
senior ANC officials and the white mayor. They were quickly arranged on cream-colored sofa sets in a large, carpeted room. The
mayor stood before them and announced, to a throng of journalists,
that the city of Cape Town wished to show the world "that there is
a movement towards peace and democracy."

Next, the Biehls were chauffeured around in a convoy of sparkling new Mercedes. They attended a memorial talk at the University of the Western Cape, packed with students who had been drawn
in by flyers plastered around campus, announcing AMY BIEHL'S FAM-
ILY SPEAKS.

"Welcome to the Struggle, family," senior ANC official Allan
Boesak said as he introduced the Biehls. Boesak and his comrades,
all black and colored with funky facial hair, raised their fists in the
ANC salute, as Peter and Linda stood stiffly nearby, hands by their
sides. By 2000, Boesak—a preacher and activist—had been sentenced to three years in prison for stealing $400,000 in donations
made to his charity by Paul Simon and other anti-apartheid supporters.

Throughout their trip, when they walked the streets, the Biehls
were followed and photographed ceaselessly, a mass of striking
blondness: Linda in her designer skirt-suits; Peter with his big
throwback glasses; beautiful Molly, as apple-pie as the popular
cheerleader in a teen drama; glum Kim, who tended to escape the
attention of the photographers; young Zach, a high school football
player with teenage vernacular and acne; and Scott, Amy's boyfriend, a gangly Stanford basketball player and law student who
wore her necklace around his neck and his pants belted high at the
waist.

Early on during their visit, the family was led by Amy's old mentor, Dullah Omar, to the spot where Amy had died. It was, according

to Peter Biehl, "obvious manipulation . . . he's got an agenda." Once there, the Biehls were surrounded by the press. The photographers ran around to get the best shots, crouching and standing on tiptoe. Amy's UWC friends and colleagues sobbed. Molly, tears streaming down her face, whispered, "I love you, Amy." There were microphones everywhere, no avoiding them.

Linda's face betrayed nothing until she laid some white lilies on the ground. "Rest in peace, Amy, okay?" she said, her voice breaking. But within minutes she had composed herself and was talking to the press about how the family intended to give back to the community and that they had high hopes for the nation. From the beginning, at least in public, Linda was impossibly composed.

"You can't fall apart, you can't take Valium and let it all seem like a blur," Linda told me, her voice edged with bitterness. People were often looking at her askew. Her stoicism was suspect. What kind of a mother doesn't wail once in a while? "People encounter horrible things all the time, and the way it is approached in society is so awful. They want to know: why don't you show more emotion? Well, you have to keep a degree of privacy and integrity. I'm not some stupid idiot! Amy would not want that."

On that first day in Gugulethu, Peter and Kim stared at bystanders, people who gathered together and craned their necks from their front yards to see what the ruckus was about. Many of these same people, Kim and Peter believed, must have seen Amy chased down and beaten. Back in the States, they had always imagined that the site of her death was more isolated. It had not occurred to them that so many people had been so close to Amy, in such a central space, but had done nothing to save her.

"How could they just watch that?" Kim, standing on NY1, asked one of the many reporters eager to get a sound bite. "Just like they were watching us is the way I imagine them watching my sister being killed."

"My God," Peter said softly. "Why didn't somebody help her?"

Everyone placed bouquets of flowers on the dry grass—irises, carnations, and native South African bird-of-paradises: the vibrant, spiky-petaled, rainbow-colored flowers in the shape of a bird in flight were Amy's favorite. She'd always hated roses. The torn lock of Amy's hair had been cleared away long ago, but the white fence was still stained with her blood. The smears looked like handprints.

On that first visit, South Africans of all colors had approached the Biehls to offer condolences. Then, almost inevitably, they followed up with a request for help.

"What can you do for us?" they asked, again and again.

"What do you need?" the Biehls replied.

The power dynamics of centuries had entered into the communal bloodstream. The relationship between blacks and whites had long been that of recipient and sponsor, so those asking for help had lists at the ready: money, donations, desks for schools, soccer balls. Plus, everyone assumed that Americans had infinitely deep pockets, as a matter of birthright. Once, a young man got into my rickety hatchback in Gugulethu, looked around, and asked, confused, "You're from America? But where is your Ferrari?"

Linda and Peter, at a loss, said yes as much as they could. They had stacks of small personal checks that had been sent by sympathizers to their home in California and they didn't quite know what to do with the money, so they began to funnel it back into South Africa. They were energized, not by hate for those who had killed Amy, but by a love for their daughter. She would have wanted this, they believed. How could they deny her? In South Africa, they felt so close to her.

After the Biehls had spent time at the spot of Amy's death, ANC and city organizers whisked them away to tour a squatter camp. As the cars disappeared, a group of local children streamed by the Caltex, singing a song.

"Settlers, settlers, viva APLA, viva APLA!"

After our first breakfast meeting, Linda and I spent the next two weeks together—"hitched at the hip," she said. The unspoken deal was that I would drive Linda everywhere in exchange for time that we could spend talking. I am a verbal person by nature and have the capacity to talk, nonstop, for hours. With similarly chatty friends, I can hold conversations for days, breaking only for sleep and shower, while quieter folks like my husband or mother have often begged me to leave them in peace. But I have nothing on Linda Biehl. By the end of a day with her, I was usually shattered into silence. It was a novel experience: I have never been out-talked before or since. She had something to say at every second of every day.

"Makhulu, she can talk, she can drink," Easy once said, shaking his head as we both slumped on a seat after a day with Linda. He recalled meeting up with Linda in New York City back in 2002 to address the conference of the American Family Therapy Academy on issues of reconciliation. Ntobeko had gone, too, and the two young men had followed Linda around the city on foot, gasping for air as she strutted ahead. "And she can walk and walk and walk."

That trip was a leap of faith for Easy: his first time on a plane, his first time out of South Africa. When Linda had offered him an all-expenses-paid trip to America, Wowo and Kiki had warned him that he was risking death or imprisonment. That Linda lady is real nice to you here in our country, but wait until you get to her country. Just wait. May as well say your goodbyes now and prepare yourself for jailhouse suppers.

Still, Easy had gathered up his courage and headed for New York. But a small part of him believed his parents. Worse, as Easy noted, "planes can crash." Upon ascent—an otherworldly sensation that Easy was not eager to repeat—he sat bolt upright in his window seat, convinced that death was imminent. He stayed that way for the entirety of the sixteen-hour flight from Johannesburg to JFK airport, never once unbuckling his seatbelt. He watched longingly as other passengers wandered around, and he wondered how he would die: as the plane tumbled toward the earth or by Linda's vengeful hand?

To complicate matters, drinks on planes were, apparently, miraculously free, and so Easy had begun to down tiny whiskey bottle after tiny whiskey bottle, hoping to pass out. Instead, he'd been unable to sleep, and his unmoving feet and legs swelled to nearly double their normal size. Upon disembarking, Easy and Ntobeko had been briefly held and interrogated by customs, on account of their criminal records, and by the time Easy reached the arrivals gate, he hardly had time to hug Linda before dropping his duffel bag at her feet and flying off into the distance, yelling, "Yho, yho, yho, I need the loo!"

"Linda has me so tired, Easy," I said, after my first week with Linda.

"I *know*! Nomzamo, I know!"

Mostly, I trailed Linda. We went to a movie set near the airport, where producers had re-created the scenes from Mandela's autobiography, *Long Walk to Freedom,* for the movie starring Idris Elba, which would come out in 2013. A fake Robben Island prison had been erected, to model the infamous facility off the Cape Town coast. Black and colored and Indian actors were dressed as prisoners, in rags. White actors were outfitted in retrograde guard uniforms. It was all so believable. One white guard, on his lunch break, smiled at me while eating a cheese sandwich. I glared back, forgetting he was not a real warder. The streets of 1950s Soweto—where Mandela spent his formative years—had been painstakingly rebuilt, little muddy lanes of red-brick houses so nice that some of the laborers, picked up from the townships, wondered if they could move in. Linda glided through the set like a pro, giving commentary to a director working on a "Behind the Scenes" featurette. He was an overweight fellow in his sixties, and he whispered that Linda was "a fox."

I followed Linda on a private tour of the real prison of Robben Island, guided by her good friend Ahmed Kathrada. Kathrada is a South African legend, an Indian Muslim activist who was imprisoned along with Mandela for twenty-seven years, and later served in

Parliament. Kathrada was then over eighty, and still considered Mandela a brother. Over the years, he and Linda had become close, and some mornings they read the paper together at the Mount Nelson Hotel.

"She grieves too much," Kathrada once told me, sitting in his modest apartment in the city center. "For Peter, for Amy, she never stops."

When I met Kathrada, on the ferry to Robben Island, he was a fragile elderly man wearing wire-rimmed spectacles, a hearing aid, and a ten-year-old promotional windbreaker that said NEW PARTNERSHIP FOR SOUTH AFRICAN DEVELOPMENT. He was accompanied by a mild-mannered white man whom he introduced as "my warder, Chris." The man who had kept watch over him for so many years in prison now helped him show visitors around the island.

Linda's American friends were with us: husky Missourians who wanted to make a difference in South Africa and had been devoted to the foundation for years. Kathrada and Linda chatted in the cabin of the ferry as we rode over the rough waters. I tried to take notes, grew queasy, and had to clamber up to the open top deck for air. Kathrada led us around the windswept island, showed us Mandela's seven-by-nine-foot cell in a cavernous empty block. Here, he slept on a thin straw mat, relieved himself in a bucket, and wore short pants and no socks, a uniform the authorities used to remind black prisoners that they were perennially boys, not men.

A professional guide, giving his own private tour, passed by, saw Linda, and doubled back. He grabbed her hand.

"It's an honor to meet you," he said.

Kathrada explained to us the organizing principles of Robben Island. Colored and Indian prisoners were allowed one ounce of fat daily, while blacks received only a half ounce. Coloreds and Indians got an ounce of jam or syrup daily, while blacks got none. Coloreds and Indians received six ounces of meat, blacks got five ounces. Blacks' main source of nourishment was a drink reserved for them only: *puzamandla,* a sour powdered energy drink that was to be mixed with water. The men wore thin uniforms, cold in the island winters, and worked in quarries, breaking down limestone—a task that eventually damaged Mandela's eyes.

"But the greatest deprivation of prison is that there are no children," Kathrada told us. You never heard the voices of children, never saw them playing in the street, nothing for nearly thirty years. Kathrada never had children of his own, anyway. He was sent to prison when he was thirty-four and released when he was sixty. But a lawyer came to visit him once, and for lack of childcare the man brought his young daughter along. Kathrada remembered that day as one of the greatest.

After the tour, we all went to lunch at the waterfront, and Kathrada ordered a tall ice cream sundae with whipped cream and hot fudge and ate it all with relish, sometimes so consumed with his dessert that he zoned out of the larger conversation completely.

Linda adored Kathrada, and her times with him were precious. But she also liked taking interviews, visiting the townships, and meeting with friends and acquaintances that passed by her office. She thought a lot about her movie option with Sony Pictures, which had been renewed for years before eventually expiring in 2013. The option had helped her out financially—plus, she was keen on getting a movie made, and keeping Amy's memory alive (in March 2016, Tyler Perry announced that he had come on board to produce a film about Amy). She treated herself to a Champagne brunch on Sundays, and favored Eggs Benedict. Though she now lived on Peter's pension, she would often buy gifts for her staff—baby clothes, suitcases, things she had gleaned they needed.

Linda also loved holding court before anyone who was willing to listen, and told a series of stories on repeat: funny stories of culture clash and misunderstanding, fascinating stories starring South African leading lights, dull stories starring her grandkids, profound stories of courage and forgiveness. There was the time Ntobeko bought a fancy teddy bear on his debit card, which signified his burgeoning success as a man in the world.

"He could've been in prison, he could've been dead," she told a reporter. "But he dared to be different. He chose to be brave and reconcile with us."

There was the watershed moment when Peter and Linda took the young men on their staff to lunch and the men said, "When we get married, we want to be friends with our wives instead of having them as property." There was the time Linda was presented with an award for her stand against racism and she talked to President Thabo Mbeki—"So tiny! And in a big chair"—for an hour, on the economy of Zimbabwe. And the time Harry Belafonte serenaded her on her birthday, when she almost lost her cool, and *he* asked for *her* autograph.

On that first day I spent with Linda, after we left the cliffside hotel, we drove to the Amy Biehl Foundation offices. Linda swept onto the floor to mixed fanfare. Her core staffers—most of them black and into their forties—approached her with the shy excitement of children, exclaiming, "Makhulu!" When she hugged them, they said "Thank you" reverently. She tried to touch base with each employee, to remember their interests ("Queen, how is your family?"; "Ayanda, the fashionista!"). The mood in the space, often tense from the battles between staff and management, lifted when Linda arrived. She always brought gifts, suitcases full of children's clothes from Walmart. In the past, she had found ways to bring her favorite employees to America once in a while. When there, she took them shopping at Target and they gained weight by gorging on chocolate croissants. She was like the grandma of Hollywood fantasies, while their own grandmas, for whom most of them would lay down their lives, could hardly scrape together enough change for a sack of yams.

Soon enough, Ntobeko emerged from his perpetually closed office with the bearing of a sullen but secretly delighted teenager, and embraced her. Easy flew in late and yelped when he saw her, throwing his arms around her neck. But the new foreign interns were not in awe of Linda, and some recently hired employees were more reticent and formal. For the most part, they were removed from the history, born in a post-apartheid world.

Linda sat in her office, a room that had not been used in many months, since her last visit. The heat had been switched off, and it was freezing, which did not seem to bother her. The walls were decorated with oil paintings of white lilies and street scenes and photographs of Peter with Kofi Annan, of Peter and Mandela, of Madeleine Albright flanked by the Biehls. Linda kept a bit of limestone from Robben Island on a dresser and a chessboard on a desk.

Outside her office, the larger, communal space was decorated without any restraint, as though by a fun-loving, deranged group of hoarders: plastered wall-to-wall with children's drawings and framed diplomas and newspaper clippings and dusty homemade sculptures and oversized promotional cardboard checks and computer print-outs of inspirational quotes, with barely an inch of orange paint showing through.

"It gives me the heebie-jeebies," Linda said shuddering, gazing at the big carpeted room.

She sat in her office sanctuary, receiving visitors, chatting, and tapping away at her iPad. There was a video of her youngest grand-daughter playing the drums, and she showed it to most anyone who walked in the door.

A middle-aged French volunteer popped in and introduced her-self. "I'm thinking of how I can maintain my involvement, Linda," she said, bursting with enthusiasm.

"Me too," Linda answered dryly.

Linda was at a crossroads in her life. She was approaching seventy. She had been ten years widowed. Her parents were no longer alive and her brother, a cowboy-type famous for founding the Arizona Trail, a scenic hike that stretches from Mexico to Utah, had died a few years earlier. Amy had been dead for nearly twenty years, the amount of time that Linda had spent traveling between two conti-nents, leading two very different existences. In America, she was a mom, a grandma, an upper-middle-class, left-leaning moderate who had lived comfortably in various suburbs from the moment she was born. In South Africa, she was the founder of a charitable foundation, an icon in the slums, the friend of many famous communists, and a minor celebrity, especially within the black township community.

Once, she had presumably liked the schism. When she arrived in South Africa, even though she did so as the result of a tragedy, the country was in the midst of rapturous change, and she had been swept up in that glory. "Free at last! Free at last!" people yelled. The leaders of the righteous revolution, the country's liberators, had embraced Linda Biehl of Geneva, Illinois, as their own, and she had suddenly been elevated to a figure in the transformation from apartheid to democracy. She had been offered a place in world history.

But after two decades, South Africa was mired in scandal and disappointment. Linda was one of millions who had dreamed of a soaring new nation and had seen the place instead falter under heady expectations, endemic corruption, flagging economic growth, debilitating rates of unemployment, excessive levels of crime, and persistent racism. There is an impossibility to South Africa, an undercurrent of aggression and tension that flows beneath the surface and bogs down everything, and Linda was up against it.

In 1997, USAID, the American government foreign aid program, had approached the Biehls and offered them significant funds to set up a foundation. But the agency only agreed to provide funding for a set number of years. By the time Peter died, in 2002, the funding had come to a close and Linda was alone with dozens of employees and no source of cash. South Africa was no longer a cause célèbre; the world had refocused its sympathies. Linda, shocked by Peter's sudden death but keenly aware that staff members and a community depended on the foundation, returned to South Africa. She sustained the organization, using foundation savings for salaries and expenses, until 2005, when they had to get serious about raising dough.

The timing was tricky: Linda had to double down on her devotion to the foundation just as her kids in the States were having more children themselves. She was by then heading into her sixties and traveling nonstop. She felt guilty about abandoning her children.

Linda told me immediately, and repeatedly, how she disapproved of her foundation manager, Kevin Chaplin—a disapproval that, over the years, would grow into what seemed to me to be unadulterated fury. Kevin was tall and soft-bodied, with a slight brown mullet, a weak chin, and a shiny white face that was arranged into a permanent toothy grin. He had a closetful of crisp pastel dress shirts, wore a gold watch, and drove a luxury SUV. He bounded rather than walked, clapped flamboyantly whenever he had a good idea, and spoke at top volume, with a rolling trill of an accent.

"I was a provincial bank manager when I was forty-one," he told me. "The U.S. ambassador called me up and said, 'I want you to meet Peter Biehl,' so I went to his office and I was so impressed with him." Peter died soon after.

Kevin claimed that he had stayed involved with the foundation on a volunteer basis, and then one day Linda called him. "She said, 'It's no pressure, but if you don't take over, I'll have to close the foundation down,'" he told me. So in 2006, he quit his bank job and took over as managing director of the Amy Biehl Foundation. Kevin was a self-professed "catalyst for change."

When I spoke with Kevin, he spent a portion of our meeting gazing at his wall, hung with medals, awards, and framed pictures of him with his arm slung around a diverse bunch of luminaries and everyday people, and he hollered merrily for the foundation's receptionist to come in and rearrange them. He bemoaned the lack of integration in South African society and recounted taking his old bank colleagues for a luncheon in Gugulethu, a prospect at which they initially balked and for which they later thanked him.

"Ninety-eight percent of white South Africans and coloreds have never been in townships," he said, snapping his fingers.

"Where does that number come from?" I asked.

"It's just something I say!"

Kevin referred to Archbishop Desmond Tutu as "Arch," and considered the bishop a friend. He said his mentor was the supermarket magnate Raymond Ackerman, a founder of South Africa's Pick n Pay supermarket chain. He considered Ntobeko Peni his protégé.

In his spare time, Kevin ran a series of networking breakfasts intended to bring together entrepreneurs of different colors. As soon as I sent him a single email, I was added to his Listserv and for years received invitations to attend these breakfasts. The guest speakers spoke on topics such as "Cultural Warmth," "How to Lead in Challenging Times," and "Embracing Diversity and Inclusion in the Workplace." To hear their words of wisdom, you simply paid 150 rand and showed up at this hotel or that conference center. The buffet breakfast was included.

These days, whatever love had once existed between Kevin and Linda had been lost, and the two were engaged in a complex, transatlantic power struggle, with Linda at the losing end. She and her board had appointed Kevin to his post but contact had since broken down. These days, she complained that her emails went unanswered and her suggestions unheeded. Linda worried that the foundation was merely an employment base for people with their own personal agendas. She feared that Amy's spirit had been washed away.

"Kevin wants the power and the name," she said.

Linda began to speak openly of her growing disdain for Kevin, telling a newspaper and a radio show that they disagreed on the direction of the foundation. Publicly, he kept mostly mum. In July 2012, when I joined Linda at the office, Kevin had planned a European family holiday for the weeks during which Linda would be around. In 2013, on the twentieth anniversary of Amy's death, the two were openly at odds.

In the mid-1990s, the Biehls had written out a statement of purpose, printed near a photo of smiling Amy balancing a water jug on her head: *The Amy Biehl Foundation seeks to encourage the peaceful study, understanding and practice of democratic principles in the lives of people and nations. Special recognition is given to gender rights and to full participation of women in the democratic process.*

To Linda's dismay, the Amy Biehl Foundation no longer aimed for such a goal. The waning media attention focused, largely, on Linda's remarkable relationship with Easy and Ntobeko. More problematic was the fact that, after a series of negative experiences, Ntobeko usually refused to give interviews. Easy, meanwhile, agreed to speak to reporters, but then skipped his appointments. He also struggled with English, which he spoke with a heavy accent. In this way, the foundation slipped closer to obscurity.

By the late aughts, the foundation, under Kevin's tutelage, stuck to a single purpose: to provide after-school programs on the Cape Flats, where two thousand underprivileged children danced, played the marimba, drew, or practiced reading. To make some extra money, the foundation offered visitors a tour of the townships and of their programs for $50 a pop.

I never had to pay to see the programs, and I was allowed to travel along with the tourists a couple of times. On my first jaunt, I accompanied a group of Eastern Europeans, who obsessively clicked and snapped away on their iPhones and iPads and Canons and Nokias and Sonys and flip-cams. The kids, hoping for attention or free pens or lollipops or hats, tripped over themselves to look extra adorable for the tourists. Township children had learned immediately to break into poses whenever a lens was trained on them. Seeing white folks hop out of a van, the kids arranged themselves into a delightful human pyramid.

"Everyone say I love—" a tourist ordered.

"Numeracy!" half the group hollered.

"Jesus!" the other half shouted.

The kids flashed peace signs. They screamed, "Cheeeeese, cheeese!"

The Eastern Europeans were taken to a dance class, and for unknown reasons I was shuffled into a room full of ten-year-old girls, who looked at me expectantly. The local staff was accustomed to showing foreigners these cute Gugulethu kids who were benefiting from the Amy Biehl Foundation programs, and the kids hammed it up.

"So, what are your names and how old are you?" I asked, at a loss. There was no teacher in sight. "What stories do you like?"

Princess and the Pea. Cinderella. Mickey Mouse. Dora the Explorer. Hannah Montana.

They were eager to practice their English. They were buoyant. Finally, their teacher, a twenty-three-year-old beauty with copious rouge and long braids, entered the room. She was fit and impeccably groomed. One little girl, frowning, reported something in Xhosa.

"She is saying to me, 'Why did I bring this woman who is saying swear words?'" the teacher informed me.

I felt my face go red.

"Sorry? We just talked about their names and ages." I imagined a scandal in which a debased American was accused of teaching innocent South African children nasty terminology.

"I believe that she is saying you said swear words because she does not understand one thing in English!" the teacher said. She glared at my accuser, who crossed her arms.

"We talked about fairy tales," I said, scanning my young audience.

"Yes, we did," one girl, my sudden ally, said.

"Speaking of fairy tales," the teacher said, dismissing the incident and looking at the girls, "tell me about your fairy-tale wedding."

My defender blushed, confused.

"There must be a cake," the teacher said. Weddings were on her mind. "And a groom! A groom. A man. A man and a woman, okay? No woman and woman. You marry a man." The girls leaned in, wide-eyed. "You get a dress."

"The white dress," I said, happy to divert attention to more pleasant matters.

"Can the dress be pink?" the teacher asked me. Suddenly, I was a wedding expert. The little girls were captivated.

"It can be whatever color you want. It's your wedding. I like cream."

"Cream? Cream is okay?"

"Cream is *in*."

"But how do I get the man?" the teacher asked. Now she looked deflated. "How do I get a proposal?"

"Threaten him. Tell him he commits or he's out!"

"But what if he doesn't come back?"

"He must! He must come back!"

The teacher wanted me to stay and counsel her on matrimonial dos and don'ts, about which I knew precisely nothing. But Easy was standing at the door, beckoning me to come along with him. I looked at my wee accuser; in a different sort of situation, she could have brought me down. At moments like that, my whiteness, my foreignness, my otherness, seemed like a grave liability. All the safety and calm that I enjoyed in the townships were exposed as fragile constructs that could be toppled.

In addition to its after-school programs, the foundation also put on summer camps and took kids swimming at the Sea Point pool overlooking the Atlantic Ocean. The kids attended traditional African dance classes, and the worst dancer in the room, a five-year-old, embarrassed me with her prolific talent. The kids also received charitable lessons from fancy schools in the suburbs, where flute teachers and ballet teachers offered their services once a week. With the exception of these outings, most of the kids rarely left the township.

The obstacles to going to town were often insurmountable for your average township parent. Specialized music or art lessons were a distant dream. Amusement parks and botanical gardens and fairs—all of which were set in the city or its suburbs—cost money. You also had to have the energy to spend your free day taking kids on an expedition, which usually involved walking some distance to a minivan taxi, loading them in and out, and traipsing to your destination, carrying what you needed. Consider also the fact that most households were brimming with children: could you really take two and leave six behind?

The logistical and financial difficulty of taking a child to a park—or a music or dance lesson—was compounded by the fact that grand-mothers often ran households; they were in their sixties and seventies, and from a time when such activities were inaccessible to black peo-ple. If parents ran the households, they often worked long and ex-hausting weeks at low-paying jobs, and had to spend any free time cleaning, shopping, doing laundry, ironing school uniforms, and cook-ing. All of these factors combined to mean that without programs like those run by the Amy Biehl Foundation, thousands of township kids would spend their summers and after-school hours either watching television, playing on the streets, or getting into trouble.

Linda knew that the kids, who had nowhere else to go after school or on holiday, enjoyed the programs. But these programs had little to do with her initial vision of a foundation devoted to nurtur-ing Amy's passions: women's rights, racial equality, democracy. How did the foundation in its current state reflect her daughter or the Biehl family values?

"Amy's legacy is not after-school programs in Gugulethu," Linda said. "It should be a much broader, more intense, rigorous kind of environment that can lead to more international understanding."

Without the strong, warm leadership of a committed Peter and Linda, the foundation seemed to lose some of its moorings. In one incident, Kevin attempted to sell expensive vitamin juice to board members. In a lengthy 2012 email to two of Linda's close friends and supporters of the foundation, Kevin detailed the miracle of Juice Plus.

> Since taking the product I have never felt better and [my wife] too. . . . [My wife] has been on Menopause tablets and her skin has been constantly coming out in a rash, but since taking this prod-uct it has cleared up for the first time and stayed clear. One of my customers in France who has been on it for 3 months recently sent me an sms to say thank you so much, it is working so well. I met a British Headmaster who, through stress as kids got naugh-tier at school and life more complicated, was constantly getting

colds and heartburn, but since taking Juiceplus for about 8 years he has never had colds or flu or heartburn.

The message was set above a signature identifying Kevin as the managing director of the Amy Biehl Foundation. Upon finding out about it, Linda forwarded it to me. "Talking about his wife's menopause rash!" she exclaimed desperately.

Foundation employees expended energy on strange endeavors. Nonmanagerial staff, for example, were usually required to spend Friday mornings at Pick n Pay supermarkets across town, hawking Amy's Bread and Amy's Wine to bored shoppers. These were items made by local bakeries and wineries that had entered into partnership with the foundation and gave a small portion of their profits as a charitable donation. Once, in the course of an interview, I accompanied a worker to a downtown location. He was a middle-aged black man in a largely white market. He looked small, bored, and humiliated. "I am here for the Amy Biehl promotions," he said uncertainly to a supermarket manager. The manager gave him the side-eye and shrugged his shoulders, so we walked over to the bread aisle and the staffer stood awkwardly by the orange packages containing loaves seemingly identical to those in blue packages but priced slightly higher. *Amy's Bread*, each package said, *The bread of hope and peace*. The staffer, who had been doing this for over ten years, tried limply to interest a few women who were eyeing other loaves.

"It's not low GI," one woman said dismissively. "Low GI is the newest thing."

"Do you have white bread?" another woman asked.

"You want white wine?" the staffer said, and the two of them raced to the wine section, where a bottle of Amy's Wine was displayed.

"No, I said white bread!" the woman said, and they raced back to the bread section.

Another woman passed by. "Sure, I remember that girl, Amy," she said, and took a package.

The staffer had sold two loaves in forty-five minutes, and he wasn't planning on sticking around for another hour. He cut out early and we went to lunch. I accompanied several other employees—none trained in sales, all with experience working with children—on similar promotions, and the same story played out. A few years earlier, Easy had stood awkwardly by while a staffer had been confronted by a shopper who asked, "What is this forgiveness you're talking about? I don't even want to look at you! What is this woman doing, hiring the killers of her daughter? For her own benefit! I would never buy the bread."

More troublingly, despite Amy's obsession with helping poor black women rise up, black women were not represented in management positions—to Linda's dismay. The officious ex-British-military woman worked as a volunteer human resources executive, while two colored women occupied positions below Kevin, but the black women at the foundation worked in relatively lowly capacities: as secretaries and program facilitators. Ntobeko, who managed the staff, told me that he had been especially bereft after Peter's death, convinced that Linda could never manage as Peter had because she was female.

"All the bigger deals were made by Peter," Ntobeko said. "I just did not think Linda would be able to shoulder it. She will spend time with you talking nonsense in a man's world."

No matter what, Ntobeko was still Linda's favored son, and one of the reasons she kept coming back to South Africa. Linda sent me emails calling him "fabulous" and "brilliant." She spoke of his "incredible intuition."

"If he had any kind of normal childhood, he could be a huge leader," she said. He knew "when to talk." He was "a strategist." She was convinced that she knew him to the core, and vice versa. "We were doing an interview at a restorative justice conference in Milwaukee, and the man wanted to know if Ntobeko had ever looked me in the eye and said 'I'm sorry,' and his answer was, 'I don't have to tell her,'" she told me. "He feels it is there without talking about it."

Later, I began to suspect that there was another reason Ntobeko never said sorry.

Ntobeko usually held a small dinner in Linda's honor when she came to Cape Town. She sent me pictures of the spread, of Champagne flutes, platters of roasted chicken and ears of grilled corn.

This dinner party is amazing as Ntobeko was released from prison 13 years ago this month, she wrote after one gathering. *How could we have imagined this ever happening???*

After another such gathering, she sent me photos of them drinking Champagne together, and of clothing piled high at the fledgling wash-and-fold laundry business he and his wife were running from their garage.

Linda loved Easy, but his struggles were a disappointment to her. He was, she said, "the child you worry about more," the "foot soldier," while Ntobeko was a "colonel." Ntobeko's triumphs were Linda's triumphs. Ntobeko was living proof that Linda's efforts mattered, that her mercy could propel a neglected young man to a meaningful adult life. Once a prisoner with neither a high school diploma nor any significant job prospects, he was now supporting three daughters and a wife. Linda had, for many years, rented a loft in downtown Cape Town, and when she gave the place up, she donated her sleigh bed to Ntobeko. He kept the bed in a guest room, which he told her was "Makhulu's room"—a place for her in case she ever wished to live with him in her old age.

But their relationship was tangled up in the foundation. Soon after one dinner party, at the urging of Kevin and his team, Ntobeko wrote Linda to rally her support for some changes. In one instance, the foundation wanted Linda's blessing on a revamped logo and website. But Linda did not want to change the logo, a rudimentary pair of black and white hands, intertwined above a retro font spelling out the foundation's name. She and Peter had helped design it long ago. Ntobeko, Kevin, and their team, however, preferred a more modern take: sleek handprints, one black and one white, their thumbs overlapped, above more contemporary lettering.

Ntobeko was dispatched to try to convince Linda. He had recently enjoyed the services of a life coach, hired by Kevin, whose specialty was helping people "find their gifts." Ntobeko had found his gift as a businessman. On a practical level he was still "lining things up," he said. But he was learning about American tycoons, and was saying things like, "I can only coach those who want to be coached!" And "I don't count mistakes, I count efforts!" In his new role as a businessman, he had begun to study the concept of brand building. In his email to Linda, he argued that redesigns had boosted the profiles of a variety of South African corporations.

Vodacom has changed colours from blue & white to red & white (many people were so interested to find out what's going on, they are now Vodacom clients), he wrote. *Standard Bank . . . slogan has changed from STANDARD BANK Simpler Better Faster to SATNDARD BANK moving forward* [sic].

Linda received the email with sorrow. Amy's name was now the equivalent of a bank or a phone company. Linda reasoned that Ntobeko just wanted a man to "nurture" him, and Kevin—who was already "authoritarian"—took advantage of that.

Still, after reading Ntobeko's email, Linda decided that though she would remain close with Ntobeko on a personal level, she wanted to remove Amy's name from the foundation. She would do so on the twentieth anniversary of Amy's death, on August 25, 2013. The foundation, Linda felt, could adopt a new Xhosa name, and continue its work without her. She worried that if she were to die, her children would be saddled with some unforeseen scandal or controversy. A few years earlier, some colored kids had accused a black facilitator of sexual abuse—a charge, it was discovered, that they had made up, stoked by racial tensions. Linda wanted to protect her own children from such a mess, and she also wanted to move on, she said. She wanted a second act. She was thinking of going back to school to study art history, as Amy had once urged her to do.

We cannot afford to part ways with a winning brand, Ntobeko wrote.

"Amy was not a brand," Linda told me, her voice raised. "She was my daughter, she was a *person.*"

But here was a contradiction: at Linda's behest, Amy's name had been strewn across wine bottles and bread bags, on charity bracelets and on the sides of vans, on business cards and mailers, before a dot-org in email addresses, on the glass door and the metal sign, on the T-shirts of the kids, on pamphlets and newsletters. By now, the simple truth was that Amy Biehl *was* a brand.

And for all Linda's talk of second chapters, she kept coming back. She would claim to be done with the mess once and for all, and then she'd book a flight and return to the office. In South Africa, Linda was able to hold on to Amy. And if you looked at how Linda conducted her life, you could see that Linda, for all her talk of moving forward, had devoted herself to never letting Amy go.

At first I was shaken, not only by Linda's closeness with the men, but by how casually the three conducted their relationship. When Linda's friends came to town Easy drove the group around Gugulethu, pointing out relevant spots. I sat in the front, in between Easy and Linda. We passed a group of boys running laps by the highway.

"When Easy and Ntobeko were little, they were training like this, but they were also training to be part of military activities," Linda announced to the car. "Isn't that right, Easy?"

Linda's friends—a Midwestern family of three kids, two parents, and two grandparents—were recording each moment, with a variety of digital devices. They had come to administer charity, see how the poor lived, and take a little safari, too.

"Yes, Makhulu," Easy said.

"You had to be fit!" Linda said.

"Yes, Makhulu."

Later, Linda asked Easy to talk about Xhosa omens. She found the "beneath the surface" beliefs in black magic and ancestors fascinating.

"The ancestors come in different forms," Easy explained. He loved telling white people fantastical tales of African belief systems and did so with great flair. "Clean water is positive. A dog is good. Ancestors can come as a bee. Also, when the little child go to the neighbor's house, to the neighbor's toilet, to do a number two, that means that visitors will be coming."

"What? Your kid poops at your neighbor's house, and it means people are coming to visit?" I asked.

"Yah." Easy nodded.

"That just shows how earthy they are," Linda said to me.

We pulled up to a field and stood in the sunshine and watched the Amy Biehl Foundation kids play soccer, Ntobeko coaching and Easy making a quick play. Linda stood to the side, with so many little hands reaching for her. The smallest of the visiting children was spirited away by five girls from the townships, who placed her on the ground and started fussing with her hair.

"Ow!" she whined. "Ow, that hurts!" But the local girls didn't care and took to fashioning pigtails.

During these moments, I usually wondered: Why shouldn't Easy have a second chance? Why shouldn't Aphiwe be born? Why shouldn't Ntobeko own a beautiful home and support three daughters? Why shouldn't Linda find some modicum of purpose, if not peace, here? Even if the process was flawed, this seemed to be the best possible post-apartheid outcome: on the small scale, these personal relationships helped everyone thrive. I could understand Linda's approach of radical forgiveness: If you stood face-to-face with the person who had wronged you, and spoke with him, and looked in his eyes, it was hard not to see him as a human being; this, I suppose, was one of the hopes of the Truth Commission. When the enemy turns from an abstract notion or a caricature or a symbol into a person—and in the case of Easy and Ntobeko, a young and confused person—it is difficult to maintain your anger at him. And when he asks for forgiveness, it is hard to withhold it. On a good day, in a good moment, I knew why Linda loved Easy and Ntobeko, and their relationship made sense. If they grew into nonviolent members of society who did more good than bad, that was another sign that Amy's death and the process that unfolded beyond it wasn't in vain, and that Amy's principles had been worth holding to. In its small way, it meant that with the Truth Commission, the country had made strides forward, and that Amy had helped.

But many months later, I stared at crime scene photographs of Amy's brutalized body. She had been healthy, young, and small. She was one female against a throbbing male mob, and she couldn't explain away her skin color. I thought of how Linda complained that some staffers, Ntobeko included, ignored her emails. I thought of how Easy so often came late to work. I thought of everyone caught up in this odd web, always congratulating themselves and receiving congratulations on their own enlightenment. And I felt like the whole thing was one big fat joke.

11.

Long you must suffer, not knowing what,
until suddenly, from a piece of fruit
   hatefully bitten,
the taste of the suffering enters you.
And then you already almost love what
   you've savored. No one
will talk it out of you again.

—Rainer Maria Rilke

After Linda left Cape Town, Easy and I resumed our days together, wandering the townships. He brought me to meet his old friends. We drove by the cemetery, so full of bodies that they were now burying family members atop one another. Easy could divide the cemetery into time periods that corresponded to sociopolitical crises: here were the people who died of the ravages of poverty; here were those who died in riots and gang violence; here were the victims of AIDS. We drove by a smashed rat as big as a cat. We went to eat barbecued meat at Mzoli's—the famous eponymous barbecue joint owned by a former butcher who had sold meat from the back of his truck and had built the business into a township empire. Ragged street entrepreneurs controlled various parking spaces, which they guarded from vagrants for a fee, and in some instances you were essentially paying a drug addict to not break into your car.

"Parking special, 9.99," a guard informed me. "Payable up front."

"Where's my one cent back?" I asked, after I handed him a 10 rand note.

His face collapsed. "We just say 9.99, like in the supermarket. Is advertising."

"Ha!" Easy said. "She joking, my friend."

I spent time with Easy's pregnant girlfriend, Ndumi, a slender woman with a beauty mark on her right cheek and perfect white teeth. Ndumi had met Easy at a party five years earlier, at which time, she recalled, "Something happen in my mind . . . and in my *body.*" She recognized him from TV; she knew he'd killed Amy Biehl, and she regarded him as something of an anti-apartheid hero. Famous friends, no matter the source of that fame, were hard to come by in Gugulethu.

I sat in the sun with Monks, Easy's paralyzed brother. I sat on the couch with Wowo. I sat with the extended family around a TV, watching wrestling in grainy black and white. Easy's great-uncle glared at me when I entered.

"Kunjani?" he said. How are you, in Xhosa. Xhosa people compulsively greet each other and inquire into each other's state of being. *How are you? Are you well? Are you fine? Are you cool?* When people addressed me in Xhosa, it was sometimes a greeting and sometimes a test. In this case, judging by the man's expression, it was a test. The unspoken question was: You come here asking around, but have you bothered to learn our language?

"Ndiphilile. Kunjani wena, tata?" I asked. I'm well—and how are you, father? I had been taking night classes in Xhosa and had been practicing the clicks and the basics. One sixth of Xhosa words are estimated to contain click sounds. For the X, you slap your tongue against the side of your upper back teeth. For the Q, the hardest click to master, you pop your tongue on the roof of your mouth. For the C, you hit your two front teeth with your tongue and quickly suck in. For native Xhosa speakers, clicks are innate. For a student of the language, they are nearly impossible to perfect.

"Ndiphilile nam, enkosi," the old man said, his face breaking into a broad smile. I'm also well, thank you. Though his bearing was stern, he was easily satisfied—which was good, because greetings were as far as I'd gotten in my classes.

No matter what we did or where we went, again and again, Easy and I circled back to Amy's death, to his days in prison, to his childhood. We retraced the day, step by step, from the still standing school in Langa, down the railway line. Easy euphemistically called the spot where Amy was attacked "Amy's last home." But after months of listening to Easy and a single interview with the stubbornly mum Ntobeko, I knew that I also needed to find the two other men who had been convicted of Amy's murder. I needed their versions of the events of that day.

First, I looked for Mongezi Manqina, the alleged ringleader of the foursome, or at the very least the man widely believed to have stabbed Amy in the heart. He would be the easier of the two to find, since his mother still lived on NY1. One day, Easy and I drove to her house, which also functioned as a shebeen. Mongezi's mother was still there, after all these years, a large, slack-jawed woman with few teeth. She sold beer and sheep's head to locals.

I had seen her in old videos, interviewed upon Mongezi's release. Her daughters were rejoicing at their brother's return home, but she sat in the corner of her living room, eyeing Mongezi apprehensively. Only three years after he gained amnesty, Mongezi was rearrested, this time for raping a sixteen-year-old mentally handicapped neighbor, and he had come out of Pollsmoor again in 2011. According to Mongezi's mother, Mongezi no longer lived at home, but she handed Easy the number for Mongezi's cell. Easy called, and we decided to meet up the next day.

Mongezi lived in Philippi, the small township south of Gugulethu, and he wanted us to come to his house. It's difficult to give directions in the townships; if a person lives on a side street or in an informal settlement, there are no roads or house numbers. So Mongezi asked us to meet him on a bridge. As we made our way, Easy turned to me and said, "Don't worry, my friend. Just throw him the question and he will relax."

As we neared the bridge, the skies opened up and rain poured down. Mongezi emerged into view: tall and gaunt and sharply dressed in a houndstooth newsboy cap and a large black leather jacket.

"So thin," I said to Easy.

"Because prison."

Mongezi hopped into the back of my car, nodded at me, and directed me to drive back over the bridge and to then turn onto a dirt path.

"I have good news for you," Easy said, turning back.

"For me?" Mongezi asked, flattered. I could see him in the rear-view mirror, his face perpetually boyish. Easy, too, had the features of a child, but brawls and accidents had marred him. I remembered that once Easy had told me, "Prison makes you beautiful." Shielded from the sun and the elements, your skin becomes baby-soft. Indeed, with his youthful face, forty-year-old Mongezi looked almost precisely as he did in old newspaper photographs from nearly two decades earlier. The only difference was that while he had been lean but muscular in his twenties, he was now rawboned. The two men switched to Xhosa, but I could understand that Easy was telling Mongezi that he could reconnect him with his ex-girlfriend, for whom Mongezi had been pining. Mongezi's face lit up.

Meanwhile, I was navigating the dirt path, which cut through a trash-strewn field, covered with tufts of anemic grass, piles of dirty diapers, crumpled paper, empty soda bottles, beer cans, used condoms, and plastic bags balled up and bouncing in the breeze like tumbleweed. The path narrowed and then led underneath the bridge, where a few destitute, drug-addled men and women seemed to have constructed a living area, with a couple of mattresses and a dim garbage-can fire. To our right was a defunct railway track.

I did not feel entirely confident that I would leave this area with my car or my wallet. Moreover, the car technically belonged to my conservative in-laws, and I pondered how, were it to go missing, I might explain that I had voluntarily driven it to a strange, informal settlement set out of view on the outskirts of Philippi.

A small shantytown rose up past the turn: a hundred tin shacks crowded together in a dip of a hill, hemmed into a triangle of land by its circumstantial borders: the main thoroughfare we'd just turned off, the tracks, and the rise of the bridge. Few cars ever took the path, as evidenced by how skinny it was. Only one resident here owned a car, as far as I could tell, and whether or not it functioned remained unclear. It was a white jalopy with red paint splashed on its doors, locked behind a steel gate secured with a padlock. My driver's-side mirror hit the swung-open plastic doors of six pit toilets. Easy peered out of the passenger side as the car inched by the walls of shacks, urging me to keep going.

Passersby gawked as they slipped around the car. We drove until we came upon Mongezi's shack, which was the last and newest structure in the area. It effectively created a dead end to the road, placed between another, older structure and the track, and was separated from its neighbor by a thin, mucky footpath. The corrugated silver tin was shiny and new, having been erected only four days earlier. We got out of the car, Easy with my cellphone protectively shoved into his pocket, and entered Mongezi's home. It was the size of two office cubicles. To the right of the door sat a bed topped with a cherubic baby propped up on pillows. Across from the bed, against the wall, was a wooden dresser. A large, crackling flat-screen TV sat atop the dresser, along with a display of lotions, men's body spray, and a lady's hairbrush. Two ancient, weathered men were sitting on the dirt floor, mixing concrete by hand. A young woman was bent over a hotplate that sat on the ground, stirring a potful of beans and chicken trimmings.

"So," Mongezi said, looking at me and holding the door open with his foot. "Why do you even want to talk to me?" He lit a cigarette and held it cupped in his hand when he took a drag. "You talk to my comrade Easy. You know everything."

"Everyone has a different story," I began, hesitating.

"Did you talk to Ntobeko?" he asked.

"A little," I said.

"She talked to Linda," Easy added hopefully. He was now smoking Mongezi's cigarette, which the two were handing back and forth. "And everyone in the office, and also Nancy from America." Nancy Scheper-Hughes, the anthropologist, had met the men many years ago.

Mongezi seemed more convinced.

"I thought maybe we could go to Mzoli's," I said. "Get some food, talk."

"I don't have a problem with that," he said, perking up. "What about Vusumzi? Have you talked to him?"

"I haven't looked for him yet but would like to speak with him," I said. We were referring to the lost Vusumzi Ntamo, the other man convicted in Amy's murder. "Are you friends?"

"From when we were small."

From there, Easy and Mongezi began to briefly reminisce about their time in jail. They sounded like old college buddies, nostalgic for youth and its antics—the good ol' days, one would almost think from the way they were talking. But it was really just the common thread connecting two estranged men, a way of finding something to say. Prison had been a nightmare for both of them.

Meanwhile, the front door kept falling shut because the shack sat on a slight slope. When it did close, the only light streamed in weakly from a single plastic window covered, for privacy's sake, by a worn towel. The ancient men smoked their cigarettes and stirred their cement. If the purpose of Mongezi bringing me here was to impress the old cement mixers, it had failed. The pot of beans and trimmings simmered on the ground. The baby fell asleep. The woman was joined by a friend, and they sat together on the edge of the bed, listening to music on a cellphone, each with one earbud. A neighbor came by and stuck his head in. He was the president of the block committee, I was informed, and wanted to check on the building progress and collect his bribe. Mongezi and I made a plan to have lunch in a few weeks, and then Mongezi and Easy stood by the car, directing me on how to back out of the tight spot in a fifty-point turn.

"Is she going alone?" asked an old man in a red sweater who was passing by.

"No, I am going with her," Easy said.

"Good. Some of those boys up ahead are not right."

Easy got in the car and Mongezi gave me a fist bump and then sauntered back into his shack. As we squeezed past the pit toilets again, a teenage boy popped out of the web of shacks, clutching a hammer in his hand.

"Just keep going," Easy said.

The boy saw a pretty girl and pretended that he was going to attack her, and they both laughed. Then he skipped up ahead and disappeared. I swerved past one of the people that lived under the bridge, sped through the trash piles, and turned onto the paved road.

"I really didn't like that," I said. "Weren't you scared?"

"No, I was not," Easy said.

"Why not?"

"I know I am ready and Mongezi is ready," he said unconvincingly. "And I'm thinking, nothing can happen, because if something happen to you, your fiancé will have a lot of questions for me."

After we met Mongezi, Easy and I went to Maphinde's, a butchery-and-barbecue joint in Nyanga East and Mzoli's main competitor. We drank sodas and ate meat while a group of ladies ordered brimming platters of sausages and popped open fruit-and-vodka coolers. Their laughter and conversation were so lively and high pitched that we couldn't possibly talk, so we sat in silence, watching. After, we parked outside Easy's house and talked about our day. Rain beat down on the roof and the car windows fogged. Aphiwe came out and tapped on the window. Easy handed her a small takeaway box of lamb.

"She is my angel," Easy said, and we watched Aphiwe walk inside, her hair pushed into a knit cap.

"The conditions of Mongezi's house were not good," I said.

"I agree. But he is a man. He want to live in his own space with his family. Not at his mother's house."

"Would you live there?"

"Is only temporary, Mongezi's house," Easy said. Of course the shack was only temporary. To say it was permanent would be to admit defeat.

I drove home, and that night I found myself at dinner with a group of well-off white South Africans. Their house was near the Camps Bay beach, in the fanciest part of the city. It was made of concrete, with marble floors and a dunk pool on the patio. Table

Mountain rose behind us. All around the home, gates hemmed us in, threaded with electrified cable. All of the women wore diamond rings on their fingers.

"What kind of engagement ring do you have?" one asked, peering at my bare finger. The ring itself still sat locked in a safe, never to be flaunted in Gugulethu. Once, I was scared of being robbed, but now I was mostly embarrassed by my obvious fortune.

"It's a sapphire."

"Oh yes, because of the blood diamonds!" she said, referring to the fact that African diamonds are often mined in conflict zones, on the backs of impoverished locals, the profits used to finance warlords. She flashed a two-carat princess-cut stone floating in a square of sparkling chips. "I also don't like blood diamonds, but I needed one for an engagement ring."

When I next saw Mongezi, he was standing on the same spot on the bridge. He popped into the car and said he didn't want to go eat, but rather that we could talk in a parking lot in Gugulethu and I could drop him at the train station. He worked as a night shift security guard. He quite clearly had devised a plan to try to eventually bilk from me the cash I would have spent buying him lunch.

"How's life?" I asked him.

"It's fucking terrible," Mongezi said. He smelled of winter air and sleep, and was wearing again his uniform of newsboy cap and leather jacket. "Work, school, work, school." He said he was studying information technology at the local community college. He was also on parole, which meant constant visits to his parole officer thirty minutes away.

"Or else they will pick me up and put me in jail for forty-eight hours," he said.

He placed his hand on the dashboard and I could see the dirt caked beneath his fingernails. We drove to Gugulethu, to the unused lot behind the Chickenland on NY1, just near the Caltex.

"I do remember the day of Amy," he said. He put a toothpick in his mouth, his signature. He spoke slowly. He had a young daughter who lived with her mother in the Eastern Cape. He had been a member of the 28s prison gang. The prisons in the Western Cape boasted three legendary gangs known as the Numbers: the 26s, the 27s, and the 28s. The 28s were known for proving their mettle by stabbing disagreeable prisoners and guards alike; they lived by a strict, complex code and divided their members into warriors and sex slaves. Sex slaves were required to have homosexual relations with 28s who so desired.

The 1999 rape for which Mongezi had been convicted after he was released from prison, he insisted, was a misunderstanding: he had no idea that the girl was developmentally disabled, and plus, she was into him, and plus, her family and his family had had a feud and so that was why they went to the police, because they wanted money and his mom couldn't give it.

"It wasn't rape, that one. I never know she is, how you say, abnormal. She's quiet and anything you say to her, she agree. But this woman wants me."

But no matter the specifics, Mongezi had done his time for that crime, too. He'd been doing his time since he was a teenager, when he used to rob houses throughout the city—he'd just slip in and steal whatever he could get his hands on. Now he was on the straight and narrow, he swore. He was happy to think back to the Struggle years, when even a petty crook like him could be part of something bigger, something that could shake history.

"In '93, everything is happening. We will rule the location, the cities, all of them, you see. We fighting for our right. So that time going from Langa, then we came back. I don't know Easy correctly. Same Ntobeko. Vusumzi, we grow up together. Vusumzi doesn't know anything about politics, but he was coming with me to the launch. In Langa, we see property of government, so we destroy the truck. We singing the song of apartheid. There is a lot of songs we are singing."

Mongezi's version of the day of Amy's murder began in Langa, as did all versions, and ended in Gugulethu, where marchers were trying to overturn and loot another truck ("It was a march of repossession") when Amy drove up.

"I see behind the truck is a white woman. Amy Biehl leave her car and I follow her and I trip her three times and it doesn't fall and then finally is falling. She fall on that pole and turn around and looks at me. We face each other. I hit her with my stone. I believe I hit her in the head. Then the others come. This other guy come running around with a knife. He borrow me that knife and I sat on her thighs and I stab her. She said, 'What did I do?' She said, 'I'm sorry.' Then they come one by one with stones, and I stepped back and watched to avoid the stones. I was not alone, but I took the lead. Easy and Ntobeko were coming after me, with others."

"Why were you so intent on killing her?"

"I don't know," Mongezi said, looking puzzled. "What I can say is I was just crazy. I was craving to do something to white people."

"Did you feel good?"

"I feel good at that moment. I thought she was a boer. Even the time I was arrested, I thought, 'No, this is cool.' It used to be that if you do such a thing to the white, the state will hang you. So I thought, they can hang me for my sin but I remain proud. I will have my memories."

"But she was not a boer."

"In the court, when they said it, I was shocked to find out this woman was not South African. I was disappointed that I did not do my job properly."

Three men strutted by on the side of the road, waving sticks.

"Do you hate me?" he asked suddenly.

"Why would I hate you?"

"Because *I* killed Amy," he said. "Me."

"Why do you admit killing her now, but you denied it in court?"

"Ma'am, when you caught by the police, you must clear your mind. You must forget."

Once he and his three co-convicted were granted amnesty, the Biehl family stood before them like a shining white beacon of hope and opportunity. Mongezi wanted a piece, but only Easy and Ntobeko benefited from these now famous Biehls; they had somehow swindled the other two out of their due benefit.

"When we come from prison, we discuss to meet the Amy Biehls. I even had a contact number for them and we make an appointment. But Easy and Ntobeko go alone. I was released and journalists come from America and London and U.K., and they want the story. Easy and Ntobeko informed me that these journalists want to make money from us and so we can get money from them. I was stupid, really. I asked for the money, and Ntobeko stayed silent. The journalists were shocked and I looked like a fool. He looked good. Later, I was interested in the foundation, and so was Vusumzi. But they kick us out.

"When we were in prison, Biehls were asked by media what they think and Biehls say they forgive us," Mongezi continued. "Say they want to support us. I came to apply for the foundation and Mrs. Biehl and Mr. Peter trust me, but then when they meet Ntobeko, they change. I knew then that I will never be part of the parcel, and I don't want to beg. They open the foundation to help all of us but now only helps those two."

"You know, the foundation was founded to help the community," I said. "Not you personally."

Mongezi shook his head dismissively. He wasn't convinced, and he also had a point: the foundation had indeed helped the citizens of the townships, but it had certainly helped its employees, chief among them Easy and Ntobeko. They were a couple of uneducated men who had spent their formative years in prison, but who now collected regular paychecks and benefits, and had traveled to Europe and America. Mongezi, seeing Easy and Ntobeko driving cars, erroneously believed the Amy Biehl Foundation had been founded in part to aid in the rehabilitation of Amy's killers, and in this sense he had been grievously wronged.

Mongezi and I spoke for an hour, and then I drove him to Heideveld station. I was heading back to town, close to where he worked. People in the townships generally relished the chance to get a free ride in a private car, rather than pay to take the dangerous trains or crowded taxis, and I gave them a lift whenever possible. In this case, though it would have been easy for me to ferry Mongezi to his job, I did not offer. Something about Mongezi unnerved me—something desperate and ruthless. I stopped by the ticket office. As I had predicted, Mongezi hit me up for cash for a train ticket, which he claimed cost ten times more than what I knew to be the actual price. I negotiated him down and handed over a few bucks, which he took, disappointed.

"Seems like only people involved in this massacre were Easy and Ntobeko," he said before he slammed the door shut and headed for the tracks.

I felt like a kid who wants to hear the same bedtime story again and again: for comfort, or to better understand, or maybe hoping that this time some detail would shift to reveal a new, improved tale. I knew, from a rational point of view, that I should get on with my work: I had my characters and I had my narrative. In New York, publishers had been particularly interested in Linda Biehl, assuming that white American audiences would relate to her heroism and her grief, and one company offered me a book deal only if I would focus completely on her, relegating the black South African characters to background noise. But instead, I kept compulsively circling back to this township, driving the streets, asking the same worn-out questions about a long-ago story that had been told, nearly word for word, for almost two decades.

One afternoon, I called to arrange yet another meeting with Easy. He sounded particularly tired on the phone, but he encouraged me to come by, so I drove over to Gugulethu and waited in my car on a strip of mud across from his parents' house. I called him again, and he directed me to stay put; he was coming.

It was one of those spring rainstorms in Cape Town, when it seems that some invisible force has lifted all the water out of the ocean and poured it down onto the land. A drenched mama dog, her teats bloated and caked with blood, passed the car, sniffing for food. After twenty-five minutes, I peered through my misty windshield and made out a silhouette weaving down the street. The silhouette wobbled its way toward me, struggled with the door, and dropped into the passenger seat, consumed by an oversized rain slicker. Sprightly Easy was gone, and in his place was a limp rag doll with shooting pains from the bleeding ulcer that acted up when he drank.

"It's okay, my friend," he slurred. "I have a good interview for you. Drive."

Easy managed, miraculously, to guide me to a tidy house with a connected spaza shop, somewhere within Gugulethu. I parked the car on the sidewalk and followed him, slowly, through the rain. Inside, a group of people regarded me impassively. Easy motioned to a couch, onto which I lowered myself. He then fell softly to the ground, narrowly avoiding knocking over a propane heater. He righted himself and stumbled over to me, sat on the next cushion, and then fell asleep on my shoulder. Within seconds, he was snoring.

I looked around the room and, for lack of anything better to do, smiled. A heavyset young woman in a pink sweater, who had been staring grimly at me, broke into a broad smile in return. A slender old man in a trilby hat sat in the corner, silent but commanding, and he smiled, too.

The house was cozy, warmed by the pumping heater, humid from the storm, bathed in cigarette smoke and the saccharine sweat of drunk folks. People walked in and out, bringing brandy and beer, mixing cheap whiskey with soda, lighting cigarettes and letting them burn to ash. Stepping out of the cold and into the warm, humid room, they all briefly emitted that grassy smell of rain-damp skin. Outside, the water flooded the streets, overflowed from the gutters, and drenched the stray piles of garbage.

Ndumi, Easy's pregnant girlfriend, was sitting in the corner, wearing her coat wrapped over a pajama top and blue jeans. On her feet were plaid socks and loafers, which gave the impression that she had simply rolled out of bed and walked across the township. She was studiously ignoring Easy and flipping through an old *YOU Magazine*.

Easy vacillated between sleep and wakefulness, occasionally leaning forward to gulp a beer. But when a certain man entered, Easy perked up.

"Justice, this is Masana," he announced. Even when dead sober, even after I had known him for many years, Easy alternately addressed me as Justice, Justin, and Justine, and remained unconcerned by any inaccuracy or inconsistency. "He was my commander."

"My sister," Masana said, in a voice like coal. He shook my hand, lowered himself onto a chair, and lit a cigarette.

Masana was forty-five years old and his mouth was set in a permanent smirk. He sported a deep scar by one eye and wore a black wool hat, sewn with the Heineken logo, pulled low. He rolled his shoulders forward, which made him look slinky and untrustworthy. Rumor had it that he once murdered a man with his bare hands in broad daylight before an audience and then strolled off. Ever since, Masana could walk alone in Gugulethu at night and even the most reckless little smokehound knew well enough to stay away.

"They come to rob me, I rob them right back," he rasped.

Masana was alternately unemployed or working hard labor on contract jobs: at the train tracks, at the electric yard, or a few months mining in Sierra Leone. According to Masana, black South African men were gathered up by mining corporations and shipped on contracts to West Africa to dig for diamonds; they were slightly more expensive to employ than impoverished Sierra Leoneans, but they were easier to manage and more skilled. But even with these inter-mittent jobs, Masana owned next to nothing. He lived in a shack in a nearby township, and he showered once in a while at his sister's house. Men like him, he noted, were the government's "last priority."

"I'm a big man," he said. "Where is my own place?"

Masana wasn't shy, and he launched into a potentially fanciful tale that deposited him in the center of the South African border wars, in exile in Zambia, and fighting for freedom in the bush as a guer-rilla. When he returned from Zambia, or maybe it was before that, he claimed that he had helped train Easy in guerrilla warfare and PAC ideology.

"Tell her, m'Africa," Easy said, using the PAC's Struggle term for a comrade, which literally means "African." Across the room, Ndumi flipped angrily through her magazine.

"I liberated people from their lives," Masana said as the old man in the trilby looked on impassively. "Killing was victory."

"You white, you classify as settler," Easy added.

"Amy Biehl didn't belong here," Masana reflected back to that day. "Why did her friends bring her here? They knew the situation in our location."

For Masana, the two black women who asked Amy for a ride home were at fault. They should have known better. He shook his head. The place was all burning tires and protests; you couldn't miss it for the world.

"You blame her friends?" I asked, incredulous.

"Yes," Masana said without pausing.

"*You* blame her friends?" I asked Easy.

Easy roused himself. "Yes," he said and nodded.

"You blame yourself?"

Easy shook his head. "No," he said. He looked past me, his eyes unfocused, and then fell back asleep, now in the crook of my arm. I moved to the side, cradled his head, and placed it on a small pillow. He let out a little sigh.

"My organization, we see white, we kill," Masana continued. "Even if you have white friend who want to come here, you must tell them no. You must say, 'I love you. I don't want to lose you.'"

The woman in the pink sweater brought out a tray of glasses full of a dense, juice-type concoction. A nearby jug did little to further identify the liquid. ORANGE SQUASH, it read.

"If you are white, you are enemy," Easy piped up again.

"Do you hate whites?" I asked Masana.

"Then yes, but not now," Masana said. He smiled. "Now I'm flexible."

I asked Masana to tell me about Easy the soldier.

He was good, Masana said: eager, and fearless. He wouldn't back down from battle or compromise a friend or comrade, but his main strength, as far as Masana could tell, did not lie in his fighting bravado. His main strength, Masana said, was cheering folks up. No matter how bad you felt, Easy could always turn it around.

"And his weaknesses?" I asked Masana.

"You seeing it now," Masana said, motioning to Easy, who had turned to one side. "When he drink, he lose focus."

"The township is full of frustrations," the woman in the pink sweater added. "We're all living this life."

Later that afternoon, I rose to leave, and the old man tipped his trilby. Ndumi shuffled behind us, grumbling, and climbed furiously into the backseat.

We rode over to a settlement called New Rest, just down the street from NY111. There, we visited Easy's aunt, a woman named Princess who lived in a simple one-bedroom set on the mud. A male nurse was sitting there, a nice guy, drinking beer. The family was constantly self-medicating for their ailments and I realized that this person, a cousin, was everyone's source for pills; tell him what you need, he'll pocket it at the clinic. This led to mass confusion over illness and cures, but I knew why nobody ever went to state-run hospitals unless they were utterly desperate.

"You get there at nine and you leave at five," Ndumi explained to me. Whenever she had a prenatal checkup, she left the house at 6 A.M. to begin queuing. If she was lucky, she'd be home by three.

I had once accompanied Easy and Aphiwe to such a clinic in Khayelitsha, where hundreds of black people sat on rows of wooden benches for the entire day. The bathrooms at the clinic lacked soap and toilet paper, though the staff, unaccustomed to seeing white people, assumed that I—in my T-shirt and sneakers—was a doctor or another person worthy of special treatment, and swept me into an employees' bathroom. After, Aphiwe had her tooth pulled by the dentist. She lay down stiffly in the chair, her toothpick legs out-stretched. In a matter of seconds, the dentist, an older bald black man dressed in a polo shirt, held out his hand. The nurse handed him an enormous hypodermic needle. The dentist squirted a substance into the air once and then, swiftly propping Aphiwe's mouth open with his hand, began to insert the gigantic needle into her gum. Her tiny body tightened immediately, she let out a shocked screech, and closed her mouth as tears began to stream down her cheeks. Easy screamed at her to "*vula*"—open. As she complied, the dentist jammed the needle in and pulled it out. Aphiwe went limp. Next, the old man reached in with a pair of heavy steel pliers and ripped her molar from her gum. For a split second, the room froze and the dentist stood still, brandishing high above his head a tooth held be-tween two prongs. Then Aphiwe let out a full-throated wail, bolted from the room, flew into the waiting room, and flung herself to a chair and then to the floor, where she let out a series of loud, bro-kenhearted moans and spat out a stream of blood. People in the waiting room calmly shuffled their chairs out of the way. Easy lifted her by the shoulders, pressed some gauze in her mouth, wrapped her school sweater across her chest to stop the blood from further stain-ing her yellow shirt, and marched her out of the clinic.

In New Rest, Princess's table was covered with bottles of lemon soda. The walls and couch were blue, the shelf dotted with a few pictures: a young girl in a school portrait, a man and woman kissing. The TV was blaring, connected to speakers with a heavy bass beat.

"See how we living?" a guy piped up, handing his cigarette to the person next to him. "Socialist."

Princess flashed me a wide smile. She was bone-tired and lonely, with close-cropped hair, no front teeth, and teary eyes. Her husband had died, followed closely by her only son, who, undone by grief, overdosed before he turned twenty-one. She worked in a factory all day and invited everyone to drink in her living room at night, beneath a blowup print of her late son at his dad's funeral. A few years earlier, the cops came to Princess's house and punched her in the face when she opened the door, but it turned out they had the wrong address. She got her picture in the paper, a sixty-year-old lady with a bloody lip, but never a payout like she wanted. Once I glimpsed her walking home from the train station after a long day. Every step, it seemed, caused her pain.

"Don't you need somebody to work as domestic, sisi?" she asked me, hopefully. This was our little routine, every time we saw each other. "A few days a week?"

"I'm sorry, Princess, but I don't need."

"What about your husband, your boyfriend?" a young guy, a relative of some persuasion, asked. "Does he have a job for me?"

"Justice is from New York," Easy said.

"Can I take a train to New York?" Princess asked.

After Easy and Masana had topped up, and Easy had offered, weakly, to cook me an egg, I decided to leave. Easy and Masana hitched a ride, since they had plans to pick up supplies for further boozing. Easy folded into himself in the passenger seat and Masana helped me navigate the road and told me to stop just before the overpass and let them out. I pulled up onto a curb and put on my hazards. My wipers were flying frantically back and forth.

"I need fifty rand for bread, my sister," Masana said.

"Bread is eight rand, Masana."

"I need money, my sister."

I sensed that Masana was a person who had no qualms about slipping a knife to someone's throat as a way to settle a difference of opinion.

"Hayi, Masana," Easy protested mildly.

"I have some change here," I said, motioning to the ashtray, where I kept loose coins to tip car guards. "I guess if you want it, it's yours."

As Masana reached for the change, Easy's hand flew out and grabbed Masana's wrist. Masana tried to pull away.

"No, no," Easy said. "I don't like it."

"It's fine," I said. "Take the change."

"I don't like it," Easy repeated, shaking his head, slow motion, and then he let go.

Masana scooped up the coins and put them in his pocket. "Thank you, my sister," he said, getting out of the car. "Bread money."

Easy followed, and stood unsteadily on the sidewalk in the pouring rain. A settlement built on a dirt patch stretched behind him, people in mud-caked shoes making their way between the shacks, followed by mud-caked dogs.

"I'm sorry, my friend," Easy said, leaning into the car. His face had collapsed into that of a child on the verge of tears. Masana was counting his take, pleased.

"Are you okay?" he asked.

"I'm okay. Are you okay?"

"Me? I'm okay."

"Well, Easy, take care of yourself."

"Yes, yes. I'm strong, Justice."

He patted the roof and moved away. He and Masana pushed against each other, waving—two small, dark silhouettes in the middle of a downpour—as I headed out of Gugulethu.

On a whim, I called the PAC offices. They were located, as far as I could tell from the party's paltry website, in some guy's apartment in Cape Town. It was a waning group of radicals, garnering 0.21 percent of the vote in national elections, but its members seemed hopelessly dedicated.

A man answered on the first ring, confirmed that his home phone served as the provincial PAC official line, and listened as I explained my project. I asked if he knew any PAC members who had been around at the time of Amy's death and who, perhaps, could share their insights with me. He called back the next day. He had found someone who was willing to meet, he explained: "He knows about Amy Biehl."

Little did I suspect then how much he knew, and how he would single-handedly shift the narrative forever.

This other man came on the phone next, mumbling his name, unintelligible, garbled through the line. He spoke softly, with a heavy Xhosa accent, and I couldn't understand what he was saying.

"Okay then," I said, flustered, pressing the phone against my ear. "Can we meet? Tomorrow, say?"

The man mumbled his assent.

"Royale on Long Street—two P.M.?"

"Two P.M., sharp," he said, a little louder. Then he hung up.

The next day, I situated myself at a table by the window at Long Street's downtown burger institution, Royale Eatery, a cozy split-level restaurant just below a popular bar and music venue. Cape Town's younger, cooler contingent, all skinny jeans and burnished skin, sat at the other tables, drinking candy bar milkshakes and eating kimchi-topped burgers, their various touchscreen devices beeping and shrilling and glowing beside them. I didn't necessarily expect my mystery man to show up, and I certainly didn't expect him to show up on time, but then there he was, at precisely two.

I knew it was him before we made eye contact, an old militant bright against a hipster backdrop. He wore military green pants, a military green jacket, a black cap, and spiffy emerald sneakers. He was six feet tall and unsmiling, with pale brown skin, a moon-shaped face, and a pert upturned nose. He scanned the room, his small, dark eyes resting on me. I was looking at him expectantly, so he walked over, gave me the African handshake—the Western grip, followed by a clasping of one another's thumbs by the fingers, back to Western grip—and sat across the table. He leaned forward, resting his elbows.

"Please inform me of who you are and what you are doing," he said.

"Of course, yes," I stumbled. People almost never questioned my intentions, so I didn't have a ready spiel. I launched into a sloppy, meandering, and oddly bubbly explanation: American, writer, Amy Biehl, 1993, people of Gugulethu, investigating, greater meaning, townships today, bring attention to cause. "And I understand you have some knowledge of the case," I said in closing. He stared at me, unblinking. At a loss, I grinned. "So, would you like a burger?"

"I am a vegetarian," he said.

"A Xhosa vegetarian?" I asked. This was South Africa, land of the *braai,* or barbecue. Charring meat on the open flame was perhaps the single tradition everyone could come together on. Heritage Day, during which all South Africans were encouraged to celebrate their diversity, had been rebranded National Braai Day. For most black South Africans, there was often an added cultural importance to meat: animals were slaughtered to appease ancestors and mark occasions. And, as for many poor people around the world, meat represented luxury—people dreamed of the day they would be able to eat steak or lamb chops or chicken regularly.

"It is in line with my Buddhist belief system."

"Well," I said after another moment of silence. "What's that like, being a vegetarian Buddhist in Gugulethu?"

"Lonely."

I scanned the menu. "What about the Yentle Express?" I pushed the page over to him. He read the description suspiciously—a lentil burger heaped with caramelized onions—and nodded.

"And an orange juice," he added when the waitress approached.

He settled into his seat, took off his cap to reveal a round and nearly imperceptibly misshapen head, shaved clean. He leaned forward, his voice low. I leaned forward, too.

"My name," he said, "is Mzwabantu Noji. But I am known, famously, as Mzi."

Mzi gave the impression of being an elder, though he was in his early forties. He spoke slowly, at length, and demanded close attention. He sipped his orange juice and laid out his life story, whittled down to fit into a lunch conversation with a stranger.

Mzi was, he explained, Easy's neighbor, one street away, on NY119. If you were to jump over the fence behind Easy's property, you would land in Mzi's backyard. When they were younger, the men had in fact commuted this way, but now left such feats to more limber adolescent relatives. Mzi was a former APLA guerrilla, introduced to politics at age eleven by a radical Rastafarian schoolteacher. He was naturally reticent, athletic, and subtle, the son of an overworked fruit vendor mother and a roaming, absent Casanova-slash-truck-driver father. His dad did well at work, mostly because he was light of complexion. Business owners trusted him more than your darker black guy. A black man with skin like a colored is called *amper baas* in Afrikaans. *Amper baas:* almost boss.

By the time he was twelve, the best day of Mzi's life had occurred when he dreamed one night of owning a bicycle and, upon waking, found just such a bicycle abandoned near his house. He was sensitive and he craved attention, which the Rastafarian teacher paid him. Mzi's first mission as a fledgling freedom fighter involved carrying a grenade, hidden in a hollowed-out loaf of bread, across Gugulethu. Having delivered the grenade successfully, he was entrusted with similar tasks, transporting weapons around the Cape Flats. Soon, he had turned his mother's house into an arms cache without her knowledge. His younger brother Steyn—equally slim, silent, swift, and impressionable—joined Mzi in his APLA activities. Later, Steyn would be one of the APLA trio—the three men indicted and released in Amy's case. All day, Steyn and Mzi's mother sat by a table of stacked bananas and broccoli down by the Heideveld train station, while her sons hid bullets under the bed.

But Mzi's mother had an inkling that her children were involved in politics, and, like mothers across South Africa, she was panicking. Boys were dying all over the township. Apartheid forces were intent on protecting the segregated state that they had created, and their tactics were becoming more brutal, desperate, and sophisticated. Black political factions were warring with each other.

Mzi's mother did not wish to see her boys killed, so she sent Mzi to stay with some relatives in Port Elizabeth. But contrary to his mother's hopes, Mzi grew increasingly politicized there. School was boring, learning rote. But politics, especially during that heady time, were irresistible.

In Port Elizabeth, Mzi officially joined the PAC and was swiftly shipped off to Lesotho, the tiny independent nation carved out of South Africa. Along with eighteen other boys, he lived in a small rural village, ran up the hills before dawn, and studied under the tutelage of a Tanzanian-born, Chinese-trained APLA commander. After, he traveled to a remote farm in the Eastern Cape that served as a training center. Mzi was a nineteen-year-old weapons expert whose hobby was bare-knuckle boxing. He helped to organize the fresh recruits from across the country, who would learn the basics of Africanist and black nationalist theory, in addition to violent resistance.

"The youngest I saw was fourteen years," Mzi recalled. "If he was or was not too young, that was not my business."

Mzi also intermittently worked as a courier, transporting arms from the Eastern Cape to Cape Town. When he snuck into Gugulethu, he faced assault by ANC loyalists, who were warring against the PAC stronghold of NY111 and NY119. The issues of gang territories had gotten wrapped up in the issues of politics, and what, exactly, everyone was fighting for often got lost in the dustups. In 1994, Mzi's mother's house was hit with a petrol bomb, thrown by those ANC kids, rendering it a burned-out shell, its every surface scorched; his mother had to leave for several years. Steyn was shot. Once, Mzi was surrounded and attacked by an ANC mob that kicked his head in—an injury he had tended to by a sangoma after escaping from a state hospital, where he was certain he'd be tracked and arrested. This perhaps accounted for his ever-so-slightly misshapen head.

Mzi and his comrades disregarded Mandela's orders for peace in the 1990s—after all, he was not their leader; their leader was Letlapa Mphahlele, APLA's militant director of operations and the current president of the dwindling PAC—and they headed down to the Eastern Cape with plans to attack a police station. There, Mzi and company were arrested and held in prison until 1995, when the PAC negotiated their release. During that time, he was tortured. His cell was flooded at night. "And I would wake up floating," he said.

Mzi had no marketable skills and little education, so he promptly joined the South African National Defence Force. The military, like other federal organizations, was undergoing massive reform. Black guerrillas were integrated into the army, along with members of the military forces of the fractured homelands. Under the sunset clause, members of the white old guard were given the choice to stay or go, and those who stayed served side by side with the men previously categorized as terrorists. But Mzi hated the integration, too, and insisted that the white officers maintain their supremacist mentality. One such officer dropped a tray of food on him in the mess hall. Mzi pummeled the man, and his career began to tank.

By 2000, Mzi had gone off the military base and was back in prison—this time for a robbery he swore he hadn't committed. The real criminal, I learned, was widely accepted throughout Gugulethu to be a wayward relative of Mzi's, a good-for-nothing young private ironically named Peacemaker, who allegedly framed Mzi to save himself. According to Mzi's convoluted story, he begged Peacemaker to take credit for his crime, but Peacemaker, in the army infirmary after a knife fight with some townies, just smoked a cigarette and crooned R. Kelly's "I Believe I Can Fly." Mzi subsequently got booted from the army and ended up behind bars again.

By his second stint in prison, he was happy to fight anyone to relieve his anger. After an altercation with another prisoner, Mzi was sent to solitary confinement. In the cell, he found a book called *Buddhism Without Beliefs: A Contemporary Guide to Awakening* by Stephen Batchelor. He had always been a loner and had always been interested in world religions. Plus, meat made his teeth hurt. A married couple made weekly trips to the prison to teach the principles of Buddhism and meditation to inmates, and Mzi joined their classes. He became a vegetarian and spent the last two years of his incarceration meditating, gardening, and earning his high school diploma. While in prison, Mzi renounced violence, a fact he did not advertise in Gugulethu. In Gugulethu, one's reputation as a dangerous man was a form of armor. Without it, you were too vulnerable.

Before prison, Mzi had been in a long-term relationship with a woman, and they had two children together. When he was released in 2005, he kept refusing lamb chops and saying things like, "I want to get in touch with my feminine side." His partner was not taken by the new, sensitive Mzi; she had preferred the "black tiger," the "silent warrior" of yesteryear. So she left him, taking his son and daughter to a middle-class suburb called Wynberg. To make matters worse, she shacked up with an ANC guy. Now, Mzi lived in a lean-to behind his mother's house, which had been refurbished since the petrol bombing.

Mzi's room, which I would pass by many times, was a tidy affair, with just a bed, a dresser, and a chair in it. His decor consisted of two pictures. In one, from 1991, he is a nineteen-year-old freedom fighter dressed in camouflage gear, sitting on a pile of red dirt surrounded by dry brush, aiming an assault rifle into the distance. The

other picture is a poster-size photo of a tank surrounded by a flash
of fire set against the black night, emblazoned with the words 3 SA
INFANTRY BATTALION. In the upper-right corner is an image of a
twenty-seven-year-old Mzi in state-issued military fatigues and a
black beret. His flat expression is unforgiving.

The Struggle, he said, had been "like a dream" when he was in it.
It was a hazy time, all that fighting and hiding, with so much bloodshed and, yes, excitement, too. He had felt so alive and full of purpose. But when the revolution was over, he found his personality
distorted and daily life difficult to navigate. Mzi had not held down
a steady job since the army. He'd applied to be a mobile phone salesman and a truck driver, "but the application was not successful." He
had worked briefly for a center that focused on reconciliation, but
funding had diminished as South Africa became less interesting to
the world, and he was eventually let go. He had started a tour company that he called the Social Nexus Consultancy, but the name
didn't draw in many clients, and he didn't know how to advertise.
Mainly, Mzi worked on a volunteer basis for the waning PAC, as the
"newly appointed Military Veterans Affairs officer." In this capacity,
he tried to secure government jobs for a ragtag group of men who
had fought in the bush for APLA. Unlike many well-connected
ANC military veterans, the APLA men were largely unemployed.

"I sacrificed my youth, my family, everything, to liberate this
country when I was young, and look at me now," he said calmly,
pushing his empty plate to the side. He had some mustard on his lip,
which he dabbed with a napkin. "I depend on my mother to feed
me."

We sat in silence for a while as Mzi sipped his orange juice through
a straw.

"So, can you tell me about Amy Biehl?" I asked.

Mzi nodded. He didn't know much about Mongezi Manqina and Vusumzi Ntamo, the other two men convicted of Amy's murder, but he knew Easy well and had grown up down the road from Ntobeko. The townships were made of little pockets of homes that were passed down from generation to generation. Plus, few people ever left the township, in part because the cycles of poverty trapped people and in part because the township, for its many problems, was also a close-knit community that could be tough to abandon. You couldn't play your music loud in the suburbs, or invite the neighbors to a big party, or slaughter a cow for the ancestors. This meant that neighbors like Mzi and Easy were intertwined with each other and, perhaps without ever discussing anything directly, knew each other's entire life stories, if imperfectly, by heart.

Mzi recalled Easy and Ntobeko when they were teenagers involved in PAC politics. Ntobeko had the potential to become a leader but was, back in 1993, too young and eager. Instead, he was appointed the chairman of the PAC student association at his high school—a position that had been announced at the rally on the day of Amy's death. Meanwhile, Easy, too gregarious to be trusted as an operative, was just a regular member of the student branch.

"APLA is for boys who don't talk," Mzi observed. The PAC was a political party, and anyone could join. APLA was the PAC's military branch, and its members were selected more carefully. The implication was clear: Easy was too verbose to operate behind the scenes.

I thought back to my earlier conversation with Easy, on the wooden bench in the Company's Garden by the ancient pear tree. I remembered his stories of the snakes in the Eastern Cape, his eight months in the countryside, shooting AK-47s. He couldn't go back there, he'd said—the old commandos would kill him. I thought back to coal-voiced Masana, who claimed to be Easy's commander, who bragged of training him.

"Sorry, but none of the men convicted was a member of APLA?"

"Well, I can say Easy and Ntobeko had a crash course in the Gugulethu bush," Mzi conceded. "But they were not APLA."

The bush of their youth, according to Mzi, was not the savage land out in the Eastern Cape. No, Mzi himself had been there, but not Easy. Easy and Ntobeko had trained with some older fellows near NY111, in a tangle of thorns and high grasses that had since been razed and developed. Ntobeko's sienna-colored house, complete with one of Gugulethu's first automatic garage doors, now sat on that land, once a barren plot that Linda had purchased for him. Easy remembered his time in the bush like people I knew remembered summer camp: he and Ntobeko and their friends and brothers had spent warm nights among the trees. There, they found a nest of eggs, buried them in the sand, and cooked them by making a fire above. There, they led a goose to a hole filled with goose goodies, and then killed and ate the goose. There, they talked about their first girlfriends and their first fights with those girlfriends. They ate snakes they'd found, which tasted like sheep intestines—a comparison that didn't help me imagine the flavor.

Most likely, Mzi noted, the boys were given some quick lessons in guerrilla tactics. That was the norm: a fighter might train a kid who might then train some others unofficially. But Easy and Ntobeko were not soldiers, he assured me; they were just students who supported the PAC cause: Africa for Africans.

Mzi heard about the Amy Biehl matter a couple of days after it went down, when he'd returned to Gugulethu from the Eastern Cape in his capacity as a courier. He went to rest at an anonymous safe house—safe shack, rather—in a triangular settlement nestled between NY111, NY119, and NY118. His comrades were there; they always were, ready with a little welcome-home dagga—the South African term for marijuana, pronounced *da-ha*—and some good gossip when Mzi swung through.

Since his brother Steyn was a member of the APLA trio, Mzi followed the case carefully. Later, when I flipped through the thousands of pages of evidence and testimony, I came upon a number of bail-out forms, all signed in a neat hand: *Mzwabantu Mzi Noji*. Mzi looked on as Terry, the young boy released into his mother's care, skipped town, and he cheered when the APLA trio was released for lack of evidence. At the very least, he believed that Steyn hadn't been part of it. His brother was a fighter, but he'd have told Mzi if he'd been at Amy's murder scene. It was something to be proud of, not something to keep secret.

"Oh yes, back then, the dream of every black boy was to kill a white," Mzi told me.

Mzi went through the day of August 25 with me, as he knew the tale. There had been five hundred or a thousand students at Langa Secondary School, both pro-ANC kids and pro-PAC kids. It was the Year of the Great Storm. It was Operation Barcelona. The student leaders made speeches and released a wave of kids out to the streets to cause mayhem. In Langa, they stoned some vehicles and got shot at by the police—nothing out of the ordinary for township protesters in the 1990s. The group then spontaneously split into two, each fleeing the cops and heading to a different train station. One group hopped the first train at Bonteheuwel and got out at Heideveld station in Gugulethu. The other group hopped the second train at Langa and arrived in Gugulethu ten minutes later. This, so far, was consistent with what Easy had told me, and with what I'd read in court and in the TRC transcripts. The later group marched up the street to NY1 to join the earlier group, which was dancing and singing and marching and in the troublemaking mood. One by one, kids broke off, turning onto their streets and going to their homes. There was only a core bunch left at the end. Most of that core lived around NY111 and NY119, since those were the last streets before Gugulethu's border. This was supposed to be the end of the rally; it just turned out, by chance, to be its historic moment.

Amy, accompanying her friends, came across the angry boys, chanting "One settler, one bullet." The kids stoned her car. She panicked and she ran, and that's when they killed her.

"Did you hear this from Steyn?" I asked.

"No, I heard from the others," Mzi said. "Steyn, he was not at the march. He was busy with other activities." It turned out that the preoccupying activities he was busy with on that day, and all days it seemed, were smoking dagga and jogging, his lifelong passions.

"So who that you know was in the march?"

"Ntobeko was a leader of one batch of students, guiding them down the road. Mongezi Manqina, the one who stabbed her, he was there. The other one, Mongezi's friend Vusumzi, he was there. Easy—" Mzi paused. He looked up.

"Actually," he said slowly, "Easy was not in the march."

"Sorry?"

Mzi was nodding to himself. "No, Easy wasn't there," he repeated. "There was an old man who owned a small shop called Viveza nearby. He paid good money to local boys who would help him go to the wholesaler and load up groceries into his bakkie. So on that day, Easy was with the old man. He was at the morning rally, but by the afternoon he was in the bakkie."

"Easy wasn't in the march?" I asked.

"When they drove back from the wholesaler, they passed the Caltex garage and Easy demanded to stop."

"This is news to me," I said, interrupting his story. I was thinking back to Easy's colorful tale: He'd trained in the hinterland. He'd worn his gear beneath his school uniform like a superhero. He'd been sleeping rough in a shack in Khayelitsha with his comrades. A young girl served them *pap*. He'd slipped around the township on a mission, with great purpose, chanting "High discipline, high morale." He had a switchblade in his sock. He was a young guerrilla fit for battle. He had mentioned Viveza, too, but there had been no mention of a wholesaler, or an errand. In his story, he marched in Langa, hopped the train, and then Viveza drove him and Ntobeko directly to the scene of the attack, where they again joined their comrades.

Now I was hearing that he might have been more interested in making some pocket money from the shopkeeper than in attending a political march, and that he may only have passed by Amy's attack, rather than been a part of it. I remembered how odd it was, considering that he claimed he had access to a militants' safe house, that Easy had slept at his mom's place on the night of Amy's murder, cuddled up with his girlfriend.

"Yah, this is not the dominant narrative," Mzi said flatly. "But no, Easy was not in the march."

"Did he attack Amy?"

"No," Mzi said, shaking his head. "He did not attack Amy."

Mzi sat across from me at Royale Eatery and continued with his story. In it, Easy had attended the Langa Secondary School rally but had then returned home early with Mzi's brother Steyn. Steyn rolled a joint in his room, laced up his sneakers, and went for a run. Easy, meanwhile, hung out on the corner with a neighborhood kid named Quinton. Viveza found them and offered them a quick buck. Quinton and Easy hopped in the back of the bakkie and headed to a long block of warehouses in the next township over. There, they filled the truck with soda, chips, eggs, candy. Then they sat in the open back, guarding the items, as Viveza navigated to his shop on NY118.

On the way, Viveza passed the Caltex where Amy lay beneath the frothing mob, unseen. From the truck, the boys could only hear shouting, slogans: "Kill the boer"; "Africa for Africans"; "One settler, one bullet."

Months later, I met Quinton and Steyn (Viveza had died long ago). Mzi and I drove to Steyn's tin shack in the settlement of Kanana, the Xhosa name for Canaan. It was a rambling collection of lean-tos built on the stinking dirt that had been smoothed over an old garbage dump site, a quarter mile from NY111 in Gugulethu.

"Land of milk and honey," Mzi said bitterly.

Steyn was a tall, rangy, bone-thin man with a vacant expression and very few teeth, the survivors just hanging loose to his gums. Quinton was a diminutive, sad-eyed man who lived with his mom and wore an old blue workman's suit. Both Quinton and Steyn were in their early forties, and neither one of them seemed to have experienced sobriety in some time. Steyn, for one, had been hit by a car a while back, and suffered from seizures. They emerged, confused, from Steyn's shack with smoke stuck to their skin, and then sat at Mzoli's eating meat and looking stricken by the noise and stimulation of the restaurant. I asked them for their recollection of August 25, 1993, and Mzi translated, as neither spoke much English. They corroborated Mzi's version of events: That Easy jumped off the bakkie after the fact, and that Steyn had been busy smoking weed. That Viveza kept driving, slowly, through the traffic. The old man had seen enough beat-downs in his time; he just wanted to restock his shelves.

After lunch, when I dropped the two men at the entrance to Kanana, they bantered with each other in Xhosa and then Steyn leaned forward.

"Justine, I can ask you do me a favor, you mind?"

"He ask if he can ask you a favor?" Quinton echoed.

"I can't pay money, I'm sorry," I said, before they could even bother, and they both shrugged. They had been defeated long ago, and they no longer had the energy to nurture anger. They left the car politely and were always friendly when I later saw them.

"What can you do?" Mzi later said when I related the story. "Give him more money for more drugs? And then? He is committing a slow suicide. So many people in the townships are committing a slow suicide." Years later, Steyn ended up in prison for stabbing his elderly neighbor in Kanana; he said the voices drove him to it.

Back in Royale Eatery, Mzi delved into a theory of why Easy may have been convicted of a murder that he didn't commit. By August 1993, Mzi noted, most people in that particular area of Gugulethu knew Easy. He'd gotten into his share of brawls, dated his share of girls, and was also, quite unremarkably, part of a local street gang. Easy attended his share of political rallies, too, since it was the norm in the township to be affiliated with a gang and a party. The distinction between pure-hearted freedom fighter and local street gangster was not always so delineated in South Africa. In fact, senior PAC members often tried to redirect local criminal energy into political fury, with great success. For disenfranchised kids whose initial sense of belonging was tied to gang membership, the meetings and marches and songs offered something to do and a sense of a greater purpose.

As a bonus, politics allowed for a rebranding of criminal enterprise. Mzi explained that during the Struggle, when you took money or items from a white person or a white-owned establishment, the PAC considered such an activity "repossession."

"Would you be repossessing this from me?" I asked, holding up my phone.

"No, I would be robbing you."

"What's the difference?"

"Only the time we are in. After the election in 1994, it's robbery. Before, it's repossession."

Mzi remembered how popular Easy had been. I thought of how, nearly twenty years on, when I drove through the township with him, he hollered or waved hello to passersby constantly.

"Everybody knew Easy. Everyone could identify Easy," Mzi said.

"Are you telling me that the witnesses identified Easy because they could?" I asked. "Not because he did anything, but merely because he was there and they could put a face to the name?"

Mzi nodded, but I was confused. From what I'd read in the court transcripts, Miss A was certain she had seen Easy Nofemela from NY111 stab and stone Amy. Why would she lie? Moreover, even if the witness had misidentified Easy, why would Easy take the blame at the Truth Commission? If he was innocent, why would he tell me—and everyone else—elaborate stories about his guilt? About Amy's long, loose hair falling in her face? About her strength and resistance?

Easy had once even led me through a reenactment of that fateful day. He led me through the events of August 25 moment by moment, taking the wheel and chauffeuring me through Langa. He pointed out the school, the street, and the train station, as I sat in the passenger seat and scribbled in my notebook. We sat by the Caltex and he detailed where they'd walked, where they'd marched, where they'd come upon Amy. If Easy hadn't been there, why would he have given me a tour of the incident? If Easy wasn't an APLA soldier, who was Masana—that man who claimed to have trained Easy in the art of war?

"Masana is a gangster," Mzi explained. Masana was also a member of PAC, Mzi added, but his main claim to fame was as a senior member of a gang Easy had been a part of. Masana really was Easy's commander, but perhaps not for the PAC, or not only for the PAC.

Regardless of the hazy separation between gangs and politics, why would anyone who was innocent go to such lengths to describe the scene of a crime that he hadn't actually committed? For twenty whole years?

"You know Easy's brother Monks, the one who is crippled?" Mzi asked.

I did: the handsome brother with the gold incisor who lay beneath the blanket in the warmest room of the house or out in the old Ford on the sidewalk in the bright sun. The brother who had been thrown clear from a taxi full of drunken friends back in 2009.

"Monks was trained by my brother Steyn," Mzi said. "He was very physical strong, very brave—a natural for APLA." He was especially natural, Mzi observed, because he was quiet. In the Nofemela family, it was true, Easy was the only loudmouth. "They are all mute, but Easy is speaking."

The thing about little brother Monks, Mzi continued, was that he was so silent and so young back in 1993 that people hardly registered his existence. At twenty-two, Easy was a chatty social butterfly, but eighteen-year-old Monks was an unknown kid from NY111, brother number five out of seven.

"So what I believe happened was, the witnesses saw Monks doing whatever he was doing and then he disappeared into the crowd. Then Easy is there suddenly, getting off the bakkie and running to see what is happening." Mzi used his hands to mime one boy slipping away and another popping up in his place.

"But they don't look alike."

"Not now," Mzi said. "But then."

I thought of the little faded photograph Easy had given me a while back, for no discernible reason at the time. The photograph of him and two of his brothers in their tiny, oversized suits. I thought of the collage Wowo had made, the enormous framed collection of photos that sat in a place of honor in the Nofemela TV room, where the boys were indistinguishable from one another.

"But why didn't the police—"

"This is South Africa," Mzi said, as if that fact alone explained the lack of a proper investigation. He sat back. "It was like this: Amy Biehl was accompanying her friends home, she came across a group of angry boys, one of them shouted 'Settler,' and she was the only settler there. She panicked and then she went out of the car."

"Monks was there, not Easy?" I asked.

"Yah, but what can Easy do?"

"Tell somebody?"

"They don't believe us," Mzi sighed. "And it's his little brother."

"But Easy always takes full responsibility for this," I said. I thought of the day on the bench in the Company's Garden, where he touched my ribs and told me where Amy had been stabbed. "He says he did it, down to the details."

"Yah, man, Easy's cool," Mzi said. "He's got heart."

12.

Once, there were two boys, Tom and Bernard. Tom lived right opposite Bernard. One day Tom stole Bernard's bicycle and every day Bernard saw Tom cycling to school on it. After a year, Tom went up to Bernard, stretched out his hand and said, "Let us reconcile and put the past behind us."

Bernard looked at Tom's hand. "And what about the bicycle?"

"No," said Tom, "I'm not talking about the bicycle—I'm talking about reconciliation."

—Antjie Krog, *Country of My Skull*

It is Tuesday, July 8, 1997, a pleasantly cool and rainless day. Easy sits before a packed room of spectators, family members, friends of both the convicted men and Amy, PAC loyalists, ANC loyalists, lawyers, judges, TRC commissioners, and Linda and Peter Biehl. The space is steamy, each seat taken, an overflow leaning against the walls. Before Easy, a black microphone and a pitcher of water. On the front edge of the pale wooden table at which he sits is taped a paper sign bearing one large typed word: APPLICANT.

A banner, in lime green and white and black, spans the wall behind him:

TRUTH.

THE ROAD TO

RECONCILIATION.

Easy is twenty-seven years old, and has spent the past five years shuttling between maximum-security prisons around the region. In 1994, he was at Pollsmoor, until he was transferred to Helderstroom, an enormous facility at the edge of the bucolic town of Caledon. There, he caught tuberculosis.

"We call it *Hell*-derstroom," he told me. "It was too much hell. The wind is cold, cold, cold, the shower is cold, the window is broken, the warders only speak Afrikaans. The mat I sleep on was wet, concrete is always wet, water came up through it. When I go to shower my body was so cold. I put soap on my cloth, open the cold water, I wait, I count, firstly I have to jog, jog, jog, let my blood warm. Then when I get there, is one-two-three and get out. With my TB, I was coughing, chest was so sore. But my father said, 'Don't be weak. Tell that mind you are not weak.'"

He only barely recovered from TB, refusing medicine he was convinced was state-sanctioned poison ("Now I think, Easy, you stupid, you torture yourself for six months"). The first day of the Truth Commission hearings, he is coming from Victor Verster Prison near Paarl.

Easy's oversized prison-issue spectacles dwarf his small, pimpled face. He has grown a squiggle of a mustache, which has the unintended effect of making him look like a teenager. His printed yellow polo shirt is tucked into his high-waisted black trousers, cinched with a belt. On his feet, he sports a pair of colossal, sparkling white Adidas high-tops.

To Easy's right, Ntobeko slumps, his skin dark and luminous, his eyes wide, his lips pressed together. He wears a printed buttercup-yellow polo shirt that pools around his neck, oversized blue jeans, and the exact same high-tops as Easy, just as spit-shined and glowing white. He, too, has managed to eke out the slightest of mustaches, and he, too, looks neither older nor manlier for it.

To Easy's left sits Vusumzi Ntamo, his hair trimmed neatly, his knees spread. His mother and aunts have pooled their money to buy him an ill-fitting beige suit and a pair of shiny black shoes. Next to Vusumzi, Mongezi Manqina leans back and chews on his ever-present toothpick, his chin raised. He wears a fitted brown leather jacket, an ironed red and black checked-plaid shirt, and his own pair of enormous, spotless white high-tops, with bubble letters spelling out AIR covering the sides.

The men sit utterly still, only the pupils of their eyes darting back and forth, as the photographers take endless shots, their lenses clicking, their flashes flashing, the cameramen jostling to get the best angles. They are lying on the floor, kneeling on tables. Journalists furiously jot down notes.

Prison was dark, and so was the truck they were transported in, with little square openings covered in a crosshatch of bars. For years, they have been numbers in the system, indistinguishable from the masses, but now the room is fluorescent-lit, with large sunny windows, camera sparks flying, and hundreds of eyes boring into them.

In the corner, a man, legs crossed, casually reads a local paper with the headline: ONUS ON BIEHL'S KILLERS TO PROVE POLITICAL MOTIVE. A head shot of smiling Amy accompanies the article. In the front row of the audience, facing the men, are Peter and Linda Biehl, and Amy's South African roommate, Melanie Jacobs. The Biehls are the only Americans to sit before the TRC. They run the Amy Biehl Foundation, which they founded in 1994, and have been rubbing shoulders with ANC elites for a few years now.

Melanie and the Biehls entered, moments earlier, to much media attention. The reporters stumbled around them, walking backward, making way. Linda, her hair at a sharp angle, wears a large gold heart locket containing Amy's picture. She smiles widely, greeting audience members, and turns in her seat to chat with acquaintances. Peter is stiff in his gray suit and red tie, his face set, just barely, to neutral. Melanie wears her black hair pushed back with a cotton band, her nose pierced with a silver hoop, her hands covered in rings, strands of pearls tight around her neck. Her face is heavy and slack, and she often places her head on Peter's shoulder. Two years later, Melanie, newly engaged, will pitch herself off a balcony and die as she hits the street below.

Wowo Nofemela, Easy's father, sits quietly a few rows behind the Biehls, on the far side of the room. His head is shaved bare, his posture erect, his beard trimmed, his wire-rim glasses balanced on his nose, his hands placed in his lap just below his bowling-ball belly. He does not shift. A few rows away, Mongezi Manqina's mother, her face bloated and her eyes hooded, absently nods her head, her lips pressed together and turned down.

Monks, Easy's brother, is mobile on that day, twelve years before he will be thrown from a taxi. He shifts around. He slides down in his chair, shrouding his face with both his hands as a camera zooms in on him and lingers.

The Biehls stand as Vusumzi's mother and aunt approach, two stout little ladies, one in her signature maroon beret. They lean in, offer their hands to the Americans. Linda beams, bright lipstick and perfect teeth. Peter does not.

"Hi, I'm Peter," he says in his earnest Midwestern twang, stiffly engaging in an African handshake, towering over the ladies. "It's very nice to meet you. We're parents, too, so we're in solidarity. Good luck today."

The Truth and Reconciliation Commission was South Africa's attempt to deal with the crimes of apartheid, lest they "live with us like a festering sore," according to Mandela. It was meant to stand in stark contrast to Germany's Nuremberg trials of 1945 and 1946, during which nearly two dozen top Nazi leaders were tried for war crimes, with the majority sent to prison or sentenced to death. Mandela's ANC government modeled the TRC on previous and lesser-known commissions across the world, in particular Chile's Comisión Nacional de Verdad y Reconciliación. Chile's commission documented the thousands of deaths and disappearances that occurred under the dictatorship of Augusto Pinochet in the hopes of ushering in a transparent and democratic government. Though imperfect, the commission was considered a successful, cathartic alternative to solely punitive measures. Mandela's ANC government hoped that a similar South African commission could approach the country's apartheid past with an aim toward transformation rather than punishment.

The TRC's mandate was threefold: to achieve a large-scale picture of the gross human rights abuses committed between March 1,

1960, and May 10, 1994 (the day Mandela was sworn in as president); to grant amnesty to any South African who could prove that
the crimes he or she committed during that time were politically
motivated; and to help victims and their families by revealing fates
of those missing or killed. The greater purpose of the TRC was to
promote national unity in a country that housed a population that
had been systematically divided for centuries.

The TRC, for all its promise, was also a political compromise,
reached as part of the overall deal leading to South Africa's first all-
inclusive elections in 1994. Its existence was the result of a negotiated settlement between the ANC and the National Party. The
settlement, also referred to as the "Liberation Bargain," was reached
after years of meetings between Mandela, his top brass, and the National Party leadership. With the fall of the Soviet Union, the ANC
lost ideological and logistical backing, but it had the hearts and
minds of the masses. And while the National Party enjoyed the
backing of a strong military and police force, they were vilified
globally and had read the writing on the wall. Rather than face a
protracted and destructive civil war, de Klerk and Mandela decided
to talk. For years, the former enemies pushed on with negotiations
until they managed to reach a settlement.

To further ease tension, and in the spirit of reconciliation, Mandela even made de Klerk his deputy president from 1994 to 1996, in
a government of national unity. The TRC was an imperfect answer
to the question of how to address the country's past, a space in
which victims could air grievances; perpetrators could admit to
their actions (but they did not have to apologize or express remorse);
and those imprisoned for political crimes could appeal for freedom.
The TRC would, in the dreams of its inventors, clear the air.

"Resentment is like drinking poison and then hoping it will kill
your enemies," Mandela said, in explaining his drive to free the nation of such a toxic sentiment.

Desmond Tutu, the archbishop of Xhosa and Tswana extraction,
was appointed by Mandela to chair the commission. He was a Nobel

Peace Prize Laureate and the son of an abusive, alcoholic father and a washerwoman mother who made two shillings a day working for a white woman—two shillings, which she gave to Tutu so he could catch a train to school. "I look like her—short, with a large nose," he said. Tutu was a social activist devoted to nonviolence, and an internationally beloved Anglican, particularly recognizable for his habit of draping himself in purple robes and for his youthful, infectious laugh. Alex Boraine, an ordained Methodist minister and ex-parliamentarian with pale white skin, bright white hair, and an impressive series of degrees, was Tutu's deputy chair. The pair gave the proceedings a strong Christian flavor.

Some have argued that the TRC also adhered to the African philosophy of *ubuntu,* which holds that a person is a person only because of other people. Ubuntu is the idea of a shared humanity, an interconnectedness of man. "A person with ubuntu . . . is diminished when others are humiliated or diminished, when others are tortured or oppressed," wrote Tutu. The TRC, then, aimed to restore that common humanity to the fractured people of South Africa.

Tutu and Boraine were, at least initially, optimistic about the TRC's purpose and outcome. It was a radical approach to dealing with and healing from the past, one that played into global and national fantasies about a new multicultural South Africa that might emerge.

"Forgiving and being reconciled to our enemies or our loved ones are not about pretending that things are other than they are," wrote Tutu. "True reconciliation exposes the awfulness, the abuse, the hurt, the truth. It could even sometimes make things worse. It is a risky undertaking but in the end it is worthwhile, because in the end only an honest confrontation with reality can bring real healing."

The TRC began with a flourish and deep pockets: $18 million annually in funds, from taxpayers and international donors. Seventeen diverse commissioners were appointed by Mandela himself, most of them lawyers and judges who had, at some level, demon-

strated against the apartheid system. Starting in 1995, victims filed
statements, and some testified at hearings held across the country.
Fresh off apartheid's dismantling, South Africa was of worldwide
interest. International journalists flew into town, filed emotional articles on the wires, rode up Table Mountain, enjoyed a couple of
days on Clifton Beach, and flew out.

Globally, the commission was hailed as a success, even as it continued on, but nationally, many people were less impressed. The
hearings often focused on personal tragedy, during which victims
and perpetrators interacted and together relived torture, murder, and
oppression. State TV played reel after reel of various sobbing South
Africans, along with photos of bombed-out buildings and corpses.
Cynics dubbed the TRC "the Kleenex Commission."

Indeed, there was an element of political theater to the endeavor,
but nobody could deny the searing moments, where the agony and
futility of apartheid were revealed—not as abstract stories, but in
human form. A former policeman, sweating in his suit, demonstrated
his methods of torture before a room, pretending to suffocate a volunteer by wrapping a damp cloth bag around his head. His victims
sat among the crowd.

"What kind of man are you?" one of the victims asked his torturer. "What kind of man uses a method like this one of the wet bag,
on other human beings, repeatedly listening to those moans and
cries and groans, and taking each of those people very near to their
deaths?"

"I have asked myself that question to such an extent that I voluntarily ... approached psychiatrists to have myself evaluated, to find
out what kind of person I am," the policeman answered politely.
Later, he added that he was still proud of his work.

APLA members who had been convicted of massacring church-
goers just before Amy's death in 1993 announced that they had
wanted everyone to "feel the pain of the children of Azania." A man
whose wife they had killed wanted the men to turn and face him.
The moment, broadcast across the country, was unnervingly inti-

mate: Did the killers remember his wife? he wanted to know. She was wearing a long blue coat. Did they remember shooting her?

"What are we doing here?" he asked nobody in particular, trembling. "The truth, yes, but—how on earth are we going to be reconciled?"

In one hearing, the mothers of men known as the Gugulethu Seven were led into the room, most in traditional African-print dresses. In March 1986, their activist sons had been lured by double agents into a trap and killed in a hail of twenty-five state bullets. The mothers sat, bewildered, in the audience, large headphones resting on their fabric-wrapped heads so that they could hear a Xhosa translation of the proceedings. For much of the time, they were sedate, concentrating. But then, suddenly, video evidence of their children's murder was played before the room. One by one, the images of the dead men, taken in grainy police video, were shown on a large TV, and one by one, the mothers began to wail.

Later, the women gathered around a table, and a black policeman involved in their sons' deaths sat before them like a child, quiet, welcoming their punishment. He was so much worse than the white perpetrators, the mothers said. He'd betrayed his own blood, "working for the boers." One mother would not look at him, her body stiff with disgust. But then another mother, a woman named Cynthia Ngewu, fixed him with a stare. She cocked her head.

"Your name, it means prayer?" she asked. He nodded slightly. They regarded each other for a moment.

"This thing called reconciliation . . . if I am understanding it correctly . . . if it means this perpetrator, this man who has killed Christopher Piet, if it means he becomes human again, this man, so that I, so that all of us, get our humanity back . . . then I agree, then I support it all," she reflected before the commission.

Face-to-face with her son's killer in the private room, she spoke again. "I forgive you, my child," she said. "You and Christopher were the same age. I forgive you."

Cynthia Ngewu and several other mothers embraced the policeman. That act of forgiveness and mercy was not widely discussed, not like the Biehls'. The women returned to their lives in Gugulethu.

Because of moments like this, many considered the TRC an imperfect success, arguing that it humanized people, offered closure, and, most critically, created a basis on which the country could move forward; in addressing its terrible, discriminatory past, South Africa was able to move toward a potentially brighter, more inclusive future. After apartheid, there needed to be some institutional reckoning, a sort of national catharsis. Many believed that the TRC worked, despite its flaws.

Others believed that the TRC was a spectacle that showcased smaller, personal crimes while hiding larger, institutional ones.

"Oh, the hurt and the harm of black people were commoditized and on display," Amy's mentor Rhoda Kadalie once said to me. "People vented and cried, but the atrocities themselves were behind closed doors."

One common complaint was that the commission largely ignored the complex issues of systemic abuse—not dramatic or sudden, but sustained and life-altering. Had Easy's grandfather Melvin stood before the TRC and announced that he had been separated from his children for years, his ancestral land stolen, his job prospects destroyed even as he worked himself to the bone so that white men could get rich, there would have been no recourse for him. Had Wowo stood before the TRC, announcing that he had only first attended school at age eleven because there was no education available to him in the homelands, there would have been no answer for him either. In this way, there was no answer for a 101-year-old black man who had been intermittently thrown in jail for political reasons all his life, the final time when he was eighty. Over a century, he had watched as his land and livestock were confiscated. In 1997, he announced to the commission that he wanted his trees back. The powers-that-be had taken his trees, and he wanted them returned, or he wanted reparations for their theft. The commissioners, abashed, looked at each other and at the man; he didn't fit into any legislated category of suffering.

The TRC also homed in on the extreme acts of a relative few white citizens (torture, murder, attacks, bombings) and largely ignored the more mundane acts of many (subtly exploiting employees, ignoring or welcoming violence and oppression perpetrated by the government, profiting from businesses built by underpaid and disenfranchised black workers, simply casting a vote for the National Party). Most whites therefore never saw themselves reflected as perpetrators, and, with enough mental effort, were able to escape guilt—self-imposed or otherwise. Ten years after the end of apartheid, a poll conducted by the Institute of Justice and Reconciliation, a Cape Town think tank, showed that one in five white citizens would prefer to return to the old regime; another poll revealed that less than a third of whites believed that they had benefited from apartheid.

"*How* did I benefit from apartheid?" Ilmar Pikker once asked me over tea. He had struggled so much in his own life that he was confused by the suggestion that he had ever enjoyed a leg up. In fact, the bloated apartheid bureaucracy was especially advantageous to lower- and middle-class whites with little education, who were almost guaranteed jobs in the civil service if they couldn't find other work. But Pikker shook his head vigorously. "No, I don't see how."

"Life in this country was far better back then," an older white man who once drove me to the airport explained.

"For you," I offered. "Not for anyone else."

"Yes, I suppose it *was* worse for them."

Political parties, too, were largely excused for their roles in apartheid. The National Party wanted blanket amnesty for apartheid, and the TRC was in part a compromise: amnesty granted on a case-by-case basis. Still, the National Party was reluctant to appear before the committee, with many senior figures echoing the cry of a famous colonel: "Me, apply for amnesty? *Se moer!*" Like hell!

When senior party officials appeared before the commission, there was a taking of overall responsibility and apologies for many of the horrors inflicted by apartheid. While these are no small concessions, it also meant that specific transgressions committed by the state and its security apparatus were left unclaimed.

But then a man named Eugene de Kock stepped forward and proved that the state-sponsored agents responsible for the worst abominations were not merely bad apples, but were in fact deployed for that very purpose. De Kock had headed Vlakplaas, a shadowy extrajudicial death squad that operated out of a sprawling farm with the same name on the outskirts of Pretoria, the capital city. The squad was made up, largely, of hard-line white cops, as well as key black and colored operatives. These policemen and their assets, on state salaries, carried out assassinations, and caught and tortured activists to only two possible ends: death or life as a double agent. Murder was a day's work at Vlakplaas. Security officers once abducted, assaulted, and shot a black operative and then burned his body on a diesel fire, a seven-hour process conducted in the bush.

"In the beginning, it smells like meat braai, in the end like the burning of bones," Dirk Coetzee, de Kock's predecessor, told a journalist. But they didn't dispose of bodies that way too often, he later added, because it was a drag: who regularly had seven free hours to just stand around, burning human beings to ash?

De Kock had been imprisoned in 1996 and was serving 212 years for crimes against humanity when the TRC got going. With nothing left to lose, and amnesty to gain, he testified before the TRC that—contrary to the denials of top-ranking apartheid government officials, who claimed that Vlakplaas was a deviant force operating on its own—he had acted on the orders of police generals, who in turn had acted on the orders of cabinet ministers, who presumably had the ear of the president. The nation watched agog as de Kock sat before the TRC and spilled all in his flat, Afrikaans-accented English.

"I do not deny that I am guilty of the crimes, many of them horrible, of which I was accused," he announced. "But we at Vlakplaas, and in the other covert units, are by no means the guiltiest of all. That dubious honor belongs to those who assembled us into the murderous forces that we became, and which we were intended to be all along. And most of them, the generals and the politicians, have got off scot-free. . . . And so it would seem that justice has been sufficiently served by turning me, a mere colonel, into a lone demon to explain all the evil of the old regime."

Following de Kock's whistle-blowing, many former apartheid-era security personnel came forward. Mostly, these were men who, having seen de Kock locked away, feared prosecution. They comprised a mere sliver of the security state, but they admitted to burning down thousands of homes. They had shot fathers in front of their children. They had sodomized detainees with broomsticks. One pair of security police applied twice for amnesty, initially confessing to sixty murders and later bringing forth nine additional murders that had slipped their minds. Nearly all of the men swore that they had acted under the orders of or with the knowledge of top leaders. Most of them got amnesty. The rest still avoided jail—they were either never prosecuted, or their cases were dismissed. Only de Kock remained in prison; though they amnestied him for the majority of his crimes, the commission decided a handful of them did not qualify as political in nature. Nonetheless, even de Kock was granted parole in 2015, and walked free after twenty-one years.

But the security police were really just glorified triggermen, violent cogs in the machine. Those in the upper echelons of power—the ministers, the presidents—didn't seem to fear prosecution in the least, nor were they sorry. P. W. Botha, de Klerk's predecessor, refused to testify before the TRC. He stood before a group of journalists and angrily announced: "I've said many times before that the word 'apartheid' means good neighborliness. I honor the soldiers, I honor the police of the past! I salute them!"

During the TRC process, the large-scale suffering of women—especially black women—was often pushed to the side or ignored outright. A black rural woman, say, who had been born into poverty, confined to a shack in an overcrowded homeland, provided with, at best, a low-level state education, who had married an absent migrant laborer and bore a child who had died early for lack of adequate healthcare, had no role at the TRC. For that matter, neither did Easy's mother, Kiki, raised in an "emergency camp," pregnant by thirteen, her only employment option to work as a maid.

Moreover, sexual violence was almost never discussed. There were nearly eight thousand submissions on mistreatment put before the TRC, but in fewer than a dozen did a woman mention being raped. On the apartheid government's part, warders often failed to provide black women prisoners with underwear and sanitary napkins. Some women gave birth in front of laughing male warders. Black female detainees, even teenage girls, were summarily beaten and shocked, and one woman was interrogated by a police officer who dangled her baby out of a window of a moving vehicle to coerce her into providing information. Another had her bare breasts slammed repeatedly in a desk drawer until her nipple split open.

I would like to see ANC training (death) camps exposed for what they were and the commanders brought to book, Pikker once wrote me in an email, after I mentioned Vlakplaas's unorthodox law enforcement methods. *I'm sure Vlakplaas will pale in the light compared to what atrocities occurred in these camps.*

Pikker was not incorrect when he pointed out that the ANC's behavior during the Struggle was hardly exemplary—a point de Klerk also made in his testimony before the TRC. Their military wing, in particular, seemed to have taken on the brutal habits of their enemy.

In the 1970s, following the Soweto Uprising, many idealistic young black South Africans slipped over the borders to attend ANC military training camps in Zambia, Tanzania, Angola, and other African countries sympathetic to the liberation cause. But the camps could be brutal outposts with their own sets of laws. The military wing of the ANC was steeped in paranoia about infiltrators, informers, and apartheid agents—and for suspected traitors, punishment was unyielding and inhumane.

Torture and assault were widespread at ANC prison camps. Even the smallest infractions by loyal male comrades were met with disproportionate and often fatal punishment. When some members protested the conditions in which they toiled at training facilities in neighboring countries, they were sent to Angolan state prisons or to the infamous ANC Quatro prison camp (officially called a "rehabilitation facility"), a filthy, lice-infested collection of dark, sweltering cells. There, according to a 1992 report by Amnesty International, the accused were beaten on the soles of their feet, hit with long sticks, and scalded with boiling liquid; stoned by guards, pushed onto nests of red ants, denied medical attention, and allowed meager rations of inadequate food and sometimes only one cup of water a day in the unyielding tropical heat; forced to defecate and urinate in a rarely emptied bucket in a crowded cell, allowed to wash with dirty water only every few weeks, and required to work hard labor on 110-degree days.

"A place where if they give you bread, you think it's cake," one survivor testified.

At other camps throughout Africa, ANC loyalists suspected to have erred reported having their testicles squeezed with pliers, their lips burned with cigarettes, and their chests burned with liquefied plastic. Prisoners dug their own graves. One prisoner, suspected to be an apartheid double agent, was put under house arrest, guarded by ANC soldiers. He died suddenly of poisoning, and nobody could figure out who did it, the ANC or the National Party. Both had reason, and both were capable.

In 1998, the ANC furiously applied for a stop on the publication of a final TRC report that implicated them in human rights abuses. The ANC argued that ills committed during the righteous fight for freedom were not comparable to those committed in the name of persecution and subjugation. But Tutu was prescient and devoted to transparency.

"We can't assume that yesterday's oppressed won't become to-morrow's oppressors," he pleaded. "We have seen it happen all over the world and we shouldn't be surprised if it happens here."

Ultimately, a court upheld the right of the TRC to publish and deliver the report to President Mandela.

"We hold up as heroes those who are not clean," Rhoda Kadalie once told me. She was referring to certain liberation leaders, hailed as demigods, who had skeletons in their closets.

In the end, of the over seven thousand amnesty applicants, 80 percent were black. Only two thousand were genuine political am-nesty applications—the rest were deemed to be from prisoners try-ing to get out of jail—and of those, the commission granted amnesty in only 849 cases, and rejected the rest. The logic behind who did or did not apply for amnesty was curious. For a person serving a prison sentence, applying for amnesty offered the possibility of freedom. For a free person, applying for amnesty meant admitting to crimes with which one had never been charged, and therefore risking im-prisonment. Because of the apartheid system, the prisons were full of black and colored men. The prisoner, far more likely to be black, had nothing to lose by applying for amnesty, but the free man, more likely white, risked everything. The government kept reasserting its plans to prosecute those whom it suspected of crimes but who had refused to apply for amnesty, but after a few bungled attempts in the early 2000s, the plans were largely abandoned. The commission rec-ommended that the new government pay victims reparations and offer them rehabilitation. But these recommendations were largely ignored.

"Now we ask ourselves, who was oppressing whom?" Letlapa Mphahlele, the current PAC president and former APLA com-mander, asked me one day in his office on a largely ignored floor of Parliament, where he occupied the PAC's sole remaining seat. It was a wide, clean space, very quiet, where the government had stationed the waning members of a number of largely irrelevant political par-ties, most of which garnered less than one percent of the vote.

Mphahlele arranged his face in an expression of faux wonder. "Were *we* oppressing *ourselves*?"

Mphahlele was a handsome, lanky man who looked younger than his fifty-two years and had a sharp sense of humor. He offered me half of his vegan almond-butter-and-avocado sandwich on seed loaf and discussed his recent spiritual voyage to India, where he had considered renouncing everything and wandering the land with only a spoon and a plate, relying on the kindness of strangers to feed him. However, his girlfriend rejected this lifestyle plan, which included a renunciation of sex. Mphahlele, now returned, seemed most concerned about transcribing his second volume of memoirs (a follow-up to his essay collection, *Shining the Searchlight Inwards;* his poetry collection, *Mantlalela! The Flood Is Coming;* and his autobiography, *Child of This Soil: My Life as a Freedom Fighter*). He wasn't great at touch-typing so the whole endeavor was taking forever. He had been late to the interview because he had been trying to return a pair of trousers to a department store, on account of the pockets being defective.

"*T* is supposed to stand for truth, but there's nothing like truth as far as interests of different classes and groups are concerned, especially if they are in conflictual relations," Mphahlele said to me. "Unless we reduce truth to mathematics—and the mathematical truth is not the same as the sociopolitical truth—your truth will always be different from mine."

"So if not truth, then what do you think was the purpose of the TRC?"

"To deepen the myth of South African magic. That we South Africans, we are special. We have done what the world never expected us to do. To sell South Africa internationally. . . . Let's get to the crux of the matter: Who still owns the means of production in this country? Whites. So then you need people like Tutu to tell you if you don't get what you want in this life, you will get it later."

While the world welcomed the myth of magical South Africa, South Africans themselves were wary. The journalist Rian Malan noted that despite international fanfare surrounding the process, the

TRC had ended up as "a sweet and somewhat muddle-headed organism cast very much in the mold of its chairman Archbishop Desmond Tutu."

Zapiro, the country's most famous political cartoonist, published a black-and-white drawing advertising "Amnesty Washing Powder," featuring a mustachioed housewife who bore a striking resemblance to a white police officer who had overseen the massacre of eleven innocent black people, mostly women and children.

"Just look at this shirt!" the housewife clucks. "Stained with the blood of eleven people!" But once the shirt had been laundered with "Amnesty Washing Powder," it emerges sparkling white. "Spotless!" she announces with a smile. "Amnesty changed my life." Zapiro had added a tagline: BLOODSTAINS IN YOUR CLOSET? GET AMNESTY ® (YOU'D BE CRAZY NOT TO!!)

Many were impressed with the commission, but others had begun to feel that amnesty had been reduced to a brand-name product marketed and sold to the masses. The TRC had been the result of a bargain struck between politicians. The people were asked to trade justice for peace, and at first they agreed. But it started to seem like a bum deal, where criminals went entirely unpunished while so many still suffered the aftereffects of their crimes. Was it enough to admit you had suffocated a man with a wet bag and inserted an electrical cattle probe up his anus? Was it enough to simply tell what you'd done? The country had avoided war and immediate ruin, and in exchange, it seemed, those who wreaked havoc on so many lives for so many decades got to retire to their beach houses while the poor still lived in soggy shacks.

One day, Mzi and I sat in his front yard, each of us perched on a plastic chair, talking about the TRC. In the back bedroom, Mzi's eldest sister was recovering from what should have been a routine appendectomy, but free government healthcare in South Africa was infamously deficient. She had been rushed to the hospital, where instead of promptly removing her appendix and sending her home, the staff had installed her in a room and kept her on painkillers. Finally, after four days, her appendix burst and was removed. A foot-long scar now ran up her belly, and she'd come to her mother's to be nursed back to health.

While she was in the hospital, some drugged-up criminals had robbed her house, and her sixteen-year-old son had returned home from school to quite a scene. Days before, Mzi and I had driven over to find the teenage boy, still in his pale blue school blazer, staring at a pile of human shit by the back door. This was the third time the house had been robbed, and the second time the perps had taken a crap. They stole small items—DVDs, a hat—and left the big-ticket items, like the TV.

"These skollies watch too many Hollywood movies," Mzi said, using Afrikaans slang for township gangsters. A lifelong socialist and black nationalist, Mzi liked to blame the West, and America in particular, whenever he got a chance.

"In what Hollywood movie," I asked, "is there a band of pooping thieves?"

"Isn't there?"

Now, while his sister recuperated, Mzi and I were sharing an egg salad sandwich from the supermarket. Mzi's five-year-old nephew was alternately doing cartwheels around us and sucking on a red lollipop that was slowly staining his white tank top. Then he changed into a green T-shirt and had a piece of cake, which he smeared on his new outfit.

"What will happen on Judgment Day?" Mzi wondered aloud, scooping another nephew onto his lap—a toddler so chubby and bald and beatific that we had nicknamed him Buddha. "What happened in South Africa, it made me look forward to Judgment Day. I thought it would be on the democratic elections, but that didn't happen. Now I'm looking forward to see Tutu answering to God. Why did he allow the TRC to go that way?" Mzi balanced the chair on its back legs, and faced the sun with Buddha. Then he lowered himself down. "No, man, judgment can't be done in a day. In South Africa, we need a Judgment Decade."

Amnesty hearings were modeled on the trial system. Defense law-yers, paid by the state or paid privately, represented those applying for amnesty. Other attorneys, often representing victims or families of the victims, acted as prosecutors, arguing against amnesty and try-ing to prove that crimes had not been politically motivated, some-times showing evidence. The judgments were made by a five-person commission comprised of judges and lawyers. While the hearings did not operate within the court system, the resulting amnesty deci-sions were legally binding.

The four young men convicted of Amy Biehl's murder were pro-vided with two lawyers: Norman Arendse, a prominent colored de-fense attorney with the face, build, and demeanor of a friendly bulldog, and Nona Goso, their junior counsel from the criminal trial.

Arendse himself was a minor figure in South African history. He'd served a controversy-laden term as the first nonwhite president of Cricket South Africa. He'd been arrested for drunk driving. He'd also helped win the freedom of a young black farmhand accused of murdering a famous white supremacist.

By 2014, Arendse had a sleek beige-and-black office on a quaint cobblestone lane in downtown Cape Town, helmed by a middle-aged blond secretary and decorated with a framed portrait of Man-dela and a large cartoon image of the famed colored cricketer Vernon Philander. He also displayed a portrait of Dullah Omar: Mandela's lawyer, Amy's teacher, Arendse's mentor, and the country's minister of justice from 1994 to 1999.

The Biehls had not secured the services of a lawyer since they did not plan on opposing amnesty (other victims' families were often represented by lawyers arguing against amnesty for the perpetrators). For much of the two-day hearing, the Biehls sat, like spectators, in the audience while an elderly white TRC-appointed advocate named Robin Brink tried to make a case against the amnesty of the four young prisoners. Brink sported a golden pinkie ring and had the pointed face of a bird. His thinning gray hair stuck to his mottled head.

The amnesty committee was comprised of four men and one woman. All had legal backgrounds and had made contributions to the anti-apartheid cause. The chairman was a gray-haired septuagenarian Indian immigrant who was the first-ever nonwhite jurist in South Africa. He was joined by a dour, pink-complected judge of British extraction; a heavyset, middle-aged black judge who seemed to be in a state of sustained, contained fury; a long-nosed, brown-haired Afrikaner advocate, who would later claim he was merely a "token with no power" and resign; and a largely silent black female advocate who wore her braids piled atop her head. These commissioners sat raised behind a high dais, their complexions tinted yellow in the fluorescent glow of the ceiling lights.

The effect, visually, was that four young black men of meager means sat far below an imposing, multiracial panel of legal professionals. Two brown-skinned attorneys argued for their release while one white attorney argued for their continued incarceration. As in their criminal trials, the young men could not adequately understand English and relied on an interpreter, who, as in the criminal trials, bungled at least a few sentences. The hearing lasted for two days; everyone changed their clothes but for the applicants, who wore the exact same outfits each time, down to their socks.

Easy and his co-accused had decided that the TRC was propaganda, since they assumed, generally, that any government-sanctioned process was propaganda, even if the government was now black-led. But eventually, prominent PAC members visited them at their various prisons scattered around the Western Cape, and convinced them to take part in the process. Despite a deep-seated mistrust of ANC government processes, the PAC leadership, led by Mphahlele, had grudgingly complied with the TRC, mostly so their imprisoned adherents would have the chance at freedom.

Though the leaders of the PAC insisted in their own submission that Amy Biehl had been "wrongly targeted," they acknowledged that those convicted of her murder were members of PAC's student branch and had been involved in a protest on August 25, 1993. *Misguided as the deed was, we support the amnesty applications of all those convicted and sentenced for the offence,* they wrote in their submission to the amnesty committee.

A few months before the hearing, the men were supplied with amnesty application forms. These were completed hastily in English in a single hand and mailed to the amnesty committee. The four applications stated the names of the applicants, their dates of birth, prison ID numbers, their victim's name, their crimes, and their political affiliations. The men identified Amy as an "aid worker" if they identified her profession at all. Only Mongezi Manqina had, additionally, completed a separate application in Xhosa in his own handwriting, listing his victim as "Amy Bill." In killing Amy, the men claimed to have been implementing actions to make the country ungovernable, as was the aim of the ANC's Operation Barcelona and the PAC's Year of the Great Storm, both launched in 1993. In Mongezi's application he claimed that he had attacked Amy to fulfill the purpose of "Oparation bhaselona" and "The Year of Cream Stone."

"Mention of 'This is the Year Cream Stone' is not correct," Arendse announced staidly before the commission.

Goso and Arendse helped the men draw up affidavits that put forth a corresponding story of the day. The affidavits were written with each point numbered and typed out. Ntobeko, Easy, and Mongezi had all been between eighteen and twenty-two when Amy was murdered, yet they were still high school students; none of them had graduated and they struggled to speak and understand English. Vusumzi, who turned twenty-two on the day Amy died and is developmentally delayed, had been attending sixth grade. At the initial criminal trial, the defense attorneys had urged the court interpreter, when asking Vusumzi questions in Xhosa, to "be a bit slow when you talk to him ... a bit slower than usual," and to use "little words," and had sent him out for a psychological evaluation.

"His mind is not normal," his attorney said. "He is not mad, but he has mental ailment."

Despite this, court psychologists declared Vusumzi to be of average intelligence and decided he had a full understanding of the charges against him and the trial proceedings.

Four years later, during their preparations for the TRC, Easy and the other two tried to teach Vusumzi a simple PAC slogan: *This land was taken by the barrel of the gun and the land must be returned.* They made him practice, to little avail.

"We sit down with Vusumzi, we tell him, 'You not going to eat until you learn,'" Easy recalled. "Just that one sentence. We repeat on and on and on and on and on. He couldn't get it."

At the TRC, Vusumzi's affidavit stated: "I have a very low intelligent quotient and I would regard myself as mentally backwards. . . . I am not able to articulate any political ideology or motivation for my conduct. I am sure however (given my limited mental capabilities) that I am a firm supporter of the Pan Africanist Congress of Azania." He signed his affidavit in a child's uncertain cursive.

When I met Arendse, he wore a fine blue pin-striped suit and intermittently yawned and checked his BlackBerry. He spoke for a while about the four young men at the TRC but eventually exclaimed that he was actually mixing up the Amy Biehl men with other APLA soldiers—those involved in the St. James Massacre—that he had represented the following day. Still, he insisted that all his clients had told the truth to the TRC.

"From where I was, what they told me, evidence under oath, they were consistent," he said. "They were all very clear that they were involved and the extent of their involvement was recorded in the statement."

PAC president Mphahlele, sitting in his office in Parliament with his almond-butter-and-avocado sandwich, disagreed. "Every story, without exception, was peppered and salted and put some condiments on. A lawyer would take weeks drilling the applicants, and I know lots of PAC applicants had their stories changed or tampered with. . . . And of course, a lot of people, their lawyers told them, 'If you say you did this, if you say you knew this, you are not going to get amnesty,' so you must say something you do not know to get amnesty."

At the hearings in July 1997, Goso and Arendse presented the men's cases, one by one, reading out loud the affidavits as the applicants listened to an interpreter through headphones. Each affidavit was between four and seven pages, and ran down the events of the day. According to the affidavits, Easy and Ntobeko had operated separately from Mongezi and Vusumzi, coming together only at the scene of the crime. The four only came to know each other, they said, either during the criminal trials, in prison, or during preparations for the TRC.

In separate statements, Easy and Ntobeko confirmed that they had attended an afternoon PAC student rally at Langa Secondary School, caused trouble on the streets of Langa, and hopped a train home. From the Heideveld train station, they walked and toyi-toyi-ed up the street until they caught a ride with Viveza the shopkeeper in the direction of NY111. When they passed the Caltex, they saw Amy running across the road, pursued by a small group and surrounded by a larger group. They hopped out and stoned her. Easy "stabbed at her about three or four times."

"You told us in your affidavit that you stabbed at her and you don't know if you stabbed her or not," one commissioner said, puzzled. "You tried three or four times and you don't know if you stabbed her. I am asking you why you did not know. You feel if you stab someone."

"Things were happening very fast," Easy said evenly. "There were more than seven, eight or more of people, so that's why I don't know whether I did stab her or not because there were many people there."

"You had the knife in your hand, you could feel if you did it. Don't say it was because there were seven or eight people you don't know. You in fact know from the medical evidence that you didn't stab her, don't you?"

"Can you repeat your question please."

"You know from the medical evidence that you didn't stab her. She was only stabbed once. You heard the evidence of the post mortem, didn't you?"

"Yes, I've heard that in court."

"So you can't give any explanation why you didn't know what you were doing?"

"No, I am sorry, I won't know whether I did stab her or I attempted to, but I can remember that it was three or four times," Easy insisted.

"I am concerned about the suggestion . . . that the applicant is now tailoring his evidence to suit the finding," Arendse cut in, and from there, the argument meandered away from the question of why Easy did not know whether or not he stabbed Amy—the answer to which Easy himself would hint at to me years later. Easy, who could so effectively play the fool, had appeared befuddled, and Arendse had redirected the questioning. The commissioner gave up, and the hearing moved on. But the commissioner had raised an important point: don't you *know* when you stab a person, when the knife in your hand pierces their flesh? If you did not stab Amy Biehl, why are you hedging? Why not just claim your innocence?

For his part, Vusumzi said that he had been hanging out with his childhood friend Mongezi, whom he followed to the Langa Secondary School rally, where, he noted, "I did not understand much of what was being said." Vusumzi then rode the train with Mongezi to Gugulethu. There, he stoned Amy. All three men testified that they had seen Mongezi trip and stab Amy, which Mongezi confirmed.

Later, Brink cross-examined Easy. Brink was arguing, to a commission whose faces were becoming increasingly stony, that the applicants were not political revolutionaries but regular street criminals
thirsting for blood. Brink, with his pinkie ring and his ruddy complexion, harked back to a different time, and he wasn't warming up
the five pseudo-judges sitting before him. Easy, meanwhile, had
gone still with fury, drawing his rage inward.

"You see what I am going to suggest to you, Mr. Nofemela, is that
the attack and brutal murder of Amy Biehl could not have been
done with a political objective," Brink said. "It was wanton brutality,
like a pack of sharks smelling blood. Isn't that the truth?"

Easy's eyes turned to slate and his upper lip twitched once. He
leaned forward slowly, burning.

"No, that's not true, that's not true," he seethed in Xhosa, as the
translator spoke his words in English. "We are not such things."

Earlier that year, the Biehls received a fax at their Newport Beach
home. The men convicted of killing Amy would likely apply for
amnesty at the Truth and Reconciliation Commission. If the Biehls
were willing, the government would fly them to South Africa to attend the proceedings.

To Mandela's newly elected ANC government, the Biehls' presence at the TRC offered some benefit. For one, South Africa was
looking for foreign investment and wanted to shine on the international stage, so a pair of well-heeled Californians would lend global
legitimacy to this national process. The ANC knew that the Biehls
were sympathetic to their cause and broad-minded, and they suspected that the family might become examples of the power of
forgiveness. For the Biehls, the TRC presented an opportunity to

honor Amy before the world and before South Africa. Since her death, Amy had become, according to Linda, "a situation." At the TRC, they hoped to make her, once again, into a person. The Biehls called Tutu for counsel, and the archbishop's advice was simple: Speak about Amy, about who she was and what she meant to you.

So on the second day of the proceedings in July 1997, after Robin Brink rested his case, the committee chairman motioned to Peter Biehl. Peter, in his freshly ironed shirt, sat before a microphone at a wooden table. Linda sat to his right, her face placid. The four young applicants, perched at the front of the room, averted their eyes.

"We come to South Africa as Amy came, in the spirit of committed friendship," Peter began. He continued:

Amy was one of our four children. Her sisters are Kim, who is now thirty-one, Molly, twenty-seven, and her brother Zach, aged twenty. We are very proud of all our children and their accomplishments. But because Amy was killed in South Africa we are here to share a little of Amy with you. . . . Amy was a bright, active child. She loved competitive sport such as swimming, diving, gymnastics among others. She played the flute, the guitar. She studied ballet. She was a focused student from the very beginning, always striving for straight As. . . . At Stanford, she evolved as a serious student and began to focus her work on the Southern African region. Her love of Nelson Mandela, as a symbol of what was happening in South Africa, grew. . . . Who is Amy and what is her legacy here? Linda and I were struck by photos which appeared immediately after Amy's death in the *Los Angeles Times* and other newspapers around the world, which showed Amy as a freedom fighter. . . . We think, in view of the importance of freedom fighting in our world, this is a precious legacy of Amy for us. We think Amy's legacy in South Africa additionally is as a catalyst, and perhaps her death represented a turning point in things in this country, with specific regard to the violence which was occurring at the time.

I was reminded of how Peter subtly martyred his daughter when I spoke to Arendse, the defense attorney. "If my friends or family go to Syria or Iraq or Cairo, where there is unrest, if you find yourself shot or blown up, for me it would somehow make a difference because it's a war zone," he reflected, sitting at a paper-strewn desk. "Wanton violence is one thing, but if the death is because of political unrest, it makes a difference." A random and haphazard death offers less comfort and meaning to its survivors. Better that a life be lost for some greater cause, in the midst of a world-altering struggle.

"Knowing Amy, knowing what I learned from her, I could see this happening to her," Linda once told me. "People said it made no sense, but it made perfect sense. She lived exactly what was happening in the country until the end."

With the help of the TRC, Amy the Fulbright scholar and researcher who accidentally drove into the arms of a furious mob could be hailed as an international liberation hero. Her death did not have to be "senseless," as Detective Ilmar Pikker believed it to be. Her murder could be more than the indiscriminate, gruesome killing Rhoda Kadalie described: "A white girl was in the traffic, they took bricks, and they smashed her to a pulp." At the TRC, the murder of Amy, who prosecutor Nollie Niehaus had told me was called a "white bitch" by the mob before they took her down, became a legitimately political act rather than an arbitrary crime. She therefore became a political figure rather than a chance victim who died because young people were bored, disenfranchised, and angry. Amy's parents and her killers and the entire post-apartheid political apparatus all agreed on how the story had played out, and so the narrative was shaped for posterity. A Diane Sawyer special would soon focus on Amy and the Biehls' new role in South Africa.

"She left all this," said Sawyer, in her husky voice, as a camera spanned the landscape of Newport Beach, where white people Rollerbladed past yachts and waterfront homes. "For *this*:" then a shot of screaming black people running from exploding tear gas canisters. "The inspiring story of Amy Biehl."

The chronicle continued, playing on TV sets across American living rooms, asserting that South Africa's "history" had begun "three hundred years ago, when settlers arrived." This common interpretation of South African history—as a creature that had appeared, spontaneously, upon the arrival of white people—reminded me of an African proverb Mzi had once related to me: "Until the lion learns to write, every story will glorify the hunter."

Peter Biehl ended his statement before the TRC by reading admiring letters that he and Linda had received since Amy's death from regular people, as well as from South African politicians and intellectuals. One man had written that "August 25th 1993 will always be remembered as the day on which South Africa came to realize we are leaning into an abyss of total self-destruction. Then Amy died and an entire nation took a step back." Dullah Omar, who died in 2004, contacted the Biehls and praised Amy as "highly regarded by all her colleagues and peers," and then added, "your beloved Amy became one of us in her spirited commitment to justice and reconciliation in South Africa." A friend of Amy's, who had removed the jewelry from her dead body, called her "a most sensitive and wonderful human being." Peter continued, noting that he and Linda could neither oppose nor support amnesty. Whether or not amnesty would be granted to Amy's killers, Peter posited, would be the decision of "the community of South Africa." He ended:

> You face a challenging and extraordinarily difficult decision. How do you value a committed life? What value do you place on Amy and her legacy in South Africa? How do you exercise responsibility to the community in granting forgiveness in the granting of amnesty? How are we preparing these young men before us to re-enter the community as a benefit to the community, acknowledging that the vast majority of South Africa's prisoners are under thirty years of age? Acknowledging as we do that there's massive unemployment in the marginalized community; acknowledging

that the recidivism rate is roughly 95 percent? So how do we, as friends, link arms and do something? There are clear needs for prisoner rehabilitation in our country as well as here. There are clear needs for literacy training and education, and there are clear needs for the development of targeted job skill training. We, as the Amy Biehl Foundation, are willing to do our part as catalysts for social progress. All anyone need do is ask.

Are you, the community of South Africa, prepared to do your part? In her 21 June 1993 letter to the *Cape Times* editor, Amy quoted the closing lines of a poem written by one of your local poets. We would close our statement with these incredible words:

They told their story to the children. They taught their vows to the children that we shall never do to them what they did to us.

When the hearing finished, Linda and Peter shook hands with the four young men who had been seated behind the APPLICANT signs. Easy claimed that they also met in an elevator, just inches from each other, and that the Biehls had smiled at them, though neither Linda nor Ntobeko had any recollection of such a meeting. Then the Biehls went back to work in Gugulethu, where they poured nearly half a million dollars in donations and funding into various services for the community. These were the early days of the Amy Biehl Foundation.

On July 28, 1998, a year after the hearing, the amnesty committee finally ruled on the case, writing of the applicants in their five-page decision:

They were taking part in a political disturbance and contributing towards making their area ungovernable. To that extent, their activities were aimed at supporting the liberation struggle. But Amy Biehl was a private citizen, and the question is why was she killed during this disturbance. Part of the answer may be that her attackers got caught up in a frenzy of violence.

The committee then reflected on Peter Biehl's speech, quoting key parts, and ended with the statement: *The applicants have made full disclosure of all the relevant facts. . . . We have come to the conclusion that they may be GRANTED amnesty for the murder of Amy Biehl.*

The Biehls learned of the news back in California.

"Even though I was completely prepared for the outcome and expecting it, I found I really missed Amy a lot that day," Peter told a reporter.

Soon, the accused had been freed. Easy heard the news while lying on his prison cot; a gardener below his window was listening to the radio.

Ntobeko, Easy, and Mongezi headed back to Gugulethu. Vusumzi went to his mom's house in Langa, and then moved with her to a little township called Delft. Within the year, Mongezi had raped his neighbor, and by 2003, he had been sent back to Pollsmoor. Vusumzi got a job cleaning the parks. He worked for a year until the contract was canceled, and nobody had seen him in a decade.

By the late 1990s, after the meeting arranged by the anthropologist Nancy Scheper-Hughes, Peter and Linda had begun to develop their relationship with Easy and Ntobeko. They'd taken them to the waterfront for dinner. They'd watched *Austin Powers* together. Peter advised the men on job training.

"At first, everyone talked about the mob who killed Amy," Linda explained. "Then four were convicted, four were in prison. They didn't have names or identities—not to us or to anyone. At the TRC, we saw what they were like. Then Easy and Ntobeko came to us, and it became the two, and we learned more about them as individuals." The Biehls had been asked by a social worker to support Vusumzi Ntamo, and had briefly entertained the possibility of working with Mongezi Manqina. But they wanted to form relationships that exemplified reconciliation, not to function purely as patrons. Easy and Ntobeko, the original pair from NY111, reached out to the Biehls, seemingly interested not simply in money, but rather in a partnership that might benefit the township.

Early on, Easy claimed that the TRC and the Biehls had also helped him to become an individual. "You take yourself out of the shoes of a young soldier," he told me when we first met, back when he insisted he had been an APLA member who had trained in the bush for months. "You become yourself. I'm not kind of person hurting some other people's family. I love another as I love myself."

The idea of new identity was certainly appealing, but it was available only if the old identity was that of a principled freedom fighter. Perhaps equally appealing were the opportunities that Linda and Peter provided Easy and Ntobeko, opportunities never before available to a Gugulethu-born ex-con and high-school-dropout: a good job, a steady salary, clothes from America, gifts, a plot of land, international travel, and recognition. Easy once explained some of Linda's finest qualities to me: "Makhulu, she spoil children. She convince people."

Nearly a year to the day of the TRC decision, the Biehls stood before a crowd at the official launch of Easy and Ntobeko's short-lived youth club in Gugulethu. Within months, Linda and Peter would offer the two men jobs with the Amy Biehl Foundation and the men would stop leading local kids on hikes.

"I'm happy to be here and pleased that my daughter's killers are doing something positive for the community and that they are not being driven by politics or economic gain," Linda said to a rapt crowd that soon broke into applause.

13.

When you were poor, you had to have luck and do nearly everything exactly right.

—Adrian Nicole LeBlanc, *Random Family*

There's no power in the world strong enough to break a man's grip on his own throat.

—Arthur Miller, *Almost Everybody Wins*

By the spring of 2012, Easy's life was unraveling. I wanted to ask him about Mzi's contention that he had not killed Amy after all, that in fact he hadn't even been a soldier, but there was never a good time. Ndumi was pregnant, and her pregnancy had sent Easy into a panic. He had always wished to build a family with one single woman, a family that would eat the same food at the same table and receive the same punishment, just as he and his brothers had. Now, Ndumi's growing belly announced that he would never reconcile with Aphiwe's mother, and that his dream of a traditional Xhosa family was dead.

Aphiwe's mother, Lucretia, had been an eighteen-year-old orphan when Easy, fresh from prison, met her. Linda called Easy Lucretia's "white knight." He'd brought her free promotional bread from the foundation and wooed her, and she soon moved away from her sisters and into the Nofemela house on NY111. She worked at a shoe store, and when she had problems with her boss, Easy met with the man. He was wild for Lucretia. Linda even helped him buy a small diamond ring with which to propose. When Lucretia became pregnant, she and Easy were equally excited and terrified.

"I don't want to tell you how the doctor checked she was pregnant!" Easy told me.

"Tell me."

"He put two fingers up vagina. She came to me and said—" Easy lowered his voice to a whisper, " *'This doctor is doing a crime.'* I say, we must ask somebody who knows if is normal. And my aunt, she laugh just like you did now."

"How did you feel about Lucretia?"

"I love her too much. She is the first who show I can make babies."

Together, the two had begun to build a life, until one day, a few months after the birth of Aphiwe, Lucretia told Easy that she only loved him like a brother, not a husband. She pawned her diamond ring and left him, an event that was the genesis of Easy's bleeding ulcer: he spent months getting drunk and eating spicy meat to forget her. Then he tried, unsuccessfully, to soothe the ulcer by drinking goat's milk.

"She broke my heart," Easy said another time, while Ndumi sat nearby.

"You also broke her heart," Ndumi spat. "Tell truth. If you don't tell truth to us, tell truth to yourself."

Easy's relationship with Ndumi, to whom he would now be forever bound, had always been less serious. She and Easy had always liked to go out drinking and carousing.

Ten years earlier, Ndumi had graduated from community college. It was the happiest day of her life. She and her family, who felt a collective sense of awe for the world of higher education, had been under the impression that a degree—any degree, from anywhere, given to anyone—was a key that opened all those doors that had until then remained shut, locked, and barricaded against them. On the water-stained wall of her one-room shack, she had posted several torn, photocopied bits of paper bearing mantras for success:

WINNERS ADMIT FAILURE AND LEARN FROM IT,
LOSERS DENY FAILURE AND BLAME OTHERS

SUCCESS REQUIRES . . . PASSION, FOCUS, COMMITMENT

7 HABITS TO CREATE SUCCESS

Nearby, she posted a photograph of herself in her graduation cap, her arm hooked with her cousin's, a woman whom she considered a sister and a best friend, and who had died of AIDS a few years back. She also kept affixed to her wall a photograph of her grandmother, the person she loved more than anyone in the world and who had raised her after her mother disappeared, returning only once the kids were grown. Ndumi's grandmother had also died and to Ndumi's great regret she had not been able to make her grandmother truly proud. She had never gotten the government job of which she dreamed, a failure she blamed on her lack of connections. Instead, she'd spent the past nine years stocking shelves and running a cash register at the Century City Pick n Pay. No promotions, no opportunities. The one thing she could say for herself was that she'd earned enough money to buy the family a TV, furniture, some pots and pans and decorations. She was proud of this. Almost everything else in her life was the cause of a great, seething frustration.

Now, as the baby's arrival grew imminent, Easy and Ndumi, who had been on and off for five years, were edging toward breakdown by the day. They used to go partying together, but on account of the pregnancy, Ndumi was off the booze, which had shifted their dynamic. She was edgy, which made Easy avoid her, which made her edgier.

"I will name that baby an Afrikaans name, one that means oppressor," Easy once told Ndumi when he was a little drunk.

"Oh, *my* baby will be named after the oppressor, while Aphiwe is named 'gift'?" Ndumi said bitterly. She believed Aphiwe was a barrier between her and a normal domestic life. What if Easy always loved Aphiwe more than the child Ndumi was carrying?

In July 2012, at the old Dutch-style Somerset Hospital down by the waterfront, Easy and Ndumi's baby was born early via emergency cesarian, weighing under four pounds, his skin so sheer that the blue veins pulsed through, and so white that Ndumi wondered aloud for months how such a creature had come from her dark-skinned self. He was called Ukhanyiso. "It mean light from God," Ndumi said. More specifically, it means "revelation."

For a short time after the birth, Easy, Ndumi, and Ukhanyiso were a family. Ndumi abandoned her shack and took up residence in her old bedroom in her father's house. The room was solid and warm, with a petroleum heater in the corner to steam it up. The child was too small to drink from her breasts, she said, and so she mixed for him formula that he suckled from a dropper. Easy and Ndumi took turns massaging a medicinal blue jelly on Ukhanyiso's small body, a sangoma's salve they believed would keep him safe and healthy. Easy, the experienced parent, taught Ndumi about changing diapers, holding, rocking, burping, and pressing the naked baby to your chest, kangaroo-style. He abstained from drink and, to Ndumi's delight, ignored his mother's incessant calls. He spent all his free time at Ndumi's place on NY78, marveling at Ukhanyiso.

Aphiwe ran straight from school to Ndumi's shack every day, grabbing her baby brother and sucking on his cheeks. She drank the fruit-flavored corn syrup Ndumi mixed for her and fell asleep on the bed with her Mary Janes still on. While Ndumi watched TV, Aphiwe paced back and forth in the patch of sun by the door, talking softly to herself, playing a solitary game. She tried on Ndumi's high heels and clomped around the dirt yard in them as Ndumi regarded her skeptically.

"She look up to me," Ndumi said, squeezing out a smile. She knew I was fond of Aphiwe, and she was trying to follow suit, but she had very little affection for the child.

When Easy arrived, he scooped up his boy and kissed his head, and Aphiwe leaned on Easy's shoulder. They sat by the door on the hand-cobbled wooden bench, and a sheet of sun warmed them.

On the day of Ukhanyiso's birth, Ndumi's father had found a minuscule and underweight black and brown male puppy with the ears of a bat mewling on the street. "I hope he does not lose his life," he said, and named the puppy Diskie. He had taken to nursing him back to health with powdered milk. Energized, Diskie often rushed into the shack, yelping for attention, only to be shooed away by Ndumi. Then, relenting, she brought him a margarine container full of formula. Ndumi felt that Diskie was some sign from above: she'd been blessed with two baby boys all at once, both born small and weak but growing big and strong every day.

The happy days were short-lived. First off, Diskie nearly died after eating rat poison from the trash that littered the streets; he survived only because Ndumi's father spoon-fed him yogurt and ferried him to a free SPCA clinic over in Philippi just in time. Tension was also growing between Easy and Ndumi. Much of it had to do with money. Ndumi and Easy were exquisitely attuned to each other's every penny. When Easy had exactly 27 rand in his pocket for Aphiwe's school taxi fees, Ndumi would demand precisely 27 rand worth of mutton for herself. When Ndumi collected cash from the backyard renters behind her house at the end of the month, Easy glued himself to her side. When Easy's paycheck was wired into his bank account, Ndumi put her hand out, demanding his debit card. All Easy wanted to do, he moaned, was to "chillax," but Ndumi made chillaxing impossible.

They had differences of opinion on the subject of how to spend money, especially when it came to the baby: Easy wanted to buy single no-brand diapers, instead of a pack of Pampers. Ndumi refused the spaza store diapers. She wrapped Ukhanyiso in a blanket dotted with stars and Mickey Mouse and spent an inordinate amount of time gazing at him and cooing. A few days earlier, Easy had found Aphiwe's old stroller in the back room, and had offered it to Ndumi. Ndumi refused, disgusted: Linda had bought that stroller years ago, and Ndumi didn't want a decade-old stroller for her kid, not when Aphiwe had rolled around in a shiny new one.

"She say she want quality," a defeated Easy moaned. "She give me headache, and her voice is very up. She is not right."

The days were clear. A pungent stink emanated from the drains in the street. Gugulethu's one white resident walked by in a red shirt, looking cracked out but friendly, talking about Marxist theory.

"Very township boy," Easy said admiringly. "He even smoke tik tik and fight on the street with his girlfriend."

In the distance, shacks burned down, the smoke spiraling up and fanning out across the township. The close-set dwellings over in the settlements were always burning, just like the shacks I'd seen leveled on my first trip to the townships. The nights were cold in July, and petrol stoves got knocked over a lot. We all leaned on the wall surrounding Ndumi's fence and regarded the fire as one might a passing car.

Ndumi was increasingly jealous of Aphiwe. She feared that Easy would favor Aphiwe, and the forensic evidence of this rift lay in material goods. Easy, for his part, claimed that times had simply changed. When Aphiwe was born, he hadn't been so saddled with debt, and the Biehls had been in and out of town often, helping him buy bottles and onesies. These days, Easy was near broke. He had natural tendencies toward disorganization and absentmindedness— he was the type of person who loses an average of three cellphones annually—and was nearly financially illiterate.

In 2002, before their friendship had crumbled, Easy and Ntobeko had approached Linda for loans. Two plots of land were available near NY111, for around $1,000 each. Linda purchased the plots outright, in Peter's memory, but that was the extent of her gift. Ntobeko had since built an adobe-style single-level place, painted a rusty red and surrounded by a tidy wall. His interior decor was inspired by his trips with Linda to Santa Fe: spare wood, clean walls. His three well-dressed girls did their homework at the kitchen table and attended prep school outside Gugulethu. Ntobeko kept his growing fleet of private school transport vans in the driveway. When Kiki walked to the train station, she had to pass the place, and her face warped with envy.

Easy, meanwhile, had failed to pay the rates on his land, and had never built on it. Aphiwe's mom had refused to move there. It was too close to the Nofemela clan; wouldn't Kiki come knocking at the door every day? So Easy ignored the notices to pay his taxes on the NY111 plot and landed a high–interest–rate mortgage on the house in Khayelitsha, overpriced at 270,000 rand (about $25,000 at that time). Aphiwe's mother moved in with him, and then, soon thereafter, left him. Easy rented the house out to a series of tenants and returned to his parents' home. For the first year, he dutifully paid the bank back. But he soon began to ignore the notices collecting at his door. His tenant was pregnant. She didn't have a job, and how could he go banging down the door and making that poor lady pay? Once in a while, she did cough up the cash, but by then he was behind. He also owed on all his other loans and debts. And it was nice to be holding a wad of money. But even if Easy had been an excellent finance manager, he had plenty of factors working against him.

As a member of a poor, close–knit family, it was nearly impossible to put away a bit of cash in an "emergency" savings account, since emergencies hit with great regularity. People living close to the ground were always laid low by circumstances; something as simple as buying a child new school shoes could tilt the monthly budget and exhaust the savings. Living in close proximity to a vast extended clan meant that everyone knew exactly how much you were making and when you got paid. They were always asking for help, and if you had any extra cash around, even in a savings account, you'd be hard-pressed to resist if your sister was in the hospital or your nephew didn't have a winter coat. Keeping an account that could be accessed simply meant that the account *would* be accessed.

Easy had also gotten his salary tangled up in a variety of over-priced and poorly understood emergency plans specifically marketed to low-income people who could not save money in conventional ways. The plans, once joined, automatically deducted their rates directly from your salary each month. First, a funeral coverage plan deducted a large percentage of Easy's paycheck. This plan covered Easy, Kiki, and Wowo, and Easy had been paying into it for a decade, though you only really benefited from the plan if you died right after you joined, since the coverage was capped. By now, Easy had paid far more than he'd ever be able to claim back and would continue to pay in perpetuity, but at least he and his family were guaranteed a proper casket and a decent celebration. Funeral coverage plans were big business in the townships, where the deepest humiliation would be to be buried in a pauper's box, and where glory might be found if not in life, at least in death.

Easy had also been convinced to help buy Kiki a sofa set on layaway, and the company deducted the payments directly from his salary. Kiki's eldest son, who had a job with the postal service, had a strict wife, so Kiki could not go to him for favors. Nobody else had a steady paycheck. And Easy owed Kiki, what with her raising his kid. Plus, how could he say no to his own mother?

Then, he paid into an education fund for both Aphiwe and his brother Monks's son. Since Monks could not work, the family had taken up his ten-year-old son's cause. The son himself was something of a phantasm, a silent, slender child whose father lay unmoving on the couch and whose mother was never around.

A year earlier, Aphiwe had needed school supplies and new school clothes all at once, which would cost over $80, which was exactly $80 more than Easy had at the time. Easy had taken out an interest-free loan that the Amy Biehl Foundation offered its employees. Over time, the foundation repaid itself the loan by garnishing wages.

Easy usually received an annual windfall, but this year's was gone. He belonged to a group of twelve staffers who each month put a portion of their pay in a communal pot—$100 each, around a quarter of their salaries. Then, once a year, each employee collected $1,200. It was a way to simultaneously save and keep those savings inaccessible, because the money went into the pocket of your colleague and thus could not simply be withdrawn on a whim. Over time, Easy had used his yearly bonanza to, variously, buy bricks to build on the undeveloped plot that Linda had purchased for him and to purchase a used turquoise VW Jetta that two of his brothers

crashed while drunk and that had been languishing at the mechan-
ic's for nearly four years. Most recently, he'd used the $1,200 to drive
to Johannesburg to see a live performance of the Nigerian televan-
gelist Pastor Chris.

Pastor Chris was one of a collection of Nigerian pastors who
traveled the continent, commanding enormous stadiums full of
mostly black believers. He claimed that he was God's vessel, and as
such he could cure cancer and HIV. More important for Easy and
his family, Pastor Chris was able to faith-heal cripples up from their
beds and onto their feet. Back in Gugulethu, Easy, Wowo, and a
couple of other brothers had lifted Monks up and laid him down in
the back of Wowo's Nissan bakkie. Unable to afford a hotel, they
powered through the Karoo to Johannesburg for sixteen hours, passing by Colesburg, that dusty desert town where Sam and I had slept
the first time I cut through the country. They stayed with family
members in a township and attended days of sermons, all with the
goal of Monks rising tall. But Monks never did stand.

So Easy was essentially skint, which Ndumi refused to believe.
But she was right about one thing: Easy did favor Aphiwe, as Ndumi
suspected. She was his "angel" and his "miracle" and his "firstborn.
He adored and doted upon Ukhanyiso, whom he called "my boy,"
but his sense of responsibility was heightened when it came to his
daughter. In Easy's mind, Aphiwe would always need protection,
whereas Ukhanyiso, on account of being born male, would be able
to make his own way. The hazards faced by a daughter in Gugulethu
were enough to make Easy particularly vigilant. He constantly worried about the day, creeping ever closer, when Aphiwe would get a
boyfriend, and he worried further about the possibility that Aphiwe's boyfriend would hit her, which was not an uncommon occur-
rence.

Ndumi was unforgiving on the matter of Aphiwe versus
Ukhanyiso. She was spending a full day every month standing in line
at the social services office for her monthly grant: 250 rand for her
baby, or around $30. Anything Easy had, she wanted. Whenever he

received the remains of a paycheck, they went shopping and she bought unnecessary items out of spite. She needed diapers and formula, but instead she bought both a strawberry-shaped pacifier and a banana-shaped pacifier, a pair of expensive bibs with trucks on them, a blue spoon in the shape of a dolphin. Then, rather than stocking up on much needed groceries, Ndumi demanded that Easy take them out to eat. She knew full well that she should have purchased staples, but she was also sick of eating beans at home for every meal. The family went to KFC and blew his extra cash on the nine-piece bucket with a mini-loaf, sides, and soda for everyone. Ndumi angrily consumed her chicken legs and sat back, semi-satisfied.

For the rest of the month, Easy had to borrow a young relative's school pass to board the train. He scrounged around the sofa for single-rand coins to buy loose cigarettes. He borrowed money from friends for beer, which he would often pay back before he helped out his family, to save face. He tried desperately to not think of his debts and his bills.

From a cultural standpoint, Easy had pressing expenses from every angle. In addition to the cash he needed to support Ukhanyiso and Aphiwe (who again owed school fees and needed a uniform), he also owed Ndumi's father for knocking her up out of wedlock; such a payment was known as a "penalty," and was standard in Xhosa culture, the reasoning presumably being that the family of a pregnant and unmarried girl or woman would be saddled with an extra burden when a baby arrived. It is also a way of showing respect to a pregnant woman and her family by making sure a father acknowledges a baby as his. Without this payment, a father would traditionally have no rights of visitation, and the baby would be raised at the mother's homestead and with her surname. But while Easy talked endlessly about the value of Xhosa cultural mores and had based his identity within the Xhosa structure, he ignored the rules when inconvenient or unaffordable, which accounted for his ability to buy beer but not to pay the pregnancy penalty. He was always going on about the beauty of African hospitality, and one day I lost my patience.

"You talk so much about the Xhosa way of treating guests, but nobody at your house has ever so much as offered me a glass of water," I said. "What is that about?"

Easy's face fell. "Is so embarrassing," he said, shaking his head, and then ran off to get me a mug of tea. That day was the only day he ever did such a thing, and I visited at least once a week for well over a year—and then on and off for three more.

One day, Ndumi, Easy, and I went to Hout Bay, a small fishing village on the peninsula, where Ndumi's sangoma lived. The sangoma was a heavyset woman who claimed, as many sangomas do, to have been commanded by her ancestors to enter the world of witch medicine. To become a full sangoma, a person had to undergo a number of otherworldly challenges.

"You go out to the ocean, you go down to the bottom of the sea," Easy once explained. "The scientists look for you but can't find you. But you are there, talking to ancestors."

This particular sangoma had met Ndumi at a shop, noted that Ndumi was in crisis, and offered her services, for a modest fee. A desperate, lonely Ndumi had come, in the span of a few months, to consider this particular sangoma a mother, a mentor, a comfort— none of which she had in her life in Gugulethu. The sangoma's daughter brought out glasses of Coke on a tray, and then we brought Ukhanyiso to the back room, where the sangoma performed a prayer to the ancestors, lit some herbs to fire, and blew a lot of heavy smoke around. Then she placed a red string around Ukhanyiso's neck, and Easy dug his last 200 rand from his pocket and placed it in her palm.

The more temperamental Ndumi became, the less frequently Easy visited her. He often drank to draw up the courage to approach her. When he did go to her, they fought. She confessed to me that one evening she had smacked him in the face with a broom and his nose had spouted blood. He pressed her against the wall and the wall cracked, but he didn't retaliate.

"She told me she hit you in the face with a broom and you bled all over the place," I reported to Easy.

"Ahhh, she joking," he said. It was a terrible shame to be knocked around by a woman, in a place where a real man would not be judged for hitting back (or hitting first) to keep his lady in line.

"I believe her," I said, inspecting the scratches, bristle-shaped, on his face.

"Womens are lying in the township," he said, gingerly touching the small scabs.

Easy missed his boy but he couldn't provide for him. He was nervous for Aphiwe, for he sensed that Ndumi was growing to despise her. Easy didn't like the person he was becoming, and he worried that he would hit Ndumi.

"She can paint me black. She can throw blames on me. Sometimes, I grabbing her and I stop myself. I say, 'Easy, don't do it.'"

He drank more, she fought harder, he drank more, she raged, and then he finally disconnected. One morning, when Ukhanyiso was five months old, Ndumi called me. She was going to kill herself, she informed me. She'd found a text on Easy's phone from a girl called Tiny: *Hey there sweetlips*. Worse, according to Ndumi, Easy had taken a loan from a local shark and used it to buy himself booze, $500 worth. Easy had dressed up smart and taken Aphiwe shopping in the city. Easy had promised Ndumi that he'd call and that she and the baby could take part in the spoils. She took the cloth off her hair and put on her wig, penciled in her eyebrows, applied blue sparkly shadow, and dressed in a purple, slinky off-shoulder top. The baby wore his cutest pair of denim overalls. They waited all afternoon but the phone didn't ring. When Ndumi called, Easy didn't pick up.

Next thing, Aphiwe's got brand-new blue jeans and long braids and Ndumi and Ukhanyiso have nothing at all. *Sweetlips.*

"He won't answer his phone," she said. "I will do a suicide."

I dialed Easy and whispered Ndumi's threats. "She joking," he said.

"I think you should deal with this rather than ignore it," I hissed.

"I know," he said, sighing. But he didn't do a thing.

"Okay, Jus, I won't do a suicide," Ndumi promised when I called back. "But I do want to leave this place, just go away."

She didn't do a suicide. Instead, after a few hours spent mulling over how she had been wronged, Ndumi grabbed her baby and marched to Easy's house, where he was drinking beer on the street with relatives visiting from Johannesburg. By then, weeks into their latest battle, Ndumi was disheveled, her eyes full of fire. She handed the baby to Aphiwe, who clutched her brother and smooched his forehead passionately. Then, as Aphiwe and the neighbors and Easy's family watched, Ndumi suddenly attacked Easy, pulling her long nails through the skin on his cheeks. Wowo put his hand to his forehead and Kiki entertained visions of throttling Ndumi herself, and the Johannesburg relatives cocked their heads to the side.

Easy felt a fury rise up inside him but he did not fight back. He suspected Ndumi of a plan: He hits her, she goes to the cops, he lands in jail, and jail can lead to prison, and prison "is not a place for anyone." Plus, Easy had stopped beating up ladies long ago, before prison, after that one time, when they were teenagers, when he stabbed his girlfriend Pinky during a dustup—just once, and not even enough to warrant a trip to the clinic.

Pinky, now in her forties and living across town, still remembers the relationship fondly, apart from the stabbing. "He was drunk when he stab, but after he was sorry and so worried."

"Just a little stab?"

"Just a little stab. And we stayed together. Even now, we are friends and I am friends with his family. And he is changed. He is grow up."

So Easy waited for Ndumi's assault to end instead of retaliating.

She then retrieved the baby, tied him to her back, and marched home, muttering. Easy's cheeks and nose were torn up. Aphiwe sobbed, holding her father, burying her face in his chest. For his part, Easy had been preparing for this moment.

"I just trust myself," he once told me. "How can you trust a human being? Better to trust a rock. You can go back in ten years and a rock is there, unless removed by a human being. You love somebody, somebody love you. When you going to close your eyes, the person is going to disappoint you. You pray to God, you want straightforward person, but is a human being. You need inside of you a room of disappointment. You have to have a disappointing room. A little space, but is not active when you love somebody. I go with the flow, but when the time comes, I got that room."

A few days after the attack, Ndumi called me again and asked me to come to her. I was living in Sea Point then, a wealthy suburb on the Atlantic Seaboard. The streets were narrow and swept clean every day by a tired army of black and colored workers in neon vests emblazoned with the words JESUS SAVES—they were employed by private companies that had won tenders with the city. The blocks were lined with homes in pale, creamy colors, hidden behind high walls. From my kitchen table, on clear days, when I opened the iron security gate all the way to get a nice view, I could watch paragliders who jumped from the peak of Lion's Head floating down to the lush rugby field near the ocean promenade.

I drove down the highway and over the Gugulethu border. Some people were burning garbage on the township's outskirts and the stench fanned out. As always, that same old man with the dented head hobbled up to my window at the same stoplight, putting out his callused hand, and as always I averted my eyes.

On hot afternoons, the township was dry and flat. All the colors melded together, a sea of pastels, hazy as an airplane strip. I drove by Kanana, that "land of milk and honey" where Mzi's brother Steyn was committing his slow suicide. By then, I had conducted a few interviews inside Kanana's borders, and each time groups of men would wander by and eye my car. And then Mzi or Easy or whoever I was interviewing would shoot them a firm yet friendly "no-funny-business" nod, and the men would wander off amenably.

Along I went to Ndumi's family home on a street lined with old apartheid-government-built houses that had been in families for generations and had been, if the families were successful, expanded, painted, and improved upon. The New & Used Tyres shop, a desolate field, a hair salon offering "eyelashes, soft-n-free, dark-n-lovely." Flyers were plastered all over light poles. "Dr. Monica" was particularly enterprising, and had posted her ad up and down the poles throughout several townships: *Abortions/womb Cleaning, Dr. Monica, For your families planning, Beware of Imitators.* Additionally, Dr. Hawa the sangoma could help you with the following issues: *Penis enlargement, Lost Lover, Man Power.*

A Golden Arrow bus ambled by. Golden Arrow is the city bus line that serves the townships. Its tagline is "The Bus for Us." People joke that Golden Arrow bus drivers must boast one simple skill in order to get hired: the inability to drive a bus. A mural of a cartoon sausage with the words *Chhsch chhsch* written below it covered a wall. Two little boys were fistfighting, cheered on by a group of kids. A bead of blood fell neatly from the nose of the taller child.

I pulled up to Ndumi's place. Two little boys approached me.

"*Umlungu,* crisps, crisps," they said, grinning wide, hands out, awed by their own wild courage. I looked in the backseat, where, anticipating this common request, I'd thrown a few little bags of Nik Naks cheese snacks. I had heard a lot of convincing arguments about why one should not give candy or gifts to poor kids—undermines the parents, creates dependency, connects white skin with privilege and charity. But I pulled a bag out and gave it to them to share.

I slipped by the gate. The old dog nodded hello and licked a wound; he always started fights with passing dogs and then had to spend days recuperating. Diskie the puppy, now recovered, bounded up to me. Ndumi's dad waved from the corner. He was wearing a mole's tooth around his neck. Why? Because a while back he'd found a dead mole in the sink, skinned it, and made a necklace from its cuspid.

Ndumi was standing up in her shack, packing up her clothes with purpose. She wore a flowered romper, her pretty face scraped free of makeup, her hair pulled back beneath a wrap the colors of the South African flag: yellow, red, green. I sat on the worn futon and picked up the baby, who had previously been lying in his blanket, gazing at the ceiling.

Today she was going to Hout Bay to stay with her sangoma, Ndumi informed me. Everyone had betrayed Ndumi, even her father, always telling her to calm down. Easy had been her best friend, her everything, and now he was cheating, leaving her alone with this baby. His baby. You look at this baby, just look, and you'll see Easy there in his face. Did you know there are other babies around this neighborhood, babies that look exactly like him, that he won't claim as his own? Maybe even five of them!

I held the baby closer. He smelled like chemicals. It could have been that blue jelly Ndumi smeared on his head to keep bad spirits away. He looked a little yellow, too, come to think of it, but he was still in a good mood. He had deep black eyes, big pools set in his beautiful face. He wore the sangoma's red string around his neck. He looked at me steadily.

Ndumi scooped Ukhanyiso up, wrapped him in his fuzzy brown blanket with teddy bear print, and pulled him to her chest. She gathered her belongings—a plastic tub of sausage, a change of clothes for herself and her child, a tin of formula—in a Winnie the Pooh duffel and announced she was ready to go. I was her ride, it seemed, so I drove Ndumi to town. She sat in the back of the car and held the baby close. She set her jaw and stared out the window. I blabbered on.

"Stay strong for your baby," I said, trying to come up with plati-
tudes but finding only clichés. "You can't let a man get you down.
You have your degree!"

It was nonsense: Ndumi was a black woman born in Gugulethu.
Her father had been fired from the potato chip factory and relegated
to wandering the township with his weed wacker, offering to trim
lawns; then the weed wacker broke. Her grandmother, who had
raised her, was dead. Her absent mother, gone for her entire childhood, spent all day at church. Her degree had gotten her nowhere,
and a decade after graduation her résumé only boasted jobs as a
checkout girl, a stacker of boxes, and a stocker of shelves. Ndumi was
thirty-three and unemployed. She lived in a shack behind her parents' house with her baby. Once in a while, she applied for a gig here
or there, and said, "Maybe today is my lucky day." It never was.

"I can't lie, Justine," she said finally, from her perch in the backseat.
"I do pray for Easy to be punished for what he did to me."

We exited the highway onto Strand Street, the broad thoroughfare that cuts through the city center. I pulled off near the taxi station and hit my hazard lights. From here, Ndumi could catch a
minivan that headed south to Hout Bay. She slid out, pulling her
bags with her and balancing Ukhanyiso. Then she leaned down
toward my window.

"He's not a good person. He really isn't. Easy is full of secrets, my
loving."

Soon thereafter, I met Easy at Mzoli's. He was half happy, half
sad. On the downside, Ndumi had blocked him from seeing the
baby. On the upside, he had a new girl, Tiny, she of the "sweetlips"
texts. Now, he explained, he wasn't saying he *had* cheated on Ndumi,
but *if* he had, it would have been because Ndumi had made him do

it. Tiny joined us for a bite. She was a twenty-nine-year-old single
mother, smart and even-keeled. When she was mad or sad, she
needed to eat chocolate cake or ice cream immediately, and her
dream was to one day open a small sandwich shop. She was under-
stated and pretty, with long braids, delicate curves, and good manners. She had pulled out her two front teeth—pulling out one's top
front teeth was an enduring Cape Flats trend—and so sometimes
displayed an oddly appealing gap and sometimes inserted her tooth
piece with one perfect fake white incisor and one gold incisor. Tiny's mother had a contract with the city of Cape Town to clean the
gutters, which meant that the family did relatively well. Tiny's twin
brother had a car and his own place. Her little sister went to school.
Tiny had thus far been paying down Easy's debts, and trying to
manage his various decrepit properties. She adored him "even with
his luggage," but she found him impenetrable.

"He has a pain," she told me. "Some deep thing, from prison or
Amy."

"What do you get from him?" I asked.

"His love, his everything."

"What do you want from him?"

"Just for him to change. A lot."

A crowd of strapping white tourists in long shorts and high socks
filed into the restaurant. A tour guide marched ahead, banging a tiny
drum.

"Your people!" Tiny exclaimed, turning to me.

"I feel like they're German," I countered.

Nearby, a white man and a Latino man, both dressed in neat
button-downs and khakis, stared at us. The white man leaned in.

"Is the food okay to eat?" he asked me.

He was British, it turned out, and his companion was Bolivian.
They were in Gugulethu to do business—though the nature of that
business was not revealed.

"But is it safe here?" the Brit asked. "Didn't that English lady get
killed here?" He was referring, I gathered, to the 2010 murder of

Anni Dewani, a Swedish tourist whose bullet-ridden body had been found in Khayelitsha. She had been in Cape Town on her honeymoon when she was murdered. Her new husband, a British citizen, had been accused of ordering the hit, which prosecutors claimed he had had engineered to seem like an unplanned carjacking. After years of court battles, he was cleared and flew first-class straight back to London. One of the hit men, now in prison, had lived on Ndumi's street.

"Safe enough," I said, and the Englishman ran off to wash his hands thoroughly.

We stayed for an hour. Our meat was delivered, pap and the spicy chopped vegetable relish *chakalaka,* too, all on a large silver plate, no utensils. A young man wearing a floral shirt with the top six buttons undone flounced by, smoking a cigarette and holding a hot mug of coffee. Easy had a gay brother, a fact he had revealed by saying, "My brother is   " and then flapping his hand from a weak wrist. Since Xhosa culture is not terribly progressive and Easy was fairly traditional himself, I asked him how he felt about his gay brother. His cousins had been around him at the time and they had all shrugged.

"Is our family so we must support him," Easy had said without any affect, and the cousins all nodded. The man in the floral shirt was a friend of the gay brother.

"I need fifty rand, I am in such love trouble," the man said. His phone was stolen a few days earlier by a neighborhood skollie.

Easy couldn't help him with cash, but he could offer advice: "Why don't you take action to get your phone back?"

"Oh *honey*, that's later," the man said, sitting down at our table and dramatically crossing his legs. "I'm waiting for the perfect moment. I'm a well-known bitch!"

Then he ran off and returned with a pile of napkins, which he dropped at the table, and continued his rounds. I had no idea if he was employed by Mzoli's or if he just enjoyed flitting about, serving and socializing.

"Can we try the story of Amy Biehl one more time?" I asked Easy. He opened a bottle of ginger beer. "I feel like something isn't right."

He picked up some lamb and chewed off the meat. Since I had bought the food, Tiny was trying to be polite by pretending she wasn't hungry and sipping some tap water. When I insisted, she happily picked up a sausage.

"Sometimes I feel South Africa divert my life," Easy said absently. "If I was not here in South Africa, maybe I be a professional."

"What happened that day? What are you not telling me?" I was hoping he might corroborate Mzi's story, but I didn't want to guide him.

"My friend, honestly, I didn't stab Amy. Because it was already people around her, a lot of people around her, and we started to make a fire to burn her car but we couldn't so the police arrive."

"If you didn't do it, why did you take the responsibility?"

"The people saw me, the witnesses they know me, each every one. They point me."

"Mongezi was the only one who stabbed her?"

"The only one."

"They say she may have died from a rock to the head, though."

"I still remember they said that she may still be alive if there was no wound in heart. There was a problem with her head, but if she could be taken to hospital, she might still be alive. But the wound to the heart, she could not be okay."

"But you did throw stones?"

"Mmm hmmm."

"And Ntobeko threw stones?"

"Yeah, we throw stones. But the person who trip and stab Amy is Mongezi. And if Amy was alive it would be easy for Amy to identify the person in front of them."

I picked up a chicken wing, took a bite, and then reeled back. Mzoli had a secret spicy sauce that he added to his meat, and it was this sauce that Easy claimed had exacerbated his ulcer. It was hard, though, to stop eating it.

Just then, two little kids shuffled up to the clear plastic sheeting that separated Mzoli's from the street. They looked longingly at our platter.

"I'm done," I said, so Easy beckoned them in. They rounded the restaurant and gathered their courage to sneak in past the bouncers. But first, they picked at each other's hair—one child had a bald patch on his head, and he was self-conscious. He pulled up his hood and took a deep breath. Then they entered with trepidation, looking at us. I estimated that they were around seven years old. Easy took all the pap and all the meat, scraped it onto a Styrofoam plate, and handed it to them, a gift they received in quiet wonder before fleeing.

Easy turned to me and smiled. "Nomzamo," he said, using the Xhosa name he'd bestowed upon me. "You will learn the truth about Amy, Nomzamo. Nomzamo. Is a big name. Is a tornado. What you need, you get. I see in your eyes."

Easy called me the following Saturday morning.

"Good news," he said. "Me and Tiny are marrying."

"What? When?"

"Nownow. Please, can you come to Gugs?"

I sped over to the house and found Easy crouched on the side of the road, wearing a blue workman's jacket, elbow-deep in a pungent pot of sheep intestines that he was cleaning.

"My friend!" he bellowed, swerving over. The proposal was a surprise, he explained. Just last night he'd asked Tiny to marry him, and today was their traditional Xhosa wedding. He was over the moon. I gave him a bottle of white wine I'd had in my refrigerator.

"Champers!" he exclaimed, and wobbled away.

For her part, Tiny was less certain about the whole ceremony. She knelt on a mat on the floor of a back bedroom, her hair wrapped in a cloth and a wool blanket slung over her shoulders. Easy's eldest brother fed her meat by hand and gave her water from a jug. Easy had not yet paid her family *lobola*, the traditional Xhosa bride price, and he hadn't really spoken to Tiny about the wedding. She was under the impression that they might get married six months later, but in old-school style he had "kidnapped" her, symbolically (she could have easily left if she hadn't been into it), and she would be living in his house as his wife from now on. She had to wear the costume of a new wife—long skirt, long-sleeved shirt, hair covered, a blanket around her shoulders—for as long as Kiki demanded, and for several months she would be expected to wake before the family, go to sleep after them, and do the bulk of household chores. Easy had purchased a six-pack of Blue Ice blueberry-flavored spirit cooler for the occasion.

"He made the decision without my permission," Tiny said. "I just came here to chill yesterday. The family was all here and I thought they were having family meeting. Then they say they want us to marry."

People came in and out of the room. There was a charcoal grill smoking up the backyard.

"Easy has to become a man, take responsibility now," Tiny said, mostly to herself. "I hope I am marrying a good man."

"All the men in my family are good," one of Easy's female cousins said to reassure her. "They don't beat women."

Outside, Easy's family was boiling mutton over a fire. A relative was also cooking *umqombothi,* a Xhosa beer made for centuries from maizemeal, corn malt, sorghum, malt, yeast, and water. Once fermented overnight and strained, the sour brew would be poured into a communal metal pot called a *gogogo* and passed around. By the time I left, at 2:45 in the afternoon, Easy was passed out in a bedroom.

"He has been overwhelmed by the occasion," his brother said.

Just days before the proposal, Tiny and Easy had engaged in a debate on love, during which he was pointedly more optimistic than his unknowing wife-to-be, who contended that modern-day township courtship came down to who could offer what. They were sitting in her mother's living room, a fan blowing, a set of copper pots displayed proudly in the armoire, as fancy pot-and-pan collections were a popular type of decor.

"You take me on a date to Mzoli's, you give me a Heineken from your cooler and some meat," Tiny said. She was talking about gold-digging on a township level: some girls slept with guys who bought them a dollar's worth of phone time, while others wanted Carvelas, a brand of imported Italian loafer—made in brightly colored patent leather and costing upward of $300—that was the ultimate status symbol of the moment.

"What about love?" I interjected.

"Black people? There's no love," Tiny said bitterly. "There's no love. It's all about money."

"There is love," Easy said. "There *is*."

Soon after the wedding, Tiny moved into Wowo and Kiki's place, and for a month or so their life was relatively harmonious. Kiki was happy to have a daughter-in-law to do her bidding, which involved demanding that every single task be completed by Tiny. Easy was happy to have a woman by his side and Aphiwe was happy to have a stepmother who would walk her all the way to school and give her a kiss on the cheek. For years, she had been watching other little girls get their cheeks kissed, and now it was her turn.

But after that honeymoon period, Tiny was less pleased that she was required to serve Kiki tea and treats day in and day out. She missed her own mother, with whom she was feuding. Tiny's mom, who was pro-ANC, didn't like Easy's reputation, and so Tiny and her mom were icing each other out. Tiny missed her young son, who was staying with his grandmother, and her twin brother. She had been nicknamed Tiny when she'd emerged into the world because she was the little twin, and her brother was named Ndlovu, or elephant, for his relatively grand size. He tried to visit as much as he could, but Tiny needed Kiki's permission to socialize, and such permission was hard to come by.

More problematic than all that was the increasingly furious presence of Ndumi, about whom rumors swirled: some people said she'd gone to jail after threatening to kill herself and the baby. Others swore they'd seen her dressed nice at church, pushing the baby in a pram. Either way, she had gotten Tiny's phone number and had taken to calling her at all hours, claiming that Easy continued to visit her at night. Indeed, Easy did slip out with increasing frequency, his phone now switched off as Tiny paced.

Ndumi also showed up at the house, threatening to fight Tiny. Tiny called the cops and charged Ndumi with harassment. Ndumi charged Tiny with harassment right back. The two women ended up at an "open air" community court held in a trailer.

Ndumi arrived alone, wearing high-heeled boots and a trench coat. Tiny wore her wife outfit and was accompanied by Easy, Easy's aunt Princess, Easy's sister-in-law, and me. Ndumi shot me a look of betrayal, then approached me and embraced me in a tight, wordless hug before pushing me away.

"She gonna key your car," one of Easy's relatives whispered.

The two women were then called into a social worker's office. Easy's aunt put her ear to the wall as the women raised their voices. She offered a running commentary: "Ndumi is yelling 'I made this baby with Easy, not you!' to Tiny," she reported with delight.

Then the social worker called Easy in, and the fight unfurled for two hours. Everyone else waiting by the trailers was told to return the next day. The social worker, a tall man, recommended additional counseling. When the door opened, we all peeked in.

"Who is that?" the social worker asked, pointing to me, the only white person around.

"She's his friend," Tiny said, gesturing to Easy.

"She used to be my friend, but not anymore," Ndumi said. She walked off alone.

Later, in the car, Easy shook his head. "For Ndumi, this is just the beginning," he said.

But Tiny and Easy thought they would be able to work out all the frustrations with time. Tiny thought she might be able to talk Easy into couples counseling, an idea he rejected.

"Too Western," he said.

"But it could help," Tiny said.

Easy shook his head. "I never went to counseling for Amy," he said. In a split second, his eyes turned cold. "How do I know this counselor person? Can a person change? My father, he is nice now but he used to be very aggressive. He was beating my mom and we sleep in the streets because we can't go in the house. But today they are too close, so people can change."

"You don't trust the counselor?" Tiny asked.

"No, I don't trust nobody." His face was tightening, his mouth pursed. I had so rarely seen him break from his cheerful demeanor. "What if you look at the past and it create problems? We must just go forward, forward."

Since the 1993 murder trial had spanned eleven months, its records were stored in dozens of cardboard boxes that could be obtained by request at the High Court. I had flipped through thousands of pages, but they were usually repetitive hard copy transcripts of the day-to-day testimony, and were largely out of order. What I needed, I felt, was some shred of evidence about the day itself—and evidence was missing from the boxes, as was the police file. At my first meeting with Nollie Niehaus, the prosecutor, he had asked his assistant to request the old file, but it was missing from the central archives— Niehaus guessed that was probably because old records were destroyed to make room for new ones.

One morning, I drove my regular way to Gugulethu, taking a road high above the ocean that led to the thoroughfare that fed onto the N2. The traffic was stopped, bumper-to-bumper, and a distance that usually took me five minutes to cover suddenly took an hour. At the main intersection, police had set up crime scene tape around a crushed white car. In the near-dawn hours, it came to light, two men had hijacked a minivan in Nyanga and then hit the highway and headed toward the city—an unorthodox choice, since any reasonable thief would head in the opposite direction. When the police began to chase them, the criminals took on speed, barreled through a red light, and plowed, at 60 miles an hour, into an oblivious hatchback ambling by. The driver of the hatchback, a woman headed to work, was killed instantly. The hijackers walked away, shackled but unharmed.

I continued on to the Gugulethu Police Department, hoping that they might have a copy of the elusive case file. On the way, I passed two separate dead dogs, lying stiff, mouths and eyes open, on two separate trash heaps. The station was filled with people waiting to report minor crimes or getting various affidavits certified. I was the only white person in line, and the black policeman at the counter called me ahead of everyone else and asked me what I needed.

The officer ordered somebody to help me find the case file. He spoke in Xhosa, but I could work out one English word nestled in the sentence: *priority*. I, in my whiteness, was a priority, no matter who I was—and the cop had no idea who I was, as he had neither asked my name nor inquired as to my purpose. A man whisked me into a back room, where another officer began searching an archaic, plodding database on a dying desktop. The background was black, the letters in white.

Amy's name never came up on the system, so I asked to scroll through the reports from August 25, 1993, one by one. Assaults, "non-white on non-white," were mentioned, one after another, followed by a robbery, an arson, a domestic complaint. At 5 P.M., a murder had been reported.

"That one," I said.

The policeman clicked on the case, and there was Officer Leon Rhodes, listed as the complainant. Amy's name was nowhere. The arrested suspects were the original eight: Easy, Ntobeko, Mongezi Manqina, and Vusumzi Ntamo, as well as the APLA trio that had been set free and the teenager who disappeared. I wrote down the case number: 447/08/93, and the police officer advised me that I could find the folder in the police archives, which were stored just down the street in the old army barracks.

"Is there anyone here that would remember anything about the day?" I asked.

"I don't think so," he said, leading me behind the booking desk. "But ask him. He knows everything."

A hulking white officer with a gelled yellow buzz cut sat at a computer in the main reception area. The officer turned toward me.

"Is it true? Do you know about the Amy Biehl case?" I asked.

"I do, but I'll never talk," he said gravely.

"Talk to her!" a secretary cajoled. He shook his head, resolute, stood up, and disappeared down the hallway. After canvassing other employees, I made my way to a series of trailers in the back of the station. I poked my head in each, looking for Officer Buzz Cut, until I came upon him.

"There you are!"

"I'll never talk," he said dramatically.

A white officer in a suit stopped in. I asked him if he knew anything about Amy Biehl, and he shook his head. "Not a thing."

On my way out of the station, I convinced a secretary to give me Officer Buzz Cut's phone number and I sent him an SMS, asking that he let me know if he ever wanted to chat. Then I drove over to the Gugulethu barracks, where the old police files were kept. They were enclosed behind a chain link fence, a sagging three-story municipal building that had once housed defense force members. It had been converted into a variety of warehouses and offices connected with the police. An elderly colored man was listening to a radio outside a room of folders. He wore a faded checked shirt and looked as though he had been running this closet for his entire life.

"I'm looking for 447/08/93," I said.

The man nodded and wandered back into a long, thin room lined with teeming shelves. After a few minutes he emerged with a parcel of folders, tied with a string. Together, we opened it up and flipped through: folder 444/08/93, followed by 445/08/93, 446/08/93, and then 448/08/93. Folder 447 was nowhere to be found. The man shrugged. Sometimes cops took folders from their cases like totems, he observed. Sometimes downtown ordered up a file and never returned it. Sometimes old papers got incinerated.

I drove to Easy's house and sat down on a roughshod bench by Wowo's Nissan. Kiki and her obese friend, dressed in an orange and green African shift, were gossiping in two chairs by the door. A herd of goats wandered by, munching on trash. The Ford was parked out on the sidewalk in the sun, with Monks inside as always, his face moist with sweat. I was trying to figure out how to approach Monks for an interview, considering Mzi's contention that Monks had in fact been involved in Amy's murder, but a neighbor was hanging out with Monks, shooting the shit in the passenger seat. The neighbor had a daughter he couldn't support, a rotten front tooth, and not an inch of fat on his body. He had been unemployed for years, "just sitting around the location," and he spent much of his time with Monks. The two had been together in the accident that paralyzed Monks, but the neighbor had walked away without a scratch.

My phone beeped. It was a message from Officer Buzz Cut.

Hey I'm not sure if I can help you. I suggest that u compile a list of questions and I may see if I can assist.

I stared at the message, got in my car, and headed home. Until I had met Mzi, I hadn't had an inkling that the case was anything other than what it seemed. My phone, sitting in my lap, buzzed again.

Back in pre 1994 the person in question were involved with organiza-

tions / people which may have made her a person of interest as she were an
activist. There may have been a file on her. I don't suppose you can expect to
much assistance with regards to finding and answers. Even after all this time.

As I turned off my exit, the phone rang.

"I am doing my daily exercise," Officer Buzz Cut said. "So I thought I'd call."

"Listen, I'd love to hear what you have to say," I said, holding the wheel with one hand. "Maybe we could meet for a coffee."

"A meeting is hard but maybe you have questions."

I pulled off the main drag, flustered but aware that this might be my only chance to talk to this curious cop. "Um, do you think somebody else committed the murder, somebody not convicted?" I asked.

"Yes."

I stopped the car. A parking guard in a neon vest tapped on my window, asking for money, and I waved him off.

"Do you think ANC knows who?" I asked.

"Let's hold on to that."

"Do you think the story at TRC was accurate?"

"No."

"Do you think the people arrested were involved?"

"Some of them may have been."

"What are you saying?"

I could hear his labored breath—I supposed he was jogging, or at least walking fast. "She wasn't very popular with the government of the day. She was an activist. That docket is gone, isn't it?"

"It wasn't at the barracks," I said. "Maybe the guy at the archives will eventually find it."

"You won't find the docket, you know the answer."

"But I *don't* know the answer. I hardly know what we're talking about."

"The problem is, you're talking to too many people. Do you think it was a coincidence that the white guy in a suit was there in my office?"

"Sure. It wasn't?" The guy had seemed like any other civil servant, just popping by.

"People want to protect their pensions."

"But what about the TRC? Isn't everything out in the open now?"

"The TRC was people getting off the hook for things. The parents did a nice thing—forgiveness, et cetera. They have that nice memorial on NY1, and that's all anyone wants to deal with from now on."

I begged the officer to meet with me, and he said he'd consider it, but I never saw him again and he never answered my calls. Many months later, he wrote: *I have been instructed to refer you to the communications officer and not to talk to you with regards to that matter. I think it is clear that you can draw your own conclusions on this.*

The next day, I went to Mzi's house and we sat outside and went over the interaction with the mystery cop. Having witnessed firsthand the evil and twisted ploys of the apartheid state as well as the dirty workings of the new ANC, Mzi was enthusiastic about any and all schemes allegedly conducted by governments, military and extramilitary forces, cabals, brotherhoods, and underground fringe groups. His email tagline was "Educate the people liberate Azania!!!!" As I detailed my interaction with Officer Buzz Cut, Mzi listened intently, nodding.

"The problem with conspiracy theories," Mzi mused, "is that you can always find a reason not to believe."

In fact, the insinuations of Officer Buzz Cut never added up to me. And months later, in the basement of the High Court, I was sorting through Ntobeko's court case file, which had its own designation, since he had been tried a year after the original three. It was a compact file box, containing documents along with two copies of the baby blue evidence folder, number 447/08/93, full of glossy crime scene pictures. Most likely, the junior prosecutor working on Ntobeko's case had plucked them from the original case files in Gugulethu and downtown, and then simply forgotten to return them.

For days, Easy had been running madly around the township. He asked me to drive him to a storefront in a Khayelitsha shopping center, where he met with a loan officer at a place called African National Bank, the windows of which displayed larger-than-life pictures of wholesome black people painting their new, high-quality homes, acquired, presumably, with a loan from that very bank. He explained that he needed extra money, but did not elaborate as to why.

A few days later, Easy prepared to take foreigners that he was always toting around for the foundation on one of their township tours. Easy and I planned to meet for lunch in town before the tour. On the phone, he was in good spirits—"fresh like a fish in water," he said.

But when I arrived, his face was ashen. He sat down next to me on some low steps off the sidewalk, and slumped forward.

"Is a big problem," he said softly.

"What happened?"

"A big problem, Nomzamo. Remember I told you my house in Khayelitsha is in arrears?"

Easy owned two properties, sort of: the run-down undeveloped plot that Linda had purchased for him in Gugulethu, and the home in Khayelitsha that he rented out. He claimed that Aphiwe's mother didn't want to live in Gugulethu so close to Easy's family, and for this reason he had put a down payment on a house in Khayelitsha. But when he and Aphiwe's mother broke up, he and Aphiwe moved back to his parents' and a tenant moved in. Then, for various reasons—including his siphoned-off salary, his hankering for alcohol, a general ability to deny financial realities, and the many demands made upon him by his family and girlfriends—Easy had not, it turned out, paid his mortgage for nearly four years. He had stopped reading the mail and was shocked when the bank called him to demand 42,000 rand (then around $4,200 according to the exchange rate at that time) by the end of the week, or they would take his house from him. He negotiated the amount down to 26,000 rand. Desperate, he dissolved his meager secret savings. The savings contained 22,000 rand, about which he had told no one. He had painstakingly stashed the money, bit by bit, in a bank account over a period of ten years; he had planned to give it all to Aphiwe. He transferred the money immediately to the bank, assuring himself that 22,000 rand was "more or less" 26,000 rand. Meanwhile, he spent the weekend hitting up every person he knew, looking for 4,000 rand to borrow. He had gathered this by the due date, and sent Tiny to wait at the bank.

All morning, he called the loan officer to say the money was coming, but the line was busy. Then, at 12:30, he received a call on his cell: the house had been sold at auction.

"The cutoff time was noon," the bank employee explained, to Easy's surprise. And it had sold for 120,000 rand—less than half the price Easy had bought the house for.

"And your 22,000?" I asked.

"Gone," he said, his head in his hands. He looked terribly small.

"Let's go to the bank. We need to understand what happened."

We walked down the street. Easy was breathing heavily. The house, he kept repeating: It was to be Aphiwe's inheritance, where she could live and raise her family. So she wouldn't be in a shack, so she wouldn't depend on a man. He always circled back to his main fear: that Aphiwe would become involved with a man who beat her. He seemed to think that home ownership could somehow prevent this from occurring, and he was not entirely off base: a woman with assets is less likely to be stuck in an abusive relationship.

We trudged to the second floor of the bank, where a neatly put together colored woman sat behind a desk at the center of a dark floor, tending to a variety of people in financial distress. A white man, missing a leg, his face covered in a dark scattering of scabs, sat in a wheelchair, mumbling for help. Next to him, an old black grandmother waited, her face covered with terra-cotta clay to protect her from the sun, her shoulders wrapped in a blue kikoi cloth. I steered Easy up to the woman at the desk. She looked upon our little coupling inquisitively.

"We have a question about a home loan," I said. "A home loan with a problem."

"Okay, what happened?"

Easy, entirely undone by the bank and the public, shameful nature of this encounter, panicked.

"They tell me my house is in arrears," he said to the woman, speaking quickly, gulping. "They say, 'Easy, the house will go to auction.' I called Mr. Mohamed and he said that I must ask Mr. Meyer at ABSA . . ." He went on, his story pouring out of him. The woman's face followed along, puzzled by the particulars but sure of one thing: this was a man in distress.

"I am just trying to think where I should put this gentleman," she said to her colleague, and then led us to her own private office, where she sat Easy before a smudged beige phone. I knew that, per some office policies, employees in South Africa often paid for such calls on their own dime, but she dialed a main number anyway, and the phone began to ring.

Easy then tried to talk with the bank officials, but whenever someone was rude or dismissive, as they initially were, he backed off. His voice was soft and uncertain and he thanked everyone. He didn't know how to reach the right department or to demand respect. Because Easy had little formal education, and because he had been steeped in a lifetime of suspicious glances cast his way and small humiliations, he had never learned to speak up to intimidating bank officials. He had not learned to ask relevant questions because he usually didn't know what questions to ask. Plus, he was afraid to expose his own inadequacies.

For some time, I sat in the corner, watching Easy meekly hang up as he was continuously dismissed, until I couldn't bear it any longer. I took the phone and demanded to be put through to Mr. Meyer.

The people suddenly snapped to. I had questions and they answered them. Within moments, Mr. Meyer was on the line. Easy sat, sweating, to the side.

I asked Mr. Meyer for an explanation of what had happened. I asked if Easy could get his 22,000 rand back.

"He owes for forty months," Mr. Meyer said in his clipped Afrikaans-inflected accent. "The bank won't give him anything back."

"He was unaware that the cutoff was noon."

"I don't know what to tell you." I imagined Mr. Meyer in some skyscraper up north, his feet on his desk, twirling a pencil. "What is the big deal with the twenty-two thousand anyway?"

I looked over at Easy. He was biting his nails.

"It's all he had saved up," I said. "It's for his children."

"Look, I feel bad for the guy, but didn't he live at the house?"

"No, he was renting it out and living at his parents'."

"But if he had at least lived at the house, he would have had free rent for years, which is not such a bad deal."

"All right," I said. "Isn't there anything he can do now?"

"You can write a letter pleading hardship, I guess. It probably won't work, but it's worth a shot." He gave me the address and we hung up.

"Sorry, Easy," I said. He nodded.

"Is okay, Justice."

We passed the lady who had lent us her office.

"I hope you get it worked out," she said to Easy. "It's your property and you should really fight for it."

We walked back to the Amy Biehl offices. Easy vacillated between blaming his ex Lucretia, with whom he'd co-signed on the loan, blaming the bank, and blaming the loan officer. He never blamed himself, at least out loud, for the years of unpaid mortgage bills. He shook his head miserably all the way down the street and then collected himself.

"Everything will come right," he said. "Steady, strong."

Then he went into the building and made his way up to the seventh floor, where he would lead a group of camera-toting tourists into a van and drive them around Gugulethu, pointing out sites relevant in the history of the Struggle. Ever since Ntobeko had stopped talking about the Amy Biehl story unless he was compensated, the foundation depended on Easy to act as the personification of a new, reconciled South Africa.

I started to wake regularly at 5 A.M. Sometimes the mournful sounds of the foghorn down on the water had me up at four, and I could never go back to sleep. On trash mornings, I peered out the front window at the band of scavengers who roamed the streets. They were homeless, most of them colored, with a few blacks and whites thrown in, their faces ragged from drink and drug. Also in the mix were some sober orphans and some hard-up refugees. In my early days, I ran from these people, terrified to be confronted by their destitution. I remember, in my first months, ducking down, slapstick-style, on a balcony as I heard the clip-clop of a man approaching my trash can on crutches. But now I merely kept reading, or watching a movie, or baking a cake. The scavengers knew the trash collection mornings in each neighborhood, and woke at dawn for the best goodies, before the big trucks powered by. Like some of my neighbors, I put my castoffs on top of the bin: flat Coke in a liter bottle, bruised fruit, stale bread, unclaimed leftovers, old T-shirts. By 6 A.M., anything I'd left out would be taken.

I took my dog—glossy, fed on imported, award-winning Canadian kibble—to the rugby field where she chased birds while a community of street people watched. The field sat directly below Signal Hill, a hill upon which the "noon gun" was traditionally fired at twelve by the South African Navy. Once in a while, one of the homeless got particularly inebriated and berated the others. They admired the dog. Sometimes, especially when the cold swept in, one of them would ask me if I might bring them an old blanket or some socks. Sometimes I did, and sometimes I didn't.

A black groundskeeper drove by on a golf cart. He asked for money. "I am desperate," he said. I didn't give him money but we got to talking. He'd come to Cape Town from a small coastal city on the Eastern Cape, hoping for better opportunities, "but there is nothing." He worked for a pittance on a three-year contract. He couldn't unionize on the short-term contract, and the lack of job security ate at him.

"The years go fast," he said. "At least before, the people who had jobs had proper jobs." When he said "before," he meant during apartheid.

He had a wife, two kids, and a 1998 Toyota Corolla. He was loyal to the white-led Democratic Alliance party, and he hoped they would take over the country. A strong opposition party, that was the key to the future, he said. As long as the ANC had no real competition, the country would continue to collapse in on itself. I was surprised that the man admitted to voting DA. It wasn't unusual for poor black people to express anger at the ANC, but they kept voting for them, or perhaps abstained, at a loss as to a better option, as if locked in a cycle of love and abuse. An inebriated retired principal whom I'd met in a shack one afternoon had told me, swaying in his oversized peacoat: "The ANC can go to hell in a nutshell. Zuma is a fuckup, drying up our funds, our taxes, fucking up the country. ANC making shit. Still I will always vote for ANC because only one movement liberate us." An old man who had lived his whole life in an old company hostel in Gugulethu—first as a laborer and later, once the companies had fled the township, as a squatter in a single, squalid room with his family and a rotting refrigerator—told me, "Must be, I vote. But for nothing. Yes, I can vote now. For nothing. How many years I vote for nothing? Where's the promise? For nothing."

The groundskeeper wanted to know what I did for a living. "Oh, a writer? Can you make money doing that?" I told him I could not, and he asked if at least my husband had a good job. He did, I answered, and this satisfied the groundskeeper.

"The wife must stay and make the home, that is what the Bible says, and that is why I soldier on to provide."

"I disagree, but then again, I'm not religious."

"Where are you from?"

"America."

"Ah, you are foreign. That is why you are talking to me. White South Africans, they think we are nothing, not even a dog, they think we are baboons. And they will never talk to us. But you are talking to me, like I am a man, and so I feel honored. Tell me, what is the landscape in America? Are there black people there?"

I went to the gourmet supermarket, situated in an upscale mall. A white man asked the attendant for a slice of lemon meringue pie. The black woman behind the counter was new, and unfamiliar with the appearance of meringue.

"Which is it, sir?" she asked.

"She doesn't know anything!" the customer said to me loudly, rolling his eyes. *What is this country coming to?*

I had become ill-tempered and easily cross, worn down by the in-your-face inequality and the general impossibility of the country. The compassion I'd once nurtured curdled and turned to irritation: irritation that I could not stop at a light without at least one hand knocking on my window. That I could not park my car without somebody in a smudged yellow vest standing by it, expecting a dollar for his troubles. When I'd first arrived, I had gasped at the sight of so many white people contained within their little pod cars, windows rolled up, refusing to acknowledge the brown-skinned unlucky ones peering in. The beggars were missing legs or their faces were bloated from alcohol or illness. They were on crutches, or they were blind, or they were mad. One woman walked on her tiptoes and hid her arm, quite obviously, inside her T-shirt so that it would appear mangled. A teenage junkie had a seizure on the sidewalk as people ambled by. Grandmothers and grandfathers hawked little pamphlets with funny facts, made by a charity to help the homeless. The people were desperate. They used lines like, "My children have got nothing to eat." They wore rainbow-colored wigs to get attention. They were pushy and obnoxious, or they were sweet and gentle; they were scammers and grifters or honestly needy or all three. I used to look them in the eye.

But after two years, I stopped. I saw that for the most part, well-off black and colored people, also secured in their pods, absently shook their heads, too, when the wretched approached. Once, I'd been so racked with guilt that I bought a bunch of dead roses from a drug addict for top dollar. Once, I'd handed out peanut butter sandwiches and smiled at every single unfortunate to make my acquaintance. Once, a beggar asked for the soda in my hand and I handed over the bottle that I'd been in the midst of drinking. But soon enough my expression was as austere as the next lucky guy's, and I had stopped giving to the people with their outstretched hands.

It felt, on some level, like playing God, a sensation both hideous and satisfying, for with money—however little—I was powerful; I could deny those I considered undeserving and reward those I dubbed worthy. I shook my head when the street children in their filthy blankets, their skin giving off the chemical scent of glue, came toward me. I shook my head when the old lady on the milk crate asked for some change. I shook my head when the cheerful man who sold periodicals told me about his sore leg, or his empty cupboards. I felt sorry for him, but not adequately sorry. He and his compatriots were screwed, royally and chronically and perhaps terminally, and what could any one person do about it? It was like drinking from a firehose.

Meanwhile, for my birthday, Sam and I dined at the Test Kitchen, one of Cape Town's most famous and overpriced restaurants. The meal, enjoyed in a light-filled, open space with soaring ceilings, cost nearly $200, and was, as far as we could tell, a series of flavored foams arranged on a series of elegant plates. The Test Kitchen was in Wood-stock, a largely colored neighborhood, with an impoverished popu-lation that lived in tenements surrounding the refurbished hipster-friendly Biscuit Mill, the shopping compound that housed the restaurant. On Saturday mornings, Cape Town's elite—all races, all ages, all with money in their pockets and nice outfits and the glow of health and plenty—gathered in a heaving crowd at the Old Biscuit Mill market. They were there to buy expensive miniature cupcakes, organic fresh-squeezed juices, artisanal smoked meats, Tai-wanese dumplings, imported Kenyan coffee. They sat around at pic-nic tables, seeing and being seen. The local children lined up just outside the wall surrounding the center, unable or unwilling to pass through the invisible barrier between their crumbling neighbor-hood and its gleaming beacon of gentrification. They rattled cups full of change and sang off-key harmonies and followed wealthy people down the street, calling them "mother" and "father" and hoping for a treat.

One night, after dinner at Sam's parents' home, where the silver had been shined by an old Xhosa woman who herself lived in Gu-gulethu, we drove by the parking lot above Clifton Beach. Earlier that day at that spot, we had met a man, his skin coffee-colored and his eyes bright blue, who had cried, saying he had no brothers or sisters and was alone in this world and needed our help.

"Please don't forget me," he begged.

We pulled into the empty lot again and called his name in the dark. We did not speak of this to each other, but I think we both imagined we would be received with gratitude, a poignant interac-tion between the blessed and the damned. But when the man crawled out from under his tent made of garbage bags, his eyes were blank. He took the offered container of soup and bread with little enthusiasm, and disappeared back to his makeshift cave. He seemed to have no memory of us at all.

14.

Igazi lomntu liyathetha.
The blood you spill will not keep quiet;
  it will not rest.

—XHOSA PROVERB

When you begin to see that your enemy is suffering, that is the beginning of insight.

—THICH NHAT HANH

On Aphiwe's tenth birthday in 2013, Tiny arrived at her classroom bearing Nik Naks cheese puffs and boxes of juice. I was in charge of bringing doughnuts. Birthdays were not yet big business in the townships, so the goodies were especially treasured. The kids jumped up and down and stuffed sweets into their mouths beneath a pink handwritten sign that said NO EATING + RUNNING AROUND. Aphiwe stood on a chair, her hair in a messy ponytail, her shoes worn. Her teacher and classmates clapped and sang "Happy Birthday" in both English and Xhosa.

"How old are you now? How old are you now? How old are you now?" they bellowed en masse. "Hip hip!? Hoo-*ray*! Hip hip!? Hoo-*ray*! Aphiwe!? Hoo-*ray*!"

"Say thank you," Tiny prompted, and Aphiwe, her face flushed with joy, muttered her thank you. She was shocked, she whispered to Tiny. Her daddy had promised her a birthday surprise, but he was always disappointing her. For a year, Easy spoke of throwing Aphiwe a tenth birthday party at Mzoli's, inviting a hundred people, handing out beer and wine coolers to the adults, passing around platters of chicken and sausage, and ordering pink cupcakes with candles. But when the day came, he'd had neither cash for a cake nor the capacity to organize anything. Tiny had saved the day.

Soon thereafter, I found Easy outside the Caltex where Amy had been killed. We had arranged to meet that morning, but he had not been at the agreed-upon spot. Instead, having failed to find him at his usual haunts, I passed him as he was weaving across NY1, wearing a heavy cardigan in the searing heat. I pulled over and he struggled with the handle, got into the passenger seat, and fell fast asleep. I slapped his cheek lightly and he opened his eyes. To the side was Amy's marble memorial. Next to the Caltex, an intricate AIDS awareness mural had been painted on the wall: the South African flag, black hands intertwined against gold rays, condoms, a bottle of booze, a needle filled with blood.

"What can sober you up?" I asked.

"Chicken."

I drove to the KFC at the Shoprite Center. A newspaper salesman stood on the median, displaying that day's *Daily Sun* headline: SAN-GOMA STOLE MY LIFE! While I went in to buy a six-piece, Easy sat atop a large paint container by the hardware store and nodded off. A young female acquaintance of his passed by and laughed at him.

"I'm not drunk, I'm exhausted from exercise," he said, miming a few punches in the air.

She laughed harder.

"Will you kiss me?" he asked.

"No!"

"We *gonna* kiss."

"We are *not* gonna kiss."

In the car, Easy ate a couple of drumsticks and perked up. I gave him a ginger soda, which he spilled on the floor. We parked outside his house and Aphiwe leaned through the window and poked her father's cheeks. She had cut out pieces of paper in the shape of long nails, doodled on them, and taped them to her fingertips. Kiki, see-ing my car, wanted us to do her errands. Everyone reached in and took a piece of chicken and Aphiwe slid into the backseat. As per Kiki's request, we drove to the Gugulethu Mall, a shining new de-velopment built in part by Mzoli, owner of the barbecue restaurant, in 2009. In addition to bringing chain stores and banks to the town-ship, Mzoli the butcher tycoon had set up an annual Gugulethu wine festival, where the black diamonds sipped local South African wines. Across the street from the mall, a man was selling fish from the back of a bakkie. Easy left me and Aphiwe in the car and stood in the long fish line. We watched him. She examined me. She touched a mole on my shoulder.

"Do you have any?" I asked.

Aphiwe shook her head. She was wearing a pair of shorts, the fly undone, and a pink T-shirt with sandals.

"I have lots more," I said, pointing to my shoulder, my chest, and finally to my stomach. She lifted her shirt to show me a small matching spot just above her belly button.

"What is your favorite food?" I asked.

"Pizza," she said softly.

"Plain?"

"With mushrooms."

"Raspberries or strawberries?"

"Raspberries."

"Math or English?"

"English."

"Soccer or rugby?"

"Soccer."

"Soccer or cricket?"

"Cricket."

"What did you do at school?"

"Played with my friends."

I sneezed. Aphiwe looked at me.

"You know what you say when someone sneezes?" I asked.

She shook her head.

"You say, 'Bless you.'"

"Bless you."

"Achooo," I said.

"Bless you," Aphiwe whispered.

Easy was across the street, chatting with people in line.

"Aphiwe, what is your favorite thing about your dad?"

She thought for a while. Then she cupped her mouth onto my ear and whispered, "Pride."

Easy came weaving back with a plastic bag dripping fish. Aphiwe

got out of the car to help him wrap it up. Then we drove back
toward NY111.

"Achoo," Aphiwe said, hopefully.

"Bless you," I said.

Once we'd dropped off the fish and Aphiwe, Easy directed me down
NY111 to a dirt yard next to the railroad. Trash was strewn across
the barren land, letting off a stink. Across the tracks, in the colored
area of Heideveld, a Kaapse Klopse band practiced. The Kaapse
Klopse are a Cape Town institution: since the nineteenth century,
troupes of colored musicians have dressed in flamboyant uniforms
and marched down the streets, singing, dancing, and playing instruments. They compete against each other in contests and at the annual Kaapse Klopse festival. Like the colored people themselves, the
music of the Kaapse Klopse players has breathtakingly diverse origins, influenced by musical styles brought over by early West African
slaves, Southeast Asian slaves, European settlers, and indigenous
Khoisan choirs. The members of the bands call themselves "min-
strels" and "coons," and the Kaapse Klopse Carnival had once been
called the "coon carnival," but tourists found the wording distasteful,
and so the city had worked to rebrand it.

"Nobody can bother us," Easy informed me as I parked on the
dirt patch. "This is my plot."

This was the land Linda had bought for Easy years ago. Dry puffs
of grass and weeds suffered in the dust and sand. An ancient brown-
and-white trailer, its exterior stained with dirt and oil and water, was
balanced on cement blocks on one side of the property. Inside, a
middle-aged man in a floppy hat—technically Easy's tenant, but I
did not imagine he paid much, if any, rent—presided over a deep-
fryer. His ripped menu, taped to the front of the trailer, offered sev-

eral confounding items: "Chips and Russians," "Gwinya and Liver," "French Polony." Everything cost around 60 American cents. There were two other structures: a red one-room shanty, no bathroom, grounded by broken bricks arranged at its borders, in which subsisted a bleary-eyed young man who, in exchange for free board, kept an eye on the land. He apparently did this poorly, for the flat-roof wood cabin next door was nearly falling in, its two windows reduced to broken shards of glass. We wandered over to inspect the dwelling. You could peek through the cracked glass, past a gray curtain that had once been striped yellow and blue, past the cardboard taped to the windows, to see a pair of unfinished rooms with cement floors and dirty walls halfheartedly painted a shade of buttercup. The rooms were strewn with dust and debris. Paper seemed to have been glued onto and then ripped off the walls. This was the house, abandoned, in which Easy and Aphiwe's mother had briefly tried to make a life together.

"What is this tattoo?" I asked Easy, back in the car. It was a faded mark, vaguely in the shape of crudely drawn letters "NTA," on his inner forearm. He had previously told me—euphemistically, I later realized—that it was a sign of local pride, though Ndumi had let slip that it was in fact a gang tattoo. "In a way, we all gangsters if we live in Gugulethu," she had explained. Easy had long insisted that he had been a political prisoner and had never taken part in any gangsterism, but time and again, people I met casually insisted that he was a member of the 28s gang in Pollsmoor. Mzi had told me that, even before his stint in prison, Easy was a favorite of the leader of the ill-famed local Ntsara gang.

"Never Touch Area," Easy said and sighed, rubbing his tattoo. "It mean that nobody can come to our area."

"And this one?"

"Cape Town Scorpions," he said.

"Which means?"

"There was fighting on my streets and other streets. These two are for the same gang. Okay, Nomzamo? Before Amy died, I *was* arrested. I stab one guy from another gang. I did get stabbed, too, when I was fifteen. I was five minutes to die, but I went to hospital. Ntobeko also was stabbed in the head. They stabbed him."

"And in prison, were you in a gang?"

"No, I just relaxing in prison."

"I don't believe you."

"Nomzamo, you will find the truth. Before, when you ask me about the tattoo, I was thinking that today, lots of ladies and boys and girls get tattoos. I didn't think it was necessary to tell why I get a tattoo."

At about that moment, a colored boy with a knit cap pulled low on his head and no front teeth popped up next to the window. Like a host on the Home Shopping Network, he artfully displayed an old taupe purse, a wallet, and a pair of lady's sunglasses. I shook my head. Some unfortunate train passenger had just been relieved of her belongings.

"Let's discuss August 25, 1993," I said to Easy as we settled back in the car. "Can we try the story one last time? But this time, the true story." I was thinking of the tale Mzi told me, of Easy Nofemela, wrongly accused, innocent, brother of the real perpetrator.

Easy spoke in a small voice: "I don't want to go back to prison, man."

"Why would you go back to prison?"

The Kaapse Klopse music was loud and bittersweet, a melody of saxophone, drums, and flute, and it traveled in the wind.

"It's not only Amy was killed. Is another person."

"It was a white guy. Killed because he was white. White, white, white."

Easy's face had gone pale, and his lip quivered. He searched for 2 rand for another cigarette and then called over a young boy, who was loitering on the street. The boy ran off with the money and returned with a loosie. Wind was whipping around the car, its windows open, and Easy was drunk, but he effortlessly lit a match, cupped it in his hand, and touched it to the cigarette.

"Amy died, just one hole was stabbed. But that guy, was too much. Was too much, my lady. Was too much."

"What are you talking about?"

"I'm talking about a white guy killed on the same day as Amy. Here in Gugulethu."

I stared at Easy. He had to be mistaken. It was impossible that another white person was killed in Gugulethu on August 25, 1993. I had read thousands of newspapers, thumbed through archives, clicked through databases. In the Gugulethu police database, one black shelter dweller had killed another with a knife and gone to prison for that. But I never saw a single mention of another murder.

"Who was he?"

"I had never met him, my love. I just saw he was a white guy. We come here near the Heideveld station and when we saw that guy, everyone say, 'Yho, God give us a target.' That guy, he died."

"But I've never heard of any such person."

"Exactly. That's the point. I never understand why. I also ask this question."

"When was he attacked?"

Easy explained that the man had died in the morning. The group that had killed him had continued on to the Langa Secondary School rally that preceded Amy's death.

"Something is burning in me. When I try to pick up my life, I don't care. I feel bad too much. Every day."

"No, Easy." It couldn't be.

"I'm telling you, one hundred percent. A white guy. I was not drunk. If you drive I can show you where."

I headed toward the train station. Easy pointed ahead. The guy, he said, was fixing power lines. He was just a nondescript white man sitting in a big truck. His colored colleagues were working nearby.

"He was... oh why? That guy... No, was too much. Was too much, Justine, was too much. Stab. Was too much. Somebody can see suffer. Stab. The voice. Just... Amy, Amy she was just, Amy she could be fine. But that guy suffered too much. Suffered." I pulled to the side and looked at Easy. He was limp, as though he'd been drained of all his vigor. "Is not fine in the township," he muttered.

I had a CD in, and Bob Marley's "Redemption Song" began to play. Amy had been a fan of reggae. Easy turned it up. *Old pirates yes they rob I / Sold I to the merchant ships.*

"My friend, I am a good person but somebody, if you push it to the limit, will become other. Was my first time to stab someone when I was fifteen. I just wanna be happy, but I don't enjoy life. Is a long story." He finished his cigarette and flicked it out the window. "Ndumi's had trauma. The white guy who died is trauma. I don't feel rest. I want rest. If I'm drunk, I sleep peacefully. Otherwise, no sleep. Mzi's place, they burned his house down. One of my friend pass away when I was young. The people who are terrible, they kill him. We run away, in the direction to go to station. We run away to get a train and my friend, he couldn't run. He just turned back and go to those guys. They shoot him here, right here. I also see him died. And his sister come and explain to the police station. But when the police said, 'We know exactly what happening, just tell us what you saw,' I lied because I don't want to be arrested. I said, 'I don't know that boy.' His sister cry, say, 'Easy, why? Tell me why?'

"Sometimes I'm thinking, alone. Worse, worse, worse. Sometimes I don't have money to go to work. I take the train, and looking at the direction of my life and feel like, 'Why?' Sometimes I sleeping and I feel angry too much, I feel too much warm, I wake up, and I see the white guy. My woman wake up and is worried, but I just say, 'Don't worry, is old witches.' That's my answer. Old witches.

"Apartheid brings problems. You find yourself in a situation that you never been expecting, and it's not easy to get out of that situation. See, Amy was exposed. Everyone knows. Parents forgive us. But that guy was not exposed. And now you ask me did I hurt Amy?"

"Did you?"

"Now I tell you what is true: No, I did not."

"Did Mongezi Manqina?"

"We told Mongezi to stand for it, and he insist that he stab Amy."

"Did he?"

"Don't ask me questions."

"Why? Did he?"

"My friend, I—"

"Just answer. Did he?"

"Everything was happening fastly."

"Why admit to something you didn't do?"

Easy went silent.

"Monks?" I asked.

"You know," he said, looking at me. "My brother was very young, but I can stand any pain."

"How old was your brother?"

"Fourteen. I stand up. I sacrifice. I don't know is a punishment now he's paralyzed."

"You think it's a punishment?"

"Maybe."

"Does he think it's a punishment?"

"Sometimes, maybe."

"Do you ever talk about it?"

"No, I don't want to stress him."

"You've never talked about it?"

"He knows. I was already named within the system. They know why exactly I'm going. They said, 'This one, I know this one.'"

"So you didn't attack Amy?"

"To me, Amy was a lady. She was beautiful. I only go to her car, try to burn her car, but to injure her or hurt her? I know, I know.

You ask me before and I never give you answer, right answer. I never give you an answer. I was involve. But I never do the Amy."

"Who should have been arrested?"

"All the PAC leadership, who use innocent people."

"After time, at the TRC, why didn't you tell the truth?"

"At the TRC, they already know me. I was already named within the system."

"And after the TRC, why didn't you tell someone?"

"Long time ago, I am not sure which journalist, but I said, 'I didn't kill Amy.' She didn't even listen to me."

"So you stopped trying?"

"People want to recognize you. They want to recognize your contribution. How many people knows me? How many people admire me? How many people acknowledge it's me? When any journalists ask to me about it, I give them what they know exactly. They know Amy was killed by the mob. So I just tell them that. I didn't see any point that I should tell them the truth. I didn't see any point. I was just telling them the story that they know."

"Easy, I'm a writer. Why are you telling me all of this? I'm writing a book about this."

"I know you a writer. I know I not supposed to trust you. But your true colors show. I know you a writer, and you want to know the truth, but there is another side of you. I can see you."

Easy sat back. He closed his eyes, and for a moment I thought he had fallen asleep sitting up. Then he opened his eyes and looked over.

"Oh, Justice, I never born a killer. I born a beautiful boy. I see to become something, but something change. I managed to change. But everything I told you is my secrets inside of me. You look sad, my friend. But what would you do? If it was you, and your little sister do this? What's your pressure?"

"I don't have a sister."

"I know. Tell me, do you have a brother? No. So then think of it this way: your little brother is me. Tell me, what would you do?"

15.

Whatever you say, say nothing.

—Irish proverb

Most people would not consider a township to be an exclusive community, but it is, by grand design, a restricted area peopled by a specific group, largely closed to the outside world. If you want to find someone in the township or learn something about the place, you either need to live there for a while or you need a guide. In the course of my research, I found that people who went by full names in the court transcripts were instead known by nicknames in the townships; their lives were fluid and often off the grid. They rarely had Facebook profiles, email addresses, or office jobs that would allow a person to find them online. They usually only had cell-phones, and the numbers were unlisted and constantly changing. But Easy and Mzi could find almost anyone anyway, through old friends or family members or common local knowledge.

Soon after Mzi told me that Easy's brother Monks had attacked Amy, I decided I was ready to track down more people who had been involved in the case in one way or another. My first order of business was to visit Easy's ex-girlfriend Pinky—real name, Linda Mayekiso. She had attended the Langa rally and had been lying in bed with Easy in the dawn hours of August 26, 1993, when Pikker and his crew pulled Easy out. She had testified to this in court, and was pictured in newspaper articles wearing sunglasses and scream-ing, as Monks—then mobile, then strong—held her back. ANGRY, began the caption, which described her as Easy's girlfriend, in the midst of attempting to throttle the photographer.

"Our parents, they are cowards for the boer," she told *The New*

York Times back then. "The youth are not scared, and they have power."

Easy knew where Pinky lived: on the other side of Gugulethu, behind an abandoned house in one of four backyard shacks, each of which was inhabited by a single woman and her children. Pinky did not have a bathroom, only an outhouse, and sometimes crossed the street to a house where Easy's relatives lived to do her washing. Pinky's most recent boyfriend and the father of her youngest child had been a nice, soft-spoken man who became convinced that his epilepsy was the result of a sangoma's curse, got hooked on a drug called the Rock ("It's more than *tik*, you *never* sleep"), and stalked the townships, robbing, raping, and murdering people. Pinky left him around that time, and he promised to slit her throat, so for a year she lived in terror. Since the police couldn't—or wouldn't—catch the man, the community eventually surrounded his house with the aim of burning him to death, and he decided to shoot himself in the head rather than face their wrath. I was told that after he was buried, community members dug up his coffin and threw his body on the road. Since then, Pinky had decided to steer clear of relationships, and now just relaxed with her female friends.

Easy directed me to his relatives' house, and they in turn pointed out Pinky's place. When I found her, she was sitting in a spot of sun, washing clothes in a big plastic tub. Two little kids sat by her. They belonged to a neighbor who had to take her third child to the hospital "because he was bleeding from the nose." She had glowing light skin, and short straight hair, and wore a purple tracksuit and slip-on sandals. She was substantial, maybe pushing two hundred pounds at five-five, a feat of which she was proud.

"I was wishing to get fat. I would see fat people and they have dignity, so I thought if I get fat, maybe I will have dignity."

"Being fat means you're automatically dignified?"

"No, because sometimes fat people also do bad things and in that case, being fat is useless."

Pinky dropped the kids at another single mother's shack and we headed to the sidewalk. Since Pinky had no space to conduct a proper interview in her shack, we would speak in the Nofemela house, where Wowo's sister lived. Wowo's sister welcomed us in and placed us in her own bedroom, me on the bed and Pinky on a chair.

Pinky was with Easy from the time she was sixteen until she was twenty-two, when he went to prison. They met on the train, and she moved into his family's home for two years, along with her baby son from another man—a child Easy loved so much that he wanted Pinky to tell everyone that the kid was his. Kiki and Wowo accepted Pinky as one of their own.

"He was a good boyfriend. He was taking care of me. He introduce me to his friends. I stayed there, like his sister, stayed there with them for two years. His mom used to support me, buying me uniforms because my mom was not working permanently."

On August 25, 1993, Pinky and Easy met up at the Langa Secondary School rally; like many poor young people of color, whose subpar education was often interrupted by life circumstances, both Pinky and Easy had attended high school into their twenties. After the rally, they separated. She returned to NY1 in time to throw a few stones at a truck, which she said drove away. Then she saw a little Mazda ambling down the road.

"And they started to shout, 'There's a settler.' I think there was two ladies with a guy. So I just stand in the corner with the other people, watching. A lot of people were hitting the car with the stones. I just saw she was running and I didn't even saw her when she was stabbed. I was far away. I just saw her far away, just a lady like your size, trying to run to the garage. I saw her fallen. I saw them trying to beat her."

"Who was beating her?"

"I saw Mongezi Manqina. I saw him. I didn't knew all of them. There were lot of people. Manqina he was one of the group that took the car, hitting her, carrying stones. I know him from the organization, but the other people who were there were coming from different school."

"Where was Ntobeko?"

"He was there, carrying stones. I did notice Ntobeko, I knew him."

"He was there, throwing stones?"

"Yes. He was just throwing stones to the car. Ntobeko Peni, I knew him a long time. He was a nice guy. He was involve politically the way we were. But Manqina, he was in front. I didn't even know that boy Vusumzi. I never saw him in our meetings. I saw him for the first time at the courts."

"What about the other guys who got arrested?"

Pinky shook her head. She remembered seeing the fifteen-year-old named Terry pluck a bag from the back of Amy's car and rush off, passing close to her. "But I didn't know the other guys there."

"And Easy wasn't there?"

"I didn't even see Easy at that time. I was just standing on the corner, watching everything. I'm just speaking honestly. He was not there. I really didn't see him."

"Was his brother Monks there?"

"Yes, yes. He was there. He was a good friend of Ntobeko."

Pinky watched the attack, toyi-toyi-ing a little, until the police arrived, and then she wandered back to the Nofemela house on NY111. There, she found Terry, who was rummaging through the bag he'd stolen. He pulled a camera out and handed it to Pinky, who took snapshots of everyone.

"Whatever happened to the camera?" I asked.

"I think Terry burned it because he found an ANC card in the wallet so he's suspecting the lady was an ANC member, and then he want to burn everything to hide the evidence."

"When did you next see Easy?"

"The one that I met later on is Easy and I asked him, 'Where were you?' and he said, 'No, I was not even here; I just pass on the train to Khayelitsha, and we did the toyi-toyi in Khayelitsha, and were beating the cars.'"

"But Easy says he went in the bakkie to get food for Viveza and passed by Amy after. Quinton and Steyn also told me this."

"Now I'm confused that the people were saying he was at Viveza store," Pinky said. "He never worked for Viveza. He would tell me if he had been there, because we always spoke truthfully to each other, so I believed him when he said he was in Khayelitsha."

"She just protecting me," Easy insisted when I later brought up the Khayelitsha angle. "I never go to Khayelitsha that day. I was with Viveza on the bakkie."

I didn't necessarily think that Pinky was deliberately lying. There could hardly be a grand conspiracy when nearly everyone had a different memory of that day. But people often have false or doctored memories of certain events, especially newsworthy ones. What they've read or repeated or heard can slowly solidify into what they perceive as real and accurate memories. Researchers have found that people routinely remember events as they want them to have occurred—slowly reshaping them over the years until they become "true" in their minds. And memories can even be created out of nothing. In one study, researchers selected a group of people they had identified as having highly superior memory—the type of person who remembered historical events as well as minute details of their lives down to the hour, years back. The researchers, when discussing the events of September 11, mentioned nonexistent TV footage of the plane crashing in Pennsylvania; later, 20 percent of the subjects claimed to remember, sometimes vividly, seeing such footage.

That night, Pinky continued, the whole area was talking about what had happened to Amy Biehl. "I was shocked, because we didn't know she passed away until later. Easy was surprised that something like that happened."

"What about Monks?"

"Monks didn't say anything."

"How did you feel about her death?" I asked.

"I was not happy, I was not disappointed. Our commander gave us the order to do what the operation was. As long as you are white, they will think you are enemy. I just told myself she went on the wrong direction at the wrong time, but she didn't do anything to anyone wrong. She just went at the wrong time."

"Was Easy nervous that night?"

"He was not nervous and I slept by him, and in the morning I hear a knock and it is the police. They didn't even want to listen that he was not there that day. They just arrested him in his pajamas."

"Pinky, why do you think that the witnesses accused Easy of being there?"

"I know exactly who the witnesses are. I know they are staying near where Easy and Ntobeko stays. When Easy was growing up, he was sort of a gangster. Maybe there is something behind it. Maybe the witnesses, they had a problem with them. Or maybe is a mistake. Easy was very active in politics in the township, and the brothers all look alike. Maybe the witness saw someone who look like Easy and told themself, 'Okay, it's Easy, it's him.' Then the witness got on the stand and said was Easy, and she cried in front of the judge."

"So you think the witness saw Monks instead of Easy?"

Pinky looked unsure. "I still don't know if Monks did anything, but I did go to see Easy in jail. I ask him about this. He said, 'It's fine. I will stand as long that my brother is safe.'"

Soon thereafter, I came across Masana, the craggy soldier-slash-gangster-slash-miner whom Easy had called his "commander" on that rainy day a year earlier. Masana, who'd drunkenly taken my loose change. But no harm, no foul. Masana was delighted to see me when we passed each other on a street in Gugulethu.

"My sister!" he exclaimed, wrapping me in a warm hug. "How are you, Justin? Me, I'm surviving." He gave me his phone number. I then called him in the hope of a second interview, to which he happily agreed.

Masana met me outside the Nofemela house on NY111. He brought with him a stern-looking man in sunglasses who introduced himself as Seven. ("Because I lived at house number 7," he said; "*Ach*, nonsense. Is because he killed seven people," Mzi later countered.) Seven, whom I would see a few more times and who always waved and smiled, hanged himself in the Eastern Cape two years later, and left no note.

The two men slid into my parked car, my primary interview location. In the townships, where most people lived with extended families and there were no coffee shops or quiet bars, the car was the only place I could ever get any privacy.

"You know, Justine, my understanding of that Amy Biehl issue is that Easy and Ntobeko and Mongezi, they were handpicked because people knew them," Masana said, settling in the front seat as Seven made himself comfortable in back. "The witnesses just pointed to the ones they knew."

"Check the characters," Seven piped up. "Easy and Ntobeko weren't violent. They were just youngsters who didn't have the capability to kill someone. Those other guys were tall, were violent." He was referring to the APLA trio. "I never understood why they got away and Easy and Ntobeko went in. Maybe those boys were younger so they were soft targets."

"We Africans have our ways," Masana said. "Even gangsters have rules we have to adhere to."

"So Masana, were you a gangster or a freedom fighter?"

"Honest? Both. First, we were in gangs. You have to be. It is peer pressure, or the others will call you a sissy. You need protection, too. It is about keeping our territory safe. In the old times, when people see us coming, they call the cops. Then the PAC leaders approached us. We had secret meetings at night with these PAC leaders, talking about the negativity of gang membership. But we can't leave the gang entirely or they will crucify us. So we became members of the PAC and the gang. We signed forms and we got membership cards for PAC. Easy and Ntobeko and their group, they were younger. They followed us, and every decision we take, they take also."

I floated the Monks story: that Monks had done it and Easy had taken the fall.

"I know that story," Seven said. "Others said it was Monks. Others said it was Easy."

"The cops could have dug deeper but maybe they just wanna show they got them, just to close the book," Masana said.

"You can never know," Seven said. "It was hear and say."

"You should go to the houses of the people who saw this thing," Masana suggested.

"Do you think if I just go by, they will answer my questions?"

Seven and Masana looked unconvinced but tried to nod politely. "Maybe?" Seven said.

Mzi was always up for an adventure, and in addition to being my guide he slowly took to acting as a historian, researcher, sleuth, and bodyguard.

Mzi may have gained his GED equivalent in prison and he may never have held down an office job, but he had the mind of a lawyer, detective, and psychologist. Sometimes, when I approached an interview incorrectly, Mzi would take over the conversation and subtly guide the subject to answer, leaving me ashamed at my own sloppy technique.

None of that organic intelligence mattered much to Mzi's daily existence. Once, we ordered two cappuccinos and a vegetable quiche to share at a spacious coffee shop near Parliament, and when I went to pay the bill at the counter, Mzi stepped outside. Within moments, a black Zimbabwean waiter approached him.

"Are you looking for something?" he asked.

"Why?" Mzi asked.

"My boss wants me to ask you to move away," the waiter said. Inside the restaurant, a woman in an apron averted her eyes. A few feet away, several white people loitered, absently staring at their iPhones or smoking.

Mzi leaned toward the waiter. "Listen here, my brother," he said. "You are an African from outside of South Africa and I am an African from South Africa."

Mzi extended his hand and the waiter, now stricken, took it.

"You remember apartheid but you won't know apartheid," Mzi continued, beginning the long-form African handshake. "Go and tell your boss I fought for this land and I have the right to be wherever I want to be. I respect all Africans, who have a right to be anywhere in Africa, and I ask that you also adopt this attitude."

The waiter muttered several thank-yous and walked slowly inside, where he sat down at a table, deflated.

"Verwoerd was brilliant, an innovator, an inventor of the future," Mzi said as we walked away. He was speaking of Hendrik Verwoerd, the prime minister infamous for perfecting apartheid. "He still rules from the grave, that guy. The waiter must be happy I am a Buddhist."

Together with this Buddhist ex-militant, I combed the township for witnesses and came up with Miss A, Pikker's star informant and Niehaus's key eyewitness. She was the woman who had handed the sheet of paper to Rhodes naming Easy, Ntobeko, and Mongezi as Amy's killers. She had not been referred to by name in any court documents, but her identity was no secret. Pinky, Easy's ex, had told me that the police had called her and revealed Miss A's real name and address, "and that's why I never trust the police," Pinky added.

"Every time there is a crime, this person is suddenly state witness," Mzi said—in other words, she was known to work with the cops.

We drove to her house and knocked on the door. An older lady, presumably Miss A's mother, pointed us to the back, where Miss A lived alone in a freestanding room. We knocked and a small, delicate woman in her mid-forties answered the door. Her face was pale and freckled, her short hair in cornrows that ended at the nape of her neck. She wore a green velour J.Lo brand tracksuit, orange flats, black socks, and dangling crystal earrings.

"How did you find me?" she asked nervously. Mzi explained that he had told me about her, and she agreed to speak as long as I didn't reveal her real name. She then welcomed us into her space. A quarter of the ceiling of her small room gaped open to reveal the corrugated tin roof. On the walls, she had pasted pictures from her modeling days: Miss A in a swimsuit on the catwalk, a close-up of Miss A's face, Miss A showing off a pixie cut. Books about the ANC and women's rights were piled up around the room. I didn't know Miss A's story, but this was a space designed with an eye looking toward the past, housing memories and photographs of herself when she was full of potential.

Miss A didn't smile and instead excused herself. Mzi and I sat, gazing at the floral couch, the muted TV. She returned, lugging a worn leather suitcase full of "evidence," which she set down on the coffee table.

She pushed the papers toward me. "You can read them and return to me with questions," she said, before she turned to Mzi. I heard her say to Mzi in Xhosa, "wrong information," and after much jabbering, they came back to me.

"She is saying that she once passed a tour guide who was discussing the Amy Biehl case with white visitors, and she tried to correct his story, but he sent her away."

"He just said, '*Suka, suka,*'" Miss A said—*suka*, Xhosa for "get out of here." "He treated me poorly. I didn't want money, I only wanted to tell what really happened."

"What did really happen?"

"Those boys were not PAC," she said, the anger still there, rising up, raw. "They just killed a woman like that. A *woman*."

The suitcase contained piles of yellowed newspaper clippings, bearing headlines from the time of Miss A's testimony:

STATE CLOSES ITS CASE IN BIEHL TRIAL

MAN IN COURT OVER BIEHL MURDER

AMY WAS KICKED, STONED, STABBED

"MISS A" TELLS COURT OF BRUTAL ATTACK

One clipping was a slender article entitled BIEHL: TRUTH MAY NOT EMERGE, which detailed defense attorney Poswa's contention that the witnesses had lied under oath about the danger they faced. He added that the witnesses—Misses A, B, and C—were "shrewd and dangerous" in giving selective evidence. Another clipping was a 9 x 11 article detailing the trial verdict: THREE GUILTY IN KILLING AMY BIEHL. Ntobeko, at that time lying low in the Eastern Cape, had not yet been turned in.

Each clipping was marked by hand with a date. The contact information for Detective Mike Barkhuizen, who had helped me track down Pikker, was written across one article. Pikker's name and pager number were jotted across two separate clippings, for Pikker was Miss A's handler, who drove her daily to court. He remembered these rides as pleasant and set to the tunes of Kenny G, while Miss A's memories were less charitable: she recalled being hauled in and out of court, paid less than promised, and, while waiting to testify, held in a small, chilly cell, near the very men against whom she was giving evidence.

Miss A had also kept her official statement, dictated to Pikker a year after the attack and written out in a tidy, girlish cursive at odds with his physique and chosen profession. Pikker had spelled out the woman's full name and age, and noted that she "states in Xhosa translated into English under Oath" the following:

1. I am not prepared to give my address for security reasons.
2. On Wednesday 93-08-25 at 16:10 I caught a train from Cape Town to Heideveld station. At Langa station when the train

stopped, a whole lot of youths mainly males got on the train.
They were very rowdy. I heard them talking about a
cooldrink truck which they had just burnt in Langa. I got off
at Heideveld station, and this group of youths also got off at
this station. They were singing but I can't remember what
they were singing. I walked a short distance in front of them
and proceeded in the direction NY1, Guguletu. As we approached NY1, I saw a truck approach towards us traveling
along NY1. The group of youths started picking up stones
and bricks from the grounds of the Apostolic Church in NY1
and attempted to throw these at the truck, but they missed as
the truck passed. I saw then a beige Mazda 323 coming up
from behind the truck and this group started stoning it with
the bricks and stones. I then saw that some of the members of
this group had pocket knives in their hands. The stoning took
place in front of the Caltex garage on the corners of NY1
and NY132. I saw how the bricks smashed the windscreen
and the driver, a white woman, was bleeding from the head.
The car stopped and she got out and ran in the direction of
No 32 or 31. A woman named Pamela tryed to assist her but
the group of youths forced Pamela away. I could see this
white woman was confused, and she ran in the direction of
the garage. The group was shouting "One settler—one bullit."
Some of the group chased after this woman, and a girl tripped
her. This girl lives in NY123 (number unknown). The white
woman stumbled and fell on the grass near the garage fence.
A person I know as Ntobeko Peni, NY111, No 4, jumped on
this woman with his feet and the woman screamed. Peni had
a brick in his hand. A youth I know by sight who lives at
NY1 No 62, stabbed the woman once on the left side with a
knife he had in his hand. Another person I know as Easy, of
NY111 (number unknown—thirty-something) stabbed the
woman at her legs. Peni hit the woman with the brick on her
head. There were quite a few people around her and there

was a lot of movement and I couldn't see everything. Some
left her alone and ran back to the car. The other occupants of
the car which I noticed, was an African woman and a Moslem
guy. They ran to the garage when the attack started. The
group was taking things out of the car and they also turned
the car on its side. I saw a person running away from the car
with a leather jacket and a black bag. It looked as if there
were books in the bag. I heard somebody calling for matches,
but the police arrived and this group ran away. I stayed there
until the car was towed away. The police put the car back on
its wheels, and also took out the remaining things in the car.
Nobody attacked the car from the time the police came to
the garage.

3. I know and understand the contents of the above declaration,
I have no objection to taking the prescribed oath and I consider the oath to be binding on my conscience.

Guguletu
94/08/31
18:40

Miss A guided me and Mzi through the day. We walked from her
house to the murder site. The wind blew fierce, but the day was
bright.

"Here they are singing," Miss A said, pointing to the spot where
the road leading from Heideveld station met NY1. Today, a cherry-
red spaza shop operated out of a shipping container there, advertising phone cards and Coca-Cola. Behind it, cordoned off by a chain
link fence, sat some of the fading old hostels. Children played at the
elementary school where the Amy Biehl Foundation operated its
programs.

"They start throwing stones they took from a pile and she was
running, confused about which way to go. They are after her. She lay
down there, where that guy's sitting." The old man who camped by

Amy's cross was, as always, sprawled on the pavement with his dogs. Linda Biehl called him Amy's Angel, since nobody knew his name or his purpose for returning day in and day out to that spot. Once, when I asked him why he sat there, he said that he was employed by the foundation as security. "Protection," he mumbled.

"The police come this way, make a U-turn, drop her in the van, take her to the police station. The boys were dispersing and then they tried to turn her car and then they jumped the gates of the houses to get away." She pointed at a pale green house that advertised BABS SALOON: SPECIALIZE IN EYELASHES ★ NALS ★ PEDICURE ME-NICURE TWIST AND STYLE EYE BROUZE WAXING. The perpetrators had hopped over the back fences to flee the scene.

"It didn't even take half an hour. Before it was white, this wall. It rained and the rain cleaned the blood, there was a lot of blood. After, maybe for an hour, my friends and I talk about that thing and then after six I just went to the police station."

We walked slowly over to the Gugulethu police station, where the men behind the desk agreed to allow us to inspect the driveway area. Miss A led us to the area where Amy's body had lain shrouded beneath a blanket. "Then I go to the charge office, then I saw Rhodes, then I called Rhodes, then I told him who I saw was involved."

"Why did you tell him?" I said. "Talking to the police in the townships is dangerous."

"Was not about me. Was just that picture of that woman, crying for help but nobody can help."

I asked Miss A to show me where she had stood on NY1. She positioned herself by a crumbling gray home, set diagonally across the street from the Caltex. I measured it as thirty-nine paces away, though the criminal case judge had said Miss A was standing only six paces from the scene of the crime. It would have been easy enough, standing at such a distance, to mistake one man for another, especially if they looked alike, especially if both were swept up in the teeming mob, especially if there were hundreds of people on the street. And Amy and the boys ran away from the car, and away from where Miss A had been standing. To keep up with the action, and to keep a really good eye on what was unfolding, Miss A would have had to quicken her pace, perhaps to a run, to follow the group. In a tumble of people, in the chaos of that moment, and from a distance, could a bystander really have made out all the distinct features of the members of a fast-moving crowd engaged in a violent activity?

"Did you know that Easy had a little brother?" I asked.

"No, I don't know his little brother," Miss A said, looking at me hard. "I only know Easy. But I *know* Easy."

As we headed back to Miss A's house, where Mzi and I would collect my car, we began chatting. Miss A revealed that she had been missing her long intestine and rectum since a 2003 operation. Now all she could eat was bread, peanut butter, and bananas. The operation, she explained without any apparent emotion, was the result of an octopus living in her stomach, which the doctors had removed and placed in a glass. Such otherworldly happenings were quite common in South African hospitals, she noted gravely.

"If you are an African person, they jump on you because they know they find a lot of things in the African people. A snake in the leg. An octopus, black, in the belly. A frog in the stomach. It depends where it was installed. It's witchcraft, black magic. If you can stay here in the township with the African people, you will see terrible things. Things you can't believe."

"So you would like me to tell my side of the story, of that special incident?" Pamela asked.

Pamela had been mentioned, by first name only, in court transcripts of Miss A's testimony, but she herself had never spoken of what she'd seen that day. She'd refused to divulge anything to the authorities, and had been quite cross at Miss A for dragging her into the whole mess. For this reason, Miss A had feigned not knowing where Pamela was these days. "She's always away, playing African drums, so you can't talk to her."

Miss A claimed that she had approached Misses B and C for me, and that they had refused to be interviewed; I had no further information with which to track them down. Mzi and I spent a day knocking on doors down the block, but nobody ever confessed to witnessing the crime. Still, Mzi mulled over Miss A's characterization of Pamela, and finally recalled that a woman named Pam, who indeed played African drums, lived just off NY1. That's how we found her.

"Molo, mama," Mzi said when we pulled up. A stocky older woman stood in the yard. He explained our purpose in long-winded Xhosa, as the woman listened silently and intently until he had finished. Then she nodded her assent and called a younger woman, who came outside. They opened the gate and extended their hands: the older woman was Eunice, and the younger her daughter, Pamela.

"Come inside, sisi, bhuti, and we can talk," Eunice said.

While Eunice busied herself in the kitchen, Pamela led us into a sitting room, which boasted wall-to-wall carpeting covered by two rugs. On the television, a black American judge was presiding over a couple in a courtroom feud. Pamela was a woman of forty with her black hair in a short bob. Judging from old photographs, her face had barely changed in twenty years: only a little rounder, a little more worn. Because the day was a holiday, she was hanging out at home in a red terry-cloth robe.

"She's very pretty," Mzi said longingly when we left.

Pamela was the single mother of a seven-year-old son, who was jousting with his friend in the front yard. She also taught arts at a public school, and had founded a program—"a little famous locally"—that taught township kids dance and music and, on some occasions, sent them on trips to perform in Europe, Taiwan once, and around Cape Town. She showed us a blowup print of her troupe, dressed in bright, woven Xhosa dancewear, assembled outside the Castle of Good Hope downtown. Pamela sat on a beige leather couch and welcomed us to sit, too. She had never told her story before. When it happened, she had been too scared to talk. And eventually interest had faded and times had changed, and who cared much about the Amy Biehl murder anymore?

Pamela had been a student at the College of Cape Town in 1993, and on that August day she had been sitting in her yard with some friends. A crowd passed by, toyi-toyi-ing.

"During that time, when you see chanting, you tell yourself it's about freedom," she recalled. "Us African people, we love music within ourselves, and the minute you hear songs, something is boiling in you and you have to move. So when I heard the music, I went with it. The music is in me, in us. So I followed them for a little."

By the time they'd reached NY1, Pamela sensed this was no peaceful demonstration. She picked the slogans out of the singing and carrying-on, and she felt the energy: dark, determined, aggressive.

"If the slogan says 'Kill the boer,' you will kill the boer," Eunice added from the kitchen, where she was stirring a pot of beans.

"I was not so politically minded and so I wanted to leave the march then," Pamela said. "They were stoning a brewery and bakery car, but those cars succeeded to drive away. But then I saw from a distance a white lady in a yellow car, and I thought, 'Oooh, I wish I could tell her to go the other way.' She was friends with two black ladies and she was not nervous. She was more in a comfort zone, but we could see it's not gonna be what she thinks it is."

"Did you recognize the people who attacked her?"

"There were many of them. I saw Easy, Ntobeko, the guys from the Amy Biehl Foundation, and especially the guy from NY1, Mongezi. But Amy, I don't think she saw anyone. I was very close to her and she was just scared, lost as to what's happening, and when you are in that place, you don't know who anyone is. Then they were throwing stones at her, pushing her, pull her hair, took her all over the places. It was very sad. There was fifteen or twenty, but some were not even students, they were just in ordinary clothes. Like Easy. We knew Easy as someone involved in gangsterism. The gang was so violent, they used to stab at each other, rob each other, use the toyi-toyi as an opportunity."

"When there is a march for rights, skollies will add in and then pretend they are also for rights, but they will pickpocket you," Eunice said, sticking her head out of the kitchen. "They will pretend they are with the people, but they are criminals."

"How could you be sure it was Easy and Ntobeko?" I asked Pamela.

"Here in the township, I knew Ntobeko by face but not by name. But Easy used to visit my classmate. I knew him before the incident."

"Did you know Easy's brothers?" I asked. "Did you know he had a brother who looked exactly the same?"

"Easy is the one I knew. I only knew some of his brothers. But I knew Easy very well. He used to come and sit and chat and make us laugh. Even when he was throwing stones, I still knew Easy. I know Easy. I know him as a good person, then and now. That Easy there, that was not the Easy that I knew. But as I said, there were many of them, but I remember that one man: *Easy*."

"Did you intervene?" I asked.

"I tried to stop what the crowd was doing. When they were throwing stones and Amy started to frighten up, she ran—or she tried to run. I said, 'No, guys, please,' and they didn't even listen. They wanted that lady. We were also trying to stop them, but we fear for our lives. After, I didn't say anything to the police. I don't involve myself."

"The police will put you in front of the enemy so the enemy can see you, and then you will die," Eunice said sagely. "When the police came, I said my daughter would not talk."

"After all that, what do you think of them getting amnesty at the TRC?"

"In my opinion, amnesty is right," Eunice said, popping out of the kitchen again. "A child can be used. The order can be coming from up high, from people you won't see or hear about. They were toyi-toyi-ing for their rights. And those that did it, they found what they did was wrong."

"But Pamela said the kids were gangsters," I countered.

"But I understand them, because I was also have that hatred," Eunice said. "I was growing up with my parents who were staying nice and progressing, and then they were moving to another place and losing everything because of the whites. So I did have that hatred for the whites."

"Mandela thought reconciliation was the only way forward, and Amy Biehl's parents reconciled so they could move forward," Pamela said. "For me, I was affected and disturbed. Something like that, nobody would like to see. To try to stop it, but you can't, and you watch a woman being killed. You know, it's very true. Where the tourists go and pray for her, by the Caltex, that is where her life ended."

16.

Remembrance of things past is not necessarily
the remembrance of things as they were.

—Marcel Proust

Because Easy and his co-convicted had spent years in prison, I had long wanted to see the institution close-up. I had tried, through various official channels, to visit the prison system, but the results had been comical. South African government employees were, in my experience, either impervious and dour and unwilling to lift a finger, or friendly and polite and unwilling to lift a finger. I consistently spoke to the loveliest people, who consistently failed to follow through on the simplest tasks and who, I later came to suspect, never intended to do so. They seemed, too, to follow a policy of simply wishing-away work: if they tried hard enough, if they pretended hard enough that I didn't exist, maybe I would vanish in a poof.

In my attempts to visit and better understand the prison system, I had first been directed to a parliamentary liaison officer, who spoke with great vigor and certitude when he said I had to simply email my request to another parliamentary liaison officer, and that the matter would be sorted. But the officers both soon disappeared into the ether, specters who had email addresses but who never seemed to be able to send a single reply. My application lingered, presumably, in various in-boxes until, after four months of silence, I tracked down a dinosaur communications chief for the national commissioner of prisons. His name was Koos Gerber, he sounded appalled at how shoddily my case had been handled, and he promised, in his clipped Afrikaans accent, to personally streamline the process. Then he disappeared. Weeks later, a man from the national commissioner of prisons office called and gave me the good news: I had been cleared to tour Pollsmoor.

Excited, I drove over to the suburb of Tokai, where Pollsmoor sat below the mountains and a few miles from the pine forest where I sometimes hiked with my dog. It was a suburb of boutique coffee shops and farmers' markets. At one such outdoor market, a baboon the size of a preteen had mugged Sam, menacingly grabbing our tote bag. The baboon rushed into the trees and called his baboon friends over to share his take; moments later, I spotted a smaller baboon sitting on a rock, smugly munching on one of my organic pomegranates.

The prison was barely visible from the road. Through the gates, inmates in orange jumpsuits worked in the shade, digging holes and patching walls. The day was blisteringly hot, and I parked my car on a lawn in the sun. I checked in at reception and was led to a small room, where I was informed by an extravagantly pleasant communications officer that in fact there was no documentation granting me access to the prison.

Soon enough, the officer's superior, a well-coiffed woman, greeted me. She, too, lacked any documentation that would allow me official access, but she was willing to circumvent the process on the understanding that indeed such documentation was forthcoming. Meanwhile, the delightful man from the prison authority, reached on his cellphone, assured me that the documentation was on its way: an official would indeed be faxing the approval "justnow."

"Justnow" is a South African term that actually means "at some imprecise time fairly soon." Its preferable counterpart, "nownow," means "immediately." My heart sank when the man spoke the words "justnow," but I was locked in a battle, and I naively thought I could persevere against one of the world's most opaque bureaucracies.

Meanwhile, the well-coiffed superior, at a loss for how to entertain a journalist sitting expectantly in her office, circled the table. "It will be a positive report, yes?" she asked me.

"Yes?" I answered.

If that was indeed the case, the superior figured that I would be able to begin the tour as she awaited the documentation. Therefore, a slight and bookish guard, fresh from the Eastern Cape, no older than twenty and no heavier than a ballerina, was assigned to my detail. I suspected that, given the right situation, I could have personally disarmed the man, and I worried for his safety in this new line of work. He led me to the records room, where a dinosaur clerk sat locked behind bars, wheeling a desk chair to and from various filing cabinets.

"Without documentation, I can't show you anything," the clerk said. This was a man from the old regime, and the old regime had, it seemed for the most part, followed the rules—no exceptions, no sweet-talking.

My guard, now increasingly frazzled, led me to another room, where a young white clerk seemed unfazed by my request for the prison records of the men accused in the Amy Biehl murders, and started combing the system. He printed out Mongezi Manqina's sentence on the rape conviction—received after he was given amnesty—but the record mentioned nothing about murder. Easy's and Ntobeko's names were nowhere in the system.

"Why would this be?" the guard asked, turning to an older white woman with teased hair and a sausage-shaped body. Everyone called her *tannie*, which is Afrikaans for auntie, and she was their institutional memory.

"Anyone granted amnesty at TRC had their records removed by the head office," she said. "They came one day and took them all away."

Disappointed, I headed for the actual prison with my young guard. Up above was Mandela's special former apartment, built for him by the apartheid government. In 1982, after seventeen years in a slender cell on Robben Island, Mandela was, without warning, transferred to Pollsmoor. He brought with him a few cardboard boxes, full of his worldly belongings, and was accompanied by three senior ANC members who had been with him on Robben Island,

and he was joined by Ahmed Kathrada months later. In 1985, after Mandela, in secret early meetings with apartheid leaders, would not agree to become the "moderate" African the state wanted in exchange for his freedom, he was separated from his comrades.

I had hoped to see Mandela's cell, but my guard informed me that it was now used to house tuberculosis-ridden prisoners, to keep them from infecting the general population. I wanted to see normal conditions of prisoners, I said, and so my guard escorted me to the maximum security section. I walked through the security checkpoint and through the puke green halls. We made our way up the steps and I could see below the line of visiting family members snaking into the guts of the building. I hoped to see the interior, which Easy had called "not a place for human being." A place run by the Numbers gangs.

But I only got as far as the office of a warden's secretary, who had arranged a little shrine to nail care on her desk, including a dozen hand creams, a pair of scissors, an orange stick, and several jars of cuticle softeners. "I'm sorry, but we need proper paperwork to show you anything," she said.

And so, four hours after arriving at Pollsmoor, I left. I sent an email to Koos Gerber, expressing my distress. Though he had promised to streamline my access to the system, he now responded curtly that I would in fact have to fill out an entirely new application to visit the prisons. I did so, at length, and six months after my initial request, multiple emails and phone conversations, Gerber finally responded simply: *Your request was considered by Management but unfortunately they did not approve of your request.*

I imagined what it must be like to be a prisoner stuck inside such a system, a labyrinth of rules and policies that were either adhered to or disregarded, seemingly at whim. As an American with a university degree, I couldn't work out how to navigate the simplest of processes: gaining visitation to an institution supported by taxpayers. I could only imagine how an inmate, typically poor and with few resources, might manage.

After my failed expedition, I drove to Mzi's house, passing, along the way, the Nofemela house, where Aphiwe was playing with a little girl who was wearing a purple shirt that said YOUR BOYFRIEND LIKES YOU BUT HE LOVES ME.

Over on NY119, Mzi was cleaning up after the previous night's stabbing, vacuuming the floor of the Spirit Horse, his beloved turquoise Toyota. At around ten the night before, a distant relative who lived down the road had hurled himself over Mzi's high iron fence and landed on the brick stoop, calling out for help, his chest and stomach punctured nine times. The relative was a pleasant twenty-three-year-old who, despite spending his days smoking *tik,* had maintained his good looks, his strong, straight nose, and all his crooked teeth. He had, however, succumbed to the main habit of *tik* users, which was stealing.

On the afternoon before, the relative was at the pale yellow single-level house he shared with his extended family, just down the street from Mzi's place. In the backyard, hanging on the wash line, he found two pairs of men's trousers, which he plucked off the line and sold for three dollars at the nearest squatter's camp. Those pants belonged to the boyfriend of his twenty-one-year-old niece, who did not take the loss of his clothing lightly. That evening, the boyfriend stabbed the perpetrator with a switchblade. After sustaining the wounds, the victim broke free and ran down the street to Mzi's small family compound.

Mzi was concerned about a new mob-justice movement gaining popularity in the townships, where terrified or impotent police have long sat back and allowed black people to brutalize each other. During apartheid, police forces were feared as indiscriminate tools of a racist state. They raided the townships and routinely tortured prisoners, sending them home blind, deaf, or mad; some people disappeared entirely after a run-in with cops. A white cop named Barnard,

who called himself Rambo of the Cape, trolled the streets of Gugulethu. Residents called him Vuil Barnard, or Dirty Barnard.

"A serial killer with a badge," Mzi recalled.

"Whenever his car appeared on the shimmering horizon leading
the yellow Casspirs, we knew: Someone dies today," a victim testified before the Truth and Reconciliation Commission, referring to
the armored vehicles driven by security forces. "We will remember
the man with the red scarf who shot dead our sons."

"He just followed the rule," Pikker told me once over coffee.
"And the rule was, really, if you can justify it, you can do it."

Today, over two decades after Mandela's election, most of the police are black or colored, but the punishment they mete out is often
no less brutal. Recently, in addition to their role in the Marikana
platinum mine massacre, the cops had been in the news for tying a
handcuffed twenty-seven-year-old Mozambican taxi driver to a police van and dragging him to his death before a panicked crowd in
a township just outside Johannesburg. His crime: parking illegally.
Vigilante-administered punishment was therefore a more popular
type of justice, though typically disproportionate and vicious, and
often mistakenly directed at innocent people.

Mzi had recently embarked on a campaign to keep NY111 and
NY119 clear of the so-called neighborhood watch committees that
roamed the dirt paths of a nearby settlement at night. They established an 8:30 P.M. curfew, even for people returning from work, and
burnished whips to punish those who broke the rules. He visited
nearby communities, bearing a laminated newspaper article describing a mob murder in Khayelitsha, during which a nameless, faceless
group had beaten an alleged young robber to a pulp and then locked
him in a portable toilet, which the group doused with petrol and set
alight as their victim wept. The article, entitled "Deathcrap," included a colorful photo of the dead man's dismantled shack below a
less colorful photo of his ash-encrusted corpse. No arrests had been
made. Mzi wanted to avoid such a gruesome scene on his streets.
What if they set upon the wrong person?

With this in mind, Mzi got out of bed and approached the gate. The thief's assailants were surrounded by women and children from the shacks and hostels down the road, demanding that he be ejected onto the street. They didn't have much, and boys like this were always grabbing their phones, their shoes, even their furniture. Let the boy walk home and face the consequences of stealing! Thieves must be punished!

"Sorry, bhuti," Mzi said to the man with the switchblade. "But I cannot allow you to kill this boy."

The crowd protested.

"Hayi, bhuti, you don't know the whole story!" they yelled.

"I don't want to know," Mzi said softly. "Go to your homes."

Some of them swore at him, but sensing that he could not be persuaded, they ambled away in the end, and nobody held a grudge the next day.

"Why were they cross with you?" I asked. "Did they want justice served, as they saw it?"

"No, they didn't want justice," Mzi said, shaking his head. "They have become accustomed to violence. To them, it is like watching a live movie. They were angry because I ended the movie before the end."

After that, Mzi had taken his relative (wrapped in garbage bags, to keep the Spirit Horse pristine) to a nearby hospital, where the man recovered. Later, Mzi and I visited him in a large, windowless room filled with beds. He lay shirtless, his stab wounds covered in bandages, a tube pulling fluid from the wound near his left nipple. He looked small and impossibly young. He wore an oxygen mask and was asking the doctor if he could have something to eat or drink. The doctor, a bespectacled white man in his early thirties, bent over a tray table piled high with bloody gauze. He was from Ohio, it turned out, fresh out of med school and on a one-month volunteer stint in the Cape Town ghettos before he began his job at a hospital in Delaware. He was telling the young man to breathe, even though it was painful, and that he could eat after his X-ray.

"So is it very violent here?" I asked.

"Very," he said, smiling pleasantly but, I sensed, only moments away from bursting into tears. "This isn't the first time I've seen multiple stab wounds like this."

"How long have you been here?"

"Two days."

Once Mzi had finished cleaning the Spirit Horse, we went inside and I plopped down on his mother's couch. His eight-year-old niece was chasing her toddler cousin through the room. The niece placed the baby on my lap and the baby began to scream.

"How will I ever get access to the prisons?" I wondered. "How will I ever get to Terry?" Terry, the adolescent thief from Gugulethu arrested and released in 1993, was now thirty-five years old and bunking in Pollsmoor on shoplifting charges.

"I believe I have a solution," Mzi said, pacing. "We can hit two birds using one stone."

Eight men had been arrested for Amy's murder. Easy, Ntobeko, Vusumzi, and Mongezi went to prison. The APLA trio was freed for lack of evidence. Terry the teenage thief was freed on account of his age. I had talked to Easy, Ntobeko, and Mongezi. I had also spoken to Mzi's brother Steyn, the only surviving member of the APLA trio (the two other men had died years earlier, one in a shootout with cops as he tried to rob the Shoprite and one from substance abuse and illness). Vusumzi lived in another township, and nobody knew what had become of him. That left Terry.

All we had to do was figure out visiting hours, Mzi posited, and we'd be able to slip in. We could see Pollsmoor and interview Terry at the same time. As Mzi and all of his neighbors and anyone with half a brain well knew, and as I was learning, the almost purposeful impossibility of South African bureaucratic processes led any sane person to simply ignore them. Clever circumvention was the name of the game.

Mzi and I drove straight to the prison that afternoon, through a series of run-down colored neighborhoods full of Cash 'n Carry shops and fish stands and homeless people, and then into upscale Tokai. A black African uniformed guard, with a heavy accent unique to that of the colored population, stood at the entrance turning people away. As Mzi and I edged closer, we noticed a pattern: this guard's attitude shifted in relation to the people with whom he interacted. He was abrupt and rude to black people; his answer to their questions was an exasperated "Read. The. Sign." But when speaking with a colored person, he was polite. Mzi walked up first and asked if we could visit. Having no experience visiting a prisoner, I'd supposed we could just waltz in.

"Not today," the guard growled, looking past Mzi. His eyes floated and landed on me, the only white person in line. "What are you needing, lady?" he asked courteously.

"I'm with him," I said, motioning to Mzi.

The guard's face fell. He ran his gaze up and down Mzi. "I have a right to know the information I'm requesting," Mzi said. "I would like to know the hours of visitation."

"That's fine," the guard said, addressing me again, spouting off the days for male prisoners and for female prisoners.

"I would also like to check the status of an inmate," Mzi continued, staring at the guard, who refused to make eye contact.

"You can go inside and ask," the guard said, again answering to me.

Once Mzi had gone on, the guard turned to me and asked what I was doing at Pollsmoor. How did I know that guy? Where was I from? Was I married? To a South African? To a black?

After Mzi gathered the proper information about visiting hours and inmate details, we walked away.

"That guy's grandfather changed his identity and now he doesn't know who he is," Mzi observed, referring to the fact that the guard spoke like a colored person despite looking like an ethnic Xhosa.

The history of South African people was all mixed up with the concept of passing and the fluidity of race. Under apartheid, black people had tried to pass as coloreds for better benefits, and colored people had tried to pass for white. Several books and movies detailed the life of one woman who, though the descendant of three generations of white Afrikaners, was classified as colored (some decades-old black gene, it was theorized, had surfaced in her, making her appear mixed-race) and thrust into a bizarro world in which she was rejected by white society, ended up marrying a black man, and became estranged from her parents.

Post-apartheid, many folks were trying to change back to their original designations, under the impression that with the new ANC government, it was more beneficial to be black. But people were also still attached to the myth of intrinsic white value. It made matters confusing from the outside—and surely much more confusing from within.

"He hates black people because he hates his real identity as an African," Mzi said of the guard.

In the parking lot, Mzi and I came upon an octogenarian Xhosa woman standing in the sun with an infant swaddled on her back and a garbage bag in her hands. Mzi offered her a lift to the nearest bus station. On the way, she explained that her grandson was in prison for robbing a lady with a toy gun. Then she got off in a nearby suburb and lined up for a minivan taxi to take her the hour back to Khayelitsha, after which she'd have to walk a mile to her shack, the baby sleeping on her hunched spine.

We continued into town. As we waited at a red light, a minivan taxi in the middle lane stopped and opened its doors. A hefty black woman climbed out and began to make her way to the median. Just then, the light changed to green, and a small hatchback bounded forward just as the woman, oblivious, stepped before it. The car swiftly hit her and just as swiftly braked. The woman slammed to the ground. As she scrambled back up, it seemed to me, frozen in my car, that her sheer bulk had acted as a sort of personal airbag. I stopped for a moment, to make sure that the car that hit her would also be stopping, but as I distractedly gazed over, a man behind me began to lean on the horn.

I looked back at him, in his shiny late-model SUV: white man, bald head, a pair of Ray-Bans shielding his eyes. He wore a polo shirt. He leaned harder. The woman who had been hit was speaking with the people who had hit her. He leaned again. Just then, some craggy part of me broke in two and a gallon of rage bubbled up.

"Fuck you!" I hollered, suddenly and to my own surprise.

The man in the SUV exclaimed something, as far as I could see in the rearview mirror, and then he swerved in front of me.

"Get out of the car!" he yelled. "Get out of the car!"

"You get out!" I screamed back, now leaning out the window.

Road rage was common in South Africa. In Cape Town, a thirty-five-year-old athlete had used his hockey stick and fists to beat a fifty-five-year-old tailgater to death. In Johannesburg, an armed motorcyclist shot an armed driver, who, wounded, returned fire, killing the motorcyclist. In the Eastern Cape, Nelson Mandela's scandal-plagued grandson, Mandla Mandela, was charged with pulling a gun on, and then brutally assaulting, a teacher who had crashed into his friend's car. The man underwent surgery for a blood clot on his brain.

This was all probably because South Africans were outraged—about race relations, corruption, ineptitude, money, class, status, politics. Beneath a thin veneer of good manners, the whole society was teeming with tension and entitlement, where people packed pistols and where everyone was perceived as either a potential perpetrator or a potential victim. Perhaps for these reasons, and because the cops rarely enforced traffic laws and happily took bribes, South Africans were notoriously aggressive, reckless drivers.

The man in the SUV now seemed to consider a potential fight. He looked at me and then he looked at Mzi. Mzi sat in the passenger seat, his camouflage hat shading his eyes. The man grumbled to himself, and sped away. Mzi and I then drove down the street slowly, in silence.

"I must tell my sisters to be careful when they get off in the street," Mzi said eventually. "Those taxis are dangerous, opening the door in the middle lane."

Three days later, I pulled onto Mzi's front lawn at 6:30 A.M. It was a Saturday, and visiting day at Pollsmoor. Mzi had recommended the early start, since the prisons were overcrowded and the lines were long. At that hour, the sky was navy. I saw Mzi's head peer slowly over a fence, the cherry of his cigarette glowing against his silhouette. He wore his UNIVERSAL MESSAGE hat and a T-shirt that said TAKE BACK THE STREETS in neon green, and when he got into the car he smelled like he'd spent the evening at a Grateful Dead concert.

"I guess *you* had a nice night," I said.

He turned to me, his eyes bloodshot, then inspected himself in the mirror. "Is it obvious?" I nodded, and he buried his head in his hands. "It is true: I have been smoking dagga with a community of Rastafarians."

Once we entered the Pollsmoor grounds, we parked by the entrance. Because most visitors came in on public transport, even on a busy day the lot was nearly empty. We gamely got in line, shuffled among moms and sisters and sons and daughters, with a dad and a brother and a friend thrown in. The women clutched Tupperware containers of food and treats. Of the hundreds of people, I counted exactly five white folks, myself included. If you had a good enough lawyer, rumor had it, she would at least get you into the fancy Malmesbury Prison instead of this place.

Once we checked in, we walked through metal detectors, were

patted down, and emerged into a spacious, pale green room, outfitted with rows of long train-station-style wooden benches. A large
flat-screen TV was bolted to the wall above the bathrooms, but it
was turned off. There were doors to one side of the room, leading to
an interior courtyard, where dozens of colored women were wandering around, smoking cigarettes. A sign reminded us of the rules:

> No short skirts (miniskirts) allowed in Pollsmoor
> No showing of half breasts (cleavage) allowed in Pollsmoor
> No short pants (shorts) allowed in Pollsmoor
> No transparent tights allowed in Pollsmoor
> No transparent pants allowed in Pollsmoor
> Your behaviour will be highly appreciated

Mzi and I were herded into a line. I gave over my passport and
Mzi presented his identity document. The document had been created in 1996, just after his first release from prison, after his participation in the 1994 attempted APLA attack on a police station in the
Eastern Cape. In the picture, he was all fury and jutting cheekbones,
his skin darker and the contours of his face sharper. His eyes were
black and vacant.

"You look rough," I said.

"They tortured me," he said, matter-of-factly. "They made me
wild."

A Nigerian gentleman with a grand belly sidled up to us. He
wore a black and neon-yellow tracksuit and a watch the size of a
cookie. He stepped on my foot and did not apologize. He was here
to visit his brother, he explained, who had been sentenced to two
years for beating a woman, but it wasn't his brother's fault that the
woman was a troublemaker, and moreover, if his brother had hired a
well-connected lawyer, *like he had advised*, instead of a state defense
attorney, he would be walking around in the world today.

"The free lawyers is *kak* lawyers," the Nigerian said, moving closer
to me, using the Afrikaans term for crap. "You find a lawyer who

went to school with the judge and other lawyers, so he was sitting next to the judge in class. They talk, you walk."

"He was trying to con you," Mzi later said, though neither of us knew how the con might have unraveled. "That's what Nigerians do."

Finally, after three hours of waiting—to enter, to be searched, to give the inmate's name, for that name to be called—we were bused, in a shiny red van, to C Section. The van stopped and we piled out before an unremarkable brick building. In the run-down entrance area, a guard stood by a small table of doughnuts, taped with a sign that said FOR SALE, 4 RAND. Mzi figured this was a side business for the guards. They were all bursting from their khaki uniforms and carrying cups of steaming coffee and tea.

On the wall, someone had pasted a sign: BE WISE NOT WEIRD SAY NO 2 DRUGS ☺. There was a small commissary, where visitors could buy smokes or candy or chips for themselves and prisoners. We bought a Baggie of tobacco and a lighter for Terry. A bag was better for prison than single cigarettes, Mzi explained, as the tobacco could be traded like currency for a longer period of time.

We were then led to a visiting room, and sat on two wooden stools, carved with hundreds of names. I carried a notebook, which wasn't allowed, but Mzi explained that we were doing work on account of the PAC and that the notebook was absolutely necessary for this endeavor. I nodded resolutely and the guards, in their confusion and laziness, accepted the explanation.

After a few minutes, Terry emerged from the back. He sat down across from us, separated by glass and metal webbing. He was small, dark, and bone-thin. His inch-long hair was working its way into matted little dreadlocks, and his arms were covered in pink scars. He was growing a scraggly excuse for a beard and wore a dirty orange jumpsuit, from which his gaunt neck protruded. A white crust was affixed to the corners of his lips.

Terry was neither particularly surprised to see Mzi nor particularly interested as to the reason behind my presence. When we asked if he would talk about the Amy Biehl case, he explained first that he had "head problems."

"My memory is not right."

But he would try to remember what had happened. On account of his being in and out of prison countless times, most of them for shoplifting, people had long stopped visiting. Any visitor broke the monotony, and Terry was a man with pretty much nothing to lose.

Terry settled in and started to walk through the day, August 25, 1993. He was fifteen then, a mediocre student. He had been in the shoplifting game for a while; stealing was already his habit.

He lived on NY111, near Easy and Mzi, and therefore had also been indoctrinated in PAC ideology. That morning, he accompanied his friends to Langa Secondary School, attended the PAC student rally, and then marched down the road. They were shouting an anti-white slogan—the slogan itself, he couldn't quite recall.

"One settler, one bullet?" I asked, and he nodded uncertainly.

Terry could remember seeing a bunch of local kids at the rally and in the march in Langa: Ntobeko and Easy and Monks included. Of the three, Monks was Terry's best friend, since the boys were closest in age. With part of the group, including Monks, Terry hopped on the train at Langa—the last he saw Monks was on that train—and hopped off at Heideveld station in Gugulethu. The crowd was a few minutes behind the first group coming from Bonteheuwel, which had already arrived in Gugulethu. From the station, the second group followed in the first group's footsteps, toyi-toyi-ing up the road. Near the Caltex, Terry saw a car. A stone had been thrown into the backseat, and the people inside the car were quickly getting out. The kids from the first group were all around.

Up until this point, Terry had been in a revolutionary mindset. But as soon as he saw an empty car, he went into his default petty-thief mode. He didn't care about slogans or politics anymore. He dove into the open door, rustled around, and took a moment to observe a cracked brick on the floor by the backseat. A heavy rucksack had been abandoned in the car, and Terry grabbed the item. Then he took off running.

Terry rushed straight to the Nofemela house on NY111. He was hoping to meet Monks there, but Monks hadn't returned yet. Easy was there.

"Easy and his other brother and Easy's girlfriend Pinky," Terry said.

"Easy was not at the march at that point?" I asked. Terry shook his head.

"Easy was home, but Monks was not home?"

Terry nodded. Everyone else I'd spoken with contended that Easy was indeed at the march. Some said he had been at the march and had attacked Amy. Others said he arrived at the end of the march and merely happened upon the end of the attack. Easy himself insisted he had indeed been there, and alternately claimed to have attacked Amy and to have done little more than toss a stone. But Terry, like Easy's girlfriend Pinky, insisted Easy was not at the march at all.

At the Nofemela house, Terry opened the rucksack. He removed a red camera, some schoolbooks, and the ID card of a student— probably not Amy Biehl, since Terry thought he'd remember if a white person had been pictured. While Pinky had told me that Terry had found an ANC card, Terry had no recollection of this. Then again, Terry's memory was, as he attested, "not right."

Terry waited for Monks, who eventually returned home, since Monks was a potential customer. Monks didn't want to purchase Terry's take, though he and the others admired the haul, and then Terry headed over to the DairyBelle hostels. Terry liked to unload his take at the hostels because you were guaranteed to find someone willing to buy stolen goods for cut-rate prices. He didn't burn the camera, like Pinky said. Instead, he sold it, along with the books, and kept the rucksack for himself. He'd look nice with a new schoolbag, he figured.

Terry looked down and closed his eyes. Then he turned to Mzi and spoke in Xhosa.

"The things that is troubling him is the voices in his head," Mzi translated. "There are voices that interrupt him when he is talking to us. The voices are talking about us."

"Are the voices a new thing?" I asked.

"From last November they started," Mzi translated.

A woman, on her way out, carried a little boy in her arms. He was looking over her shoulder, repeating, "Bye dada, bye dada, bye dada!"

Terry resumed his story. After he had sold the items, he returned home with his new bag slung across his shoulder. His mother and grandmother were sitting in the living room, watching TV, and they informed him that a white lady had been killed on NY111.

"Get rid of that bag, Terry," his mother advised. And so he went to the backyard and burned the bag.

Terry was soon arrested anyway—presumably somebody had given up his name—and taken to the local police station. He was in the second group of suspects that had been swept up, and he met the APLA trio at the station. Then, because he was underage at the time of arrest, Terry was released to his mother's custody, on the expectation that he would appear in court.

But in October 1993, six months before Mandela won the nation's first democratic elections and while the apartheid government was involved in negotiations, a team of twelve South African commandos stormed a house in the nominally independent homeland of Transkei, part of today's Eastern Cape. The state claimed that the place was an arms cache for APLA members and that eighteen militants were harbored there. In fact, the only inhabitants of the house were five sleeping children, ages twelve through seventeen. Commandos shot each one in the head with an Uzi, then searched the premises and found no weapons. De Klerk announced that he had ordered the raid.

The PAC, incensed, bused students and supporters to attend the boys' funeral, and Terry rode along. Monks went, too. They discussed the best plan of action for Terry, who was scared of being tried. They decided that he should hide out in the Eastern Cape until things cooled down. Terry didn't return to Gugulethu, and instead ingratiated himself with APLA members in the bush. He trained for a few months, once in a while meeting up with Mzi, who was in the midst of planning the police station attack that would result in his first imprisonment. At one point, Terry stole a party member's petty cash and bought some booze; he was subsequently relocated to another member's house. The man he considered his commander was killed. His last words to Terry: Do not surrender to the enemy.

"After that, Terry went underground," Mzi explained.

"Is he still underground?" I asked.

Terry and Mzi laughed.

"Ever since I was underground, I never came up," Terry said.

Eventually, Terry did return to Cape Town. The murder charge against him was withdrawn, for reasons unknown to Terry (the prosecutor Niehaus noted lack of evidence), but by the time he was eighteen, he would enter the prison system anyway. Mostly, he was arrested for stealing, which he did often and not very well, probably because he was usually high when he committed his various offenses. He was currently serving a year for stealing a pair of trousers from a mall, though he had no idea how far into his sentence he was.

"But the voices are saying I get out next month," Terry added without enthusiasm.

That's when a guard came by and informed us our time was up.

As we drove away from the prison, I remarked on Terry's downward trajectory. Grappling with drug addiction and mental health issues, the man bounced aimlessly between the township and the prisons.

"We have a saying in Xhosa," Mzi said. "*Indlala inamanyala.* Poverty makes you perverse."

I had now spoken to five of the eight men arrested for killing Amy Biehl: Easy, Ntobeko, Mongezi, the lone surviving member of the APLA trio (Mzi's brother Steyn), and now, finally, Terry. Since two of the men were dead, only Vusumzi eluded me. This was because Vusumzi came from Langa, a different township, and therefore a different ecosystem. Mongezi, who had been childhood friends with Vusumzi, and who had brought him to the site of Amy's murder, was my closest link to the man. Mzi accompanied me to meet up with Mongezi, and Mongezi agreed to help us look for him. We spent a couple of days bopping around Gugulethu, as Mongezi led us to various empty houses that he said had previously been inhabited by Vusumzi's relatives. We even once drove over to Vusumzi's aunt's house in Langa, but nobody was home. Vusumzi had fallen off the grid, if he had ever been on it.

"What do you think of Mongezi?" I asked Mzi. We were sitting in the car as Mongezi knocked on a door.

"I think apartheid created monsters," Mzi said philosophically. "Anyway, he doesn't want us to find Vusumzi."

"He doesn't? But he says he does. He's even helping us now."

"No, he's lying," Mzi said. "He is hiding something. What, I don't know. We're going to have to find this Vusumzi on our own."

"Sorry, ma'am," Mongezi said, sliding into the backseat. "Nobody is home."

Having given up on Mongezi, Mzi and I tried to retrace our steps a few weeks later, back to the aunt's Langa house. As Cape Town's first township, Langa was a more contained neighborhood, closer to town. Its population was a bit over 52,000—as compared to Gugulethu's nearly 100,000 and Khayelitsha's 400,000-plus—and most families lived in cement apartheid-era houses on neat lanes, with small, well-tended front lawns or gardens. It had the feel of a small, pleasant, very poor neighborhood.

Mzi drove my car—he liked driving, and was better at navigating the townships; this allowed me to take notes from the passenger seat. Finally, after an hour driving up and down the same streets, we recognized a small spaza shop and decided the house was on this very street. Mzi asked a passerby if he knew where the Ntamos lived, and the man pointed at a home with an orange door. We parked and knocked, and an ample-chested woman, wearing a tank top and no bra, welcomed us in. This was Vusumzi's aunt. She had a mole the size of a raisin over her left eye and a curly gray bob. The room's central decor was a portrait of her striking a pose in a large sun hat. Her blaring radio was competing with a blaring radio down the street. She sat at her pink kitchen table eating goat stew directly from a pan, listening as Mzi did his standard, long-winded, explanatory pitch. They were shaking hands like old friends, immediately familiar, and Mzi was lowering himself into a chair.

"Mmmm," the aunt said when Mzi was done. "Vusumzi did say he threw a stone, but he never did stab Amy. He can talk to you, but he is not staying here."

The aunt's son, a skinny thirty-year-old wearing a knit yellow T-shirt and baseball cap, was sitting with her, fiddling with an ashtray. He had kind eyes and crooked front teeth. Mzi whispered that I should give the man a few rand to buy minutes for his phone, which I did. He then made a quick phone call and said he would be most pleased to take us to see Vusumzi, who now resided with his mother in Delft township, near Khayelitsha. The cousin needed a lift that way anyway, so he packed a quick duffel bag and hopped in back, leaning over the seat to offer directions.

We took the N2 to Delft, a desert: no beach, no water, only sand, in great quantity. Sand blowing across the flats, stuck in the weeds, coating the paved streets, surrounding the houses. Sand, and whole neighborhoods of tidy, beige, single-story block homes on small plots, the same design repeated again and again, differentiated only by small touches: a Bible verse painted by the door, a colorful window treatment. Set behind and around the government houses of Delft were the typical cracked pastel structures, the backyard dwellings, the shacks, and then, peppered among them, the built-up, improved-upon houses of the tentative middle class, those township-born professionals who, at least for this generation, couldn't leave their roots but could certainly beautify and modernize them. The area was home to a mix of black and colored people, and when a colored truck driver blocked our path down a one-way road, Mzi leaned out the window and pleaded in Afrikaans, which the driver heeded.

"Broer, asseblief!" Brother, please!

Finally, we pulled off onto a dead end and parked to the side. We knocked on the metal door of a blue one-room stand-alone house, and a boy of twelve or so let us in, uttering a few words in Xhosa before he shuffled back to sit on his bed, set a foot away from a bright TV. The dim dwelling contained two neatly made beds, separated by a wooden armoire, and a barren kitchen with a hotplate and three pots. The toilet, set alone in the backyard, was shared with several other houses.

We loitered in the house as the boy ate cereal before the TV, until the cousin saw a woman whose age I estimated to be somewhere between sixteen and twenty-six. She was short and wore a powder-blue housecoat and slippers. She approached, and he grabbed her face, examining the acne covering her forehead.

"There's a very effective pimple cream available at the pharmacy," he said. "It only costs five rand."

While the cousin was conducting a dermatological consultation, an emaciated older man shuffled into the house: small, with bits of close-shaven gray hair and a sunken, hollow face, his body—just skin pulled taut over bone—disappearing beneath a baggy maroon pajama top and black athletic pants, his oversized flip-flops exposing gnarled dark toenails. But I recognized those features: the handsome younger man he had once been, the man I had seen staring, uncomprehending, from newspaper photos and captured on old video.

"You must be Vusumzi," I said, offering my hand. "I'm Justine and we've been looking for you."

"Hello, ma'am," he said, averting his eyes.

Vusumzi was only forty-two, but he could have passed for ten or even twenty years older. His hand was clammy, and though the day was hot, he smelled cool and smoky. We were heading to his mother's house, I was informed, and as we turned to leave, the young woman in the housecoat admonished Vusumzi for going out in sleepwear. He turned at once, shuffling to the armoire. In the corner, facing away, he pulled off his shirt. I glanced over to see his curved back, every jagged rib visible, as he slipped into an orange tank.

From there, we drove to the house that belonged to Vusumzi's other aunt, one of those beige government-issued places. The old lady—a short, fat, light-skinned woman in a navy maid's uniform, her hair pulled back under a purple-and-white scarf—met us at the door, addressed me as "lovey," and pulled my hand to her lips to kiss it. A placid, developmentally disabled teenage girl, wearing a bright orange minidress, stood behind her. Vusumzi's aunt, the girl in the orange dress, Vusumzi's cousin, and Vusumzi himself headed out to my car. As the group was arranging itself into the small backseat, Mzi leaned to me.

"Is strange family, this," he whispered. "They all seem to be mentally challenged."

We drove farther into Delft to another collection of government dwellings.

"Straight, m'Africa," Vusumzi mumbled to Mzi. "Straight, m'Africa, straight, m'Africa, straight, m'Africa, straight, m'Africa. 085, 085, 085, 085, 085."

We pulled up at house 85 in another government development. A heavily pregnant black dog slept on the sand beneath a roof overhang. Vusumzi's mother opened the door. She was a tall, warm woman with a nagging dry cough and a broad, open face, dressed in a blue-and-white blouse and long denim shorts, her hair braided tight to her head. She welcomed us into a spotless, spartan room, its main furnishing an enormous home theater console that boasted a disconcerting pair of life-size white ceramic terriers, a ten-strong DVD collection that included *Dreamgirls* and *Mr. Bean's Holiday,* and a flat-screen TV.

The house was unfinished, its walls and floors bare cement: the state provided the structure, but no tiles, frills, or finishings. There were also neither chairs nor tables, so the older ladies sat on a couple of ottomans, while Mzi and I balanced on a narrow hand-hewn bench. The cousin settled onto a yellow jerrican in the corner. The girl in the orange dress pulled up a wooden stool. She was sweating heavily from the temples. A drill sounded outside, metal boring into concrete. Vusumzi lowered himself to the floor, took off his shoes, and pulled his knees to his chest. He rested his arms on his knees, and then lay his head in the crook of his elbows, the posture of a small child who has been punished.

First, Vusumzi's mother and aunt began the intricate Xhosa way of greeting me and Mzi, that long and tender conversation that has the capacity to quickly turn strangers into friends. Then they reminisced about their meetings with the Biehls—the handshakes and murmurings of solidarity at the TRC, and that time in 1994 that Linda took them to lunch and asked them not to cry. They were crying because she had lost her daughter, and *she* comforted *them*.

"We are happy you are allowing Vusumzi to finally tell his story," the aunt said. "The new generation can learn not to repeat these old mistake."

Somebody started banging at an interior door, and the mother got up to let a six-foot-tall teenage girl out of the bathroom—it seemed that the door could only be opened from the outside. The girl ambled into the room and sat on the floor. Vusumzi began to run through his memory.

Vusumzi had never been involved in politics. Rather, he had known Mongezi Manqina since he was a child, and had followed Mongezi's lead. The two were friends, then, and Vusumzi didn't have many of those on account of him being different, and slow. Still, he recognized a dark and wicked side to Mongezi. When they were teenagers, one day, after smoking no small amount of dagga, the two had wandered by an old lady selling meat.

"She was working only to survive, and Mongezi stole the meat from her. We argued but the meat fell to the ground. Mongezi, he was born that way."

Mongezi, deep into petty crime, was also involved in radical student politics and he had invited Vusumzi once before to a PAC youth gathering. The politics of the PAC appealed to Vusumzi, he claimed. "I was just learning the PAC then, but I still believe," he said. But the rally that resulted in Amy's death was only his second march. It was a convenient one for him to attend—after all, he lived in Langa then, less than a mile from Langa Secondary School—and Mongezi invited him along.

Vusumzi was following Mongezi, singing freedom songs and toyi-toyi-ing, when somebody yelled that a settler was in their midst. Vusumzi saw the white lady and, spurred on by the group, picked up a stone and hurled it toward her car. Her windshield shattered, but she was not hit. She drove a bit more, until the group descended upon her. Vusumzi stood watching as she ran, and as his friend Mongezi tripped her and stabbed her. Others had begun to step back, but Mongezi was committed.

"Who else was there?" I asked.

Vusumzi didn't know Easy or Ntobeko then. The first time he saw Ntobeko was at the Langa Secondary School rally, but he didn't recall seeing him at the scene of the crime. The first time he saw Easy, he said, was when Easy was trying to burn Amy's car.

"How did you recognize Easy if you'd never seen him before?"

"I saw that he was small and had a light complexion. Later, in prison, the guy I met looked the same as the guy I saw when Amy was attacked."

After Amy's death, Vusumzi, like dozens of others in the mob, hid at his family home in Langa, hoping that nobody would come for him. But Mongezi had been picked up, and had given Vusumzi's name. Mongezi had reason to be frightened of retribution from others—you could not safely be an impimpi on the local gangsters or the militants—but he knew Vusumzi couldn't hurt him. Vusumzi didn't belong to a gang or, officially, to any political group, and he wasn't capable of enacting revenge.

"Mongezi directed them," Vusumzi said. "He is the reason I went to prison."

"How do you feel about Mongezi now?"

"There's no friendship," he said, and set his mouth.

"Why?"

"I have *got* a reason. My own reason."

"Tell me more about Mongezi."

"Mongezi has no values, no respect. He is bad company. I remember very well that in prison, Mongezi said to me, 'I've been longing to be alone with you.' He planned it all. He wanted to destroy me. In prison, he wanted me to be a 28 with him, a gangster, but I didn't become a gangster. I stuck to my guns. Only me. Mongezi was a 28. Then Easy had convinced Ntobeko to join."

"What happened in prison?"

"I share this secret for the first time . . ." Vusumzi said. Then he stopped. He shook his head back and forth and began to mutter: "Mongezi, uwrongo, uwrongo, uwrongo." *Mongezi, he's not right, he's not right, he's not right.*

"That was why Mongezi doesn't want us to find him," Mzi later theorized. "Perhaps Mongezi did . . . things to him in prison." I recalled that Mongezi had raped his developmentally disabled neighbor in 1999.

When the police tracked Vusumzi down in 1993, he was sitting in the living room while his aunt washed clothes in the bathroom. He heard the police vehicle pull up in front of the house, and he heard the officers enter. They told Vusumzi's aunt that he had been involved in Amy Biehl's murder, that big story she'd read about in the papers. Vusumzi was considering making a break for it, but a black officer entered his bedroom speaking in Xhosa.

"He said, 'Small boy, what are you running away for,'" Vusumzi testified before the court twenty years earlier. "He added by saying,

'I'm going to shoot you so that you shit,' my Lord . . . he said, 'Small boy, you killed a white person.'"

The policeman dragged him to a van full of other officers, and shoved him inside. He sat on the bench, but they pushed him to the floor and then drove to an isolated area on the outskirts of the township, where they beat him and interrogated him. They then drove him to the Bellville police station, where Pikker was based, and presented Vusumzi with a confession, which he signed, and then later denied, on his lawyer's recommendation. The confession held up in court; because no eyewitness could identify Vusumzi, it was this confession that sealed his fate.

"There were a lot of white people, speaking Afrikaans" was all he remembered of the interrogation. Vusumzi didn't understand Afrikaans.

"Vusumzi, you only threw a rock?" I asked. "Nothing else?"

"Nothing else," he whispered. "But I did throw that first stone."

"Did it hit her?"

"No, I only hit the car. I break the windscreen."

"Are you sure you never hit Amy?"

"Yes. But after my stone, she was driving low and she can't see right. Then the mob came for her and everyone is throwing stones."

"Did you deserve to go to prison for what you did?"

Vusumzi paused. His aunt let out a series of loud burps. "Yes, I did deserve the sentence. I broke the law and I was found guilty, so I did deserve my time."

"Do you *feel* guilty?"

Vusumzi nodded. The room was silent, and all of Vusumzi's relatives stared at him.

"Do you think Amy would still be alive today if you hadn't thrown that stone?" Mzi asked.

"Yes," Vusumzi said. He looked at Mzi and his eyes turned wet, and then he bent his head into his arms and began to weep. In all my time interviewing people about this crime, I had never seen anyone shed a tear. Vusumzi looked up and wiped his cheeks. "She was running and yelling 'Help me, help me!' I saw Mongezi doing it, and I wanted to stop him but I was too far."

"Why did you get involved?" I asked.

Vusumzi sighed. "It was the mood of the moment."

In the more current moment, Vusumzi was unemployed and lived with his girlfriend in the one-room hovel where I'd found him. I asked if he had children, and he answered that he did, at which point everyone burst out laughing.

"You?" his aunt said between guffaws. *"You?"*

"Well, I don't have children of my own, but I am a good man and take care of the children of my girlfriend," he said softly.

Vusumzi's dream, he said, was to get a job so that he could help his mother. She was straining, you see. Usually, he made money by gardening—he was "good with a spade"—and cleaning people's cars. The last real gig he'd had was ten years earlier, cleaning municipal parks until his temporary contract ran out. If given the opportunity, he would clean the parks again, "with a passion." Or, in his dream world, he would work at the Amy Biehl Foundation, where you could make good money, where you worked in an office, where you could imagine a future.

"It is because of me that there is now a foundation called Amy Biehl and I believe I deserve to be there. But I only see Easy and Ntobeko working there. Maybe this is because they had a better education?" He slumped back against the wall. In 1993, he had lied to police officers, claiming to be in grade nine, and then admitted to being in grade seven. This was because, as he explained to the court, "I wanted to give the impression that I am attending a high school. I did not want to make a disgrace of myself to say I am in [grade seven] . . . because I am too old for [grade seven]." In fact, at age twenty-two, Vusumzi had just barely made it to sixth grade.

"Why is he not included?" his mother asked me, palms up. "Even as a family we cannot help him. We try to tell him that his time will come. We have faith. But people make him so many empty promises, from the PAC up to the Amy Biehl Foundation."

"Even the public thinks I am a fool," Vusumzi said. "I don't benefit like the others. It takes my confidence."

It was an unusual logic that the family shared, and that Mongezi
had previously expressed, as well. All of Amy's killers were, in a sense,
responsible for the creation of the Amy Biehl Foundation, and so
shouldn't they be rewarded with jobs? And yet, to their befuddle-
ment, only two of the convicted killers had benefited. They didn't
understand that Easy and Ntobeko had taken the first step by approaching Linda and Peter, and had slowly proved themselves willing to work for a salary, continually demonstrating that they did not
expect charity and that they understood the foundation's stated
mandate to help the townships. Vusumzi's continued lack of employment was, according to his family's rationale, an injustice. When
I suggested that the foundation had not been founded to help Vusumzi, they stared at me, unconvinced.

The evidence they had gathered—watching Easy and Ntobeko
drive new vehicles, often containing white people, around town—
was that the foundation benefited its employees most of all. More
than the kids. More than the community. The community had enjoyed some free bread, but Easy got a plot of land. Ntobeko was a
manager. And this foundation would never have maintained its
prominence were it not for the services of Easy and Ntobeko, the
reconciled, redeemed perpetrators. So why, then, had Vusumzi not
been included in this radical form of rehabilitation? Had he not, too,
served his time for the exact same crime? If Amy's killers got jobs to
make a grand point about South African redemption, and if he was
a killer, then why didn't he have a job?

As we got up to leave, I spotted a minuscule brown puppy in an
overturned milk crate by the back door. He looked to be only a few
weeks old, too young to be separated from his mother. I stuck my
finger into the crate and he stumbled toward it. His fur was dry.

"What's his name?" I asked.

"Chester," the aunt informed me. Presumably he was named for
Chester Williams, one of the first colored rugby players to play for

the beloved Springbok national rugby side, a traditionally white sport. "My friend give me this puppy." She clasped my palm in her cool, soft hands. "When you come back, lovey, bring the book you are writing . . . and a big bag of meat."

"I am thankful that my story won't die," Vusumzi said as I stood by the door. "The story can educate children of Africa, to empower our minds."

"Vusumzi was denied his right to work with the Biehl family," Vusumzi's mother said, as a final word. Vusumzi lingered behind her, his shoulders dragged down. "What perplexes our minds is that Mongezi said he stabbed and Vusumzi admitted he threw a stone, but there is nothing to connect Easy and Ntobeko to the incident. I'm not saying that Easy and Ntobeko don't have the right to benefit from the Biehl Foundation, but in court, the evidence only pointed to Vusumzi and Mongezi. Easy and Ntobeko, nobody knows what they did on that day."

Monks may have known what Easy and Ntobeko did that day, but he was difficult to interview. I was accustomed to meeting people on neutral ground, in a private space, but Monks was immobile and surrounded, at all times, by people. He hated his wheelchair, and could not use it. Though he had some mild movement in his arms, he rarely visited a physical therapist and so in the six years since his accident, he had lost muscle tone. Therefore, he functioned essentially as a quadriplegic. He would have needed an electric wheelchair to gain some independence, but he had only a basic, unwieldy manual number that required he be pushed by another person. Monks had no interest in this, and so he was restricted to his home and driveway, to the places where he could be lifted and comfortably set. And because his parents feared that he might need something, and he was frightened to be left alone and vulnerable, either Wowo or Kiki was always within a few yards of him. Even when he slept, one of his brothers was nearby, in the next bed over. His friends, many of them unemployed and at loose ends, liked to come sit with him and shoot the breeze.

I found him alone on one occasion, laid out in the sunny car where he liked to bask in warmth to avoid pneumonia. He had that one gold front tooth and a beautiful, chiseled face.

"Can we talk?" I asked.

Whether or not he had much of a choice, confined as he was to the car, I don't know, but he said yes. To my questioning, which was rushed and nervous, he was agreeable but evasive. He was at the rally and in the march, yes, but that was all. He was walking with his friend Ntobeko. His brother Easy was around, yes, he was. He did see Amy in the distance, but he couldn't say much more than that.

"Did you throw a stone?"

He paused. "No."

"I heard from many people that you did throw a stone."

"No," he said. Then with more emphasis, as if convincing himself: "I could not have thrown a stone. No. No."

Just then, a neighbor got in the back of the car; I knew him from the area. "Justine, let me tell you about my new tae bo training center," he said with excitement. "I call my method GetFit." I'd only managed five minutes alone with Monks.

Months later, Easy, Monks, and I sat together in the Nofemela living room. "Lucky day, I find some photos for you," Easy said, absently dabbing the sweat from Monks's forehead. Monks's head was wrapped in a white terry-cloth towel, the effect of which made him look like a nun.

Easy left the room and returned with a red leather album with gold trim, so worn and cracked that it looked like a relic from some archaeological dig. I opened it. A yellowed newspaper clipping had been pasted on the interior of the front cover and then ripped out.

I could make out the headline: ANONYMOUS TIP ... LED POLICE TO AMY MURDER SUSPECT. Above the ripped article were words written in labored, flowery capital letters: THIS IS MY HISTORY IT BELONGS TO EASY NOFEMELA.

Another line of writing had been crossed out frantically with a black marker. The first three pages of the album were blank. On the fourth page, upside down, was a photo of a white woman whom I recognized as a friend of Linda Biehl's and a teenage boy whom I had never seen. The next three pages were blank, and then a photo of what looked like a choir of young black men in black suits and white shirts, Easy nestled among them in a sweatshirt and sneakers. Peter Biehl stood to one side. Linda Biehl, in a gown, stood to the other, grinning.

In one picture, Easy crouched down, saluting the camera, with two friends behind him, while Ntobeko, skinny and sulking in a red cap, looked off to the side. Another picture, askew on the page, was a portrait of Easy's late aunt. On the back interior cover was a color photo clipped from a paper of three APLA militants who had bombed the St. James Church in Cape Town. The men had applied for and received amnesty, with Norman Arendse as their attorney. Across from the militants, Easy had pasted a picture of the 1990s pop star Brandy, her lips slicked with red gloss, wearing a shiny baby-blue jacket.

The end of the album contained haphazardly arranged photos from a few separate days, it seemed, of a post-incarcerated Easy and his friends running around Cape Town, playing soccer, and hiking up Table Mountain. They posed in front of fancy houses and in parks, exuberant. There was a small kid, younger than the rest, in a turquoise shirt, barefoot and dancing. Monks was in the picture, too, wearing khakis and a white T-shirt. I recognized him, his sharp cheekbones and dark eyes. In one picture, he and Easy are caught mid-stride, their steps mirroring each other's: left leg down, right leg up. They have the same shaved round head, the same pale skin, and the same scrawny build.

Monks lay still on the sofa.

"Monks, can I ask you again about the day Amy Biehl was killed?" I asked.

"Yes," he said pleasantly.

Then, as though possessed of some maternal antennae that received radio signals from her boys, Kiki entered the room and made her way to her favored chair. She lowered herself down and turned toward the TV, though she was pointedly listening to us.

"Again, do you remember what happened? You were there, right?"

"I was there—" Monks began.

Kiki let out a short, angry command in Xhosa. Monks immediately shut up.

"What did she say?" I whispered to Easy.

"She says we must stop talking about the dead and the past," he said. And so we did.

Two years later, when I had known the Nofemelas for a total of three years, I was finally granted access to Monks. I appealed to Wowo, who arranged for me to meet with Monks in the Ford the next day. At the agreed-upon time, Monks was lifted into the car. One of his brothers provided me with Monks's water bottle and a towel with which I was to dab his sweat, and then Wowo shooed everyone away so we could have some peace and quiet.

Monks, reclining in the sun-drenched passenger seat, wore a constant, winning smile, and had clearly been a heartbreaker before his accident. Now he was a cheerful, quiet man, dressed in sports pants and a striped polo shirt. He had dropped out of high school, then dropped out of a computer course, and then dropped out of an electrician-training course. Finally, he'd gotten a job driving a bread truck, and then a job driving a truck for the post office. He and a girlfriend had a son. Then in 2009, he was in the accident.

"I don't feel nothing," he said of his condition, as his younger brother bent in to wipe his brow. "Because nothing can change."

"Let me ask you about your involvement in politics," I said.

"I was involve too much. I go early in the morning to learn about PAC and APLA. I believed in PAC, and I still believe. Land first, and all shall follow."

Monks had been close friends with Ntobeko, who was his age—around eighteen—in 1993. He considered Ntobeko his leader, since both boys attended Langa Secondary School and Ntobeko had been the chairperson of the school's PAC student organization. He remembered learning PAC theory from older militants. He remembered training with Ntobeko on the outskirts of Gugulethu in the night.

When Monks thought back to August 25, 1993, the day of Amy's death, he remembered attending the rally and then toyi-toyi-ing through Langa. After the cops chased them, the boys boarded the train. Monks was together with Easy and Ntobeko, and they all hopped on Viveza's bakkie. Monks did not recall Quinton, the neighbor, being there, just as, months earlier at our meeting at Mzoli's, Quinton had not recalled Monks's presence. Monks never mentioned going to a wholesaler with Viveza. But Monks's memory was fuzzy twenty-one years on, so it was hard to tell when he was being purposely evasive and when he was simply forgetful.

As Monks recalled, he, Easy, and Ntobeko rode to NY1 on the bakkie and it was there that they saw Amy running down the street, pursued by a gang of young men. Monks had seen the APLA trio at the rally, but he didn't see them among the crowd, he said.

"I just saw the lady already jumping out to the car. I saw a lot of guys chasing with the stones. I saw Amy was crossing from the church, then running across the road and after she cross the road, I saw Mongezi Manqina stabbing her."

"Who else was there?"

"There was a lot of guys there," he said. "I can't know every guy's name. They were from Langa and Khayelitsha and Gugulethu, but the other side of Gugulethu." He claimed to recognize nobody in the mob, all of them from different areas whose residents were not familiar to him.

"Did you join?"

"No, no. I didn't throw the stone because she is already bleeding. You can't throw the stone because already she is bleeding and want to collapse because she haven't got the power. Then the police come through and everybody going."

"What did Easy and Ntobeko do during Amy's attack?"

"I know Easy and Ntobeko said they throw the stone. But really, really, really serious, they didn't throw the stone, because is already bleeding, Amy. Serious."

"Why would a witness point to Easy and Ntobeko if they didn't do anything?"

"Maybe was politics. I don't know."

"Well, why did Easy and Ntobeko themselves say they throw the stone if they didn't do it?"

"You know, if you said to the TRC that you didn't throw the stone, they will say, 'No, you are lying' and you can't come out of prison."

"What were you doing the morning of Amy's death?" I asked Monks.

"Morning I was going to school."

"But there was no school. There was a teachers' strike."

"Hmm," Monks said.

"Did you take the train to Langa with Ntobeko and Easy that morning?"

"I was with Ntobeko, but Easy was not there." Monks said that he had accompanied Ntobeko to help set up for the rally, and Easy had arrived later.

"Did you see a white guy that morning?" I asked, wondering if anyone had any memory of the purported attack that Easy had told me took place on the morning of Amy's murder.

"I didn't see a white guy."

"In a big truck?"

"Hmm, I remember that guy but I don't remember what's happening that guy. What is that guy doing there in that station?"

"He was there in a big truck. Two colored guys were helping to fix the electrical."

"Oh God, I don't remember. I don't remember exactly what happened. But I remember now a white guy. I saw that guy. I did see him on the way to Langa. But I don't remember more."

"Did you see people attacking him?"

"That time I didn't remember that. I know that guy but not more."

"When you got to the school, was Easy there? Or did he come after? Or did he come with you?"

"He must come later. I don't think was come that time doing the preparation."

"What did you and Easy and Ntobeko do when you came home after witnessing Amy's death?"

"I don't remember."

"Is there anyone around here who might remember that day in more detail?"

"I don't remember."

"You went to the TRC, right?"

"I don't remember."

"You don't remember the TRC?"

"TRC?" He smiled. "Okay, I was there. In the chairs."

"When the camera came, you hid your face."

He burst into laughter. "I remember that! I was shy! Also at the High Court this guy came with the camera and I said, 'No, I will break you camera, don't take a picture, please man.'"

"What do you think of Linda and Peter Biehl and their act of forgiveness?"

"I don't think nothing."

"Monks," I said. "You don't remember too much."

"I'm sorry," he said.

"How do you remember that Easy and Ntobeko didn't throw stones at Amy?"

"I was there together with them. I was there on NY1. I saw that lady is already bleeding. Seriously, they didn't throw the stone. I don't know why they said to the court they throw the stone. Maybe is the lawyer or what, I don't know. But that time, I was there, they didn't throw the stone. Maybe that time I didn't see clearly?" He paused and tried to access some old image, stored in the recesses of his brain. "*Ach*, no, man, I was standing there together with them. They didn't throw the stone."

Because she had directed us to shut up about the past, among other reasons, I had long avoided talking to Kiki. Of all the people I'd approached to interview—from convicted killers to members of the police force—Kiki was the person who most intimidated me, and it took me years to find the courage to speak with her. Maybe it was because she had never once engaged me in conversation and the only time she had ever looked happy to see me was on a single occasion when I brought her a large bag of Ethiopian coffee, which she grabbed, saying "Give me!" and then, almost as an afterthought, added, "Thank you." The most attention she paid me was when she realized that Easy was in my car, and that I could therefore ferry him across the township to pick up groceries. Local cockroach taxis—low-lying jalopies that crept around the townships—cost at least $2 one way, and once in a while, skollies stole the taxis and then picked people up only to rob them. Kiki, in addition to not having a spare $2 and not wanting to get robbed, was also a homebody who didn't even like leaving NY111.

Eventually, I would realize that Kiki, though indeed fundamentally suspicious of outsiders, didn't want to speak to me mostly because she hated speaking English, a language she hadn't come close to mastering, even as she raised three white children over twenty-five years in her capacity as a domestic worker. She spoke fluent Sotho and Xhosa, but English had proved elusive.

"Justine is coming and now is just English, English, English," Kiki complained to her family.

Once I understood this, I was less daunted by the woman and one day I arrived at the house with a purpose. Outside, sprawled upon some lawn chairs, were Tiny and one of Easy's sisters-in-law. They were complaining about their partners, Kiki, and their own moms.

"Justine, you have pimples," the sister-in-law observed benevolently upon seeing me, and she pointed to a zit on my forehead. This was not meant to offend me. For Xhosa people, it wasn't rude to exclaim, for example, "Wooh, you got *fat*!"

Wowo was fiddling with his Nissan bakkie, which was dripping water for some unknown reason. In the TV room, Monks and a neighbor were watching TV. Easy was lying on the couch hungover, complaining that his body didn't "feel right." One of Easy's younger brothers was nonchalantly mopping the main room in his underpants.

Kiki was washing dishes all alone. This was highly unusual: her various grandchildren were forever slumped on her, using her breasts as elbow rests, leaning on her shoulders, and lying on her lap. She was a fan of sugar, meat, fried foods, and soap operas, and her solid frame reflected this list of pleasures. She desired neither adventure nor novelty. She smiled rarely, commanded often, and liked to make her point by shouting orders at her family.

I sat down on a chair as she eyed me, the water running over the plate in her hand. I took a deep breath and decided to forgo pleasantries.

"Kiki, can you tell me about how you remember the Amy Biehl case?"

I expected her to dismiss me. Instead, she put down her soapy rag and faced me.

"My child not kill Amy Biehl," she said.

"Why do you say that?"

"I know in my heart my child."

Kiki began to recall, in halting English, Easy's arrest. The officers crashing in and hauling her boy away. They knocked him in the face, she said. They slapped him. It was the middle of the night, and she was standing in her nightgown, confused, and her elder sons were itching to fight the cops, while Wowo was ordering everyone to stay calm. Then Easy was hauled off.

Kiki was hardly the first mother to see her kid marched away in cuffs, and she was hardly the first to believe her boy was innocent. In fact, a few of Kiki's other sons had been in trouble with the law: a little robbery, a bit of fighting. But none of her family members had ever been charged with murder. And black people in South Africa knew that historically, when you killed a white person, you'd feel the full weight of the law come crashing down on you. For killing another black person, you might get a few years in jail, but for killing a white, you'd be hanged. So from that day on, Kiki lived in fear that Easy would be executed.

"My heart was sore."

"Did Easy ever tell you anything about the case?"

"He say he don't kill Amy, and me, I'm believe Easy. Me, I'm know Easy."

"If you don't think he killed anyone, why do you think he was arrested?"

"Yes, was there. Yes, was child of the PAC. Maybe is bad luck. But he no kill. Lot people was there. Why only four people go to jail? The people point Easy because they know Easy."

Easy had always been a good son. He always did his chores. He rarely got in trouble. He loved people. He had a short temper but it was so easily quelled—the boy couldn't hold a grudge. He was clever and sociable. And he liked to garden with her; how could a boy who liked to garden with his mom kill a woman?

Kiki stayed home from work for weeks after Easy's arrest, "sick, sick, sick." Pinky, Easy's girlfriend at the time, brought her food and water. After his sentencing—and Kiki could not bear to attend the trial, a dubious honor that belonged to Wowo alone—she visited him at prison. Every weekend for five years, she took a bus to Tokai, or to Caledon, or to Paarl, depending on the prison in which he was kept, hours on public transport and expensive to boot. Once, when the bus broke down on the way to Caledon, she slept on the side of the road.

Though Easy boasted of "relaxing" in prison, and many claimed he had been a member of the 28s, Kiki remembered her son's experience differently. He was so small and so scared, his face drawn and yellow behind the glass, she said. At the beginning, he was desperate to get out and had hatched a plan in which she need only to provide a fraudulent certificate to say he was a juvenile so he might be transferred to a less violent facility.

Kiki had been devastated that Easy was found guilty, but relieved that he wasn't given the death sentence. Then the Truth and Reconciliation Commission came along, a process Kiki hardly understood. All she comprehended, really, was that Easy would perhaps be released from prison due to some political shifts and backroom deals, and indeed, even before she received the official news of his amnesty approval, she knew he was coming home. She was sitting in her living room when a bee flew around her head. Bees were, according to Kiki's belief system, a sign of her ancestors, and the bee's presence was a message: her son was on his way. She ran to prepare a bath with medicinal soap obtained from her sangoma, which would allow him to wash the stench and evil of prison from his body. He could start afresh. The next day, Easy was released.

"How do you feel about the TRC?" I asked.

"I'm happy because I don't like my child in jail, but I'm sad for his name. Easy say he kill at TRC, and so I'm sad, yho!"

"Yes, Easy says he did kill Amy. He tells—"

"—other story," Kiki cut in.

"Why is that?"

"He tell me it's for the commission. But I never understand."

I nodded and Kiki turned back to her dishwashing. "I know Easy," she said softly. "My child is not kill Amy Biehl."

Did Kiki's child kill Amy Biehl? If so, which child? According to everyone I'd asked, except for Terry the thief and Pinky the ex, Easy was, at some point, present during Amy's attack and subsequent death. I had searched the area for other witnesses and most, if they saw Easy at the scene of the crime at all, remembered him holding a stone in the vicinity of Amy's car near the end of the incident. Easy confirmed this. Nobody, except for Miss A in her statement and the supportive Misses B and C, remembered him standing over Amy, stabbing her. And in any case, Amy received only one wound, by all accounts delivered by Mongezi Manqina. Why, then, had Easy told the commissioners that he had "stabbed at her"? Why would he have said, "No, I am sorry, I won't know whether I did stab her or I attempted to, but I can remember that it was three or four times."

Neither Vusumzi nor Ntobeko admitted to a stabbing, and they were given amnesty, so having thrust a knife in Amy's direction was not a prerequisite for release. Moreover, whether or not Easy had a knife didn't affect his ability to shield his brother from prosecution, if he was indeed protecting Monks, who claimed that neither of them had joined in on Amy's assault. Plus, the contention that Easy had thrust a knife at Amy only confused matters, since the medical examiner's report proved that Amy had been stabbed just once.

For the longest time, I couldn't figure out this detail, threaded through so many stories. In the course of my work, still confused, I reread Miss A's account of August 25, 1993, as well as Judge Friedman's final judgment in October 1994, in which he found the defendants, who were maintaining innocence, guilty of Amy's murder.

"Ntobeko repeatedly jumped on her and hit her with a stone on her head. Mr. Manqina and Mr. Nofemela approached the deceased while she was lying on the ground and both of them were on her left-hand side with knives, stabbing her," Miss A told the court, hours after breaking down on the stand, explaining that testifying "made the whole picture of what happened that day come to my mind . . . as if I am presently experiencing the events of the day." The lesser witnesses, Misses B and C, knew Miss A socially and were rumored to be fellow ANC members. They corroborated Miss A's testimony, each mentioning Easy's role in stabbing Amy.

The confessions of Mongezi, Easy, and Vusumzi were weak, and only placed them near the scene. They had also all retracted their confessions, though only Mongezi's confession was thrown out. Nine months of the eleven-month trial were spent arguing whether the accused had been coerced or abused into confessing. Also, there were no photos or videos of that day. After potential witnesses got scared and pulled out, six people remained: Amy's passengers and the three Misses. Unfortunately for the prosecution, most of them were of little use. Amy's friends either hadn't seen anything because they were too busy defending themselves against assault, or did see the perpetrators in the chaos, but then could not definitively point them out in a lineup. Judge Friedman liked Miss B, but found Miss C to be unreliable. Miss A, however, was his favorite witness, and she claimed to have seen the entire attack play out before her eyes. She stood up beautifully to cross-examination, explained what she had seen eloquently, and was impossible to intimidate.

"She made a very favorable impression on the Court," Friedman announced soon before handing down his verdict. "She struck the Court as an entirely honest witness, upon whose testimony the Court could rely."

Without Miss A, there were neither trustworthy witnesses nor adequate evidence linking the defendants to the crime. Friedman would have had no choice but to acquit. In his judgment, Friedman then adhered most closely to Miss A's clear, well-told version of events. It occurred to me that Miss A had therefore essentially decided what had happened on August 25, 1993. She had made the first move in pointing out who was guilty. Of the four defendants who were imprisoned, three names—Easy, Ntobeko, and Mongezi— were on the original slip of paper that she had handed to Officer Leon Rhodes; Vusumzi had been hauled in after somebody, most likely Mongezi, gave him up to investigators. Miss A may indeed have seen the men attack Amy. Or she may have been convinced that she had seen them, but she may have made a mistake. And she was not aware that Easy had a lookalike brother.

Or Miss A may have had her own agenda: to rid the streets of troublemakers and to stick it to the militant PAC. She was receiving compensation in return for her testimony. Despite her claims that she was apolitical, rumor had it that her mother's house often functioned as an ANC salon, and Miss A herself was known to be active in ANC-aligned women's groups. In her short life, she had seen enough violence to make anyone sufficiently angry. Most of this violence was committed by young gangsters, and perhaps she had nurtured a burning hatred for such young men, the kind of hatred that would motivate her to seek out a little well-intentioned revenge. Maybe she was telling the truth. Or maybe she was just telling her truth.

Friedman dismissed inconsistencies and deficiencies in Miss A's testimonies as reasonable, considering the chaotic scene she was describing. He noted that there was indeed one stab wound despite claims of multiple assailants with knives, but deemed this irrelevant.

"Having regard to the number of people who were surrounding the deceased and attempting to attack her at the same time, the fact that the deceased had only one serious stab wound is understandable and does not detract from the reliability of the eyewitnesses' testimony," he announced.

Three years later, Nona Goso and Norman Arendse, representing the men at the Truth and Reconciliation Commission, were in a bind. Their job was to obtain amnesty for their clients by allowing them to present a consistent, sincere rundown of August 25, 1993. But first, they had to come up with a single set of events to explain the chronology of the day. The "Truth" in the commission's title (along with proving that the crime was political) was the main prerequisite for obtaining freedom. I knew that learning the perfect truth about Amy's murder was impossible. Goso and Arendse probably chose to follow Miss A's version of events because this version constituted the recorded, accepted, official truth of the circumstances surrounding Amy's murder.

And besides, the Truth and Reconciliation Commission was an institution with an overwhelming mandate—to bring the atrocities of the past to light. The commission required that applicants admit to their crimes, not deny them. If a person had been falsely imprisoned, he would have to appeal the case in the criminal courts, not before the TRC. But the criminal courts had already found the men guilty once; and if in fact Easy was wrongly identified, he could hardly explain the case of mistaken identity to a judge without implicating his brother in the crime. Nor was he likely to successfully argue that while he had been involved in Amy's death, he had not been sufficiently involved to warrant a murder conviction. Moreover, where would Easy find a pro bono lawyer?

In contrast, the TRC was a ready-made forum in which applicants were supported by a political party and provided with attorneys. The TRC dangled before the prisoners the possibility of liberation and a clean slate. Possibly better, a hearing at the TRC allowed them to solidify their reputations as righteous freedom fighters, not as street gangsters or hooligans. The TRC could potentially provide the men with new, appealing, official identities. In this way, the TRC had an awesome power: It could create, rather than expose, history.

At the TRC, each man admitted to a version of what Miss A said happened. Miss A said Mongezi had stabbed Amy, and Mongezi admitted to stabbing Amy, and took the blame for the fatal wound. Miss A said Ntobeko had hit Amy with a rock, and Ntobeko said he had thrown rocks. Miss A said Easy had stoned and stabbed Amy. Easy agreed, but used the term "stab at"; this technicality could help him hedge if questioned as to why his supposed victim had only one puncture between her ribs. Miss A didn't mention Vusumzi, so Vusumzi echoed his own confession at the criminal trial, in which he admitted to throwing rocks. It's possible that in a perverse twist to the standard justice system, the men, or at least some among them, had been found guilty for a murder they didn't commit, and the only way to freedom was to officially accept the blame.

But this brings up another question: what is guilt in the context of mob violence? If we are to believe that Easy was at the scene of the crime but did no more than stone Amy's car, does that mean he is guilty nonetheless? He says he hopped off the bakkie, saw the throbbing crowd, and joined in pelting the Mazda with rocks as others pummeled a woman on the ground a few yards away. Can he be innocent if he was there but did not personally harm Amy? What about Ntobeko and Vusumzi, who always maintained that they only threw stones?

If they are guilty for simply being part of a mob, then every member is guilty. They all contributed, by sheer mass and intention, to Amy's needless death. If this is the case, then Ilmar Pikker was right when he said, "There was thirty people there that day, and I would have liked to see them all in prison. . . . The four we got are just a weak consolation prize."

Or were the men who actually attacked Amy the real killers, and those who pelted her car merely vandals? In this case, some might consider Mongezi Manqina the real murderer, since he admitted to Amy's stabbing. However, the medical examiner believed that the first stone to the head may well have been the crowning blow.

Then the question is: who threw that particular stone? Vusumzi broke the windshield, but he was certain he had not made contact with Amy. Evaron Orange, sitting next to Amy in the passenger seat, remembered a pop of glass, and then stones pouring in, cracking Amy's skull. So then the real murderer is a person who stood on NY1, hurling rocks and bricks at Amy with devastating aim. After twenty years, or even after twenty seconds, would anyone in a throbbing, adrenaline-laced throng be able to tell who cast that deadly stone?

And if they could, would that exonerate those who stood by as an innocent woman was beaten to death? Would it exonerate those who cheered as she was stabbed? Would it condemn a system that sought swift, inexact justice? Would it condemn those who told a false story as if it were true?

17.

No foreign sky protected me,
   no stranger's wing shielded my face.
I stand as witness to the common lot,
   survivor of that time, that place.

—ANNA AKHMATOVA, *Requiem*

On the day that he told me of the white man killed by the train station, I left Easy propped up and sleeping on a couch at Aunt Princess's house. I drove out of the township, over the bridge. On the way out, I called Pikker, who was again in South Africa from Abu Dhabi, this time for some operation on his legs that never took place, as the doctor decided he was too likely to perish while under anesthesia. Did he know of this white man, attacked the same day as Amy? No, no, Pikker said. He had never heard of such a thing. I called Niehaus, the old prosecutor. Did he recall a second attack? Oh my, he said. It was a long time ago, but he certainly did not. Maybe the cops would have a record, but he probably would have gotten wind of it had another white been killed.

I called Mzi. "No, Justini, I don't remember this," he said.

I figured that Easy had been mistaken, or confused. His mind was scrambled from a long night drinking crummy brandy. There had been no white man, no worker. Certainly Amy Elizabeth Biehl was the only white person attacked in Gugulethu on August 25, 1993. If she hadn't been, the police would have investigated the other murder, would have connected the two crimes. I knew the killing of a middle-aged white male South African municipal worker wasn't as intriguing as the killing of a young white female American activist, but surely the papers and news programs would have reported on them together, at least a bit. According to Easy's telling, the attack occurred less than a half mile from where Amy was killed.

I tried to put this out of my mind. I had things to do: I was getting married two weeks later, on a vineyard in Stellenbosch, in the Cape

Winelands. The main building was an Old Dutch-style hall, white stucco and swooping lines, beside a small man-made lake, where a family of ducks lived. The vineyard sat beneath rugged black and green mountains. I had flower arrangements to look at, Chinese lanterns to consider, the evil grande dame of wedding caterers to meet with and be admonished by.

While I was picking out the perfect casserole pot from an online catalogue, I tried to convince myself that I didn't believe in the mystery white man. But his hazy face, featureless, burned in my mind. The memory is a strange and unreliable creature indeed, but Easy was neither insane nor suffering from dementia, and drunkenness could not explain the complete conjuring of an incident, along with the accompanying detail and emotion.

So that evening, I sat in the kitchen at my computer. I typed in Amy's name and ran through articles I'd read a few times already. I looked everywhere for a second murder. I scanned township news and articles in the international media. By 2 A.M., after hundreds of pages, I still had nothing.

Assuming the murder was true, I thought, what did I know about it?

I typed what I knew into the search bar.

The white page flashed open, the results in black type: *DE VIL-LIERS, DANIEL. A municipal worker fixing street lights who was severely assaulted by PAC-aligned students in Gugulethu on 25 August 1993. An American student was killed that same day in nearly identical circumstances.*

"I found out the name of the white guy," I told Easy a few days later. I was drinking a takeaway coffee and he was sitting, again, in my passenger seat. Easy's phone had been going straight to voicemail, so

I had gone stalking around NY1 and, with the help of one of his brothers, finally plucked him out of a smoke-filled house on a sandy back lane. An old lady, slumped against a shack and barefoot, nodded when I asked her, pointlessly, to keep an eye on my car while I extracted Easy.

"Who?" Easy asked.

"The white guy."

"What white guy?"

"*The* white guy."

"Hmmm."

"The white guy you said was killed."

"No, I never said."

"You *just* told me all about it."

"Maybe you hear wrong. Maybe you make mistake. I don't know a white guy."

"You also told me how you weren't involved in Amy's attack."

"Myself and Ntobeko, we were involved. And Mongezi and Vusumzi. Honest, Justice."

I let Easy out at his parents' house and drove home, where I began an all-out search for Daniel de Villiers, with no luck whatsoever. I suspected that he was alive, because the TRC report, which contained thousands of other similar entries, tended to state if someone had been killed or merely injured. I tracked down a salesman with the same surname, but he claimed no relation. I ended up calling a few people who were related to the salesman, and they also had no link to Daniel de Villiers. Searching further, I found a too-old Daniel de Villiers who according to the newspapers had been shot dead up near Johannesburg back in 2004; a Daniel de Villiers who lived in a small town in the middle of the Netherlands; and a bevy of young, handsome Daniel de Villierses who were scattered across France.

After about a month, I found a twenty-eight-year-old banker with the last name de Villiers on Facebook. I messaged him continuously until he sent his phone number.

"Ja, I do have an uncle named Daniel," he said, when I called. He had an Afrikaans accent, since the early French Huguenots who had settled in South Africa had melded into the Afrikaans population. His Facebook profile showed a plump man with hair gelled into spikes. "He used to work for the municipality until some blacks attacked him."

"That's him!" I said. Daniel de Villiers was not dead after all. "Do you know how I could reach him?"

The banker hadn't seen Daniel since he was a kid and had no idea where the guy was. But his grandmother would know more, he was certain. Here was her number. I dialed immediately, but Grandma denied knowing anything about Daniel.

"No, sorry, my dear, we're very distant family," she said, before hanging up.

I dialed the banker again. "She says she doesn't really know Daniel."

"Ach, of course she does," he said. "She's lying." Unbothered, he gave me the names of his various "aunties," though he wasn't really in touch with them, as the de Villierses were, I would learn, a fractured bunch. There were five aunties, and he could come up with only one phone number and one address. But she would know more, he was certain.

Over another month, I tracked down some of the aunties. I called them at work and at home and all the way in Port Elizabeth, a small city along the Indian Ocean. I even found a de Villiers working at a bookstore in Canada. For the most part, they were confused by my calls. One lady had no clue who Daniel was. Another was certain she wasn't related. A man had never heard of him. Another knew he was a cousin, but that was it.

I ran expensive searches on a real estate database and found only a wealthy restaurateur from Pretoria who had the middle name de Villiers. The trail ended there. As a last-ditch effort, I dragged myself to the Department of Home Affairs in the city center.

Like most South African government departments, the Department of Home Affairs is notoriously inefficient and corrupt. I had even once gotten caught up in one of their schemes. I already had a visa that was valid for three years, but I had needed to provide, within six months of its issuance, proof that I had no criminal record in my home country. I was a few months late in my delivery of such a document. When I did deliver it, a group of employees—who, judging from the human contents of the waiting room, were accustomed to taking advantage of desperate Zimbabweans—seamlessly attempted to bilk me for $250 for "staying in the country illegally." It was a false claim, as my visa was valid even though my clearance was late. After I threatened to see a prosecutor about the situation, they miraculously canceled the fine. A friend of mine, along with most of his rugby team, had simply purchased their driver's licenses, and the undocumented migrants I knew spoke of handing over $80 to the right person and obtaining a South African birth certificate.

Because of this culture of corruption, terrorists loved the South African Home Affairs office. You could get a real passport with a fake name for a fee, if you knew the right guy. In 2002, a Home Affairs employee was arrested in connection with the theft of four thousand passports. In 2004, a Tunisian al Qaeda leader confessed to possessing a South African passport. In 2006, the Pakistani mastermind of a plot to blow up airplanes with liquid explosives was arrested with a South African passport. In 2011, an al Shabaab and al Qaeda leader was killed in Mogadishu, a fraudulent South African passport in his possession. In 2013, the "White Widow," a British woman involved in Kenya's Westgate Mall massacre, traveled to the scene of the attack on a fraudulent South African passport purchased from Home Affairs officials. With help from her extremist cronies, she allegedly helped murder 67 shoppers and shopkeepers and wound 175.

The lax attitude of such officials made it easy for a journalist to seek out information. I knew a guy who knew a guy whose brother-in-law worked at the department, and so I wandered into his office and he agreed, quite easily and without demanding so much as a dollar, to search the database for Daniel de Villiers. Without an ID number or date of birth, we didn't have much luck, but I did leave with three notecards scribbled with names, phone numbers, and addresses of possible de Villiers relatives.

One of these contacts led me to a friendly teenage girl who lived at boarding school, loved horses, and had no known relation to Daniel. One led me to a man named Philippe, who lived out by the beach and had never heard of Daniel. And one listed an Alfred Devilliers, no space between "De" and "villiers," whose phone number was no longer working and whose listed address was abandoned.

Finally, I reached a cousin of Daniel's, who remembered that about twenty years earlier he'd been attacked.

"He showed me the shirt, full of holes, full of blood! You couldn't see the color of the shirt," she said.

Though the cousin had no idea where Daniel was, she had a brother named Gareth who had once nurtured a real friendship with Daniel. But she wouldn't be able to help me find Gareth: she hadn't spoken to her brother for years. He lived somewhere in the Cape, she figured, and he had a son named Alfred—whose disconnected phone number and abandoned address I'd gotten from my connection at Home Affairs.

Since I'd run through nearly every de Villiers in the country, it seemed that Gareth was, indeed, my last chance. But he wasn't popping up on any Internet searches or in any property record pulls. I asked a police source to look into the matter, and he found a possible family member in police records: In 2001, one "Gareth Devilliers" had been arrested for disorderly conduct. The cop popped by the address listed in the police file, but all he found was a different family who had been living there for years. Six months of looking for Daniel, and he remained a shadowy figure—there was no trace of him alive, but there was also no trace of him dead.

I nursed a hope that old TRC records could help me find Daniel. The Department of Justice, it seemed, held old files from the TRC— odd, I thought, as the TRC was comprised of public hearings, and its main mandate was to bare the many secrets of apartheid atrocities before the country and the world. But they were kept behind lock and key now. To see the files, you had to partake in an arduous and often futile process: a South African law called the Promotion of Access to Information Act allowed anyone to request documents from the government. You paid a fee of about $25 (prohibitive for many poor people, who may have been collecting only that amount in welfare checks every month), filled out forms stating your needs, and applied to the relevant government official.

When I first put forth my request for the back records from the Amy Biehl TRC case, I ran it by a woman I knew who worked for a foundation that advocated for government transparency. She gave a sigh of world-weariness. Between 2012 and 2013, a mere 16 percent of the Promotion of Access to Information Act requests made by civil society organizations had led to the full release of records. In 2014, an NGO conducted a small survey, sending out 223 PAIA requests to municipalities rather than the federal government. They requested nonsensitive information on local budgets that would take ten minutes for an employee to access and send. But only 30 municipalities responded. After the NGO appealed, they received 13 more responses. The vast majority of information officers simply did not bother to honor the law.

"The bigger the amount of docs, the more likely they'll make a badly grounded refusal because they don't feel like scouring them," the woman from the government transparency foundation told me. Some people suspected that PAIA requests for files related to the TRC were refused because current high-up ANC officials were mentioned in those files, along with the atrocities they may have committed in the name of the Struggle, and powerful people didn't want those old skeletons let out of their closets.

Indeed, the Department of Justice seemed as devoted to avoiding my request as the Department of Corrections had been when I wished to visit the prisons. Month after month, they ignored emails and only intermittently returned calls—usually somebody enthusiastic contacted me, made big promises, and then disappeared. Eventually, after five months, during which I repeatedly called and emailed a number of officials, the department sent me an email. All I had to do, they said, was obtain permission from Amy Biehl's next of kin, as well as from each of the men amnestied, and I would be rewarded with the files. The permission, they noted, had to be filed on an affidavit stamped by the South African Police, and sent back to them. This demand led me to write Linda Biehl and ask if she would allow me permission to access the files, something I would come to regret.

As I grew more enmeshed in the South African side of this story, I had stopped calling Linda as often, and we no longer emailed regularly. I had seen her last in Pittsburgh in September 2012, when I visited her at the home of her son, Zach, for three days in order to comb through the family archive, a mountain of photo albums and letters and records and newspaper clippings kept in tidy plastic file boxes in the basement.

Pittsburgh was a grim and gray place when I visited, depressed and acutely aware of its status as a third-rate city. Linda stuck out against the grit—wearing all white, her toenails painted crimson. In the cab from the airport, I'd passed a roadkill raccoon, a collection of trailers warmed by coal smoke, a freestanding bar, and lots of old Pontiacs. I'd stayed two nights in a chain hotel plopped between strip malls, and lay in bed at night watching episodes of *Here Comes Honey Boo Boo* with my mouth agape. After over a year in South Africa, with no TV, no streaming, and slow Internet, I was out of the American pop culture loop.

Zach, the keeper of the family archives, lived in a new house in a small development among other McMansions and nouveaux country clubs. His refrigerator, peppered with magnets and kids' drawings and school photos, was filled with gallons of milk and bags of baby carrots, the cupboards stuffed with Goldfish crackers and Oreos. The counters had little boxes full of disposable pop-up napkins and plastic pump bottles of hand sanitizer. The floors were spotless, despite a band of dogs: one soft-nosed black mutt and two hysterical little mushy-faced creatures.

Hemmed in by his own impeccable manners, Zach was compelled to drive me to and from the hotel, but he wasn't happy about it. I suspected that he allowed me into his home because I was a human being on a quest for knowledge, because his mother wanted this, and because the Biehls never denied those whom they could help. But I also suspected that I represented something dark, old, and unwelcome to the family. This was the contradiction, too: the Biehls let people keep coming, but they hated opening up those boxes of memories time and again.

By June 2013, Zach's family had relocated to New Jersey for his wife's job and I had written Linda an email requesting her permission for access to the TRC records, a request she granted with a caveat: she wanted a copy of the records for herself. When I relayed this information to the Department of Justice, the official I spoke with noted that in order to secure a copy, Linda would have to make her own official Promotion of Access to Information Act request.

I called Linda to explain further about the process. On the other end of the line, Linda was waiting for her granddaughter's school bus somewhere in Jersey. Linda had started doing the Bar Method classes, and her other granddaughter, an actress, would be starring in *Matilda* soon. But she was in a sour mood, having been at odds with the foundation for years now. Her youngest daughter was also embroiled in a divorce.

Plus, my waning attention, I think, had caused Linda to wonder what I was really up to. For so long, I'd hung on her every word. Now I was entrenched in a different story, one she didn't know existed, and I had disappeared into it. I could not explain to Linda, or to anybody, really, that I was following an entirely new lead, searching for a ghost of a municipal worker. I could not tell her that I was no longer sure who had killed Amy.

Worse, Ntobeko was growing to despise me, without directly in-
teracting with me more than once. According to people who spoke
with him, he wanted to write his own book, and felt I might be
stealing his story for profit. Whenever he saw me, he put his head
down and slipped by, seething. He thought I was up to no good, and
I wondered if he had begun to share his suspicions with Linda.
Months later, as I was leaving South Africa, I wrote Ntobeko one
last time. I informed him that I would be writing about him, and
that it would be good to get his perspective, and I asked for a final
interview. I had written him many emails over the years, all of which
had been ignored. But to this one, he replied: *I will not grant you an
interview. I HAVE NEVER GIVEN YOU ANY AUTHORISA-
TION TO WRITE ABOUT ME AND I WILL NEVER DO
THAT, I AM NOT AS STUPID AS YOU THINK I AM. Your email
has evoked all the devil instincts that I have.*

On the day I called Linda about the TRC files, I had not yet
evoked anyone's devil instincts, and Linda was still feeling ever so
slightly gracious toward me. She answered the phone and began
talking about how she wished to extricate herself from the foundation and focus on issues in America. She wanted to make a "graceful
exit," she said, her voice breaking. But the foundation management
team—" *'management team . . . '* if I hear that term again I will throw
up"—still would not agree to drop Amy's name. She was planning
two trips to Cape Town in the coming months.

"July is gonna be awful," she said. "I am hoping by August I will
have my ducks in a row and it will be my swan song."

At this point, I should have backed away from a seventy-year-old
widow who was overwhelmed by personal issues and mourning a
foundation, her life's work and a monument to her daughter, that
had turned away from her and her original intentions. Instead, so
dogged was I in my determination to get the TRC files that I said:
"I'm just hoping you could maybe write up this affidavit for the
Department of Justice. All you have to do is write it out, then go to

a police station, then have them stamp it, and scan it and send it to me."

That's when stoic Linda Biehl began to cry.

"No! I don't want to have to run around looking into how she was killed in Gugulethu," Linda said, her voice raised and broken. "I can't keep doing this anymore. I just want my life back. Twenty years is enough."

I stared at the blank Skype screen, Linda's number glowing.

"Why did you talk to me?" I asked, scrambling. "Why do you help me?"

"I don't know why. Because you seem like a nice young woman and Amy was a nice young woman. I thought you were trying really hard to discover. But I don't care about your book."

"What *do* you care about?"

"My family is important. The proper truthful legacy of who Amy was is important. I want my privacy. I want to grow as a person. I am stuck in South Africa. I am seeing more and more how this has affected my family. The time has come, and there is no one there to carry on. I have no one really to turn to. I cannot keep doing this to my family. They have got to be able to live their lives. They have their issues, their interests, and their cares and their concerns. I don't want this to be on their necks anymore. I want to get my own place. I am really at a point where I want to move on."

Linda grasped for composure. She lowered her voice, and I could hear her drying her face. I imagined her mascara running down her cheeks. "Nobody wants the truth," she said. "Those TRC records aren't the truth. They are graphic and ugly. The truth is that the country was still in turmoil. She represented the oppressor, and her white face was all that was wrong with the country, and she was killed."

At that moment, I heard the school bus pull up and the sounds of children's voices—and then her granddaughter. Linda put the phone down, but didn't hang up.

"You're carrying lots of stuff, do you need help?" she asked the girl.

"Thanks!" her granddaughter replied in her small, determined voice. "I had a big party to go to."

Linda picked the phone up, and now she was calm.

"You write me an email, tell me what you want me to do, and I will do it," Linda said, and then she hung up.

I stupidly wrote that email, explaining the complicated steps toward acquiring the release of the records, to which she replied:

> This is a mess. I have worked with you in the spirit of Ubuntu (generosity of spirit) but I am not aware of what you are planning as you are not particularly forthcoming. If I can be more helpful when I am in the country, let me know. . . . Linda.

So I explained to the Department of Justice that Amy's next of kin was a woman of advanced age who lived in a far-off country, and that it would simply be impossible for such a person to officially grant permission using the complicated channels required by a clunky government. Easy wrote me out a signed and stamped affidavit. I didn't bother to ask Ntobeko, Mongezi, or Vusumzi, and mailed in Easy's permission. For whatever reason, after so much tangled red tape, this alone seemed to satisfy the bureaucrats, or perhaps they had simply grown tired of fielding my calls. Seven months after I'd begun the process, a heavy red cardboard box arrived in the mail, full of papers from the TRC. Daniel de Villiers's name didn't show up anywhere.

Sam and I took our honeymoon in Botswana, where we paddled down the Okavango River Delta at dusk, and watched the hippos lolling in the water. Then we traveled to Lesotho, where we trekked on horseback to the remote, untouched mountains. Back in Cape Town, I drove Easy, Aphiwe, and Aphiwe's two cousins to a park by the water. It was a new development built by the city in conjunction with the soccer stadium, which hosted games during the 2010 World Cup. In keeping, the park, a World Cup "legacy project," was a small sliver of utopia in the city. It abutted the Mouille Point golf course and the rugby fields where I ran my dog, and sat just east of the stadium.

"The World Cup went off flawlessly," a friend of mine remarked. The event had been slick and crime-free and precisely orchestrated, as finely coordinated as any event in London or New York. "It's a disgrace, because it proves that the government isn't even inept, like they pretend to be. It proves that if they want to do something perfectly, they actually *can*."

The fields, dotted with picnickers straight out of a Benetton ad, were broad and viridescent, covered in flocks of geese. A tiny footbridge ran over a salty stream. In the middle of the park was a small biodiversity garden, planted with the region's indigenous flowers. Easy and I sat on a picnic blanket, where Aphiwe and her cousins had left a pile of pink and purple sandals. Aphiwe was the skinniest, while one cousin was medium-sized, and the other was fat. They had dressed up for their day in town, since they left the townships only a few times a year: white capris, patterned shirts, and the fat cousin donning a plastic tiara. They popped in once in a while, to have a piece of fruit or some chips, but for the most part they tore about the state-of-the-art playground, exploiting each and every slide, swing, and jungle gym. I had taken my Israeli niece and nephew, ages five and seven, to this very playground a few weeks earlier. They were children whose parents sought out fun, educational activities every weekend, and so the kids had wandered the playground unenthusiastically, having been-there-done-that all their lives. But not Aphiwe and her crew; they wanted to experience every single part of that park.

But try as I might, I couldn't shake my obsession with Daniel de Villiers. One night, I searched Facebook for the twentieth time. Again, I typed in "De Villiers" and scrolled around. Nothing new. Then I typed in "Devilliers," no space. Finally, I came upon the profile of an Alfred Devilliers, the name on that piece of paper from Home Affairs and uttered to me by the de Villiers cousin. He was the son of the elusive Gareth, the only de Villiers who might have an idea where Daniel was. The profile bore no picture, just the anonymous blue-and-white Facebook icon of a man's head. Boasting thirty friends and zero photos, Alfred's page had the look of a Facebook profile that had been set up and then abandoned within weeks as the owner lost interest. But since I had officially exhausted all my other leads, I sent Alfred a friend request. Then I clicked on his friends list.

Facebook had introduced a feature within a person's friends list called "People You May Know," which used an algorithm to suggest connections you might have with someone, no matter how tenuous. I clicked on the link and found a single viable suggestion: a man named Ruben Atkins. Beneath Ruben's name and photo were the words: *1 mutual friend.* I clicked to find out who this mutual acquaintance might be.

Rito Hlungwani.

Much of my South African existence had involved hanging out with Sam, eating, sleeping, and walking my dog in Sea Point. I spent the rest of my time in Gugulethu with Easy and Mzi. But in the early days, I'd made a single friend, a Canadian named Aimee-Noel. Aimee-Noel had studied at the University of Cape Town, where she'd met her Xhosa husband. They now lived a six-hour drive away in Port Elizabeth, where her husband played professional rugby, but they often visited Cape Town, and stayed with the husband's best friend: Rito Hlungwani.

Rito Hlungwani—nicknamed Shangaan, for the small Southern African tribe of his roots—was a six-foot-five former professional rugby player currently working as a quantity surveyor. Rito lived just down the street from me in Sea Point, and I saw him once or twice a week. I dialed Rito's number. "Yo cuz," he said in his baritone.

"Cuz," I said, "I need your help desperately."

"Shoot."

"How do you know Ruben Atkins?"

"Ruben? We played rugby together. Why?"

I explained to Rito that Ruben seemed to be connected to a person I needed to interview for my book. Alfred de Villiers, I said, was possibly a relative of a man I'd been trying to track down for months, and I just needed a way to reach him. Okay, Rito said—he would send Ruben a message asking about Alfred.

Five minutes passed. My phone pinged. *Ruben is Alfred's relative.*

I stood up and started pacing back and forth in my kitchen. I could see Ruben's picture on Facebook. He was colored, as were his siblings, which led me to believe that Alfred, identified only by his blue-and-white Facebook icon, was therefore also colored. This was a hitch, since the de Villierses were white.

I messaged Rito: *Could Alfred be the colored son of a white father?*

Rito was chatting with Ruben, relaying my questions. After a brief pause, my phone lit up.

His dad is white.

The next morning, I woke up early and spent the next few hours refreshing my phone. Finally, a tiny red flag popped up: Alfred Devilliers had accepted my Facebook friend request. A moment later, another tiny red notification beeped, a message from Alfred:

Hey, wu u n whre did u get my contact?

I immediately wrote him back, using a series of exclamation points, but I could see, as I frantically circled back to the message throughout the day, that he had not checked his account. After nine months of searching, I was achingly close to finding Gareth—and therefore, I hoped, Daniel. After Gareth, I was out of all other options.

I clicked around impatiently. I inspected the profile picture of Ruben, Alfred's cousin and Rito's friend: it was a poorly lit desktop selfie, probably taken with a PC video camera. He was a handsome, powerful fellow grinning wide in his cubicle, wearing a green-and-white T-shirt. Around twenty-eight, I guessed, with that rugby player neck and a head that had taken some serious knocks. I hit "request friend." An hour later, the red flag appeared.

You are now friends with Ruben Atkins.

I looked through Ruben's profile for information on getting in touch with him. He managed the help desk for an IT company out in the suburbs, I discovered. I called and asked to be put through.

"Hallo, dis ek Ruben," came the voice. Like most of the colored population, Ruben's mother tongue was Afrikaans. His English was studied and formal.

"*Ja, mam*," he said when I introduced myself and explained the situation.

Alfred was Ruben's nephew. Ruben's sister had married Gareth. He would call his sister and explain the situation. Twenty minutes later, he called back: his sister's number wasn't working.

"Could you maybe find her new number?" I asked. "I'm sorry but it's urgent."

"Ja, ja. Maybe I must call my father."

Another twenty minutes passed and the phone rang again.

"Hi mam," Ruben said. "I have the number and you can call."

"Ja? This is Gareth."

He had a gruff voice and an Afrikaans accent: the rolling *r*'s, the heavy inflection. He had been expecting my call, I could tell.

I launched into my explanation: I'm an American journalist, I am working on a book about an important—major, significant, *huge*—part of South African history, and I've been trying to find you, Gareth, for quite some time. You simply can't imagine how happy I am to have finally tracked you down. You do have a cousin named Daniel de Villiers, do you not?

A long pause.

"Ja, Daniel, he is my cousin," the man said slowly. "But I haven't seen him in years."

My heart sank.

"Do you have a phone number?" I asked.

"*Ach*, no, man, nothing, hey. Last I saw him was back at the Shoprite in Kraaifontein, a few years ago. He was looking thin, and he said he lived over the bridge in Brighton but I never did see. I don't know why he didn't invite me over. He used to always invite me over."

"So you never saw the house?"

"No, man, and Brighton is big, hey!"

"Well, do you know his parents' names? Maybe that would help me track him down. Nobody can remember his parents' names."

"I think his mother's name was Evelyn. I think Evelyn, she never liked me, and maybe that's why he didn't invite me to his house. Maybe she was there. Now that's what I'm thinking."

"Does he have siblings?"

A long pause, a grumble. Silence.

"Any other family? Anyplace I might find him? Any idea at all? Maybe if I had the name of his sister or his brother—"

"Listen, it's complicated," Gareth said, cutting me off. "Can't you come see me?"

An hour later, I veered off the N2. I was practically in the Winelands, out by Cape Town Studios, the soundstage that a couple of South African–Indian tycoon brothers—friends of Linda Biehl's—had built on a vast plot of undeveloped land. This is the place where Linda and I had wandered around the set of the Mandela movie, where a little fake Soweto had been painstakingly re-created. Now, in the distance, past the tough prairie grass, a couple of miles from the most isolated shacks along the highway, rose a vast pirate ship and a French medieval village.

I turned away from the studios and headed into the working-class colored neighborhood of Eersterivier, a collection of little cracked houses surrounding a central strip of shops: a butcher, a market, some hardware stores, a burger place. It was a sunny day, pretty and bright, and Cape Town was showing off, as she did, with the endless blue sky, the rolling hills, Table Mountain clear and snowcapped in the distance. I had written down the address but the streets either had no signs or had their names written only in small black letters on the curbside. Twice I circled around, finally making my way past a bodega and over a hole in the road patched, by enterprising locals, with bricks piled to street level. I pulled up to a lawn full of people who appeared to be braai-ing while stoned, and asked for directions. After three minutes of shouting animatedly to each other in Afrikaans, one turned to me.

"Sorry, lady!" he said. "We don't know!"

"Maybe you must continue that way?" another motioned.

I drove straight and weaved around the small streets until I arrived at a cul-de-sac. The house numbers were arranged seemingly at random. I drove back and forth: 76, 43, 21, 78. I rolled up to a house where an old man was standing on the porch.

"Do you know where number 45 is?" I asked.

He shook his head, put his finger up in the universal sign for "wait a second," and hobbled indoors. A younger woman came out. She spoke English, it seemed, but she didn't know where number 45 was.

"Well, do you know anyone named Gareth?" I asked.

"Sorry, I don't know no Gareth," she said.

"A white guy," I clarified. "With a colored wife? And a kid maybe, a teenage kid."

The woman thought for a moment. "*Ja,* there is a guy who is white of complexion down that road," she said, pointing. "End of the street, to the right."

I pulled up to a pale house by a patch of dry grass. A gate ran around the property, secured with a chain and padlock. I rattled the gate and waited. Silence. I looked around. Some kids ran by with a basketball. Two doors down, a fuzzy dog chained to a laundry carousel curled up sorrowfully on a barren lawn.

A man in his early fifties emerged from behind the pale house, accompanied by a honey-colored American Staffordshire terrier. He was slender, with squinty eyes, a big nose and big lips, and crinkled leather skin. He wore black shit-kicker boots, a turquoise T-shirt over a white long-sleeved shirt, and black jeans. He had tucked his curly gray hair, which hit the middle of his neck, beneath a black cap emblazoned with the words I REGRET NOTHING. He held a cigarette between his right thumb and forefinger and had his left hand shoved in his pocket.

"You must be Gareth," I said. His dog, sleek and muscled, wagged her tail.

Gareth cocked his head and regarded me with exaggerated suspicion.

"I'm Justine," I said, extending an arm through a gap in the gate. Gareth warily took my hand in his and shook once. Then he opened the gate and led me into his house, a swept-clean, single-level four-room number with a flat-screen and two love seats covered in leopard-print throws. He walked to the open kitchen and looked over at me. He poured himself a small glass of beer.

"So. My mother says I must not talk to you," he said, giving me a sidelong glance. "There are a lot of scams out there."

"But my friend Rito knows your brother-in-law. So you know I'm a real person." He nodded slowly, amenable to my point. "Anyway, what would the scam be? I don't want money from you. I just want to find your cousin Daniel."

He nodded more vigorously. Then he stood to the side, pondering for a little while.

"So tell me why you want to find Daniel then?" Gareth asked, sitting down and leaning back, legs spread. I also sat down, unbidden, on an adjacent couch. I explained to him that Daniel had, I believed, been brutally beaten in Gugulethu in 1993 and was, perhaps unknowingly, involved in a significant event in South African history. Did he know of Amy Biehl? I asked.

"No," Gareth said. He looked up briefly. "Oh wait, that student the blacks killed?"

Daniel was also beaten on that day, I said. Maybe by the same person. Daniel was important.

"Daniel wasn't in Gugulethu, though," he said. "Not Daniel."

"I believe he was. I believe he was injured there."

"But what was Daniel doing there?" Gareth wondered aloud, shaking his head. "He's scared of black people!" He lit another cigarette and explained that he hadn't seen Daniel in years. "There is something about Daniel you have to know," he said. He leaned back, inhaled, and exhaled. "Daniel was of another world."

"Daniel, he's got hair like a colored. When you look at him, you know something's not right. He could never get a girlfriend 'cause he had hair like steel wool and he had a complex about himself. 'Cause he knew where he came from."

"Where did he come from?"

Gareth lit up. "My father, François, was the brother of Jacques de Villiers. Jacques had a wife and a daughter. Now, Jacques molested the daughter, and the daughter had Daniel. And it was a whole big scandal and they covered it up, and we only figured it out years later."

And with that, Gareth, who had gone from zip-lipped to confessional in under three minutes, started to tell a story of a man of tragic origins.

Let's go back to the 1940s. The de Villiers family were "poor whites," a sort of variation on the American term "white trash," except that over time the South African poor whites have had their many champions, including a number of Afrikaner nationalists who wished to protect them and raise them up. The de Villierses were descendants of the cast-off French Huguenots. Jacques de Villiers was a sadistic dockworker who lived in a damp wood house on Ebenezer Street by the port. Today, the port has been remodeled into the opulent Victoria and Alfred Waterfront, with a Gucci boutique and an artisanal food market, but back then the white dockworkers lived there in working-class squalor and were paid by the government. It was by those docks that Jacques raped his daughter for years. In her teens, the girl gave birth to a child. She continued to live in her parents' house and her parents raised the child as their own, pretending that he was just her little brother and not also her son. That child was Daniel de Villiers.

Eventually, the abused daughter married a widower. The widower had three kids of his own, and Daniel and the woman he believed was his sister moved into the widower's home. One day, the widower fell ill, and on his deathbed he uttered what Daniel had always suspected: that Daniel was the product of incest and abuse. Confronted, the woman confessed.

After the widower died, Daniel's mother-sister met with tough times. Gareth recalled that a few years earlier, she had been profiled in the Afrikaans daily *Die Son*, talking about all her problems, minus the incest bit, and asking for financial help from readers.

Gareth pulled himself up and plucked an old snapshot out of the corner of a larger frame: six skinny little girls in various states of dishevelment, and one baby boy shaped like a potato, in the short shorts and the high striped sports socks of the 1970s. They were leaning back against an old rusted car. He pointed out his sisters. I had talked to nearly all of these women, each one claiming not to know where Gareth was.

"Daniel had the most terrible hair you ever saw in the world," he said happily. "Like a Brillo pad!"

He noted that he and his family had spent some time with Daniel, but after the deathbed revelation, the family split apart. Nobody wanted much to do with the boy after that.

"Sorry, but why don't your sisters or your mother want to see Daniel anymore?"

"How can you ask?" Gareth said, aghast. "Now you know why!"

"But it's not Daniel's fault if his grandfather abused his mother. It doesn't mean anything about him."

Gareth considered this. "That's true," he said, thoughtfully.

Then he continued on about Daniel. In apartheid South Africa, Gareth had been drafted in the army, like all white men of a certain age. He'd shot Cuban commies over on the Angola border. When Gareth was discharged, and before he knew Daniel's terrible secret, the two were pals. Daniel got him a gig at the dockside store, selling parts. But how long could that last when Gareth was not exactly a model employee? He had long hair and wore bell-bottoms and was terribly fond of drugs. Meanwhile, Daniel was straitlaced and diligent. For a while, he worked fixing the lights down at the docks.

"So Daniel *was* a municipal employee," I said. "This is him. Your cousin is the man I'm looking for."

"Who says he's alive?" Gareth asked. "Last time I see him, he's thin. And if he died, no one's gonna know."

I thought someone would have heard, I said. If Daniel had died, the news would have made its way down the grapevine of the big, fractured de Villiers family, I felt certain of it. And now I knew for sure that he had lived through the beating in Gugulethu, if Gareth had recently seen him over at the Shoprite in Kraaifontein. So who's to say he hadn't survived a further three years? What else could Gareth remember about Daniel?

"Well, let's see," Gareth said, walking to the kitchen and opening a fresh tall bottle of beer. "He fell in love with a whore and he bought her a ring and everything. They were busy jolling"—a casual South African term for having fun—"but meanwhile she was busy with the Japs and Chinese with the docks. He bought her an expensive ring but nobody liked him because of how he looked, and he wasn't a nice build. Daniel, he liked his cakes and cookies and chocolates. He was round. Did I mention his hair and how it was the wildest hair you ever seen? He had to spend money to get girls and I had to go along also. He was very helpful and he had a very good heart. He don't drink, he don't smoke, he used to buy alcohol for us all just for the company."

"But you were his friend?"

"Nah, man, I was using him, too!" Gareth said. "You know, I think his mom was colored and so he was part colored. He had some relatives who looked like coloreds. And you see his mom, you'll see she doesn't look white. And Daniel, he couldn't get friends on his own on account of his hair, I telling you."

"Maybe they *were* part colored," I suggested.

"Any fool can see they're colored! Maybe it's in their genes, even though they mostly have straight hair, maybe the colored hair is in their genes and so he got it." Gareth had a crude bicycle tattooed on his hand, a spider tattooed behind his ear, and a long left thumbnail.

"The whole family is alcoholics. They drink and drink. I mean, I drink, too."

"Are you an alcoholic?"

Gareth gave me a knowing look. "No alcoholic is gonna say he is an alcoholic."

"So are you an alcoholic?"

"Nah," he said, sipping his beer. "And Daniel, he was no alcoholic, just sweets. He was a very scared guy, who carried a big .38. He was so, so scared. We would sometimes go to spend time with coloreds and he looked so scared and I said, 'Why you scared?' And he said, 'We are white people,' and I said, 'Don't worry, these are our friends.'

"Once, he got a flat on his truck. Usually you have a colored guy to help you change it. But the guy was sick so Daniel did it himself. There was a spring he didn't know about so it came out from the tire and hit him smack in the face, and it scarred him. After that, he was depressed and wanted to take his own life. You know, if Daniel is dead—and he may be dead—he can die in his house and nobody will know. He is going to leave a will and he said he'd leave it to me, but I don't even want his money. And he has money! He retired, good pension. Poor Daniel, he found out he's a bastard, you see? He's very heartsore. People always used to laugh at his hair. They asked me, 'Is that your cousin? He looks like a colored!' He's a lonely guy, Daniel. He had one friend and that guy is probably dead."

"What was that friend called?" I asked.

"A long time ago, I was smoking drugs, so I don't remember much," Gareth said.

"Somebody must know," I said. "Nobody has his number?"

"Let me see the phone book!" Gareth hollered. From behind a door, somebody tossed the white pages out onto the couch. I tried to peer around into the hallway, but Gareth continued on. "I did see him at the Shoprite in Kraaifontein a few years ago. I said, 'Hi, how are you? Where are you staying?' He says he stayed in Kraaifontein, over the bridge, toward Brighton, and then he just runs off, never told me more. He did have a red Ford, which means he has a license. Maybe he stayed with his mother. Maybe he was supporting his mother. He had money, see?" Gareth flipped through the book. "*Ach*, he had his phone number in the book and then he unlisted it."

A heavyset colored woman emerged from a back room, bright lipstick slicked on, her hair combed back.

"This is my wife," Gareth said. "Sarah."

Sarah smiled. She was a nurse at a local hospital, and Ruben's sister, and the thrower of the phone book.

"You could look for him around Kraaifontein," she suggested. "I remember Daniel." She put a dish in the microwave.

"Ja, ja," Gareth said. "You know, when I got older, everyone used to lie to me about that side of the family. They sure looked colored but everyone said 'No, no, they're white, white, white, white, white.'"

Gareth walked over to the empty wooden bookshelf and picked up a photo of his son, Alfred. The boy had pale chocolate-tinted skin, corkscrew curls, and freckles. Gareth shoved it into my hands.

"My son asks me, 'Dad, what am I?' And I say, 'Son, you're white!' He's white. His ID book says he's white."

I smiled dumbly, holding the frame.

"Alfie!" Gareth shouted. "Come out here!"

Nobody emerged, and Gareth went to fetch him. A few moments later, a bare-chested teenager, all sinew, with a head of wild black ringlets, emerged.

"Alfie, this is Justine," Gareth said.

"We met on Facebook," I explained.

"Ja, we did," said Alfred.

"You asked me who I was and how I found you," I said.

"Did he? He asked who you was?" Gareth asked. "That's my boy! Good boy! Always find out!"

Then Gareth turned to me, and motioned to Alfred. "So what is my boy? What is he? White or colored?"

"What does he think he is?" I asked.

Alfred stood before us, bored. Sarah was milling around the kitchen.

"He thinks he's white!" Gareth shouted happily.

Alfred smiled and wiped some toothpaste from his mouth.

"Nice to meet you, Justine," he said as he turned back to his room.

"You, too."

"White, white, white," Gareth said.

"So, Daniel—" I said.

"So, Daniel—" Gareth perked up, took another glass of beer. "It's funny, after all these years no one ever came to ask me about Daniel, and then you come as a stranger and ask me."

"So Daniel never got attacked?"

"No, no, I don't think so. Anyway, twenty years ago, the townships weren't so bad."

"Twenty years ago? That was the end of apartheid."

"Oh, right, there were the riots! But not Daniel. Daniel was boarded because of the tire spring scarring him, and he had a lot of policies, a lot of money from them. They boarded him because of how the spring hit his head and then he was rich. Six or seven policies!"

"I'd like to find him," I said. "I have to find him."

"Maybe we can go looking," Gareth suggested hopefully.

"You want to come look for Daniel with me?"

"Well, ja, if you free. I know Kraaifontein. He always does the same thing so I bet we find him at that same Shoprite. I bet he slips in and runs out. He's a real scared guy. Or maybe he's sitting alone at the pubs or the brothels. You free tomorrow?" Gareth asked.

Sarah was sitting at the counter, looking at us. She took a bite of her lunch. Her shift at the hospital started in an hour.

"Sure, what time?"

"Real early," Gareth said. "He'll come in before the crowds and run out. Ja, ja, and we'll track down Daniel," Gareth said excitedly. "Over by Brighton, Belmont Park. There are lots of pubs there, lots of whorehouses. He's gonna need company somehow."

That night, I met up with my Canadian friend Aimee-Noel, who had settled in South Africa with her Xhosa husband and their young daughter. I'd been intermittently updating her on the progress of the story, and over dinner I told her about the day's discoveries and our plans for finding Daniel. I didn't really know Gareth, nor did I trust him entirely, so Aimee-Noel offered to accompany me on our outing.

It was August 23, 2013. In forty-eight hours, it would be the twentieth anniversary of Amy Biehl's death. Linda was in town for the memorial, though I had not seen her much. When I had met up with her, she'd greeted me with tepid enthusiasm. Neither of us mentioned that I'd made her cry and lose her temper, but something between us had shifted. During her previous trip, I hadn't left her side, but now I was distracted, and so was she. The foundation still wasn't giving up Amy's name, and Linda was at a loss; she was considering getting a lawyer involved. She had recently screamed, "You have no respect for me or my family!" at Kevin, before storming out of a meeting.

"I can only think this is twenty years of pent-up grief making its way out," Kevin told a California reporter who had been trailing Linda and had thus witnessed the blowup.

People kept writing to Linda about Amy as August 25 edged nearer. A few days earlier, she had read me some emails aloud, her voice shaky.

"Now, this person wrote me such a long email. It says: *Amy's death shook the ground.*" She let out a heavy sigh.

"Does it annoy you?" I asked. I found her opaque; I could never figure out what touched her and what irritated her.

"I don't know what it does," she said. "You know, there is no such thing as real closure."

I woke up early on the 24th, and picked up Aimee-Noel at Rito's house at eight sharp. We arrived at Gareth's place an hour later, and he bounded out of the door, wearing his I REGRET NOTHING cap, his boots, and a black T-shirt that displayed an enormous, disembodied mouth sticking out its pierced tongue. He was stone-cold sober.

"Come inside for a second," Gareth said, excitedly.

Aimee-Noel and I followed after to find Sarah sitting at the table in her dressing gown, face scrubbed bare, just home from her night shift at the hospital. She held a scrap of paper in her hand, all-caps written in ballpoint pen, at an angle:

DANIEL DE VILLIERS 7/5/2009
LOOP STR 8
EDGEMEAD

Below was a phone number. After listening to my conversation with Gareth in the living room, Sarah had been intrigued by my search for Daniel. That night, when she wasn't dressing wounds or inserting catheters, she had made her way to the records room. She'd opened the patient database. She scrolled through the Ds, one after another, until it popped up, bright text against a black screen: Daniel's name. He had been a patient at that very hospital, brought in back in 2009. Sarah called Gareth again and again all night, so excited by her discovery.

"But we tried the number all night and day, and it don't work," Gareth said. "Plus, it must have been 2010 when I saw him in Kraaifontein, so this address was before then. Must have moved."

We could always try it, I said. I didn't want to get my hopes up, but it was an address. Things were going my way, courtesy of an intrepid nurse-cum-detective.

"Ja," said Gareth. "First, let's see if he's at the Shoprite in Kraaifontein. He's a creature of habit, slips in to do his shopping and slips out. But if he's there, I'll recognize him."

"Because of his hair," I said.

"The hair!" Gareth exclaimed. He turned to Aimee-Noel. "He had hair of a colored. Nobody could forget his hair! You know, once he dyed it orange, so it was like a bright orange Afro, that's what I remember."

Aimee-Noel sat in the back and Gareth hopped in the front. We drove twenty-five miles south to the Kraaifontein Shoprite center, a collection of shops and fast food restaurants organized around the supermarket. Gareth had a plan: I was to park in the front lot of the Shoprite, facing the market. Aimee-Noel and I could scan the pedestrians: Remember to keep an eye out for a red Ford or a terrified-looking freak with the craziest hair you'd ever seen. Meanwhile, Gareth would get out and search for Daniel on foot. He would *become* Daniel, in a sense, trying to inhabit his cousin's psychology.

Gareth slipped out of the car and stalked around the parking lot before entering the market. He saw a few old friends and greeted them exuberantly. He patted the hood of my car and leaned on the side. His friends stared at me and Aimee-Noel, confused.

"He's showing off," Aimee-Noel muttered from the back.

Gareth smoked and rocked on his heels. He ran into the market and walked the aisles. No Daniel. He stuck his head out to the back parking lot.

"No, he wouldn't park there," he reported back. "Blacks are drinking back there, he'd think it was dangerous."

Aimee-Noel and I surveyed the foot traffic. An elderly white man plodded by, followed by a small black boy, who clutched his hand.

There was a guy with a mullet. "That's bad, but not steel-wool bad," Aimee-Noel said.

A man stumbled around, sporting a deep blue bruise around his eye.

"His eye is messed up, but his hair looks unremarkable," I said.

A gentleman strolled up to a friend to shake hands. He was bald, so the quality of his hair remained unknown. "Too young though," Aimee-Noel offered.

Finally, Gareth came out, his spirits high despite the fact that he'd had no luck. He leaned into the car as a red-faced woman in a neon vest walked by, carrying a whip. She smiled broadly at me.

"Why does she have a whip?" I asked.

"I dunno," Gareth said. "These people is all crazy."

After an hour, Gareth circled back. "*Ach,* man, he may be dead," Gareth said. "If he was here, I'd see him."

"Should we try the address Sarah found?"

We drove back onto the highway and got off at Edgemead, making our way through a row of shops and into a quiet residential neighborhood. We turned off onto a tiny dead-end street with six single-level houses, each set on a tidy lawn. Here was the place Daniel had lived four years ago, number 8, a pretty stone house with a brown wooden door. It had no garage, and there was no car in the driveway. It didn't look like anyone lived there. Or at least, it didn't look like anyone was home.

The next house over, a young blond woman was unloading groceries from the back of her car.

"Do you happen to know if a man named Daniel ever lived next door?" I asked her.

"Hmmm, the man who lives there is named Clinton," she said. "I don't know a Daniel."

"How long has Clinton been there?" I asked.

"Oh gosh, has to be six years or so."

"And nobody named Daniel even stayed there?"

The woman shook her head. Actually, she said, she didn't live here. It was her parents' house and she was merely visiting for the weekend. If we would give her a moment, she'd go ask her parents about this Daniel character.

She returned a few minutes later.

"You know, there was a boarder there some years back," she said. "A small guy, real quiet, kept to himself. He could have been named Daniel, my parents also recall."

"Did he have strange hair?" Gareth asked.

"I don't quite remember his hair," the woman said. "He was just a nice little man. He always wore jerseys and walked to do his shopping."

I looked again at the stone house, its blinds drawn. I thanked the woman, turned the car around, and parked. Unbidden, Gareth hopped out and started off toward the front door. I imagined my own reaction were I to open a door and find Gareth standing before me.

"Do you think I should go, too?" I asked.

"Definitely," Aimee-Noel said. "And fast."

I rushed after Gareth. He knocked loudly. After a few moments of silence, we heard footsteps, followed by the voices of children.

"Daddy!" they were yelling. "Daddy, the door."

Then the mumblings of a man, a rustling of keys, steps, and the door pulled open. Two little girls peered out from behind their father.

"Can I help you?" he asked. He was a tall colored man in his early thirties. He inspected me and then looked back at Gareth, who lit a cigarette and flipped his chin.

"Are you Clinton?"

"I am."

"I'm sorry, this is probably a strange question," I said. "But do you know Daniel de Villiers? This is the address we have for him, and I've been looking for him for some time."

"Daniel?" Clinton said, craning his neck to look out at Aimee-Noel in the car and then shifting his gaze from me to Gareth and back. "Ja, Daniel was a renter here."

"Did you know him?"

"Ja, ja, lovely guy . . ." He paused. "Do you mind if I ask who you are?"

"Of course! I am writing a book, and I think Daniel was involved in a serious incident in South African history."

"And I'm his relative," Gareth explained.

"Daniel? In a serious incident in history?" the man said, taken aback. "Daniel?"

"He got beaten up in Gugulethu back in 1993," I said. "Did you ever know about that?"

"Ja, ja, everyone knew about that."

"They did?"

"Sure, that's why he retired from the municipality."

"Hrmph," Gareth mumbled.

Clinton's sister was a taxi driver, and Daniel had worked a bit with her, which was how he'd come to rent this room, Clinton explained. But Daniel had moved out a few years back, and unfortunately Clinton didn't have a phone number for his old tenant.

"Any idea where he stays?" I asked.

"Well, I did see him last year."

"And, where was he?"

"At the old-age home in Bonny Brook. He was at the old-age home with his mother, I think." He told his daughter something in Afrikaans and she left the room only to return a moment later. Amazingly, she was holding a photograph.

"Daniel was really a lovely guy. He is the girls' godfather. Here's a christening." Clinton passed me a faded, low-quality 3 x 5 snapshot.

This was the first time I'd seen Daniel de Villiers and I inspected the picture. Daniel stood beside a priest in the sunlight, outside a brick church. He was a small person, of average weight, wearing charcoal slacks, a white short-sleeve button-down shirt, and a maroon striped tie. His face rested in a neutral expression. He wore round, unfashionable sunglasses. In short, Daniel de Villiers was perhaps the world's most nondescript man, right down to his gray hair, styled in an unremarkable buzz cut.

Gareth directed me to the old-age home in Bonny Brook. We doubled back for forty minutes toward Kraaifontein until we arrived at the three-story white building on a quiet street, protected by gates. I pressed a square orange button and the buzzer sounded. Gareth, Aimee-Noel, and I filed through and opened the lobby door. There was a small sitting area immediately before me, but no signs of life. I planned to find some sort of office, where perhaps a receptionist or administrator would be able to confirm whether a Daniel de Villiers resided here.

A lady with teased blue hair plodded over on her walker. She was a full foot shorter than me. She looked up and asked if she could help me.

"Do you know if a Daniel de Villiers lives here?"

"Daniel? De Villiers? Sure, just upstairs. Here, I'll show you." She gave Gareth a once-over. We followed her up a long wheelchair ramp to the second floor, hung right, and looked ahead. There was a plain wooden door, slightly ajar. On it was taped a white paper sign with computer print:

D. DE VILLIERS
DIABETIC

Nine months of searching, and here he was: D. de Villiers, diabetic. I knocked. No answer. I knocked again.

The woman teetered around nearby.

"Just go in," she urged. "He can't hear a thing."

Gareth courageously pushed the door open. Past the hospital bed and the little bathroom with a dim light, near the small window, sat a frail figure hunched over a table, facing away from the door. Before him was a tray of mushy, brown foods arranged in little indentations. He was bent close to the tray, spoon in his hand, toiling away at his meal. The room was silent. He had no reaction to the squeak of the hinge or the sudden presence of three unseen visitors behind him.

Gareth strode over and touched the shoulder of the man. The man looked up and his mouth opened wide. He was a waiflike creature, wasted and pale, with wide black eyes. He was missing the bulk of his teeth, without whose support his mouth had collapsed inward, pulling his face with it. He wore enormous glasses and a white hoodie that said BILLABONG in bright red script across the chest. The same man as in Clinton's picture, but a hundred years older. He had very plain white hair, cut short.

Gareth put his hands on his hips and raised an eyebrow. The man stared at him in wonder. Then, screwing up his face, he said with a rasp, "What the hell are you doing here?"

The day after I found Daniel was the twentieth anniversary memorial, to be held in St. Columba Anglican Church in Gugulethu. Linda Biehl, along with the anthropologist Nancy Scheper-Hughes, a reporter from *The Orange County Register*, and the foundation staffers were all preparing for the celebration of Amy's short life, as Gareth, Aimee-Noel, and I sat on a few hard couches in an open lobby that smelled like bleach and overcooked vegetables.

"We started off thinking we were going to check out the whorehouses, and we end up at an old-age home," Aimee-Noel whispered. Gareth jiggled his leg.

I thought we'd be waiting for a while, as Daniel had needed to freshen up, but in under a minute he was making his way down the ramp with surprising speed, balanced on his curving metal cane.

Daniel and Gareth stood facing each other at the end of the stairway. They tried to exchange pleasantries, but neither was a skilled conversationalist and they just ended up talking briefly about a relative who had pancreatic cancer that needed to get "cut out of her." Then they lapsed into silence.

"Last I saw you, you were by the Kraaifontein Shoprite and we didn't speak about nothing," Daniel said.

"Ja," Gareth agreed. He dug his hands in his pockets. Then, for lack of anything better to do, he suggested that Daniel take a seat near me. Daniel obliged. Light streamed in from the tall picture windows, warming the room. A few framed landscape prints had been arranged high up on the wall. A small palm plant was flourishing in the corner. I turned to Daniel and introduced myself.

"You have to speak a bit louder," Daniel said. His glasses, with their thick lenses, had a magnifying effect: His eyes seemed extraordinarily large, and he therefore wore an expression of perpetual shock.

I started again, raising my voice. Amy Biehl, the attack, Gugulethu, 1993.

"A bit louder still."

"Do you remember the Amy Biehl case, the American girl?" I said, as loud as I could without embarrassing myself.

"Ja," Daniel said blankly.

"You were also in Gugulethu."

He stared at me. "I used to stay in Kraaifontein, I was also there for six years."

"Can I talk to you about this attack that happened twenty years ago. Do you remember?"

"Ja. Vaguely."

"At the train station," I said. *He doesn't remember*, I thought. *His mind is gone.*

"Ja, ja . . ." A pause. "You have to speak a bit louder."

I looked around. A few people had stopped and were gaping. I pushed off my embarrassment and took a breath. "The train station!" I hollered. "The train station! Where you were attacked! They stabbed you!"

Suddenly, his eyes bulged.

"*JA!*" he said. "Ja! You know Amy Biehl?"

18.

I am what time, circumstance, history, have made of me, certainly, but I am, also, so much more than that. So are we all.

—JAMES BALDWIN, *Notes of a Native Son*

When Daniel spoke, he let out low gurgles and gargles. He was missing his left lung, he said, which had been taken out at the hospital after the attack by the railroad. They'd saved his right one, just. His breathing was labored, and he wheezed perpetually. Talking was a significant effort, but he was energized, and now he leaned forward, held his cane in one hand, and began to tell us a story he had never thought anyone would come around looking to hear.

"What I heard is that instead of taking that Amy Biehl to a hospital, they took her to the police station, and that's where she died," he said. "I don't know why they took her to the police station of all things. There is a hospital in that area. Even though there were colored people staying there, the hospital would have helped her. She was attacked there, opposite Heideveld. I can't think of the name, where the blacks lived. Gugulethu, you say? Yes, that's it. She was attacked there in the afternoon and me, in the morning. I heard about her first when it was in the news. I was laying in a hospital and the patient next to me, he lent me the paper."

"What did the newspaper say?" I hollered. Daniel didn't hear me, but he nodded and continued on.

"It was only about two, three lines where they spoke about me. And her business was right down the whole newspaper. Amy Biehl. I was left out of the picture altogether. All they said was a driver was attacked. I don't know why. The reporter who put that piece in didn't go around to find out who is this other person. Then they would have had the whole story from beginning to end.

"I was a supervisor, fixing the lights. I had two colored guys working with me. They were on the street. I'm driving. When they attacked me, it was about eleven. I was alone in the truck. One minute, I was sitting there. The next minute, this whole group of characters came toward me. There were forty of them. Without a word, they forced my door open and they took me down. They said, 'Get out. Get out of the truck.' I refused and they pulled me out. They were shouting 'PAC!' 'ANC!' 'Viva PAC!'"

According to Daniel, the ANC kids had been part of these groups, too—just like Rhoda Kadalie and Mzi believed.

"They pulled me to the ground and then they stabbed me so many times. They started with screwdrivers, axle blades, and daggers. It happened so quick, it took me completely by surprise. The way they attacked me, you could see on their faces they wanted me dead."

"Do you remember their faces?" I yelled. Daniel looked at me.

"Do you remember their faces?" Gareth yelled louder, into Daniel's ear.

"No, I don't. There was too many of them. They weren't even men, more like schoolkids, high school kids. I do recall they had thick shoes on. This is why I'm deaf. They kicked me on the head. That is why my hearing is gone. If you had seen those people, you wouldn't have believed it. They were just out to murder because of the color of your skin. I was lying down and they only got me in the back. They kicked me like that as if they were playing soccer. They stabbed me in the lungs, which is why I still can't breathe right. They counted there was ten stab wounds in my back. And because they stabbed me in my pancreas, I'm a diabetic. They were like a couple mad things. I hope you never meet something like that.

"After they pulled me from the truck, railway police came off the train that was coming in. These guys ran and disappeared in three different directions. The police called on the radio for the ambulance to come but the ambulance refused to come. Said it was too dangerous. So my guys used the radio in my truck and called my boss. He was all the way over in Salt River. He picked me up an hour later and took me to the hospital.

"My doctors struggled to keep me alive. I hope you never meet something like that. I went into shock. I stayed in hospital for two and a half months. My bill for the time being there was two thousand rand short of a million rand.

"Later, I spoke to the police. I don't remember now the police station I opened the case at. It was long ago. The policeman said, 'We will never solve this case, there's too many of them.' But then Amy Biehl came into the picture and they got these guys and they took them to court. I said to the policeman, 'Can I go to the court and see if it's them?' He said, 'No, they will kill you right there, right in the court. We will leave it as an unsolved attack. We will leave the case open.' And it's still open."

"Did you go to the TRC?" I shouted.

"TRC!" Gareth yelled.

"In late '97 I think it was, I went to the TRC," Daniel said. "I spoke to them. Brought details. I had to write down all the details word for word. Then Tutu came into the act and we all were paid thirty thousand rand, but we were promised more." The TRC had, in its final report, recommended that the government pay each victim reparations in installments for six years. Only a select few received any reparations at all; like Daniel, they got a one-off payment.

"The Amy Biehl guys were there. They got freed. A lot of people thought it wasn't so wonderful at all for them to let them go like that after they killed her. I don't know about those people and those political parties. Never once, ever, did anyone say to me, 'Sorry about that.' If you get hold of anyone in leadership, tell them I can't sleep at night. If somebody attacked you, wouldn't you be nervous, wondering when someone will come and finish the job off? Maybe in the day I can shut my eyes, but I haven't slept at night since 1993. You know, we could have all been killed if Mandela had not taken that action, but we're all still alive today."

"What action did Mandela take?" I yelled.

"He could have caused a disaster here. In those years, every time in the paper, it was so many people killed: this many blacks, this many whites, this many coloreds. But it was so many more blacks than anyone else. For every white person, there were twelve blacks. What did Mandela have to gain by letting us go? If not for him, you and I wouldn't be around to tell about it.

"But me, I was destined to be attacked. The St. James Massacre, you know?" He was discussing the church attacked by APLA cadres just one month before Amy's death. "I went to that church. I was supposed to be there that night that the militants killed the parishioners. There was a storm so I said to my mother, '*Ach*, forget it.' You see, they reckon the militants were watching for six weeks. How can they attack a church? What is there in a church for them? There is nobody there to fight them back. I should have been killed there in church on July 25th of that year. I would have died then. But instead I had to wait till August 25th to get killed."

Daniel had grown tired, his breathing more labored, the gurgling more pronounced. I shook his hand, cool and bony. We decided to meet again that week, when I would be able to speak to his brothers. He entered my number into his small cellphone, across the screen of which ran the sentence ALWAYS BE HAPPY DANIEL. On the drive back with Gareth, Daniel called. His cellphone was set to high volume, and so for the first time, I could speak fluidly with him. He had already asked his stepbrothers to tell me the whole story of his attack. Would I come back in a few days?

That night, I fell into bed at ten and woke with a start at 4:15. In my dream, a man was being brutally stabbed. He sat ramrod straight in a wooden chair at an office desk. He was an innocent son stabbed by his father. Then he was a father stabbed by his son. The son stabbed him with a screwdriver. It took such effort for that thin round of steel to pierce the skin and sinew, to run deep into the flesh of the face, the muscle, and then to penetrate the skull, boring through into the folds of the brain. Finally the man in the chair was dead.

Then I was the assailant, armed with the screwdriver. I put my strength into it, feeling nothing but determination. The metal went in and out of the man's body, leaving wounds as perfect as hole punches. The man, alive again, but not for long, sat at that desk the whole time, his posture straight. He didn't utter a scream or raise a hand in self-defense. He looked like a mannequin, but he was real.

When I sat up, in the dark and out of breath, I could sense Daniel's chilly hand—how it felt clasped in mine. I could hear the ocean in the distance, the waves crashing on the shore. Late at night, when no traffic ran along the streets, the sounds of the water were clear. It had rained at some point, I supposed, and I could hear, too, the drops dripping through the ceiling cracks in the kitchen, hitting the linoleum.

That morning was the twentieth anniversary of Amy's death. I wrapped myself in a parka and picked up a friend of Linda's at his hotel—he was an academic who had come all the way from Georgia to observe this memorial. Linda had arranged for some out-of-town visitors to travel in the foundation's van but there was no room for him, so Linda had asked that I drive him. Then I met Easy at Linda's hotel. He was waiting in the parking lot next to the van, and was wearing an entirely new outfit: brown loafers, black trousers, a pale pink polo shirt, a white scarf thrown jauntily around his neck, and his Africa cap, which displayed the continent.

"I'm Italian," he said, striking a pose to show off his new look. Someone had taken him on a shopping spree, either Tiny or Linda, it was unclear, and Easy would not divulge the information.

Then he loaded up Linda, a reporter and a photographer from

The Orange County Register, some of Linda's friends, and the anthropologist Nancy Scheper-Hughes and her husband. They all stopped to buy white lilies, which Linda liked to lay beside Amy's memorial every year. We drove in a two-vehicle convoy to Gugulethu, where the church memorial for Amy would begin.

After I had parked behind the church and everyone had gotten out of the van, I walked over to it and slid into the passenger seat. Easy had parked on a grassy mound by the church, turned the van off, and was fiddling with his phone.

"I found Daniel de Villiers," I said.

"Who?"

"The *guy.*"

"And?" His expression revealed nothing.

"He's not dead."

"Where did you find him?"

"In an old-age home in Bonny Brook."

"Is he okay?"

"Not really." I fished out a photo of Daniel I'd taken on my phone the day before, drawn and blind, gazing vaguely at the lens. He leaned upon his little cane. His face was deeply lined, his eyes sad and unfocused, his mouth set in a mild, uncommitted grimace. Easy took my phone and studied the picture.

"Now you see, Nomzamo, I really tell you the truth. What I tell you is true."

Just then, an old colleague of Easy's tapped the glass and mimed a kiss.

"I'm coming now," Easy said, and hopped out of the van.

We walked down the street, everyone with the fabric hearts made to honor dead women pinned to their shirts, some holding flowers. The children sang songs and played the marimba. Linda, holding her AMY BIEHL, OUR COMRADE sign, clutched the hand of Ntobeko's daughter in her purple dress. Kevin, the foundation director, was nowhere to be seen, and Ntobeko had slipped off into the township,

far from the glare of the little group of journalists. Amy's former colleague cried in Linda's arms. Mzi met me, and we leaned on the car
and watched Nancy's twenty-minute address. She called Amy an
"accidental hero." She called her death a "Shakespearean tragedy."
Mzi's hands trembled.

After the service, Linda's American friends treated the staff and
the hangers-on and the dribbles of media to a meal at Mzoli's. They
ordered vats of sausage and chicken and staked out a long plastic
table that ran through the room. Since it was a Sunday, Mzoli's was
in "Sunday Chill" mode, as it was called. The place was pumping, full
of people ending the weekend on a high note. Easy and I sat by each
other on one end, and Linda sat far away, surrounded by admirers.
The table was peppered with sodas, wine bottles, beer bottles, and
Styrofoam plates.

After they'd finished eating, Easy and the other staffers got into
the spirit. He was shaking his ass to a pop hit, circling his colleagues,
who were bopping to the lyrics: *What do they make dreams for / When
you got them jeans on.* From her seat at the end of the table, Linda was
grooving, too, sipping her Chardonnay, eating sausages daintily with
her hands.

Two days later, the foundation held its "Youth Spirit Awards" in a
near-empty hall of the University of the Western Cape. They awarded
three young people with checks of varying amounts for their community service. A colored boy won first prize, a white girl won
second prize, and a black girl won third prize.

"Is not right," Easy muttered. "Look who win and look who is on
the committee. Never a black person."

Kevin, in a blue shirt and red tie, his face rosy, stood behind the
podium, talking about how his staff "aim to inspire the youth of
South Africa . . . to greater heights of service."

Linda followed and Kevin averted his eyes. Easy clasped my hand,
terrified that she would make him stand before the room, but she
skipped over him. "Sometimes I feel like I've lost Amy's spirit," she

said, losing her train of thought in the midst of her speech. "Sometimes I feel the foundation has lost Amy's spirit . . . but it's changing
is what it is. . . ."

The foundation's choir, kids in yellow and green shirts, harmo-
nized as the South African opera diva Aviva Pelham led them in
John Lennon's "Imagine." Linda and the crowd waved their hands in
the air. When the evening was almost finished, Pelham treated the
audience to an unrequested encore, directing the choir to sing a
song about Mandela called "He Walked to Freedom," and making
everyone do a march in the aisles.

The next day, before Linda's departure, I stopped in at her office
to bid her farewell. We had both been busy during this time—me on
my quest for Daniel, she in her endless, if uncertain, quest to cut ties
with South Africa while keeping Amy's story, and her own story,
alive. Linda was holding court before an Irish filmmaker and the
journalist from her hometown paper. As we said goodbye, Linda
hugged me lightly, patting my back once, and said, "We'll talk."

That was the last time I ever had contact with Linda Biehl. Three
months later, my publishing company received a letter from Scott
Meinert, Amy's old boyfriend, who worked as a lawyer for wine
estates in California at that time. I had interviewed Scott that August, after Linda had given me his number; he'd sent me scans of old
photos of Amy and connected me with some of her dearest friends,
who shared their memories. Now the letter was written on behalf
of Linda and Ntobeko, and it demanded that I cease and desist writing my book, explaining that I had misrepresented myself as working with Linda's permission and was engaged in "the worst type of
profiteering. . . . Her continued attempts to exploit Mr. Peni's participation in the story have caused him much harm due to her in-
cessantly acting as if she has the privileged right to publicly exploit
his personal story without his permission, which is unfortunately
reminiscent of the tactics of the Afrikaans regime."

The next I heard of Linda and Ntobeko was in April 2014. They
had been invited to an interview on St. Louis Public Radio, before

participating in a panel at an American university: "Nelson Mandela's Legacy of Reconciliation: Lessons for Leading an Inclusive Community." In a snapshot on the radio website, they stood next to each other, both dressed in blue, smiling broadly.

"You realized you were taking somebody's life?" the interviewer asked Ntobeko.

"We were prepared to die for the cause, and in the process of that we automatically became prepared to kill for it," Ntobeko answered in his soft voice. "I am prepared to give my life for the cause, and in the process I will pursue the target."

"Um, Ntobeko is quite amazing," Linda interrupted a few minutes later. "We often learn from each other when we talk like this, and I have to say that one of the things I've learned is that he took responsibility for this act because he was elected the leader of that particular youth group at the time. He was not maybe a perpetrator that actually committed the crime, but their whole process of how they dealt with rats and ratting on each other is really quite amazing, and I've learned so much about that. So you use the word killer, but I don't use the word killer. I think he was one of the disenfranchised young males who Amy had talked about. . . You know, as much as we tell the story cut and dry, there are all these little sidebars and things that say many of them could have wielded a knife or thrown a stone, but eyewitnesses came forward and kind of picked out some. Ntobeko ran away, was not tried with the other three. But it's more complicated than just—"

"These stories always are," the interviewer said, "They get picked up and repeated and perpetuated. So my apologies for using that word, but that is basically the way it had been presented to us here."

"No, I understand, I understand," Ntobeko said.

I may never know what Linda and Ntobeko believed I was up to, but I thought of their sudden legal letter as the perfect coda to the general impossibility of South Africa, a place that had tried to divide each facet of life into black and white, and had succeeded only in creating a land where everything is rendered in shades of gray. Just

as you thought you were coming to comprehend something or
someone, you'd get thrown for a loop. There was no shortage of
mystery and conflict here.

"Look at Daniel," Easy had told me soon after the twentieth anniversary memorial. "Look at Pikker. Look at all the members of
PAC. Look at ANC, a destroyer. We try to build together pieces. But
is broken. Heartbroken."

19.

The world asks of us
only the strength we have and we give it.
Then it asks more, and we give it.

—JANE HIRSHFIELD, "The Weighing"

South African winters are merciless. Outside, it was chilly but not unbearable; it had nothing on American East Coast winters, or Midwestern winters, or European winters. No snow, no ice. The problem, rather, was that one could never get adequately warm, since the country was in denial about the existence of its most terrible season. Residences and offices had neither central heating nor fireplaces, and the cement walls of most structures held the chill inside. The sea air floated up the mountains and across the Cape Flats, burrowing into the bones of every structure, dispersing little droplets of dampness through the air. I wandered the house clutching a space heater, plugging it in wherever I went. I lay in bed in the mornings, trying to find the courage to poke a toe out from under the covers. People, rich and poor alike, shivered from June to September. My in-laws wrapped their parkas over their fleece bathrobes, and sat watching television, bundled up like a pair of Eskimos. Easy's entire family gathered in a single room, warmed by their petroleum heater, and refused to leave except to fetch more food from the kitchen. Others in the townships kept gas stoves burning into the night, and when they tipped over, houses, streets, whole neighborhoods burned.

On the day I went to see Daniel for the second time, Linda Biehl had just left town. The Western Cape was not only freezing, but it was also in the grips of a merciless rainstorm. In the informal settlements surrounding the townships, people were emptying their homes with buckets. The portable toilets flooded, and raw sewage seeped out onto the dirt pathways. Shacks were scattered with pots and pans to catch the water dripping through porous tin ceilings; moldy furniture and linoleum tiles floated off. A man died sleeping rough somewhere in the province, the radio announced. The water pounded down on my windshield and I had to press my face close to the glass to see the road.

Daniel had been waiting at the door and came out of the building straightaway, balancing on the cane and maneuvering through the rain, wearing a Christmas sweater, short black corduroys that exposed his ankles, and large, heavy-duty sneakers. He sat in the car and directed me down the curving streets, past tidy suburban homes with trim lawns. We would visit his stepbrothers, Daniel said. They could tell me the full story.

"Do you have any brothers or sisters?" Daniel asked, and when I shook my head he seemed comforted. "You're an only. Just like me."

It had grown dark, and the windows of the homes glowed yellow and orange. Daniel peered out from behind his glasses, largely silent unless he wanted to direct me. When we weren't speaking, the sounds of his wet breathing, gurgling up from his bum lungs, filled the car.

"Did you ever marry?" I asked.

"No, never did."

"Why not?"

"Didn't find a suitable girl." He shrugged. His legs were just bones, silhouetted by the ill-fitting pants.

After a few minutes, we pulled up to a modest white ranch house, surrounded by a chain link fence behind which a brown-and-white Dalmatian growled ferociously. Daniel shakily exited the car and began to rattle the fence, which caused the dog to erupt into vicious barks. A fifty-something man, round and balding, poked his head out the door.

"Let us in, would you!" Daniel said.

"Wait a minute, for goodness' sake," the man said, before dragging the dog into a garage and locking the door behind it.

"This is Stephan and this is Willy," Daniel said, when the man finally opened the gate, followed by another man. "They can tell you all about what happened to me."

Stephan, wearing a striped fisherman's sweater, shook my hand and led me into his sitting room, a cozy space filled with worn sofas and the verdant smell of split pea soup boiling on the stove. Willy, in a puce shirt and brown tie, was about five years younger and twenty pounds thinner, with a ruddy complexion and hair styled in a short, spiked mullet common to a certain set of white South African male. Daniel balanced on a small chair to the side, grasping his cane, and I sat next to Stephan, turning to him to explain myself. I hoped, I said, he could tell me about Daniel. Stephan nodded.

"To start with, Daniel is my stepbrother, but we at first thought that he was the brother of my stepmother," Stephan said, settling into his seat. Without glancing at Daniel, and without raising his voice to make himself audible to Daniel, he summarized precisely what Gareth had told me: that Daniel was a child born of incest, raised to believe his mother was his sister. As Stephan spoke at length, I gazed over at Daniel. He was an interiorized person by nature, rendered more so by his inability to properly hear or see. The world around him was a blur of sounds and sights he could not entirely make out.

"Daniel, that must have been shocking," I shouted, trying to confirm that he had been listening.

"You must make contact with *YOU Magazine*," he announced, referring to the tabloid-run ladies' rag. "This story is perfect for *YOU Magazine*."

"What Stephan is saying, I mean. That must have been shocking."

"*YOU Magazine* will expose the truth of my attack," he said. No, he couldn't hear me, and he hadn't heard Stephan.

"Why would she put your attack in *YOU Magazine*?" Stephan shouted.

"Ja." Daniel nodded.

Stephan shook his head, and continued on with Daniel's biography, while Willy sat stiffly in his seat. Back in the day, according to

Stephan, Daniel was quiet and withdrawn, and he found it tough to make friends. Once Daniel moved in with Stephan and Willy's family, the boys all attended high school together. Daniel was a decent student, a wallflower. At nineteen, he graduated and started working for the state—first at the docks, where he kept the lights in good order, and later around town, where he fixed streetlamps and such. He was a dedicated worker, entirely peaceful, the type of man who'd be twenty minutes early before he'd be a minute late. After eight years, he resigned, with a plan to drive taxis—presumably with the sister of Clinton, the man whose house I'd first approached with Gareth and Aimee-Noel. That didn't work out, so Daniel drove a hearse for a while. But eventually, unable to eke out a proper living, he returned again to the docks and the shadow of his father.

"Do you have good memories of the docks?" I hollered to Daniel.

"No ..." he said uncertainly. "What about when they attacked me?"

"How do you feel about your father?" I shouted.

"Two lines about me in the *Cape Times,* and Amy Biehl got pages and pages," he said.

"How does he feel about his father?" I asked Stephan.

"When he found out about the abuse that had taken place and linked it to how he had lived as a child, he hated his father. He was tasked with getting rid of the old man's remains, and he's done something with it, something ... not honorable." Stephan let out a stifled laugh. "He never told us what exactly."

"They attacked me like it was nothing," muttered Daniel in his corner. One of his fingernails was ridged with a fungal infection.

"They targeted him," Willy said, moving the conversation away from Daniel's family and toward the assault. "He was like a red flag to a bull."

"It's true." Stephan nodded. He thought back to 1993. He'd married by then, and had four kids, so he didn't see Daniel much. Maybe at birthdays and braais, but nothing regular. But on August 25, Daniel's hysterical mother—by then, the secret was out—learned that

Daniel had been beaten severely and was in the hospital. Stephan and Willy drove over and found Daniel encased in a plastic oxygen tent, his smashed-up face a pale shade of gray where it was not black and blue and purple, his hands shaking. He could only moan and wheeze. His eyes darted back and forth, his ear was encased in a bandage.

"He was all open," Willy recalled. "They split him open."

Daniel's family didn't quite understand what had happened. The police said that there had been a riot in Gugulethu, and the crowd had targeted government property. They intended to burn the truck, and had pulled Daniel to the ground and hacked away at him.

"The PAC—" Daniel said.

"I don't call them the PAC," Stephan interrupted. "I always think of them as just blacks. Just blacks. Anyone with any grievance can say it was political. But it was thuggery."

"They stabbed me in the pancreas!" Daniel exclaimed. "That's why I have diabetes."

"I don't think the stab in the pancreas caused diabetes," Willy said to me.

"Nearly three months in the hospital," Daniel said.

"You weren't in the hospital for three months!" Willy scolded.

"My hospital bill was two thousand rand short of a million rand," Daniel said softly.

"He did develop pneumonia from the wounds to the lungs," Willy said. "And all that went with it."

Willy remembered that before the attack, Daniel used to go to the bars with a couple of friends, perhaps have a beer and listen to some music. But after the attack, he stayed at home, unwilling to brave the outdoors unless necessary.

"The PAC owes me for twenty years," Daniel added. "They haven't paid me a penny."

Stephan thought of the TRC, when Daniel had been promised restitution. "This Tutu, he's such a big man. This great archbishop, His Eminence. Nothing was ever pursued.

"The TRC washed its hands of this matter," Stephan continued. "They never investigated. They washed their hands like Pontius Pilate. Maybe I should be more forgiving, but I never liked Tutu."

After he had recovered as much as possible, Daniel was forced to retire.

"The lousy thing was, he was earning a decent salary," said Willy. "He could have worked until he turned sixty-five and he would have had a fantastic pension. But he couldn't do labor anymore."

In the late 1990s, Daniel bought a little flat in a modest beach town north of the city, and invited his mother to come live with him. In a few years' time, he'd fallen behind on his payments and gave the place up.

"What were his politics?" I asked Stephan. "Politics!" I screamed toward Daniel.

"Working-class people, you don't really have a say," Stephan insisted.

"I'm not interested in politics," Daniel piped up. "Politics up and killed me."

After losing his flat, Daniel had moved to a one-room rental in the back of a house in a nearby suburb, a place he rarely left but to do some shopping. A few years later, Daniel didn't answer his phone for two days, so Stephan and Willy went to his place. They heard his voice, weak and small, from within. They tried to peer into the windows, but the entire space was high with papers and debris, old milk cartons and greasy plastic bags, a place of squalor and chaos. Daniel had become a hoarder.

"I'm no psychologist, but in my humble opinion, he was scared of losing what he had," Stephan said.

The brothers broke off the burglar bars covering the window with a spade and pulled Daniel out from the mess. His diabetes, uncontrolled, had sent him into a coma, and he had lain, unmoving, on the floor for days. They took him to the hospital, where the doctor dictated that he could no longer live on his own. Willy and Stephan cleaned out his apartment, trashing his epic collection of junk, including his meticulously kept case folder on his assault. My sudden and impossible-to-predict appearance in Daniel's life only confirmed his great conviction: that this crap was truly precious, no matter what anyone said, and that someday, somebody was going to come looking for the valuable pile of papers underneath the perfectly good cracked hamper full of totally fine used coffee filters.

"*You* threw it away like it was nothing," he hissed at Stephan and Willy, who tried to explain that there was just so much, and how could they have possibly known?

A year before our meeting, Daniel was placed in the old-age home, which garnished 92 percent of its inhabitants' pensions, no matter the amount. That left Daniel with 300 rand, then a bit less than $30, a month. He couldn't afford new clothing or even, some months, toothpaste. The stepbrothers, themselves supporting families on salaries and pensions that were hardly generous, tried to bring him soap and socks, but that was all they could manage.

"His health seriously deteriorated after that beating," Willy said.

"I don't know how," Stephan said, shrugging, "but Daniel never became bitter."

It was pitch black outside and I still had a long drive back home. "Do you think Daniel's case and the other case from that day were related?" I asked.

"Well, he's the missing link that nobody speaks of," Willy answered. "We also wonder why nobody has drawn a link with the Amy MacBiehl case."

While Daniel was in the hospital, the Amy Biehl story had dominated the news. The media knew a good story, and Daniel was not that story. Daniel, a working-class white South African citizen employed by the National Party government, was "a nobody," as Stephan said.

"Plus, *she* died," Willy added thoughtfully.

"It was not through their efforts that he didn't die," Stephan said. "They wanted him to die."

Daniel and I said goodbye and walked to my car. "You really must get in touch with *YOU Magazine,*" he said as he shuffled to the passenger side. "*YOU Magazine* can do an article on me."

"Eish, man, why does she want to get in touch with *YOU Magazine!*" Willy said from the doorway. "She's writing the story herself."

As I pulled up at the old-age home a few minutes later, Daniel turned to me.

"Give this to Patricia de Lille," he said, handing me a few pieces of paper covered in tight, tidy handwriting. De Lille was the current mayor of Cape Town and a member of the center-right Democratic Alliance, the ANC's official opposition. The DA was favored by whites and well-off people of color, among others. But back in the 1980s and 1990s, de Lille, who is colored, had been a high-ranking member of the PAC.

"I don't know Patricia de Lille," I said. "I made a bunch of interview requests but she won't speak to me." Her office had told me that she simply had no time, ever, to see me and, presumably, discuss her radical past.

Daniel opened the car door and shakily stepped out onto the sidewalk. "Now don't drive away until you see I am in there," he ordered. "Don't leave me standing here on the street at night."

I watched him make his way through the rain, now falling in a light and steady drizzle, illuminated by a streetlamp and a strobe by the gate. He buzzed, waited nervously, and then pushed his way in. He continued on unsteadily to the glass door, never looking back, and finally disappeared inside, fading into the lobby.

I did a U-turn, back past the Shoprite and over the little bridge and onto the highway, bound for Sea Point. For forty minutes, the highway was bathed in darkness, punctuated only by tiny lamps in the secluded settlements along the way. I let out a sigh of relief when I hit Century City, that monstrous mall lit like Vegas. I could see the city in the distance now.

I curved down off the exit ramp where the highway ended, and drove past African Mama tourist restaurant, where in the mornings the refugees waited against buildings for trucks to come by and hire them to work for a few hours. I headed up toward Lion's Head, past the luxury car dealership where homeless people slept huddled beneath a brightly lit showroom for Ferraris and Maseratis, and into Sea Point. A man stood on a corner, drenched by the rain, unmoving.

The bogeyman was everywhere in this country, alive in the horror stories that never stopped: a friend of a friend was carjacked and her baby driven away with the car (the baby was found, still strapped in his car seat, down the road, but other children had been killed in similar incidents); a neighbor was mugged on my block; a friend's elderly father was tied up, beaten, and left for dead by three day laborers he'd hired to help clean out his office. There were smash-and-grabs (at a stoplight, someone might smash your window and grab your purse from the seat). There were these people who threw bricks from highway overpasses in order to cause a crash below, so they could loot the victim's car before the ambulance arrived. There was a lady who slept with her window cracked, only to find a man in her bedroom. He warned her to be more careful, stole her valuables, and left without touching her.

What was particularly strange about my reaction to all this was that I felt increasingly paranoid in my upscale neighborhood of Sea Point and increasingly safe in Gugulethu. The statistics showed that Gugulethu was the more dangerous place: in 2012, Gugulethu saw 120 murders, while Sea Point saw 5. I was traveling between Ethiopia, where Sam had been posted for work and where I would soon move, and Cape Town, and so I was often alone in our cottage for a month or two at a time. Even the dog had moved across the continent. All along the ritzy Atlantic Seaboard, the streets seemed eerily empty and silent, and anyone could be hiding in the shadows, and

who would hear my howls? Not the family across the way, in their
secured mansion. Not the deaf senior citizen next door. But in Gugulethu, there were at least twenty people upon whom I could depend to extricate me from a situation. Then again, I had never had
to make my way back to the township in the dark.

One day, on the way to visit Easy, I drove over a large plastic jerrican that had just fallen from an open truck onto the highway, and
the can became wedged beneath my car's chassis. I pulled over and
tried to kick the thing out, but it would not budge. To my left was a
barren field and then an informal settlement. To my right were six
lanes of highway and then a tangle of trees and bush. I flashed to the
many stories of stranded motorists swiftly losing their cars to
criminals—this, despite the fact that Sam had earlier broken down
on a highway and been helped by a stranger from Khayelitsha, who
pulled over and happily fixed the problem without asking for any
compensation, despite telling Sam he had just been let go from his
job. I glanced around, took a breath, and calculated that I was just
five minutes from the township, and there I knew plenty of people
who, through necessity, could repair most anything when it came to
cars.

I began to drive again, making a horrible racket. A bakkie with a
white man driving and a colored man sitting next to him pulled up,
and they motioned for me to stop and pointed down at the jerrican,
but I waved them off and headed to the Gugulethu exit. The men
frowned and shook their heads, and I imagined that they were wondering why a white girl with a can stuck to her car was dimly driving off into a township. But I dragged the can along until I reached
NY111, where I spotted one of Easy's brothers. I pulled over. He
peered under the car and then kicked very hard and the can dis-
lodged. Gugulethu had become for me a peculiar little sanctuary.
When I finally moved away from South Africa, I would rarely yearn
for Clifton Beach or the palm-lined streets of Camps Bay. But I
missed Gugulethu all the time, and it was the first place I stopped by
whenever I circled back.

After visiting Daniel, I called our security service when I was five minutes from home. The South African police, common knowledge dictated, were neither reliable nor trustworthy, and so each and every house in wealthy and middle-class neighborhoods, and even some homes in working-class areas, displayed the plaques of various security companies on their external walls. The country boasted nine thousand such companies, which employed 400,000 armed guards— more than the combined members of the police and army. These services typically installed burglar alarms, handed out panic buttons, and sent an employee to meet you at the entrance to your home and usher you in if you so desired. Were your alarm to sound, they arrived with guns cocked.

A private car, AVENUES RESPONSE stamped across its side, awaited me, its lights cutting through the drizzle. A guard stood under an umbrella as I opened my gate and turned into my drive. I can't say I trusted him entirely; there were reports of the guards themselves committing crimes, but he drove off once I had closed my front door behind me. I checked the windows, the iron bars mounted over the front door, the grates pulled across the back door. Then I wrapped myself in a blanket and studied Daniel's letter.

Across the top of the page, Daniel had printed his identity number and his address: *Bonny Brook Old Aged Home*. Then he laid out the facts, or his version of them.

DATE: 25 AUGUST 1983

PLACE OF ATTACK: HEIDEVELD STATION

PERSON CAUSING ATTACK: HIGH SCHOOL STUDENTS, BEING ATTACKED
   BY +40 STUDENTS.

WEAPON USED IN THIS ATTACK: HACKSAW BLADES—DAGGERS—
   SCREWDRIVERS

The specifics were shaky—1983 crossed out, 1993 crossed out, 1983 reconsidered and rewritten. Details deemed especially important were underlined in red. Daniel's handwriting was labored and meticulous, except nearing the end, when he seemed to grow tired, and the letters sat on a rushed diagonal.

THEY STABBED THE TRUCK WHEELS TYRES FLAT WITH THE WEAPONS THEY WERE ARMED WITH. BEFORE THEY ATTACKED MR DANIEL DE VILLIERS. MAKING ALL THE FILTH INTO MY STAB WOUNDS.

I envisioned Daniel hunched over that desk with his felt-tip pen, recording the memories as they came to him.

I LOST A CONSIDERABLE AMOUNT OF BLOOD. RUNNING OUT OF MY BODY!

I had fantasized about a different narrative: a wise old man who perhaps hoped only to make peace with those who had hurt him.

THE POLICE CAME AND FOUND ME IN A BLEEDING STATE.

After the forgiveness of Mandela, there was a perpetuating myth of magical South Africa, place of forgiveness and fortitude. The impossible could happen in this country, and the world would be inspired. Except that wasn't the case. Not here, not now, and really, not anywhere.

THE AMBULANCE REFUSE TO COME THERE BECAUSE OF WHAT WAS HAPPENING!

Daniel had never seen justice. He had never experienced truth and he was not interested in reconciliation.

MY PANCREASE WAS PENETRATED BY ONE OF THE WEAPONS THESE STUDENTS HAD!

When Daniel had adequately cycled through the events of that day, twenty years earlier, he laid out what he wanted from the PAC.

It was all the worse for its impossibility. The PAC was a near-dead party that employed practically nobody. Most everybody I'd met who worked with the PAC was like Mzi: dead broke, unemployed, mired in disappointment, and marginalized.

I DANIEL DE VILLIERS REQUIRE FROM THE P.A.C. BECAUSE OF WHAT THEY DID TO ME:

1. THEY PAC TO PAY THE RENT AT THE OLD AGED HOME UNTIL I PASSAWAY IN DEATH.

2. A HEARING AID BECAUSE THE WAY THEY KICKED ME ABOUT MY HEAD.

3. IF AT ANYTIME I NEED TO ATTEND A HOSPITAL FOR ANY REASON THE PAC MUST PAY FOR MY HOSPITAL ACCOUNT

4. PAY ME DANIEL DE VILLIERS BACK FROM 25 AUGUST 1983!

5. URGENTLY A PAIR OF SPECTACLES. (EYEGLASSES)

Months later, Mzi organized a roundtable at the community center off of NY111 to discuss what had happened on the day of Amy's death, and he convinced his old militant friends to come, a group of five men who ambled in, distraught, ragged, and high. Another man arrived, pudgy and round-faced in a leather jacket: when he was twelve, wearing his high soccer socks and standing on the field by the Caltex, he had seen Amy murdered; it was his dog whose stomach had been sliced open, and his mother who had refused the U.S. government's offer of a new life in America. An old lady who had been walking by joined us, mostly to offer her memories. An incentivizing bucket of KFC and a package of white bread sat in the center of the room, and people helped themselves.

Mzi passed around a smooth wooden stick that he called the Talking Stick, and each man held it as he recalled the day, helping me to piece together a picture of the crime. Easy stopped by at the end, wearing a newsboy cap and drunk from attending a funeral. He spoke of his role as a freedom fighter, his involvement in Amy's murder. He was used to changing his tune for his audience. For the white tourists and journalists, he had been caught up in a maelstrom of violence, and Amy's death was the regrettable result. For these haggard old radicals, it was a different story.

"I am an African who can serve and suffer and sacrifice just for the benefit of the people," he said. "They've seen me do it."

When it was over, I drove Mzi home. It was late afternoon, and we attended a small birthday party for his niece Nanha. She was the daughter of Steyn, Mzi's broken brother who lived in Kanana and smoked dagga all day long, the man arrested in the murder of Amy and then set free. Nanha's mother had skipped out when Nanha was a baby. She lived with her extended family and slept next to her grandmother. Her teacher, impressed by her academic performance, had given her a pink notebook, which she hid beneath her grandmother's mattress. She motioned me into the room, lifted up the bed, and fished it out.

"Nobody knows it is here," she whispered. "It's my birthday Saturday. I turn nine."

"That's great news."

Nanha made her eyes into slits and pursed her lips, slipping the notebook back to its hiding place. "Don't breathe *any* word of it!"

A family friend had baked her a multilayer magenta cake covered in sprinkles and candles and she was wearing a new dress and new shoes. Her cousin, a confident four-year-old, walked over to me. Her hair was pulled into two tidy Afro puffs.

"Do you want popcorns?" she asked, shoving a handful at me. Then she pushed her face close to mine. "I like your dimples," she announced, a compliment I appreciated despite the fact that I don't have dimples.

After we sang "Happy Birthday," I left Gugulethu, but instead of returning to Sea Point, I took an alternate route. I drove off the highway, over the bridge, and turned left on a sleepy street. I buzzed in, walked past the walls covered in glitter and the other detritus of Christmas cheer, and arrived again at a barren brown door.

D. DE VILLIERS
DIABETIC

His phone had stopped working a while back, so I hadn't bothered to call. I didn't bother knocking either since he couldn't hear me. I opened the door to find Daniel in exactly the same position in which I'd found him when we'd first met: back facing the door, hunched over a shallow bowl of soup. I walked to where he could see me. He paused and looked up, unsurprised.

"Hello, Justine," he said in a soft warble.

I motioned to the hospital bed covered in a green and dark red cover, the only place to sit, and Daniel nodded.

"Can I ask you some questions?" I shouted.

"What?" he asked.

"Can I ask you some questions?"

"Can you speak up?"

How could this possibly work? I looked down at the notebook in my hand. I opened to a blank page and wrote, CAN I ASK YOU SOME QUESTIONS?

I held it up. Daniel leaned in.

"Sure," he said.

HOW DID YOU GROW UP?

"How I grew up? In Green Point, near the Traffic Department, they had the houses in back, that's where I grew up."

WHY THERE?

"My father worked on the railways."

HOW WAS YOUR FAMILY LIFE?

"Family was all right. Only my father was the troublemaker. Me and him could never see eye to eye."

WHY?

"He was just like that," Daniel said. As always, his face stayed in one position, betraying no emotion.

WHAT THEN?

"I was at the high school and then I went to work on the docks. That time, anybody that worked for the state, that person's relative got a job immediately, no questions asked. I stayed there and kept the electricity working right. I start about seven in the morning and turn in at half past eleven at night. This went on for nearly ten years. Somebody came with a rumor, saying the Suez Canal will close and this will be the end of it. Now me, like a fool, listened to that, so I left there and went and drove a taxi for a while. I saw there was no life in a taxi. Went back to the docks, they took me back, and then I started driving to help fix up the lights all over town. Stayed there till 1994, when they boarded me." He stared at me, his eyes made immense by his glasses. I stared back. "So that's how my life went," he said, finally.

DID YOU LIVE ALONE?

"I stayed with my mother and her husband. Me and my father couldn't get along so I said to hell with him and I stayed with my mother."

Here was what I was getting at. It was clear, now, that Daniel hadn't heard a thing that his stepbrother had told me. His stepbrother had revealed Daniel's secrets before Daniel's face, and Daniel hadn't been able to hear it.

YOUR MOTHER DIVORCED YOUR FATHER? I wrote.

"No. She was married at that time. Her husband, he died a couple of years later. He had that smoking disease—emphysema. But I stayed mostly around with her and then I moved on my own."

TELL ME ABOUT YOUR FATHER.

"My father died in 1975, I think. My grandfather came from France during the war. He was a doctor on the warships and he jumped ship and met a woman here and died here. This is something you don't put in there. My . . . that's classified."

WHAT IS CLASSIFIED?

"What I'm gonna tell you, your ear will fall off. My father raped her. She was my sister, supposed to be. But he raped her and that's where I come in. Don't write nothing about that in there. That's my business."

WHAT IF I USE A FAKE NAME FOR YOU? I scrawled. He leaned in and made out the letters.

"Ja, you can use another name," he said, shrugging.

AND THEN I CAN TELL?

"Ja. But make it a French name."

For this reason, Daniel de Villiers is not his real name. Nor are any of his family members identified here by their real names. Most other details surrounding Daniel's life, including where he lives and his former profession, have also been changed.

WHEN DID YOU FIND OUT? I continued.

"I had a dirty habit of walking very quietly," Daniel said. He turned toward me. Next to him was a grimy fan. He had a funeral announcement on his bulletin board: his mother pictured, presumably, a decade before her death, a lady with her gray hair in a short set perm. According to the dates, stamped in gold cursive, she'd died only a few weeks before. "Nobody knows I'm there and they're having a vicious argument, that's how I found out. I told him everything that happened. After that, his hate for my father was immense."

HOW DID YOU FEEL? I scribbled.

"I was highly disgusted. Imagine yourself finding out something like that. I found out when he was still alive and I threatened him often, very often." I recalled what Daniel's brother had intimated: that Daniel's father was hard and cruel. "One day, he came to hit me, and I grabbed his hand, and I put my foot on his throat. I said, 'If you ever, ever lay your hands on me again, I'll kill you.' He said, 'I'll leave you nothing.' I said, 'You take your money, and you shove it where your mother never kissed you. And another thing, I am going to wait to Judgment Day, and on that Judgment Day, I'm gonna put all the things that you have done to me, and you will pay for it, you'll go straight to hell, and I'll make sure you get there.'"

His face, normally pale, was pink now. He stayed sitting in his wooden chair.

"I says, 'A person like you doesn't exist. Why do you do these things to me?' From small, he ill-treated me, hitting me for nothing. Most of the time he was drinking. But I stood my ground and he turned me nearly into a murderer."

An aide strode into the room then, a young colored woman with shoulder-length black hair. She took a step back—seeing a visitor there, I supposed, was a shock—and then composed herself. "Hello, are you done?" she asked.

"I haven't touched anything," Daniel said, motioning to the bowl of thin soup. The woman smiled and left.

DO YOU HAVE FRIENDS? I wrote.

"Friends can cause a lot of trouble, saying things they know nothing about. People must be kept in the dark."

WHY IS IT SO IMPORTANT THAT THIS IS A SECRET?

"Put yourself in my position. My father is the one who instigated this nonsense. You would also keep your head under your arm. It's not my fault but wherever I go, fingers get pointed. It's damn embarrassing."

HOW DOES IT FEEL TO KEEP IT TO YOURSELF?

"It doesn't feel nice at all. I've got to walk around with this guilt that what her father did. Justine, you put it in your back pocket but one day you're gonna take it out of your back pocket and you're gonna be careful when you take it out, that nobody knows. Then your whole life will be uncovered. It's a complete charade that you have to play, not to let anybody else know what's going on. But I said: Judgment Day, he will answer for that. He won't get away with it."

MAYBE IT WOULD HELP TO TALK TO SOMEONE? I wrote. He shook his head. A FRIEND?

"You think you know a friend. Turns out this friend is a somebody else, a Judas in disguise. Rather carry your own cross. It's a helluva life, but what can I do? Look, I'm in this place. I'm safe here from anybody outside and they will only know what I tell them. I leave out where my father was concerned. That is blocked out. They know nothing about it. That's how things go."

BUT THEN NOBODY REALLY KNOWS YOU.

"Better that way, than walking around with people pointing at you, talking behind your back. There is no such word as love when somebody finds out the truth about you. Then he puts it on a scale. Somehow afterwards, you'll find he starts to back out."

Daniel paused here and sighed. He sucked in his breath.

"It's a helluva life to live, but what can I do? I wanted a family of my own, but if I got involved with a woman, this had to come out. Children are given to you, and they got their lives to live, and they can't live the results of your nonsense, your troubles, the trouble you cause them, and all that. That is how I look at it. Ja, Justine. I must be the strangest case you've ever written up."

YOU'D BE SURPRISED AT HOW MANY SECRETS PEO-PLE HAVE.

"Yeah? I thought I was the only one."

NOT EVEN CLOSE.

"The wicked things, the evil things that men can think of," he said.

After a bit, I got up to leave.

"Justine, what do I get out of this?" Daniel asked hopefully, standing with me.

"What do you want?" I shouted.

"Some clothes. Size extra-large."

I looked at his diminished frame and told him I might not be back for a year. I was leaving the country to join Sam across the continent. Daniel nodded. He was used to waiting. He followed me out to the hall and took my hand briefly in his—as always, a cool and brittle hand. As I made my way down the wheelchair ramp, he waved.

"Don't forget about me," he said.

It was hard to conjure up a more forgotten individual. Daniel had never enjoyed the support of a world superpower, a major political party, or even a pair of devoted parents. He was "a nobody," as his stepbrother said, so while everyone still remembered Amy Biehl, Daniel's own family hardly gave him a second thought. Daniel's triumph was that he escaped death, but his reward was a meager pension and a worn-out hearing aid.

Nelson Mandela's lack of bitterness and his willingness to forgive had permeated all strata of society. South Africans were encouraged to follow suit and reconcile with those who had wronged them. But how could Daniel reconcile with a ghost, a fleeting image, criminals who had targeted him arbitrarily? In this, Daniel had unwittingly joined an unfortunate brotherhood, the majority of them black: people suffering from effects of apartheid—unable to pin their suffering to a precise person or group, but nonetheless expected to move forward with grace. Most of these people were victims of the entire apartheid system that stripped them and their forefathers of their basic human rights. But Daniel was a white government employee, who had quite literally benefited from apartheid before he was also taken down by its creations: a group of furious, poor, politically aligned young men from the township.

Despite going to TRC hearings to state his case, Daniel had received neither truth nor reconciliation. He trudged before the commission, but he did not really take part in any process—not like the Biehls had, or those who were involved in bigger, more captivating cases, where the perpetrators sat before the victims, answering questions, explaining themselves. Daniel couldn't remember the faces of his attackers. They were only black schoolboys in heavy shoes. He was paused in time, living in the moment of his assault, unable to sleep for decades—waiting and wondering, as he said, "when someone will come and finish the job off."

Daniel's case at once proves the necessity and the insufficiency of the TRC. One theory behind the TRC was that if a victim and a perpetrator could face each other in a controlled setting and discuss the circumstances of the crime in which they occupied opposite roles, each would see the humanity in the other. The victim could begin to heal because his trauma would be recognized, his dignity reclaimed; he would no longer be a tortured body, an abstraction, making unbelievable claims; rather, he would become an individual again. Then the perpetrator, too, might take off the torturer's hood, and maybe he could also be restored to humanity.

But Daniel, glossed over by the police and the courts and finally the TRC, had nobody with whom to reconcile. He was just a name entered in a log, nestled in the "D" section, between two other little-known victims of human rights violations, both of them black young men killed by unnamed cops during protest rallies in the 1970s and 1980s. After I went to speak to him, Daniel was reduced to writing letters to the former head of the PAC, a woman who, unbeknownst to him, was now the mayor of Cape Town, a former African nationalist lefty conveniently affiliated with a whole new, far more relevant, center-right party that garnered most of the white vote. Daniel wasn't thinking about truth and reconciliation. The only justice he could wish for was an acknowledgment, perhaps an apology, and some token to improve his days: if not a hearing aid, maybe the PAC could get him a pair of spectacles?

Mzi and I once spent a day searching for some official record of Daniel's beating. The Gugulethu Police Department pulled up nothing from August 25, 1993, or the days surrounding it. We sifted through the archives in the old army barracks off NY111, to no avail. Daniel, who had lost track of the department that had handled his case, suggested it may have been processed at Manenberg, the colored township next door to Gugulethu. We drove over the border and sat in the room of the station's captain, an older white brigadier who knew how to click in Xhosa and welcomed Mzi in so politely that Mzi and I chattered on about him for hours after the fact. The captain was intrigued by our little mystery and seemed eager to help us solve it. Finding no evidence on the computerized database, he ordered an officer to bring to his office all the old physical files from the time in question. Together, we sifted through piles of mildew-stained papers. We inspected each one, but to judge by the old records, the assault on Daniel had never occurred.

20.

Penetrating so many secrets, we cease to believe in the unknowable. But there it sits nevertheless, calmly licking its chops.

—H. L. Mencken

"We want to talk to you about the Eastern Cape," Easy's uncle Taku said, taking a deep breath. We were in the living room of the other Nofemela house on NY41, where a bunch of relatives were huddled together, watching a Nigerian soap opera in which a murderous motorist hits a cyclist on a sandy street and the cyclist obligingly falls to the ground and dies with a flourish. The glossy violet paint covering the walls was cracking, and the unfurling tendril of a potted plant had been affixed to the wall with Scotch tape. One particularly friendly child with a particularly snot-covered face reached up to me, smiling broadly, and demanded to be picked up. The child was heavier than you would imagine and its gender was indeterminate and it kept giggling in my arms. An elder of some sort was wrapped in a plaid blanket next to a petrol heater, on top of which a steaming pot of water had been placed.

This was the house the family had been given after eight years in the shack on the open field, where all twelve of them, and then husbands and wives, had lived until one by one the brothers got their homes. This was the house in which Wowo and Taku had grown up. This was where I had interviewed Easy's ex, Pinky. Now only two of Wowo's siblings, and their multiple children and grandchildren, still lived there: an older brother who lived in the backyard and the eldest sister, the old woman who slept beneath blownup photo portraits of her deceased son, her deceased daughter, and her deceased mother.

Taku and Wowo, both wearing eyeglasses and sitting on a couch, stood and herded me to a corner of the kitchen, where they sud-

denly looked, for all their age and wisdom, like bashful schoolboys.
Taku was a retired teacher. "The principal gave his friends jobs,"
he said. "While we were twenty years in the field, that new chap
will be our manager. So I decided to take my pension." He was
now studying to become a preacher. Wowo was the older one, a
man inclined to silence, who had left school to work any and every
job: on the assembly line at a steel factory, as a janitor at a nursing
college, "putting dead people in the fridge" in the tuberculosis
hospital morgue, stocking shelves at a grocery store, and finally
working as a cleaner and then a gardener at Old Mutual Insurance.
He had also played drums in a band of other gardeners, called the
Cape City Kings. After thirty years, he took retirement on February 14, 2009. On February 15, his son Monks was thrown from a
car and paralyzed. Upon retirement, Wowo got a one-time pension payout the equivalent of around $14,000 for three decades of
service.

"You can't do nothing on that money," he observed. "When I
think of it, I want to cry."

Easy, who regressed to boyishness around older relatives, had followed us and was staring at the fridge as Wowo and Taku gathered
up their courage to talk to me. I leaned against a kitchen counter,
gazing down at the three short Nofemela men before me.

"We're all going, right?" I asked. "You, too, Wowo?"

"I don't know," Wowo said.

"Why not?" Easy and I had been planning a trip to the Eastern
Cape, which had absorbed the former Transkei homeland, to see
where the Nofemela family had come from. Wowo and Taku, who
had spent some boyhood years there, would accompany us and act
as guides.

"We don't have any pocket money, not even for a cool drink,"
Wowo said apologetically.

"So, we can't fund petrol," Taku added. His shoulders slumped.
"We don't know if you are expecting that."

Taku and Wowo had worked for white governments and white-owned corporations and then for black governments and corporations still run by whites, from the time of their youth until old age. They had stayed away from drink and drugs and all the temptations available to frustrated people in the depths of poverty. They had raised black boys in Gugulethu, none of whom was dead or in prison; they had lifted paralyzed adult children up on bad backs and slept in beds with little grandsons and taught neighborhood kids soccer and fed their hungry nieces and nephews; they had nurtured marriages for fifty years; they had built and improved family homes with their bare hands. These were the respected elders of their communities, heads of overflowing families. And here they stood before me, a young white American female thirty years their junior, chastened, admitting they were too broke to pay for the gas necessary to make it out to their ancestral land.

"I expect five thousand bucks each," I said. "Three gourmet meals a day and a bottle of wine from everyone."

For a moment, the room was quiet. Then Easy began to laugh, and the men followed.

"It's my research trip and I am grateful you will come as my guides. I have already arranged funding."

The two breathed out. Then they looked a little bit excited.

"Well then, we will be happy to show you our roots," Wowo said.

A few days later, I woke at dawn and drove up to High Level Road, which ran parallel to the ocean but far above it. I passed the palms of the N2, the power plant, all the familiar landmarks, and entered Gugulethu. The shacks in the marshlands looked flat in the morning light. At such an hour, the township was more lively than town: these were the nannies that had to arrive before Mom left for work or yoga; the clerks who had to open up shop; the security guards

changing over from the night shift to the morning shift. And before
all that, everyone had to bathe, dress, and feed their own kids. The
nine-to-five jobs were for the fortunate, the middle-class-plus. Those
people were served. These were the people who did the serving.

On the morning of the road trip, I walked into the Nofemela
house on NY111 and found Wowo sitting expectantly by his suitcase in the living room. Wowo's two-year-old grandson, perched on
a plastic motorcycle, was glaring, alternately at me and at Wowo. The
child slept against Wowo every night of his life, and he sensed that
the suitcase meant that he would be abandoned. He mumbled
something in Xhosa and cocked an imaginary gun, which he aimed
at me, and then at his grandfather.

"What did he say?" I asked.

"He say he will kill me and you as well. He say he will shoot us
dead."

Easy, in a puffy jacket and a knit cap, came from the back room
with his own suitcase, as well as a small binder of CDs.

We loaded up the car and drove to Taku's tidy house, which he
had been improving whenever he had money. He had managed to
build two tasteful and contemporary back rooms, which he hoped
to rent out, and had gutted his sitting room, though he was waiting
for the next cash influx before he could fit in finishings and floor-
boards. For now, the windows were covered in plastic and the floor
and walls were bare concrete.

Taku finished quarreling with his eldest son, a hollow-cheeked
twenty-something with a tik habit, and loaded his own small bag
into the trunk. He hopped in back with Wowo, two upright old
men with legs short enough to be comfortable in the small confines
of a hatchback. They were stocky, though Wowo was more rotund,
where Taku made efforts to keep his belly at bay. Where Wowo's
nose was flat and round, Taku's was long and sharp. Wowo was light,
and Taku was dark. Wowo kept his gray beard trimmed and his head
shaved, while Taku kept his face shaved and his gray hair trimmed.

On that day, Wowo was dressed in his long woolen overcoat, a green polar fleece, a white cap, and fancy leather shoes. Taku wore a plaid flannel shirt and a plaid flannel scarf, nylon sports pants, sneakers, a brown corduroy jacket, and a beanie cap. Easy was wearing a tan jacket, tan pants, a tan sweater, and a knit cap. These would remain their outfits for the next several days, as it turned out their bags contained—in addition to changes of socks, T-shirts, and underwear—blankets and towels and soap, in case they had to bed down on the floor. I was swathed in a down parka and sheepskin boots, and had packed an oversized sweatshirt and a sweater; I was prepared, for some reason, for an arctic journey. Easy had agreed to drive the first leg, and then I would drive the next.

On our way out of Gugulethu, we passed people standing along the main road.

"Toilet protesters," Wowo said, unimpressed.

The toilet protesters were the ones who had thrown poop at the mayor's van, a questionable tactic to communicate how sick they were of relieving themselves in open containers. Now here they stood, assembled in little crowds along the sidewalk, displaying their buckets full of excrement and demanding flush toilets be installed near their shacks.

"They are disturbing people," Taku said.

We drove east, toward the apple orchards of Grabouw, passing through the mountains, the dry bush, the rocky landscape dotted with pine trees. We ignored hitchhikers, 10-rand notes in their hands if they were willing to pay for gas. We passed an ostrich farm. We passed a rumpled group of men and boys holding out crates of grapes beneath a billboard that warned: BEWARE OF ROBBERS SELLING STOLEN GRAPES.

We played oldies, which Wowo and Taku liked, especially Ella Fitzgerald, Nina Simone, Louis Armstrong, Grover Cleveland, and the Zimbabwean superstar Oliver Mtukudzi. Easy sang along badly and inaccurately to every single song.

South Africa is a physically epic place. It contains deserts and seas, rivers and lakes and towering mountains. To drive across the country is to pass through ecosystem after ecosystem, each one ancient and boastful. We drove by vineyards and cut through the mountains, zig-zagging up and out. There were swaths of dry bush and miles of rocky terrain dotted with pines. A troupe of baboons trotted along the road, engaged in the many dramas of monkeys, who kvetch and fight and love like they're on a reality TV show. At one point, a forest of enormously tall trees bordered the highway, the trunks reaching up like skyscrapers, covered in smooth, white bark and topped with deep green leaves. We burst out from the flatlands and before us stretched the sparkling Indian Ocean. We passed through the wealthy vacation town of Plettenberg Bay, where Capetonians kept summer homes. Slate-and-white mansions cascaded down to the famously immaculate beaches. Just as suddenly, we passed the township on its outskirts, pressing against the highway, shacks and a crumbling wooden church.

"This is the N2, the National Road," Easy said, observing the township. "Is embarrassing."

We stopped at a KFC. Easy had cobbled together a couple hundred rand, which had been burning a hole in his pocket for the entire morning. He jumped out of the car, rushed into the franchise, and ordered three boxes of chicken and three mini white loaves from a weary, middle-aged colored woman in a little red cap whose name tag announced her as Maritsa.

"What does that mean?" Easy asked, pointing at the tag.

Maritsa ignored him, punching at her register.

"Does it mean you love me?" Easy asked, leaning in. Maritsa didn't look up. "Does it mean you hate me?"

He collected the chicken and sprinted to the table, where we sat and ate. The three men eyed me as I picked at my food and finally Easy informed me that the family had recently been engaged in a debate about why I was slender, with Kiki arguing genetics while Wowo argued that maybe it was because I didn't eat hot dogs all day, *like someone he knew*, and then Kiki spitting back that Wowo was one to talk.

"For me, fried chicken is just . . . unhealthy," I said tentatively.

"What do you mean?" Taku asked.

"Fried chicken . . . It's really bad for you."

I had long assumed—naively, I now realized—that people in Gugulethu knew, but did not care, that their diets were generally unhealthy. The staples tended to be fried or barbecued lamb, goat, or skin-on chicken; slice after slice of fluffy white store-bought bread; fried potatoes; boiled-to-death carrots and green beans; *pap;* a variety of processed meats; soft drinks; packaged cakes; candy bars; maybe a wan apple or cucumber here or there. Looking at Wowo and Taku across the pile of fried chicken, I realized that for a large portion of the population, nutritional education had been elusive, while fast-food advertising had been plentiful. Health food was unavailable, out of reach, while the spaza shops dotting the township sold cheap chips, sweets, and fizzy drinks.

"What is healthy, then?" Taku asked.

"Like, grilled chicken," I said. "Um, brown bread? Fish."

He nodded. "Baloney?"

"Not baloney."

"No more fried chicken for me," Taku decided. "I don't want to die of Kentucky."

Months later, when I visited him at his house one afternoon, Taku would still be abstaining from fried chicken, a decision his wife found baffling, since fried chicken was, she said with a shrug, "very tasty."

The earth turned red and yellow when we reached the Eastern Cape, and the traffic thinned. Once there, we were often the only car in sight. There were no mansions or industries. Time turned back. The plains and hills were dotted with horses and cows. We saw the silhouettes of sheep walking across a craggy hilltop in a perfect line. "Like soldiers," Easy said. We bought a sack of oranges on the side of the road, and Wowo prepared each orange with his pocket-knife, cutting off a perfect spiral of peel in one piece.

We passed a fake Khoikhoi village, advertised with billboards—we could see the collection of straw-roof rondavels from the road. The Khoikhoi, the first to encounter white settlers, had been largely destroyed or absorbed into other communities so we supposed the endeavor involved a few Xhosa people dressed as ancient pastoralists, willing to pose for a tourist picture if the opportunity arose.

In the Eastern Cape, a white police officer pulled us over for a standard check. He peered into the car. Wowo, Taku, and Easy nodded hello. I handed over my New York State driver's license, which he examined.

"Where are you going?" the policeman asked.

"Lady Frere," I said.

"Why?" He was not asking in an official capacity; he was simply overcome by curiosity.

"To visit some friends."

The policeman returned my license and stood to the side, unsatisfied, as we drove away.

In the Eastern Cape, the main towns were few and far between. They contained Shoprites and Pick n Pays, sneaker stores, cheap clothing shops, run-down auto shops, and gas station franchises. In one such central town, we stopped and bought groceries. As we strolled through the store, Taku asked me to point out healthy foods and unhealthy ones as he took mental notes.

We finally reached Lady Frere, where Wowo and Taku were born. Lady Frere was now a town, spread out over thirteen square miles, of around 2,500 people, nearly 99 percent black Xhosa. Lady Frere's main road contained little more than a police station and a few shops. The surrounding lanes were built with run-down single-level ranch houses that had once been owned by white government employees and teachers, until they found themselves contained within a homeland ruled by a semiautonomous chief. Then they booked it out of there.

This was the general feeling of Lady Frere: of a place abandoned, first by the whites and then by the blacks, who headed to the cities to eke out work. Anyone who could get out, it seemed, did get out, for there was simply no opportunity here. No jobs, no universities, no money, no nothing. And so the streets had a vaguely mournful quality, as they do in any ghost town.

Wowo and Taku directed me to the house of their late brother, close to the police station. He had died a year earlier, leaving a widow and assorted sons and daughters and grandchildren. The house itself was low and beige. It had once belonged to whites, Taku told me with an inkling of pride, and now his family owned it.

The living room into which we entered was painted fuchsia and decorated with framed photographs hung high up on the wall, so that one had to crane one's neck to see them—a common aesthetic choice in many Xhosa homes, and one I never understood. At the center of the living room sat a gigantic, severe widow. This was the Xhosa custom that always threw me: it was up to the guest to greet, to welcome herself into the home, to say hello to everyone, and then to take any place she could find. It was the opposite of Western etiquette, in which the host stands, welcomes, and offers the guest a seat, and I almost always screwed it up. I grew shy, or awkward, or greeted the wrong person, failing to properly identify the matriarch or patriarch, using the incorrect honorific, admiring a cute baby first (acceptable in America, but discourteous in black South African households).

Xhosa people were unfortunately accustomed to much grander offenses by whites, and generally received me with generosity and

good humor. As far as I could tell, though I certainly deserved multiple helpings of disdain during my time bumbling around a new
culture, I was never once corrected harshly or subjected to any
grudge holding or even judgment.

"You do try," Easy once said, and it seemed that this was what
counted.

The five rugrats running around the house were immune to social mores, and they promptly tackled me and then, when I stumbled
to a seat, climbed atop my lap, and those who could not fit hung
over my shoulders. When I looked any one of them in the eye, he or
she collapsed into a fit of giggles. As Wowo and Taku and the widow
caught up, a teenage girl served us milky tea. In the corner, Easy had
reunited with a cousin, and the two of them were laughing up-
roariously.

Dinner was two loaves of bread that Taku and Wowo had brought,
and a cooked chicken I had picked up on the way, having been advised that the family would have a hard time feeding us. Everyone
ate on individual trays balanced on their laps. An American sitcom
called *The First Family,* which as far as I could gather centered on a
fictional black family living in the White House, played in the background. In the kitchen, various young women cleaned up, and children flew around. Nobody spoke much, not to me or to each other.
The lone table was worn and cracked. In the living room, the widow
held in her lap an ice cream carton full of change and toilet paper,
and anybody in need of either item approached her meekly, and she
handed out the goods accordingly. It was the norm, where bathrooms were shared and toilet paper was expensive, for people to
keep their own rolls in their rooms, which meant that when I used
a bathroom at somebody's house, I was usually first provided with
the roll. As the evening wore on, the matriarch put down the carton
and picked up a baby, whom she cuddled to her breast. At one point,
she ordered the children to assemble and sing a song for Wowo and
Taku.

"Jesus loves me," they warbled.

That night, the family informed me that I would be sleeping elsewhere. Wowo and Taku planned to sleep on the floor with their woolen blankets, as all beds were taken, but they were all concerned that I would be unable to survive such a night, and so had arranged, without consulting me, to send me to the neighbor's. The neighbor was a retired schoolteacher who ran a sort of bed-and-breakfast, except without the breakfast part or any advertising. Basically, people in town knew she had some extra space and you could pay what you liked.

Easy and Wowo escorted me out the back door to the car, where each of us grabbed our bags. It was very dark and frigid, but as my eyes adjusted, I could make out a human shape in the shadows, weaving around and then crouching by a rusty car.

"There is someone pooping there!" I yelled, alarmed. "He is pooping!"

"Yes, that is our relative, who is very drunk," Wowo said, heading back inside. "Good night, Justine."

The figure pulled up his pants and scampered away.

Easy guided me down the dirt road and we knocked on a door. The neighbor, a plump and smiling woman of about fifty, ushered us through an empty, darkened hall to a living room area, where three young women and a couple of babies were hanging out, warmed by a paraffin stove. The house was low but long, and all of it, save for this area, seemed to have been shut off, to preserve heat and save money. It was like the town, this house: largely deserted, its remaining citizens concentrated in a desolate little cluster. After exchanging pleasantries, we sat and spoke like old friends, about the dying town of Lady Frere, about how it felt to live as women in this lonely house. There was a great deal of crime out here in this barren place, she said, and no jobs. The unemployed boys and men were bored and broke, and, stuck here, had turned to petty crime within the community.

"They are robbing grannies on pension day," the neighbor said. "Here in South Africa, white people act like they are the victims of crime only. But everyone is scared."

After giving us glasses of Coca-Cola, she led us to a bedroom, which had been interpreted quite literally: the long space was painted teal and contained eight twin beds, arranged along the walls. At the end of the room, two such beds, with wooden backboards, had been made up with multiple woolen blankets and blue flannel sheets. A space heater pulsed out some warmth. There was no hot running water, the neighbor said, but she had been heating the samovar for the past hour, and I would be able to take a bucket bath. I nodded uncertainly. She presented me and Easy with towels, and left. Easy set down his bag.

"Are you staying here, too?" I asked.

"We don't want you to be alone in Eastern Cape, in strange house," Easy said, sitting on one of the beds and taking off his shoes. "Also, is better for my back."

That evening, I tried to wash, shivering, haphazardly splashing water here and there from a tub my host had filled for me. This was the way so many township and rural residents still bathed: with a plastic basin full of water. Everyone I'd spoken with preferred it to a shower; they didn't feel clean otherwise. But I was hopeless at bathing this way, until Tiny later explained to me the system: wash face first with the cleanest water, plenty of soap, and a washcloth, then rinse and dry; next comes the neck and the chest and the arms; and you work your way down the body, scrubbing and rinsing and drying piece by piece until you finish with your feet. After, cover yourself in Vaseline; it keeps the warmth in.

When I returned to the bedroom, I found Easy tucked in, talking on his phone to Tiny, giddy as a teenager. They had not been married long, and this was the first night since their wedding that they'd been apart. I nestled under the blankets but my nose was still icy. A car passed, its lights swiping over the room. Eventually, Tiny's airtime ran out and the phone call ended. Easy turned over and looked at the ceiling. His phone beeped. He read the message, swooning, and passed it over for me to admire: *I luv u my bby u r the best hubby a woman could have gudnight.*

Then we lay in our little beds, telling stories. Easy, his voice heavy with sleep, told me of his teenage years, of getting stabbed on the streets, of shebeen fights and recovering in his mom's living room. It was almost like he was telling a fable, and we both grew sleepier, until Easy finally let out a loud yawn and closed his eyes. The room was bright, lit by a fluorescent bulb.

"Should I turn off the light?" I asked.

"No, no," he muttered. "Is good this way."

"Wait, do you sleep with the light on?"

"Yes, I prefer like this because this is another people's house."

"So?"

"I prefer it."

"I'm not sleeping with the light on. Who sleeps with the light on?"

"Me."

"Always?"

"Not always. At my place, I switch off the light because is my place."

"What is the benefit of the light being on?"

"When you go to somebody's house and somebody is not your family, you never know if maybe the ancestors will come."

"What? What are you talking about? If you're scared of someone coming to kill us, we can lock the door."

"And then? Ancestors don't care for locks."

"Look, if you're scared of their angry ancestors coming, those ancestors will come if there's a light on or not."

Easy considered this. "Okay, we can switch off."

I made my way to the switch in the hall and then used my cellphone as a flashlight, navigating the many beds back to mine.

"Easy, are you scared of the dark?" I asked.

"Is true, Nomzamo, I don't like the dark. But we must sleep

tightly now, relaxing, because we have a long day tomorrow. Yho, it's far away, this Transkei. Far, far, far away."

In the crisp morning, Easy and I walked down the street to meet Taku and Wowo. There, by the ever-simmering fire, a cousin served us bowls of warm *umphokoqo*, a porridge of maizemeal boiled with salt and water, and then mixed with a kefir-like sour milk called *amasi*. While staying at one of London's finest five-star hotels, with its entire culinary repertoire available to him, Mandela was so desperate for *umphokoqo* that he insisted a visitor from South Africa bring along the necessary ingredients—in her hand luggage no less, to ensure their safety. He then instructed that if she were to encounter any trouble at customs, she was to call Tony Blair directly.

After breakfast, we headed to the driveway. The town was still, the sun slowly rising up in the distance. Outside were various buckets, sheds, a car on blocks, the detritus of country living, some chickens a few houses over, pecking about.

"Now we are getting to our roots," Taku said excitedly as we loaded into the car.

Easy drove, with Taku and Wowo barking directions from the back and me taking notes in the passenger seat. We left the main strip and headed toward a stretch of empty one-lane highway, flanked by open plains of dry yellow grass, dotted with thousands of molehills. Here the summer rains were followed by a long and arid winter. Piles of dung were being sold by the side of the road, to be used as traditional floor polish and to stoke fires. Two cocks fought in the yard of an isolated house. A brown-and-white dog lounged in a spot of sun nearby. Some women walked along the road, thumbing a ride. One wore a long purple dress. Here and there, bits of litter glistened by the side of the road. A piglet tied to a doghouse was eating from a tiny bowl.

"Yho, Justine, in 1971, I took a bicycle from Queenstown all the way to here," Taku remarked.

We passed a green sign signaling a turnoff to a place called KwaPercy. In Xhosa, this meant Percy's Place, a strange name in a land where the villages had either African names or Afrikaans names.

"Who's Percy?" I asked.

"Percy was a white man, and he is famous because he was rumored to be good," Taku said. "There was also a white man in our area who sold groceries, general goods, firewood. If I wrote a letter to my family from Johannesburg, it arrived at the white man's shop. But when they made the homelands, the laws brought by the government caused all the white people to leave this place."

We turned off the main way and entered a rocky stretch of dirt road. The car bumped along. To one side rose a vertical expanse of brick-colored rock where the locals used to graze their cattle.

"Nowadays, these areas are not as alive as before," Taku reflected. "When the whites discovered gold and diamonds, they took the people who were capable and left behind mothers and young babies. Our main destruction came when the diamond mines and gold fields were discovered. What happened here, you cannot really rely on historians to tell. They write with their perception, so you must learn to read between the lines."

"Sometimes if I think too much about this, I feel other way," Wowo said evenly. "But then I think, I'm still alive, so why worry?"

We drove along the dirt road for nearly an hour and covered only a few miles. Our pace was slow, the terrain difficult and twisted. We passed through clusters of houses set in the midst of obscurity: a dozen or so homes constructed out in the boonies, and then nothing for a half mile, and then another dozen homes. Finally, we curved onto an enormous field and stopped near a village of about twenty-five houses. Sheep roamed the prairie. It reminded me of Wyoming, open and melancholy. The wind whipped across the exposed land, loud and constant. Taku and Wowo led me and Easy to a large pile of rocks by a low tree. Upon this space had once sat the home of Melvin and Alice Nofemela.

Melvin had been born here and was well known locally as a skilled stick fighter. Stick fighting was a waning Xhosa tradition, though one that had once been an important way for a boy to prove his valor.

In his twenties, Melvin had attended his brother's wedding. His brother was marrying a woman from a village over the hill, and the people from her area came with their offerings of cattle for the celebration. Included in the crowd was a teenage girl named Alice, to whom he proposed that very day.

"That very day?" I exclaimed.

"You don't believe in love at first sight?" Taku asked.

"You are too much white," Easy said.

Melvin and Alice had lived by the tree in a traditional rondavel, a thatched-roof hut with a floor that smelled of grass. But soon enough, as the family grew larger and the region offered little in terms of opportunity, Melvin left for the cities to find work.

"If my father had money, he would like to live here," Wowo said, meaning that his father had always dreamed of returning to his birthplace—the place where his umbilical cord was buried. "He cares too much for this place." But Melvin had never made it back to stay.

"Can you imagine, to leave this beautiful place with warm homes, to go live in shacks in Langa?" Easy asked, surveying the land.

Wowo sucked in his breath, thinking of his father. "That man. He work hard and have too much pain."

We left the empty plot and headed back to the car, and then drove farther away from town, and upward, until we stopped at a pale pink house sitting alone on the top of a hill. A crowd of people were milling about. The women wore skirts, sneakers, and aprons, their hair wrapped with cloths. The men wore hats and sweaters and slacks.

Wowo, Taku, and Easy pushed their way through to find an elderly man in a cardigan and a knit cap, sitting at a table. The man, a cousin, threw his hands in the air and began to greet the Nofemelas with handshakes and hugs.

It turned out that the man was a widower, his children far away, and his church group made the long trip weekly in taxis and buses and cars, from Lady Frere or even Queenstown, to visit him and bring him groceries. They chipped in money from their small pensions and salaries, and the ladies cooked him food and scrubbed his pots and pans. The men helped him plant vegetables and tend his garden, and kept him company. When we arrived, everyone was sitting down for a meal of goat meat, pap, and boiled carrots.

I was, as usual, an oddity in these parts. In Gugulethu, women usually played interior roles in the family: in the house, in the kitchen, cooking and cleaning and watching the children. Men, meanwhile, milled about outside, fixing cars or smoking and talking. Automatically, due to the subject of my research and my relationship with Easy, I had ended up with the men, hanging in the sunshine and shooting the breeze. My whiteness, my foreignness, and my profession as a journalist separated me, placing me in a sort of gender-role limbo. Here in the Eastern Cape, where such roles were more strongly entrenched, especially with the older set, my presence was an even more confusing matter.

I was herded to the border separating men and women, where I sat awkwardly on a bench, literally half in the men's room and half in the kitchen area. When lunch ended, the men streamed outside, and I followed. A long-drop outhouse made of corrugated tin sat atop a bluff, overlooking the biblical stretch of land below. A white clay structure with dark floors contained a chicken and newly hatched chicks. The air was very clean. I held in my hand a novel by the famous South African author J. M. Coetzee, and I absently flipped through its pages.

A man approached me. "We want to know if you are Coetzee," he said. He was not familiar with the bearded, male, septuagenarian

Nobel Prize winner, and Coetzee is a common Afrikaans surname. Here I stood: a white writer, holding a book. Could be.

"No, I wish," I said. "Anyway, I'm not Afrikaans. I'm American."

"Serious? Please take me there in your suitcase!"

After lunch and chatter and warm goodbyes, we drove farther up the mountain to another cousin's house. This house, despite also lacking electricity and running water, was a sleek, fresh little number, a new white three-bedroom with shining peach-tiled floors, an expensive sofa set, and gauzy curtains. Its owner was originally from this village, though he now worked and lived in Durban—apparently doing well, if his late-model Mercedes and house back in the city were any indication. But his dream had always been to build a place of his own in his native village, and this house was the realization of the dream.

The man was surrounded by his rural relatives, and he was simultaneously treating them to a braai and displaying his good fortune. Now, with us there, he had even more people to spoil and to strut before. He laughingly challenged Taku to a push-up contest, which Taku won. Easy, meanwhile, had become obsessed with a lilliputian fellow who was hanging around. The man was just over five feet and small-boned, and this delighted Easy, who never got the opportunity to tower over another man. He demanded that I take multiple pictures of him with his arm slung over the agreeable man, and later ran around Gugulethu showing off the prints I had made at his request.

We stood outside as the sun began to set, congregating around the grill, as the relative turned the meat. He was at least six-foot-three, and I couldn't see how the diminutive Nofemelas and this towering fellow shared any DNA. Somebody had brought a bottle of whiskey, which was summarily shared—though Taku and Wowo, teetotalers, refused. Once the cousin had cooked the first batch of meat, he put another batch over the fire, to be tended by a friend, and everyone filed inside. The sausage and pork chops were set out on a communal silver platter and the six men gathered around, their faces grave. This was serious business, the business of sharing the fruit of the braai. Each pulled from his pocket a switchblade and helped himself. A lady entered, took her own piece, and settled to the side, on an overturned bucket. Once the first helping had been polished off, another platter was brought in. The men, who had been steadily eating for twenty minutes, looked tired, but then the cousin flipped open his knife and started at it again, and everyone followed suit.

The sun was now a flame across the horizon. A larger group of men had gathered outside, and they were deep into their drink. They held cigarettes between their thumbs and forefingers. Dusk fell, and with only candles lighting the earth for miles, everything was bathed in navy. For my benefit, this group, which I had joined in the open air, was speaking to each other in halting English. Then suddenly, one young man, who had been particularly enthusiastic about the whiskey, stopped mid-sentence. He stared at me and then spit out some words in Xhosa. I shrugged innocently and the group waited for him to break the silence.

"You must speak Xhosa here," he said harshly, in English.

I looked at Easy and considered the situation. He returned my gaze, steady. Everyone else fixed me in their sights.

"*Ndisafunda ukuthetha isiXhosa,*" I said slowly, like a schoolchild. *I am still learning to speak Xhosa.* They had taught me this in my class, and it was among the few sentences I could remember.

Everyone continued to stare, and I shifted in place.

Then, just like that, my accuser broke into a smile. Everyone else smiled, too. They started talking again. I stepped away.

"It's time to go," I whispered to Easy, and we made our way back to the house, where we said our goodbyes.

Once in the car, Easy took the wheel, with Wowo and Taku in back. A dark blanket was slowly pulled across the plains. Wowo and Taku, bellies full of meat, let out burps. The hatchback lurched down the hill.

"Wowo, tell me about Easy, as a son," I said.

Wowo shifted in place. "What I like, he respect even my brothers. I like that. All my sons. And if someone fighting, they were not scared to fight. Especially if they not started the fight."

"I can't imagine you angry," I said to Easy.

"Is like Truth Commission here!" he exclaimed.

"What I like with Easy, he was not a skollie," Wowo explained. "But if you provoke him, want fight, you get it. Is like me. Like me, yho, I fight, don't worry. Other day, we were there in Langa, me and my brother—"

"Was 1965, and they want to check Wowo's strength so they come to me and take my money," Taku interrupted. "So we go together to them."

"We fighting straightaway, they run away. Yho!"

"Now is terrible. They have words like bullying, but was playing to us," Taku said.

"Fighting is part of playing," Wowo said.

"Then in 1976, there were people staying in Gugulethu," Taku said. "They were trying to help the government to stop us from stoning the property. Those people were having weapons but we are not scared of them. We fight with them. We won the battle! We won the battle!"

Now only our headlights guided the way down the hills, passing over the villages and, once in a while, a solitary pedestrian.

"When it was governed by the white people, it was a better town, it looked nicer then," Taku said absently. "But when Africans took over, tsho . . ."

"Tell me, Wowo," I said. "Do you remember when Easy was arrested for Amy Biehl?"

"He was sleeping on the back side, with Pinky. They go to the back and caught him. Arrest him. Then he gone. Tomorrow, the police come back. Again they check. I don't know what. They see a lot of pictures, PAC pictures, the flag of PAC."

"Did you think he was involved in Amy's death?"

"I was not there. That day was a riot. He wasn't there, or was there, I don't know. I don't know nothing about what he do outside. I was in house."

"Ntobeko was also at the march? And Monks?"

"Rumors saying, but we don't know," Taku said. "It's hearsay. All of them were mentioned, but Monks wasn't caught."

"People say Monks hurt Amy," I said.

"I think they are confused," Wowo said.

"I can't say," Taku said. "We didn't see them. But the information that we are getting, some people are saying some things. I don't say if we will ever know."

"Monks was there," Easy said. "We see this white lady running towards the garage. She was already outside the car, already stoned. I think from there, people say they saw Monks."

"Did he and Monks look alike?" I asked Taku and Wowo.

"But not exactly," Taku said.

"One theory is that Monks was the one at Amy Biehl," I said. "Easy came after and they pointed him out because he was well known in the area. I talked to the main witness. She doesn't even know who Monks is, but she knows Easy. Maybe she saw Monks and thought he was Easy. But nobody will confirm."

"I never heard this story," Wowo said.

"What we heard, we heard Easy is the one," Taku said. "But maybe the witness was scared of the mob. She might never notice exactly who did what."

"And Monks, he didn't tell us they make mistake," Wowo said. "If he is scared to go to prison, Monks can tell us, and Easy also can tell us, 'Was not me, was Monks.' We don't know nothing. We only know Monks and Easy was there in riot. We can say is possible or not possible, we don't know. I don't know nothing."

"What happened that day was beyond our expectations," Taku said. "Maybe was Easy, maybe was Monks. He knows, Easy does."

"The one who was there must know everything," Wowo said.

"And I told you, Justine," Easy said.

I will never know for certain who killed Amy Biehl on August 25, 1993: who cast the fatal stone, who stabbed her in the chest, who stood above her as she begged for her life, and who snuffed that life out. Was it Easy, his little brother Monks, or neither? Did Ntobeko hit her with a rock, or did he watch from afar? Did Mongezi Manqina, gangster-cum-freedom-fighter-cum-rapist, pierce Amy's heart and her lungs with a blade, or did he take the credit because he was hungry for some taste of glory in his decidedly inglorious life? Was Vusumzi Ntamo—impoverished, easily manipulated—a guilty part of the frothing mob or just an easy-to-arrest black man? How many others surrounded Amy, and how many of them slipped back into the township forever, to be swallowed by the place? Was Amy a naive student who made a bad choice? Was she a rights fighter who died as she made a stand for equality? Were her friends, who wanted a ride home so badly, victims as well, or had they acted irresponsibly when they brought her into the volatile township?

Linda, it occurred to me, knew about the uncertainty of the South African narrative. She had said as much to that radio interviewer in St. Louis, months after she cut contact with me. The interviewer had called Ntobeko a killer, and Linda had intercepted.

"He was not maybe a perpetrator that actually committed the crime," she said. "So you use the word killer, but I don't use the word killer. . . . You know, as much as we tell the story cut and dry, there are all these little sidebars and things that say many of them could have wielded a knife or thrown a stone, but eyewitnesses came forward and kind of picked out some. Ntobeko ran away, was not tried with the other three. But it's more complicated than just—"

The interviewer, apologizing, cut her off. "These stories always are," he said, and the conversation veered away.

People, myself included, have a blind spot just here. When Easy, questioned before the TRC in 1997, insisted he had "stabbed at"

Amy, but could not be sure if he had really stabbed her, one commissioner had tried to clarify Easy's actual role in the crime, but Easy's lawyer led the hearing away from that suspicious detail. I had read the term "stabbed at" many times, and regarded it curiously, but for at least the first year of my research, I simply justified it to myself as the verbal quirk of a court interpreter. White detectives, followed by a white prosecutor and a white judge, had decided Easy's role in the crime and convicted and imprisoned him; later he admitted to that crime before a diverse group of sympathetic commissioners. And after that, he and Ntobeko had built lives upon this version of the past. They were reformed killers and ex-radicals making good with their victim's parents; this was recorded for posterity. How could it be otherwise?

Linda also knew that the old records weren't the whole truth. She had told me this when I was haranguing her for them over the phone. "Nobody wants the truth," she had said. "Those TRC records aren't the truth. They are graphic and ugly. The truth is that the country was still in turmoil. She represented the oppressor, and her white face was all that was wrong with the country, and she was killed."

Newspaper articles and official papers did their part in shaping the story. But they never told of Daniel down the street, his head stomped in. They never mentioned Monks, the lookalike brother. Miss A didn't figure in as a multidimensional person—a feminist with ANC proclivities, sick of the gangsters in her community, in contact with the police. Nonetheless, the written word—by the court, by journalists—became the mold, and history was solidified within it.

The Truth and Reconciliation Commission also created history, a reality for the new schoolbooks. The ANC-aligned progenitors of the TRC wanted to reclaim the past from the National Party, to wipe clean decades of propaganda. Men and women who had once been categorized terrorists were rebranded freedom fighters, and hidden atrocities were brought to light, all captured on color TV and in multivolume reports. But the TRC, despite its name and its marketing campaign, was not purely an exercise in truth telling, nor was it a vehicle for exposure. The TRC, the result of a negotiation between former enemies, was actually designed to circumvent a civil war and help build a nation. Nearly a quarter century has passed since the events took place, and as Easy told me long ago at the Hungry Lion franchise in the mall in downtown Cape Town: "The truth is not anymore existing for years and years."

The countryside had been so black that once we reached town, even the pitted paved roads and feeble streetlamps seemed like luxuries. We drove to the Nofemela family house in Lady Frere for a quick supper of samp and beans. Wowo wanted to wake at 4 A.M. to drive back to Cape Town, since he was worried that Monks might need him. I negotiated him up to a 6 A.M. start time, and then Easy and I walked down the street to the neighbor's place. Only a few houses let off a faint yellow glow, and the sky was clear, starry, and infinite.

"Remember in one of our first meetings, when you told me you trained out here for APLA?" I asked. "And you told me you could take me to the training camps?"

"I remember."

"You never trained for APLA, so what was your plan?"

Easy began to chuckle and hooked his arm in mine. "Nomzamo, no, I will take you exactly to the place. I know exactly what's going on. I will tell you exactly the place that the people used to go and train."

"People, maybe, but not you."

"Me also."

"I don't believe you."

"Serious, serious. I know exactly what's happening here years ago."

We knocked on the door of the schoolteacher's house, and she welcomed us in. She had warmed the samovar so that we had hot water. We brushed our teeth and washed in shifts. The little oil heater pumped out as much heat as it could manage, but we each dressed for a night in an igloo, me with a hood tied around my neck and Easy with his hat pulled over his ears. We climbed into our respective twin beds, and huddled beneath woolen blankets.

"In Xhosa we say: Don't talk the truth on top of the fire," Easy said. "It means don't ever try to talk the truth, even if they hold you over fire. The fire make you strong so you never surrender. But I know you, Nomzamo. You did find out the truth. I tell you a straight truth. I'm not now joking."

It was silent in Lady Frere, set in a former homeland, the birthplace of the Nofemela clan, not far from Nelson Mandela's ancestral village. The borders had been drawn and rearranged by Europeans, and the town had been named after the wife of a Welsh colonial employee who had warred against Xhosas and Zulus for the British cause. It was situated on a bleak plain, hemmed in by red hills, dotted with sheep. The low-lying house in which we were staying had been set on land once belonging to blacks, then ceded to whites, and then abandoned and given back to blacks, who still had to leave to work in the far-off cities so their families could survive. It was dark in the room, and peaceful.

"No, I'll never know the true story," I said from beneath my mountain of blankets.

"I told you before: Is life, this. Full of tricks, disappointment. Love directed in the right direction. Love directed in the wrong direction. People have two side or three or more side. Don't listen too much to what anyone is saying," Easy said.

"Including you, apparently."

"Including me," he said, and laughed loudly, and then we went to sleep.

ACKNOWLEDGMENTS

I am deeply indebted to the people of Gugulethu.

Of those people, Mzwabantu "Mzi" Noji was my translator, historian, and investigator. For years, he shared with me his hard-won wisdom, offered me protection, and was the truest friend. Without Mzi, I would never have been able to write this book.

And without Easy Nofemela—big-hearted, unapologetically himself—there is no story. Easy started out as my subject, but also became a teacher, a guide, and, as so often happens in these unexpected situations, a friend. I am forever grateful to him and to the Gugs branch of the Nofemela clan who shared their lives with me—in particular, Tata Wowo, Mama Kiki, Uncle Taku, Asange, Mongezi, and Aphiwe.

I also owe thanks to Ndumiso Bolo; the Nojis; Ilmar Pikker; Mike Barkhuizen; Chris Malgas; Dianna Healley; Zahira Adams, Yasmeen Mitole; my high school English teacher James Bucar; Peter Gastrow; Tracy Randle; the historian/revolutionary Madeleine Fullard; and my insightful Xhosa expert Oscar Masinyana.

Aimee-Noel Mbiyozo offered conversation, perspective, and analysis. Mpho Mbiyozo, Rito Hlungwani, Jo Goyen, and Nyasha Karimakwenda helped me navigate a new land and the many cultures within. Jenny Vaughan kept me sane in Addis Ababa while I wrote.

Percy and Irene Choritz, my parents on another continent, welcomed me into their family with remarkable generosity.

Cindy Spiegel saw, in the raw proposal for this book, its potential. She gave me the freedom to follow my nose, and supported this project from beginning to end. I admire her courage in the way she goes about choosing and publishing books. Simply put, she's my dream editor.

At Spiegel & Grau/Random House, Annie Chagnot, Fred Chase, Vincent La Scala, Rachel Ake, and Greg Mollica seamlessly brought together all the pieces required to turn a manuscript into a book.

Anna Stein, my lovely and amazing agent, had faith in my ability as a writer before she had reason to.

Mary Marge Locker has kept things in check. Andrew Kidd, John McElwee, and Alex Hoyt helped shepherd the manuscript into the world.

I thank my mother, Patricia van der Leun, for everything, as always.

Samuel Choritz—my South African, my first and most valued reader, my toughest critic—has walked beside me every step of the way. When I met Sam, I knew he would be my partner in life, but I didn't know that he would become my partner in my work. This book is our collaboration.

ABOUT THE AUTHOR

JUSTINE VAN DER LEUN is the author of the travel memoir *Marcus of Umbria*. She has written about South Africa for *Harper's* and *The Guardian*. She lives in Brooklyn, New York.

ABOUT THE TYPE

This book was set in Bembo, a typeface based on an old-style Roman face that was used for Cardinal Pietro Bembo's tract *De Aetna* in 1495. Bembo was cut by Francesco Griffo (1450–1518) in the early sixteenth century for Italian Renaissance printer and publisher Aldus Manutius (1449–1515). The Lanston Monotype Company of Philadelphia brought the well-proportioned letterforms of Bembo to the United States in the 1930s.

9-1-16
28.00